CORPORATE GOVERNANCE IN THE COMMON-LAW WORLD

The corporate governance systems of Australia, Canada, the United Kingdom, and the United States are often characterized as a single "Anglo-American" system prioritizing shareholders' interests over those of other corporate stakeholders. Such generalizations, however, obscure substantial differences across the common-law world. Contrary to popular belief, shareholders in the United Kingdom and jurisdictions following its lead are far more powerful and central to the aims of the corporation than are shareholders in the United States.

This book presents a new comparative theory to explain this divergence and explores the theory's ramifications for law and public policy. Christopher M. Bruner argues that regulatory structures affecting other stakeholders' interests – notably differing degrees of social welfare protection for employees – have decisively impacted the degree of political opposition to shareholder-centric policies across the common-law world. These dynamics remain powerful forces today, and understanding them will be vital as postcrisis reforms continue to take shape.

Christopher M. Bruner is an Associate Professor at the Washington and Lee University School of Law. His teaching and scholarship focus on corporate law and securities regulation, including international and comparative dimensions of these subjects. Bruner's articles have appeared in a variety of law and policy journals. His comparative study of corporate governance in the United Kingdom and the United States, *Power and Purpose in the "Anglo-American" Corporation*, won the 2010 Association of American Law Schools Scholarly Papers competition.

Corporate Governance in the Common-Law World

The Political Foundations of Shareholder Power

CHRISTOPHER M. BRUNER
Washington and Lee University School of Law

CAMBRIDGE
UNIVERSITY PRESS

CAMBRIDGE
UNIVERSITY PRESS

32 Avenue of the Americas, New York NY 10013-2473, USA

Cambridge University Press is part of the University of Cambridge.

It furthers the University's mission by disseminating knowledge in the pursuit of education, learning and research at the highest international levels of excellence.

www.cambridge.org
Information on this title: www.cambridge.org/9781107013292

First published 2013

A catalogue record for this publication is available from the British Library

Library of Congress Cataloguing in Publication data

Bruner, Christopher M., 1972–
Corporate governance in the common-law world : the political foundations of shareholder power / Christopher M. Bruner, Washington and Lee University School of Law.
pages cm.
Includes index.
ISBN 978-1-107-01329-2 (hardback)
1. Corporate governance – Law and legislation. 2. Common law. 3. Stockholders – Legal status, laws, etc. I. Title.
K1327.B78 2013
346′.0666–dc23 2012042747

ISBN 978-1-107-01329-2 Hardback

For Lia, Cullen, and Claire

Contents

List of Figures

Acknowledgments

At the risk of understatement, I have run up big debts in numerous quarters to bring this work to fruition. I hope that in time I can repay those debts. In the meantime, my deepest gratitude will have to suffice.

This book is the product of a long-term project that directly builds upon a series of articles written over the last few years, notably:

- *The Enduring Ambivalence of Corporate Law*, 59 Ala. L. Rev. 1385 (2008), where I developed the argument that U.S. corporate law remains fundamentally ambivalent regarding the role of shareholders in corporate governance and the consistency of their interests and incentives with the public good;
- *Managing Corporate Federalism: The Least-Bad Approach to the Shareholder Bylaw Debate*, 36 Del. J. Corp. L. 1 (2011), where I applied this argument to the debate regarding the scope of the shareholders' authority to enact, amend, and repeal corporate bylaws;
- *Power and Purpose in the "Anglo-American" Corporation*, 50 Va. J. Int'l L. 579 (2010), where I developed the U.K.–U.S. comparative argument linking their differing degrees of shareholder-centrism to differences in the degrees of extra-corporate social welfare protection available to employees in each country; and
- *Corporate Governance Reform in a Time of Crisis*, 36 J. Corp. L. 309 (2011), where I applied this comparative argument to the debate regarding U.K. and U.S. corporate governance reforms in the wake of the global financial and economic crisis that arose in 2007.

I remain deeply grateful to the editors of these fine journals, as well as to many colleagues and friends for their helpful comments, suggestions, and conversations regarding the subjects addressed in these articles. They include John Armour, Stephen Bainbridge, Barbara Black, Bryan Camp, William Casto, Brian Cheffins, John Cioffi, Alan Dignam, Susan Fortney, Brian Galle, Martin

Gelter, Joshua Getzler, Andrew Gold, Catherine Howarth, Lyman Johnson, Brett McDonnell, Russell Miller, David Millon, Donald Nordberg, Dean Pawlowic, Gerhard Schnyder, David Skeel, D. Daniel Sokol, and Robert Vandersluis, as well as workshop participants at the Association of American Law Schools 2010 Scholarly Papers Competition awards panel, the Indiana University–Bloomington Maurer School of Law, the Southeastern Association of Law Schools 2010 Annual Meeting Panel on Shareholders' Role in Corporate Governance, the Texas Tech University School of Law, the University of Cincinnati College of Law, the University of Oxford, the Virginia Junior Faculty Forum (University of Richmond School of Law), and the Washington and Lee University School of Law 2010 Faculty Enclave.

Whatever its strengths and weaknesses, the book is immeasurably improved because of the time that I was able to spend conducting comparative research in Australia, Canada, and the United Kingdom. Many thanks to the Centre for Corporate and Commercial Law at the University of Cambridge, where I was a Visitor to the Faculty of Law in the spring of 2009 (and to the Texas Tech University School of Law for financial support of this component of my comparative research); to the University of Toronto, where I was a Visitor to the Faculty of Law in the summer of 2011; and to the Ross Parsons Centre of Commercial, Corporate and Taxation Law at the Sydney Law School, where I was a Parsons Visitor in the summer of 2011. For guidance, suggestions, and encouragement in my comparative research on Australian, Canadian, and U.K. law, I am deeply grateful to Anita Anand, Helen Anderson, John Armour, Joanna Bird, Brian Cheffins, Aaron Dhir, Alan Dignam, Jennifer Hill, Edward Iacobucci, Ian Lee, Jeffrey MacIntosh, Christopher Nicholls, Luke Nottage, Ian Ramsay, Joellen Riley, and Jacob Ziegel.

I am particularly indebted to Jonathan Eastwood, Martin Gelter, and D. Daniel Sokol, who provided valuable comments and suggestions on the whole manuscript. For advice, suggestions, and encouragement to pursue this project, many thanks to John Berger (Cambridge University Press), Robert Danforth, Sunit Das, Mark Drumbl, Joshua Fairfield, Brant Hellwig, Margaret Howard, Lyman Johnson, Timothy Jost, Russell Miller, David Millon, Elizabeth Oliver, Doug Rendleman, and Ben Spencer. Thanks also to workshop participants at Boston College Law School, Florida State University College of Law, Melbourne Law School, and Sydney Law School, for feedback on numerous aspects of the project at various stages of its development.

Throughout the writing of this book I have been a member of the faculty of the Washington and Lee University School of Law. I could not imagine a more supportive faculty and institution. For generous financial support, I am grateful to the Frances Lewis Law Center. Thanks also to Alana Dagher, Parker Kasmer,

James Moore, and Jillian Nyhof, who provided excellent research assistance; Linda Newell, who expeditiously tracked down numerous sources; and Diane Cochran, who provided superb administrative assistance throughout.

I am most grateful of all to my family. My parents, Richard and Sharon Bruner, always expected me to work hard and think for myself. I dedicate this book to my wife, Lia Pierson Bruner, and to our kids, Cullen and Claire, who have supported me in this endeavor with patience, optimism, and grace.

Lexington, Virginia
September 2012

CORPORATE GOVERNANCE IN THE COMMON-LAW WORLD

PART I

SHAREHOLDER ORIENTATION IN THE COMMON-LAW WORLD

1 Introduction and Overview

The global financial and economic crisis that arose in 2007 has led to widespread debate regarding the adequacy of decision-making processes in financial and nonfinancial firms alike. Lawmakers and regulators, in particular, have asked whether corporate boards of directors ought to be more directly answerable to their shareholders, rendering comparative study of differing regulatory approaches to corporate governance a matter of vital public interest. This book presents a theory explaining the varying degrees of shareholder orientation historically exhibited by corporate governance systems in the common-law world – including Australia, Canada, the United Kingdom, and the United States – and explores the theory's practical ramifications for contemporary law and public policy.

The comparative literature tends to place corporate governance systems[1] in one of two broad categories. Throughout most of the world, the stock of large companies is generally concentrated in the hands of controlling families, banks, corporate groups, or governments. In such countries, the corporate governance system typically aims to balance the competing claims of various "stakeholders" in the corporate enterprise – notably, shareholders and employees. In common-law countries, conversely, publicly traded stocks are often held by widely dispersed, passive investors, and the corporate governance system typically places greater emphasis on their interests – a shareholder-centric approach to corporate governance often described as uniquely "Anglo-American," "Anglo-Saxon," or "common-law" in orientation.[2]

[1] Although definitions vary considerably – see, e.g., PETER ALEXIS GOUREVITCH & JAMES J. SHINN, POLITICAL POWER AND CORPORATE CONTROL: THE NEW GLOBAL POLITICS OF CORPORATE GOVERNANCE 293–95 (2005) – I use the term "corporate governance" to describe the rules that govern decision making in public corporations, whether arising from corporate law, securities regulation, exchange listing rules, or elsewhere.

[2] *See, e.g.*, Ruth V. Aguilera, *Corporate Governance and Director Accountability: an Institutional Comparative Perspective*, 16 BRIT. J. MGMT. S39, S41–S49 (2005) (contrasting "Anglo-Saxon"

Common-law jurisdictions – so called because they trace their legal origins to English judge-made "common law"[3] – undoubtedly exhibit substantial similarities in their business cultures, financial structures, and corporate governance systems.[4] Generalizations regarding the "Anglo-American model," however, tend to obscure the truly substantial differences exhibited by corporate governance systems in the common-law world – differences of great theoretical and practical significance. Simply put, shareholders in the United Kingdom and jurisdictions following its lead are far more powerful and far more central to the aims of the corporation than are shareholders in the United States. This central divergence – observable both in law and in market practice – has embarrassed all previous efforts of which I am aware to devise a comprehensive theory of corporate governance in widely held public corporations of the sort that predominate in common-law jurisdictions.

In this book I survey the vastly differing positions occupied by shareholders in public companies across a category of corporate governance systems too often lumped together in the comparative literature.[5] I then explore the political factors leading these otherwise similar legal and business cultures to part ways on the governance role of shareholders, and trace the consequences of this divergence for corporate governance theory and practice. I argue that external regulatory structures affecting the interests and welfare of other stakeholders in public corporations – notably the form and degree of social welfare protections available to employees – have had a decisive impact on the degree of shareholder orientation exhibited by corporate governance systems in the common-law world. Specifically, stronger stakeholder-oriented social welfare policies and legal structures have permitted the U.K. corporate governance

and "non Anglo-Saxon" corporate governance contexts, while acknowledging distinctions within the former category); JOHN W. CIOFFI, PUBLIC LAW AND PRIVATE POWER: CORPORATE GOVERNANCE REFORM IN THE AGE OF FINANCE CAPITALISM 192 (2010) (describing German "ambivalence toward the Anglo-American variant of finance capitalism" following the financial crisis); Rafael La Porta et al., *Legal Determinants of External Finance*, 52 J. FIN. 1131, 1142 (1997) ("[C]ivil law families have much smaller stock markets than those in common law countries, presumably because of inferior investor protections."); Jean Tirole, *Corporate Governance*, 69 ECONOMETRICA 1, 3 (2001) ("The popularity of the shareholder value concept is much higher in Anglo-Saxon countries....").

3 *See, e.g.*, BLACK'S LAW DICTIONARY 276–77 (6th ed. 1990).

4 *See, e.g.*, John Armour & David A. Skeel, Jr., *Who Writes the Rules for Hostile Takeovers, and Why? – The Peculiar Divergence of U.S. and U.K. Takeover Regulation*, 95 GEO. L.J. 1727, 1751 (2007); Geoffrey Miller, *Some Points of Contrast between the United States and England*, 1998 COLUM. BUS. L. REV. 51, 51 (1998).

5 *See, e.g.*, Ruth V. Aguilera et al., *Corporate Governance and Social Responsibility: A Comparative Analysis of the UK and the US*, 14 CORP. GOVERNANCE: INT'L REV. 147, 147 (2006) (observing that "[l]ess attention has been paid to differences in corporate governance within the 'Anglo-American' system").

system to focus more intently on shareholders without giving rise to political backlash. The same generally holds true, I argue, in other common-law jurisdictions including Australia and Canada, which pursue broadly similar policies both in their corporate governance systems and in the provision of state-based social welfare protections. Conversely, weaker stakeholder-oriented social welfare policies and legal structures have inhibited the U.S. corporate governance system from doing the same, resulting in a starkly different balance of power between boards and shareholders.

I begin with a discussion of methodological problems encountered in comparative study of corporate governance, problems widely ignored in the extant literature. The challenge, explored in Chapter 2, is to avoid two extreme postures, each of which effectively undercuts the utility of comparative study – strict functionalism on the one hand and strict contextualism on the other. By "functionalism" I mean an analytic approach that assumes that corporate governance regimes have been crafted to manage identical, or at least very similar, sets of broadly defined problems. This approach often animates economic theories of corporate governance, which accordingly style corporate governance as chiefly concerned with the minimization of agency costs. This assumption obscures very real differences in how various systems function, and diverts attention from the possibility that differing degrees of shareholder orientation reflect more deep-seated differences in social views and market structures. At the same time, however, excessive "contextualism" threatens to render meaningful comparison impossible by focusing heavily or exclusively on idiosyncrasies of history, culture, and politics. I aim to steer a middle course between strict functionalism and strict contextualism by selecting the prevailing politics of social welfare as my explanatory variable. In this manner, I effectively assume the common necessity in each country to achieve some form of broader political compromise addressing employee interests, while highlighting the potential for strikingly different forms of political equilibrium to emerge in various countries – with divergent impacts on their respective corporate governance systems.

Chapter 3 provides an overview of significant differences between the principal corporate governance models in the common-law world, emphasizing the far greater power and centrality of shareholders in Australia, Canada, and the United Kingdom relative to their counterparts in the United States. For example, whereas shareholders in the United Kingdom possess unqualified legal power and practical capacity to remove public company directors without cause and to accept hostile takeovers without board interference, U.S. shareholders – including in Delaware, the principal jurisdiction of incorporation for U.S. public companies – possess neither. Similarly, U.K. company law focuses quite intently on maximizing return to shareholders, defining this by statute to be the overriding purpose of the U.K. corporation. U.S. corporate law, by contrast, has long remained ambivalent regarding the degree to which shareholders' interests proxy for the larger public interest, adhering to an ambiguous formulation of fiduciary duties owed simultaneously to "the corporation and its stockholders," and giving boards substantial discretion to favor the interests of other stakeholders in responding to hostile takeover attempts. The practical upshot is that shareholders loom much larger in U.K. boardrooms than in U.S. boardrooms. Although U.S. shareholders undoubtedly possess far greater capacity to sue after the fact for breaches of fiduciary duty, the considerable corporate governance authority possessed by shareholders in Australia, Canada, and the United Kingdom permits more direct and substantial shareholder influence over corporate affairs than one finds in the United States.

The book then turns to the prevailing economic and political theories of comparative corporate governance, examining in some detail their strengths and weaknesses, and endeavoring in particular to expose the limits of their respective explanatory domains. Economic theories, explored in Part A of Chapter 4, tend to focus on minimization of "agency costs" arising from misalignment of the board's and shareholders' interests. The corporation is often depicted as a "nexus of contracts," with corporate law tending toward those rules that rational shareholders, employees, and other stakeholders would agree upon in a hypothetical *ex ante* negotiation. In these respects, such theories reflect an inherent functionalism grounded in the scientific pretensions of the "law and economics" movement, a tendency contributing to a convergence bias – an expectation that rational actors grappling with the same (or substantially similar) problems in different countries will eventually converge on the optimal regulatory response. This, I argue, is contradicted by enduring differences in levels of shareholder orientation across common-law jurisdictions, and particularly by the fact that the corporate governance system of the United States – the world's predominant capital market – has remained a consistent outlier in this respect for several decades.

The turn to politics, I argue, is inevitable, given the shortcomings of economic theories of corporate governance. However, while I acknowledge the relevance of certain institutional factors identified in the extant comparative literature – notably the earlier rise to power of U.K. institutional investors, and their greater proximity and homogeneity in the London marketplace – in Part B of Chapter 4 I explore the inability of prevailing political theories of corporate governance to provide a complete explanation for the core divergence that I identify. Theorists emphasizing historical origins – for example, common-law versus civil-law orientation – find themselves unable to explain variations within a given category of countries, let alone why a given system might remain politically stable, or change, over time.[6] More generally, theorists purporting to identify a consistent political trend across both concentrated and dispersed ownership systems effectively sacrifice nuance for parsimony, finding themselves unable to explain the differing impacts of politics on corporate governance in these radically different settings. Mark Roe's "social democracy" theory[7] – perhaps the preeminent comparative political theory of corporate governance – is representative, associating ownership concentration and stakeholder-orientation with stronger social democracy (e.g., Germany), while associating ownership dispersal and shareholder-orientation with weaker social democracy (e.g., the United Kingdom or the United States). This approach would appear to have considerable explanatory power at the global level and is certainly capable of explaining the position of either the United Kingdom or the United States vis-à-vis numerous other countries. It cannot, however, explain the position of the United Kingdom and the United States vis-à-vis each other – because the United Kingdom (like Australia and Canada) simultaneously exhibits both greater shareholder-centrism in corporate governance and a greater commitment to social democracy in its prevailing politics than does the United States. My discussion of this and other prevailing political theories of corporate governance[8] exposes the inability of each to account for this striking divergence between the United States and other capital market-based corporate governance systems.

In Chapter 5, then, I analyze the varying approaches to social welfare policy embraced by the common-law jurisdictions in question, presenting evidence that the degree of shareholder orientation exhibited by the corporate governance system, on the one hand, and the degree of external "welfare state" protections,[9] on the other, reflect a single, broader political equilibrium

[6] *See infra* Chapter 4.B.i. (discussing the "law matters" theory built on the work of economists Rafael La Porta, Florencio Lopez-de-Silanes, Andrei Shleifer, and Robert W. Vishny).

[7] *See infra* Chapter 4.B.ii.

[8] *See infra* Chapter 4.B.iii–vii. (discussing John Armour and David Skeel's work on the role of institutional shareholders, the "Varieties of Capitalism" literature pioneered by Peter Hall and David Soskice, Alan Dignam, and Michael Galanis's work on macroeconomic context, Peter Gourevitch and James Shinn's work on coalition formation, John Cioffi and Martin Höpner's work on party politics, Pepper Culpepper's work on political salience, and Martin Gelter's work on the impact of employment protections).

[9] By "welfare state" I refer generally to a baseline set of protections relating to income, health insurance, employment insurance, and various other "social services." *See* Sanford Levinson, *The Welfare State*, *in* A COMPANION TO PHILOSOPHY OF LAW AND LEGAL THEORY 553, 555 (Dennis Patterson ed., 1996); Allan Cochrane et al., *Comparing Welfare States*, *in* COMPARING WELFARE STATES 1, 5–7, 12–14 (Allan Cochrane et al. eds., 2nd ed. 2001).

within each country. In the United States, social welfare protections – notably including access to health care – have historically been linked to employment status, whereas the British welfare state has, since the late 1940s, provided such protections primarily through government programs. These structures, I argue, have impacted the trajectory of each country's corporate governance system in profound ways. For example, the emergence of a shareholder-centric takeover regime in the United Kingdom – where board interference with hostile takeovers is prohibited, absent shareholder approval – reflects confidence among Labour leaders in the 1960s that the welfare state could mitigate the effects of job loss on employees. Conversely, in the United States, the emergence of a stakeholder-centric takeover regime in the 1980s – giving target boards substantial discretion to deploy potent defenses, regardless of shareholder wishes – reflects a powerful alignment of manager and labor interests, drawing substantial force from larger political concerns regarding the welfare of employees vulnerable to the loss of health care and other benefits linked with their jobs.

These political dynamics, I argue, remain as powerful in each country today as in decades past, and their relationship is further reflected in Australia and Canada, which have adopted social welfare models and struck larger social and political equilibria broadly resembling those in the United Kingdom, even if each has arrived there by its own path because of unique legal, economic, historical, and cultural factors. In Australia, for example, courts responded to the advent of hostile takeovers in the 1970s and 1980s in a manner resembling the approach taken in the United States, giving managers substantial latitude to deploy defenses. This reflects the fact that moves toward state-based social welfare remained hotly contested and incomplete during this period. Since the 1990s, however, Australia has adopted a far more shareholder-centric position on hostile takeovers, sharply limiting defensive tactics in a manner strongly resembling the approach taken in the United Kingdom – a move that was not inhibited by the social concerns of prior decades because by the mid-1990s Australia's state-based social welfare programs were firmly established. In Canada, however, a relatively substantial state-based social welfare system predated the major efforts to modernize its corporate laws in the late 1960s and 1970s, constituting part of the background social and political conditions before which corporate legal reforms took place. Canada's adoption of a social and political equilibrium resembling that in the United Kingdom remains remarkable, however, insofar as it required overcoming the substantial influence that U.S. models exerted because of the cultural, commercial, and geographic proximity of the United States.

The remainder of the book addresses limits to the theory's explanatory domain and explores various factors that the theory suggests will be likely to reinforce stability, or bring about change, in these corporate governance systems moving forward. My claim that social democracy correlates with shareholder orientation will naturally prompt critics to ask why, then, we observe less shareholder-centrism in continental European systems, rather than more. In Chapter 6 I take this potential objection as an opportunity to reiterate and explain further my theory's focus on the common-law world. Returning to the political theories explored in Part B of Chapter 4, I explain how the impact of politics on corporate governance differs between the concentrated ownership systems prevailing on the continent (and elsewhere around the world), on the one hand, and dispersed ownership systems such as those in the United Kingdom and the United States on the other. In countries with concentrated share ownership, as I explore in Part A of Chapter 6 principally by reference to Germany's bank-dominated system, the key regulatory aim of corporate governance is to constrain the innate power of controlling shareholders in order to bring corporate affairs into focus with the perceived needs of other stakeholders. One consequence in Germany has been substantial employee participation on the boards of large companies – so-called codetermination. Conversely, in countries with dispersed share ownership, the principal regulatory aim is to protect minority shareholders in order to incentivize the development of deep, liquid equity markets – hence the relatively greater emphasis on shareholder interests in U.K. and U.S. corporate governance. My analysis, however, suggests that the process of ownership dispersal – which unfolded over the course of decades in both U.K. and U.S. capital markets – requires a constant recalibration of emergent shareholder and stakeholder protections to balance shareholders' comfort with minority status and stakeholders' comfort with shareholder-centric corporate governance rules. Again, stronger stakeholder protections outside the corporate governance system allow it to focus more exclusively on the shareholders' interests by blunting political resistance, whereas weaker stakeholder protections outside the corporate governance system permit political opposition to arise, inhibiting the emergence of strong shareholder-centrism in favor of maintaining some flexibility to accommodate stakeholders' interests within corporate governance itself.

I then test the descriptive power of this binary distinction through examination of borderline cases. China, the Netherlands, and Japan, for example, arguably exhibit high levels of private share ownership dispersal, yet have not straightforwardly exhibited the traits that I associate with dispersed ownership systems. In each case, however, de facto control has been considerably more concentrated than it appears at first blush, because of substantial government control in China, the separation of control from cash-flow rights in the Netherlands through the placement of stock in "trust offices" (rather than with investors directly), and the *keiretsu* system of cross-shareholding in Japan. Over recent years, however, Japan has moved toward genuine share ownership dispersal, giving rise to a natural experiment. As long-term, stable shareholdings have unwound since the mid-1990s, a nascent market for corporate control has arisen, effectively requiring Japanese lawmakers to evaluate the U.K. and U.S. takeover regimes. As explored in Part A of Chapter 6, Japan's adoption of an approach to takeover defenses resembling that of Delaware – rather than that of the United Kingdom – reflects the fact that Japan's employer-based approach to social welfare provision more strongly resembles the approach historically taken in the United States, resulting in a similar need to buffer employees from the risks of job loss following the advent of hostile takeovers.

In contrast with China, the Netherlands, and Japan, which have exhibited high levels of private share ownership dispersal, yet have not straightforwardly exhibited the traits that I associate with dispersed ownership systems, Australia and Canada appear to present the opposite conundrum – each exhibiting somewhat higher levels of ownership concentration than the United Kingdom and the United States do, yet similarly exhibiting strong shareholder orientation. This suggests that the political factors that I describe may be impacted by other dynamics – including cultural, commercial, and geographic proximity to influential foreign regulatory models. In the case of Canada, as previously noted, what is truly remarkable is the degree to which reformers deviated from influential U.S. models, further suggesting that Canada struck the social and political equilibrium that it did because of social welfare–oriented dynamics resembling those at work in the United Kingdom. With respect to Australia, then, crude assertions of "path dependence" on U.K. models are flatly contradicted by Australia's unique approach to social welfare provision, long based on a national wage arbitration system, as well as the fact that its approach to corporate governance has evolved considerably over the course of recent decades – in a manner mapping quite coherently onto the evolution of its social welfare environment. Ironically, Australia arrived at a social and political equilibrium resembling the U.K. approach only following a long and complex process of domestic policy evolution – in multiple regulatory fields – that in fact bore little resemblance to the U.K. experience prior to the new millennium.

The remainder of Chapter 6 further tests the descriptive power of my theory by examining recent events potentially altering the fundamental conditions giving rise to the dynamics that I identify. Part B of Chapter 6 investigates the impact of changes in the composition of the shareholder base. In the United

Kingdom, pensions' and insurers' stockholdings have diminished over recent years, and foreign ownership has increased. Given that the relative proximity and homogeneity of the U.K. shareholder base have historically contributed to the willingness of U.K. regulators to rely on market-based self-regulation of areas such as takeovers, the shift toward greater foreign ownership may tend to undermine confidence in the traditionally shareholder-centric U.K. corporate governance model. Conversely, Australia's compulsory "superannuation" program, requiring virtually all employees to contribute approximately 9 percent of earnings to pension investments selected by the employees themselves, may tend to promote a stronger and more widespread "investor" identity across the population – a culture shift strongly encouraged by aggressive marketing of the program. In effect, this program blurs the traditional boundary between "employees" and "shareholders" to an extraordinary degree, merging state-based and private social welfare provision in a manner that actively facilitates shareholder-centrism. In this light, Australia's broader social welfare regime defuses anti-shareholder sentiment by reducing the stakes of the employment relationship through programs such as universal healthcare, while at the same time actively promoting an "investor" identity among the voting population through compulsory superannuation – mutually reinforcing policies rendering it all the less surprising that Australia has adopted strongly shareholder-centric corporate governance rules in recent years.

Part C of Chapter 6, then, argues that postcrisis austerity measures, if substantial and sustained, could undermine shareholder-centric corporate governance rules by threatening erosion of the strong social welfare protections that historically insulated U.K. corporate governance from stakeholder-oriented political pressures. Although the fate of U.K. welfare reform initiatives remains uncertain at this writing, there is already evidence that postcrisis concerns regarding the vulnerability of employees may prompt reassessment of certain corporate governance structures – notably in the context of takeovers. Kraft's takeover of the British confectioner Cadbury in 2010 provides a vivid example, prompting wide-ranging inquiries regarding the effects of the shareholder-centric U.K. takeover regime on employees.

In Part D of Chapter 6 I examine regulatory responses to the financial and economic crisis that arose in late 2007, observing that recent corporate governance reforms in the wake of the crisis in both the United Kingdom and the United States (considerably harder hit than Australia and Canada were) have sought to empower shareholders in various ways. In light of the dynamics described in Chapters 3 and 5, shareholder empowerment would appear status quo–oriented in the United Kingdom, while representing a striking departure from the status quo in the United States. I argue, however, that in fact the political dynamics that I describe loom large in the apparently anomalous U.S. crisis response, effectively amounting to a populist backlash against managers, fueled by middle-class anger and fear in an unstable social welfare environment. Postcrisis shareholder empowerment initiatives in the United States reflect the same dynamics that drove the creation of a stakeholder-oriented takeover regime, although toward a different outcome. Just as the wave of antitakeover measures in the 1980s was supported by the employees' coalition with management, reflecting the perceived threat posed by shareholders desiring to accept premium takeover bids, recent postcrisis reform measures have been supported by the employees' coalition with shareholders, reflecting the perceived threat that reckless management poses to the financial and social welfare stability of the average middle-class family. In this light, postcrisis shareholder empowerment initiatives in fact provide fresh evidence of the significant impact that employee interests can have on the evolution of U.S. corporate governance. Moreover, their emergence at a time when external social welfare protections have likewise been enhanced – notably through far-reaching health insurance reforms – may suggest that the United States is moving, however tentatively, toward a new political equilibrium more closely resembling that in Australia, Canada, and the United Kingdom.

Chapter 7 concludes with brief reflections on the normative implications of my analysis. I reject the simplistic notion that any of these systems could be said to represent an "optimal" political equilibrium, given the historical and cultural contingency of the balance struck in each country. Nevertheless, I emphasize the tension between calls for corporate decision making to focus exclusively on the interests of shareholders, on the one hand, and to limit or eliminate stakeholder-friendly social welfare protections on the other. In their various ways, each of the countries investigated in this book demonstrates that such an approach likely could not stand the test of time – a reality suggesting that policy makers must approach the domain of corporate governance with a far more embracing conception of its role in the political economy, and its deep relationship with other regulatory domains affecting the interests and well-being of all the stakeholders in the corporate enterprise.

2 Comparative Theory and Corporate Governance

All comparative legal analyses are at least implicitly built on the assumption that placing legal rules and regulatory structures from various countries side by side, and then cataloguing apparent similarities and differences, can be expected to generate useful information. Precisely how it does so, however – and more specifically, how we know relevant "similarity" and "difference" when we see them – too often go unexamined. Ralf Michaels, for example, laments the rarity of "methodologically explicit studies,"[1] and David Clark observes growing concerns regarding the "lack of methodological reflection and theoretical foundation" in modern comparative law.[2]

This chapter endeavors to lay bare the practical difficulties and methodological challenges of comparative legal analysis generally, and comparative corporate governance in particular. By specifying up-front the critical assumptions, I am willing to make in order to render meaningful cross-border comparison possible – that is, what I am willing to hold constant in drawing comparisons among corporate governance regimes from different countries – my aims are twofold: to facilitate the critique of extant corporate governance theories presented later in this book, and to facilitate the reader's critique of my own theory. As I argue in this chapter, the scope of justifiable claims – both positive and normative – that can be advanced through such comparative study is heavily impacted by the plausibility of one's assumptions and the methodology built on them. Accordingly, I set out my views on comparative methodology here to permit greater refinement of the claims made later regarding the corporate governance systems of Australia, Canada, the United Kingdom, and the United States.

[1] Ralf Michaels, *The Functional Method of Comparative Law*, *in* THE OXFORD HANDBOOK OF COMPARATIVE LAW 339, 341 (Mathias Reimann & Reinhard Zimmermann eds., 2006).

[2] David S. Clark, *Developments of Comparative Law in the United States*, *in* THE OXFORD HANDBOOK OF COMPARATIVE LAW, *supra* note 1, at 175, 210.

A. FUNCTIONALISM AND CONTEXTUALISM

The traditional impetus motivating comparative legal study has been an abiding faith – widely shared among comparative scholars – that fundamental similarities across national legal systems are there to be found, so long as one looks long and hard enough for them. Typically termed "functionalism," the core assumption is that various regulatory systems tend to develop a range of broadly similar institutional solutions – described as "functionally equivalent" – to problems universally encountered by societies the world over.[3] Konrad Zweigert and Hein Kötz, for example, declare that "as a general rule developed nations answer the needs of legal business in the same or in a very similar way," suggesting that "it almost amounts to a '*praesumptio similitudinis*', a presumption that the practical results are similar."[4] This provides a good, concise statement of the functionalist working hypothesis, which Zweigert and Kötz conclude provides a sound methodological basis for developing knowledge through comparative study – a framework through which to draw both positive and normative conclusions about a given country's law. Comparative legal study is "best done," they argue, "if the author first lays out the essentials of the relevant foreign law, country by country, and then uses this material as a basis for critical comparison, ending up with conclusions about the proper policy."[5] This approach appears to be reinforced by the prediction that legal harmonization will increasingly occur as an empirical matter, and that convergence on superior ways of tackling common problems naturally ought to be favored. On this view, comparative legal analysis is an expression of globalization itself, simultaneously reflecting and systematizing the growing consciousness of foreign law, while aiming ultimately "to discover which solution of a problem is the best."[6]

[3] Michaels, *supra* note 1, at 341–42; Russell A. Miller, *Comparative Law and Germany's Militant Democracy, in* US National Security, Intelligence and Democracy: From the Church Committee to the War on Terror 229, 236–37 (Russell A. Miller ed., 2008). Such use of the term is akin to, although not identical with, its use in the social sciences more generally. *See, e.g.*, James Mahoney, *Path Dependence in Historical Sociology*, 29 Theory & Soc'y 507, 519 (2000) (describing functionalism as explaining "institutional reproduction" by reference to "its functional consequences"); Paul Pierson, *Increasing Returns, Path Dependence, and the Study of Politics*, 94 Am. Pol. Sci. J. 251, 263–64 (2000) (similarly describing functionalism as reflecting an "assumption that an institution arose because it serves some particularly useful purpose").

[4] Konrad Zweigert & Hein Kötz, Introduction to Comparative Law 40 (Tony Weir trans., 3d ed. 1998).

[5] *Id.* at 6. *See also* Miller, *supra* note 3, at 237.

[6] Zweigert & Kötz, *supra* note 4, at 3, 8, 24–26.

Perhaps nowhere has this convergence bias more strongly taken root than in comparative corporate governance scholarship emerging from the "law and economics" movement, proponents of which style the corporation as a purely private undertaking defined by a single universal problem – minimizing "agency costs" that arise when one set of actors (management) controls the use of resources belonging to others (the shareholders' money), without necessarily sharing the others' incentives.[7] "Modern economic theory," Klaus Hopt observes, "has developed the principal–agent problem as its basic question," with the normative upshot that "company law reform initiatives in all industrialized countries have tried to address this problem."[8] Hopt rightly attributes "a new and increased interest in comparative company law" to the law and economics movement,[9] which strongly reinforces the universalizing tendency already present in the functionalist approach to comparative scholarship.

Economically oriented theories of corporate governance are evaluated in some detail in Chapter 4,[10] but as a threshold matter, more remains to be said about functionalism generally. As a methodological matter, functionalism effectively treats the purported common problem as the independent variable – that is, the explanatory variable – whereas institutional responses to that problem are treated as the dependent variable – that is, what the scholar endeavors to explain.[11] As Helen Callaghan aptly reminds us, however, "no model is better than its assumptions"[12] – and on this score, functionalism no sooner articulates a method than it begins to unravel. Critically, how can we

[7] *See, e.g.*, FRANK H. EASTERBROOK & DANIEL R. FISCHEL, THE ECONOMIC STRUCTURE OF CORPORATE LAW 14–15 (1991). On agency costs more generally, see Michael C. Jensen & William H. Meckling, *Theory of the Firm: Managerial Behavior, Agency Costs and Ownership Structure*, 3 J. FIN. ECON. 305 (1976). *See also* Deborah A. DeMott, *Shareholders as Principals*, *in* KEY DEVELOPMENTS IN CORPORATE LAW AND TRUSTS LAW: ESSAYS IN HONOUR OF PROFESSOR HAROLD FORD 105, 105–08 (Ian Ramsey ed., 2002) (observing that economists often apply the term "agency cost" to relationships not fitting the legal definition of agency, notably the board–shareholder relationship); Simon Deakin, *The Corporation as Commons: Rethinking Property Rights, Governance and Sustainability in the Business Enterprise*, 37 QUEEN'S L.J. 339, 359–60 (2012) (same); LYNN STOUT, THE SHAREHOLDER VALUE MYTH 33–46 (2012) (same).

[8] Klaus J. Hopt, *Comparative Company Law*, *in* THE OXFORD HANDBOOK OF COMPARATIVE LAW, *supra* note 1, at 1161, 1166.

[9] *Id.* at 1172, 1184–86.

[10] *See infra* Chapter 4.A.

[11] On the use of these terms in statistical studies, see ROGER BAKEMAN & BYRON F. ROBINSON, UNDERSTANDING STATISTICS IN THE BEHAVIORAL SCIENCES 48 (2005). Although this terminology was traditionally "reserved for true experimental studies," today these terms "indicate not necessarily experimental manipulation, but simply how investigators conceptualize relations among their variables." *Id.* at 48–49 (emphasis removed).

[12] Helen Callaghan, *Insiders, Outsiders and the Politics of Corporate Governance: How Ownership Structure Shapes Party Positions in Britain, Germany, and France*, 42 COMP. POL. STUD. 733, 757 (2009).

know that we have identified a true common problem? The universality of the purported problem must be assumed to permit straightforward cross-border comparison of regulatory institutions, and claims regarding the optimality of any given approach, predictions of convergence, and so on, inevitably rest on this assumption – a shortcoming that critics describe as the "functionalist fallacy."[13] Correlatively, functionalists must assume that specified regulatory institutions in various countries respond to that problem in some straightforward, singular fashion – that is, they must assume the "mono-functionality" of regulatory institutions in order to render them amenable to comparison with purported functional equivalents in other countries.[14]

The instability of these assumptions is most clearly reflected in the degree of abstraction to which functionalist scholarship often must resort to locate the hypothesized similarity. Zweigert and Kötz state that "the solutions we find in the different jurisdictions must be cut loose from their conceptual context and stripped of their national doctrinal overtones so that they may be seen purely in the light of their function, as an attempt to satisfy a particular legal need."[15] This is effectively tantamount to assuming that "the social and economic conditions are similar" across the countries studied.[16] Notwithstanding the acontextuality advocated,[17] however, they inevitably confront the impossibility of so detached a perspective in any but the most simplistic circumstances. Just as an issue addressed through one body of law in Country A might be addressed in Country B through another body of law, an issue addressed through the legal system in Country A might be addressed in Country B by structures that fall entirely outside the formal legal system. "Often a solution is provided by custom or social practice," Zweigert and Kötz rightly note, "and has never become specifically legal in form." They continue, "[t]he same is true if there is something about the structure of the foreign society which makes the adoption of a legal solution unnecessary."[18] The point is entirely sensible – although observe the degree of departure required from the acontextuality that they present as the functionalist ideal.

Indeed, such appeals to history, culture, and politics will ultimately reveal the outer boundary of the explanatory domain of any functionalist legal

[13] Günter Frankenberg, *Comparing Constitutions: Ideas, Ideals, and Ideology – Toward a Layered Narrative*, 4 INT'L J. CONST. L. 439, 444–45 (2006). *See also* Ruti Teitel, *Comparative Constitutional Law in a Global Age*, 117 HARV. L. REV. 2570, 2570–78 (2004) (reviewing COMPARATIVE CONSTITUTIONALISM: CASES AND MATERIALS (Norman Dorsen et al. eds., 2003)).

[14] Michaels, *supra* note 1, at 351. *See also* Caroline Bradley, *Transatlantic Misunderstandings: Corporate Law and Societies*, 53 U. MIAMI L. REV. 269, 275–76 (1999).

[15] ZWEIGERT & KÖTZ, *supra* note 4, at 44.

[16] *Id.* at 45.

[17] *See* Miller, *supra* note 3, at 237.

[18] ZWEIGERT & KÖTZ, *supra* note 4, at 35.

analysis.[19] As Caroline Bradley explains, a given country's perception of the problems it faces, as well as the regulatory responses fashioned to address them, will invariably be "interlinked" with prevailing "social, economic, and political structures" – the context in (and through) which the legal system takes shape.[20] Legal rules invariably derive some measure of meaning from other rules in the given legal system, as well as from the ways in which the legal system as a whole is understood and operationalized on the ground – what Katharina Pistor calls the "living legal system."[21] This means that social needs and regulatory responses to them will necessarily be defined by reference to one another and bound together in fundamental respects, reflecting the unique contexts from (and through) which they emerge.[22] It is critical to acknowledge that these observations effectively deny the possibility of identifying truly universal problems or straightforward mono-functional regulatory solutions to them – the twin pillars of functionalist comparative methodology.[23]

In response to the manifest shortcomings of strict functionalism as a comparative method, an alternative approach has emerged. Aptly styled "contextualism," the core idea is that historical, cultural, and political context drive the formation of law and the life of legal systems to such an extent that countries could not meaningfully converge on some purported "best" law even if they genuinely sought to do so.[24] In this manner, contextualism clearly seeks to avoid the pitfalls of functionalism, in opposition to which it is effectively

[19] *See* Pierre Legrand, *The Same and the Different, in* COMPARATIVE LEGAL STUDIES: TRADITIONS AND TRANSITIONS 240, 261–63 (Pierre Legrand & Roderick Munday eds., 2003). *Cf.* JOHN W. CIOFFI, PUBLIC LAW AND PRIVATE POWER: CORPORATE GOVERNANCE REFORM IN THE AGE OF FINANCE CAPITALISM 48–49 (2010) ("The integration of political economic analysis with comparative legal theory can ameliorate these theoretical problems [of functionalism] by showing how the functions and meanings of law vary according to systemic differences in politics and economic organization.").

[20] Bradley, *supra* note 14, at 314.

[21] Katharina Pistor, *The Standardization of Law and Its Effect on Developing Economies*, 50 AM. J. COMP. L. 97, 98–99 (2002).

[22] Michaels, *supra* note 1, at 353–69. *Cf.* Frankenberg, *supra* note 13, at 447–51 (similarly arguing that constitutions be viewed as "reflecting *and* shaping the imagination of political unity and collective identity").

[23] *See* Christopher M. Bruner, *Power and Purpose in the "Anglo-American" Corporation*, 50 VA. J. INT'L L. 579, 586–91 (2010). Similarly reductionist theoretical claims, and similar responses to them, can be found in the broader literature on social and political institutions. *See, e.g.*, Jonathan Eastwood, *Reflections on the Implications of Evolutionary Psychology for the Theory of Institutions*, 8 J. INSTITUTIONAL ECON. (forthcoming 2012) (arguing that evolutionary psychology cannot fully eliminate the need for a theory of institutions because it cannot be shown that the core features of most institutions are truly universal).

[24] Zweigert and Kötz identify this approach with "legal sociologists," whose rigorous scrutiny of purportedly universal problems Zweigert and Kötz confess to finding "a bit worrying." ZWEIGERT & KÖTZ, *supra* note 4, at 10–11.

defined.[25] But this perspectival shift only trades one set of problems for another. "If the contextualists are right and context thwarts the borrowing that functionalism sought to promote," then, as Russell Miller rightly observes, "comparative law runs the risk of being reduced to little more than socio-legal tourism."[26] Put differently, to the extent that "it takes a theory to beat a theory,"[27] contextualists can hardly claim methodological victory merely by poking holes in functionalism. Assuming that scholars, practitioners, and policy makers alike will continue comparing legal regimes – and there is every indication that we will[28] – justified skepticism regarding functionalism's utility ought to lead not to rejection of the comparative enterprise outright, but to hard thinking about alternative methods through which comparative legal analysis might draw meaningful cross-border comparisons among legal regimes while acknowledging and grappling with the significance of historical, cultural, and political context in the formation and application of any given national law.

B. FAILING BETTER

As noted at the outset, comparative legal analysis – like any form of comparative activity – involves perception, analysis, and resolution of similarity and difference. As we have seen, functionalism is heavily preoccupied with the former, whereas contextualism is heavily preoccupied with the latter. What potential might there be for a coherent comparative theory acknowledging the necessity, and building on the strengths, of both perspectives?

As a threshold matter, it should be borne in mind that the challenge of perceiving relevant similarity and difference is in no sense unique to "comparative" law as such. In fact, this intellectual and psychological challenge lies at the very heart of the common-law concept of "precedent." As *Black's Law Dictionary* explains it, "[p]rior cases which are close in facts or legal principles to the case under consideration are called precedents," defined more

[25] *See* Miller, *supra* note 3, at 238. The methodological approaches referred to as "functionalism" and "contextualism" here are sometimes referred to as "universalism" and "particularism," respectively. *See* ABDULLAHI AHMED AN-NA'IM ET AL., GLOBAL LEGAL TRADITIONS: COMPARATIVE LAW IN THE 21ST CENTURY 5 (Lexis/Nexis, forthcoming) (manuscript on file with author).

[26] Miller, *supra* note 3, at 243.

[27] On the use (and abuse) of this phrase in law faculty colloquia, see Lawrence B. Solum, *Legal Theory Lexicon: It Takes a Theory to Beat a Theory*, LEGAL THEORY BLOG, Mar. 14, 2010, http://lsolum.typepad.com/legaltheory/2010/03/legal-theory-lexicon-it-takes-a-theory-to-beat-a-theory.html.

[28] *Cf.* AN-NA'IM ET AL., *supra* note 25, at 2 (encouraging "a cosmopolitan education for a generation of lawyers who are destined to encounter laws and legal actors from other legal cultures in our globalizing world and profession").

specifically to mean judicial decisions "considered as furnishing an example or authority for an identical or similar case afterwards arising or a similar question of law."[29] In this sense, analogical reasoning is fundamental to the practice of domestic law, most obviously in common-law jurisdictions such as those studied in this book, but also more generally in any embracing "the precept that similar cases be treated similarly." This requires practitioners and scholars to perceive, analyze, and in some fashion resolve, similarity and difference.[30] In this fundamental respect, then, one might imagine that this core process of domestic legal analysis could offer productive insights toward the development of a coherent comparative theory.

Unfortunately, however, analogical reasoning in and of itself offers little useful fodder for comparative theory. As Jefferson White observes, "[i]n legal argument from analogy the similarities . . . support a normative, not a causal, inference, that is, an inference about correct legal outcome."[31] Put differently, argument by analogy within a given legal regime presumes a system of normative preferences to guide the identification of relevant similarity and difference. This, however, is precisely what contextualists compellingly argue cannot be taken for granted in cross-border comparison of distinct legal regimes.[32] More fundamentally, however, the analytical mechanism by which the resolution of similarity and difference occurs in legal reasoning by analogy itself remains poorly understood. As White explains, a given case might easily be analogized to multiple lines of irreconcilable precedent, depending on the criteria chosen as a basis for comparison. This inevitably creates a "problem of choice" among competing criteria that can be resolved only by reference to normative values.[33] The process by which judges accomplish this remains unknown, however, and perhaps unknowable. White emphasizes that "we do not understand how similarity recognition interacts with normative legal judgment," concluding that "[u]ntil more progress is made in scientific and philosophical understanding of these cognitive functions and their interaction it is likely that some purely conditional or stage-setting conception . . . will control accounts of analogical reasoning in law."[34]

Perhaps surprisingly, then, it would seem that reasoning by analogy within domestic law provides no clearer a picture of the resolution of similarity and

[29] BLACK'S LAW DICTIONARY 1176 (6th ed., 1990).

[30] Jefferson White, *Analogical Reasoning*, *in* A COMPANION TO PHILOSOPHY OF LAW AND LEGAL THEORY 583, 583 (Dennis Patterson ed., 1996) (quoting JOHN RAWLS, A THEORY OF JUSTICE (1971)).

[31] *Id.* at 584.

[32] As Clark observes, this has rendered quite controversial the practice of citing to foreign legal materials as persuasive authority in U.S. judicial opinions. *See* Clark, *supra* note 2, at 178–80.

[33] White, *supra* note 30, at 585.

[34] *Id.* at 589.

difference than the functionalism/contextualism debate in comparative law does. The nature of the failure, however, as White describes it, is nevertheless illuminating. At rock bottom, we are talking about exceedingly complex cognitive processes that (at least for the time being) passeth understanding. A fascinating and, to the comparative scholar, tantalizing corner of the cognitive neuroscience literature suggests that the mental processes involved in resolving similarity and difference may lie at the core of how we sense the world around us, evaluate it, and choose to behave in response to it.[35] Such cognitive theories remain nascent, however, none claiming to provide a comprehensive account of how the mind resolves similarity and difference.

To the extent that developing a coherent comparative theory requires such deep comprehension of similarity and difference – how we determine which similarities are relevant to decision making, how the mind resolves relevant similarities and differences, why some might systematically fixate on the former whereas others fixate on the latter, and so on – it would seem that we are doomed to fail. Even this limited insight, however, may prove useful in a way. Perhaps the defining characteristic of comparative scholarship by those mindful of the twin challenge that functionalism and contextualism present is methodological humility – most notably with respect to the strength and defensibility of the claims advanced through their comparative analyses.

[35] *See, e.g.*, Katharina Henke, *A Model for Memory Systems Based on Processing Modes Rather than Consciousness*, 11 NATURE REVS. NEUROSCIENCE 523, 525, 528–29 (2010) (developing a model of memory distinguishing "slow encoding of rigid associations," the basis for "procedural memory formation, habit formation, category learning, classical conditioning and the formation of new representations in semantic memory"; "rapid encoding of flexible associations," the basis for "mental time travel, foresight, planning and creativity"; and "rapid encoding of single or unitized items," in which even a single exposure to an item results in "priming" and "feelings of familiarity for the perceptual, spatial or conceptual aspects of an item"); Dwight J. Kravitz et al., *A New Neural Framework for Visuospatial Processing*, 12 NATURE REVS. NEUROSCIENCE 217, 223–24 (2011) (reviewing studies linking the capacity for navigation with a part of the brain that "responds strongly to visual landmarks and to the recall of familiar locations," and that "shows evidence of generating representations that extrapolate beyond the borders of the image" of a partial landscape); Marius V. Peelen & Paul E. Downing, *The New Neural Basis of Visual Body Perception*, 8 NATURE REVS. NEUROSCIENCE 636, 638–39 (2007) (reviewing studies suggesting that a particular part of the brain "has a body representation that is abstract across specific visual features," but that its "response . . . to non-human animals is significantly lower than to humans, but higher than to objects, and . . . higher to mammals than to birds and fish, suggesting that this area is partly activated by objects with a body plan similar to that of humans"); Friedemann Pulvermüller & Luciano Fadiga, *Active Perception: Sensorimotor Circuits as a Cortical Basis for Language*, 11 NATURE REVS. NEUROSCIENCE 351, 355–57 (2010) (reviewing studies indicating that words conveying appearances, scents, and sounds stimulate visual, olfactory, and auditory areas of the brain, respectively, whereas "action-related words" similarly stimulate areas related to performing those actions, suggesting that "action-perception circuits are necessary for, and make an important contribution to, semantic processing").

For example, Michaels urges caution in advancing claims about the best or optimal law, not least because the multifunctionality of regulatory institutions within particular social and legal contexts "makes a comprehensive evaluation almost impossibly complex."[36] Even if functional analysis offers some potential for identifying ostensible "alternative solutions" to a given problem, "it cannot tell us whether those alternative solutions are better or not." Michaels observes that it can, however, "provide us with a view of our own law from the outside," thereby "revealing the contingency of any one doctrine" – an insight suggesting that evaluation limited to criteria internal to one's own legal system may, at least in this limited sense, be enhanced through comparative legal analysis.[37]

Miller takes this approach further, advocating a "discursive" comparative methodology that deemphasizes the issue of whether a particular norm or rule could be transplanted from one country to another – a fixation of functionalists and contextualists alike. Rather, Miller encourages the comparative scholar to focus more intently on "the social milieu" from which that norm or rule emerges. Consistent with Michaels's approach, Miller observes that "the sociology, history, economics and politics the comparatist discovers in the foreign context might come to inform the comparatist's understanding of the sociology, history, economics and politics of her or his own socio-legal culture." As opposed to transplantation, the apt biological metaphor would be the potential for something resembling parallel evolution. "Comparative law," Miller suggests, "might inform the growing of our own norm as a bottom-up process."[38]

For Pierre Legrand, this enhanced self-awareness is itself the ultimate goal of comparative legal analysis. His "contrarian comparativism," as he terms it, aspires to achieve a sort of social "archaeology or genealogy" of difference, "such as will *sustain* otherness."[39] Consistent with Michaels and Miller, Legrand suggests that comparative analysis permits "a new awareness of difference," a "productive tension" that reveals more vividly "a vital aspect of social existence which helps to define selfhood."[40] The effort to know oneself, one's social context, and one's legal system in this deep way – let alone to achieve the truly "cosmopolitan gaze" upon others that he advocates – may well be doomed to failure as a literal matter. But for Legrand, it nevertheless remains a worthy goal to "*fail better*."[41]

[36] Michaels, *supra* note 1, at 375–77.

[37] *Id.* at 379–80.

[38] Miller, *supra* note 3, at 243.

[39] Pierre Legrand, *Antivonbar*, 1 J. Comp. L. 13, 30 (2006).

[40] *Id.* at 34–36. *See also* Legrand, *supra* note 19, at 287-88 (arguing that comparative legal scholars "must make themselves into difference engineers").

[41] Legrand, *supra* note 39, at 25, 35.

Phrased in such terms, my aim in this book will be to "fail better" than extant economic and political theories of comparative corporate governance have done. As a methodological matter, I consciously steer a middle course between strict functionalism and strict contextualism, endeavoring to balance the need for commonality sufficient to permit meaningful comparison with the need for nuance sufficient to reflect the significant impact of distinct histories, cultures, and legal contexts.[42] This, as I see it, requires transparency regarding the assumptions that I am willing to make (or not, as the case may be) in order to facilitate cross-border comparison, and conscious scrutiny of the nature and defensibility of the claims advanced based on the comparative analysis provided.[43]

In the chapters that follow, I argue that the common-law jurisdictions investigated – Australia, Canada, the United Kingdom, and the United States – in fact differ on fundamental issues of corporate governance to a much greater extent than is typically recognized in the comparative literature, and that comprehending why requires placing corporate governance in the context of a broader political economy, of which it is but one part. Specifically, these jurisdictions vary considerably in the relative degrees of shareholder-orientation that they exhibit – both with respect to power (i.e., the capacity of shareholders to make decisions affecting corporate governance) and purpose (i.e., the degree to which their interests are prioritized over other competing interests). I then argue that a critical – but widely overlooked – factor impacting the degree of shareholder-orientation exhibited in each country has been the larger social welfare landscape faced by employees at key points in the historical development of that country's corporate governance system.

Developing this argument requires discerning various ways in which corporate law relates to other regulatory fields – including labor law and, most critically, social welfare policy. My core claim is that greater regard for the interests of employees in other regulatory domains has tended to insulate certain corporate governance systems from political pressure to show regard for employees and other "stakeholders," permitting more exclusive focus on shareholders without precipitating backlash – a key political determinant of the relatively higher degree of shareholder-centrism exhibited in Australia and

[42] *Cf.* Peter A. Hall, *Historical Institutionalism in Rationalist and Sociological Perspective*, *in* EXPLAINING INSTITUTIONAL CHANGE: AMBIGUITY, AGENCY, AND POWER 204, 204–06, 214–19 (James Mahoney & Kathleen Thelen eds., 2010) (similarly steering a middle course between "rational-choice approaches to institutions," emphasizing "Pareto-optimal equilibria or subgame perfect solutions to collective actions dilemmas," and "approaches associated with historical institutionalism . . . more attentive to problems of institutional change").

[43] *See* Bruner, *supra* note 23, at 591–93.

the United Kingdom, and to a lesser (but nevertheless substantial) degree in Canada as well. Conversely, weaker regard for the interests of employees in other regulatory domains has tended to result in greater political pressure being brought to bear on corporate governance to do so, inhibiting exclusive focus on shareholders – a key political determinant of the relatively lower degree of shareholder-centrism exhibited in the United States. In light of the comparative analysis provided, I conclude with various predictions regarding how and when varying levels of commitment to shareholder-centrism might change in these countries. I then explore certain normative implications of the argument as well – particularly in the United States, my home country. It is nevertheless my hope, however, that the comparative analysis provided might usefully contribute to corporate governance policy dialogues in other countries as well.

It will be immediately apparent to scholars of comparative corporate governance that my approach requires rejecting various assumptions commonly made in this field, while relying on others. As explored more fully below,[44] economically oriented comparative theories typically embrace (at least implicitly) a functionalist approach in which all systems are said to grapple with a single universal problem purportedly defining the field – managing "agency costs" arising where boards and officers control resources belonging to others, notably the shareholders' money. In styling public shareholders as "principals" to which corporate "agents" are (or should be) answerable, it is effectively assumed that corporate law universally does (or should) prioritize the shareholders' interests over all others – an assumption that effectively forecloses meaningful examination of the varying ways in which common-law countries approach issues of corporate purpose. Although I acknowledge certain broad structural similarities of the sort that preoccupy functionalist corporate governance scholarship – and that such similarities are, in fact, heightened among common-law jurisdictions – I reject the more sweeping assumption that corporate law performs perfectly coextensive sets of legal and social functions across the countries investigated.

In essence, the independent variable in my comparative analysis is the broader political economy faced by employees – a dynamic set of legal and social processes that I believe permits a more nuanced examination of why the divergence in shareholder-orientation has arisen among these otherwise similar systems, and how corporate governance has changed over time within them. At the same time, to avoid lapsing into excessive contingency, I focus on that aspect of the political economy that I consider a particularly operative, and

[44] *See infra* Chapter 4.A.

overlooked, driver of this divergence – the politics of social welfare, including both state-based social welfare systems and related structures that impact social welfare protections available to employees. For similar reasons, I focus my analysis on just four common-law jurisdictions – Australia, Canada, the United Kingdom, and the United States. This approach permits in-depth analysis through a manageable range of comparisons,[45] while embracing the large jurisdictions typically identified as exemplars of equity market-based corporate finance[46] – four countries that, by any reckoning, represent some of the largest, best-developed, and most consequential economies and capital markets in the world.[47]

Mine is not remotely the first political theory of comparative corporate governance – in fact, a number of important contributions have been made by legal scholars, political scientists, and others over recent years. As I explain below, however,[48] those theories have tended to pursue broader – and in some cases, global – explanatory power, contrasting a stylized "Anglo-American" (or "Anglo-Saxon" or "common-law") system that strongly emphasizes equity market financing and shareholder interests with other systems that place greater emphasis on a range of corporate stakeholders. Although I build quite directly on important contributions made by a number of these political theories, I nevertheless reject the implicit assumption that a holistic global theory can account for the varying degrees of shareholder-centrism exhibited by the common-law countries investigated here. In essence I conclude that extant

[45] *Cf.* Zweigert & Kötz, *supra* note 4, at 40–41 (urging "sober self-restraint" in the selection of jurisdictions and observing that "as soon as one tries to cover a wide range of legal systems the law of diminishing returns operates"). The geometric growth in complexity bears emphasis. For example, whereas two countries give rise to one comparison, four countries give rise to six, and six countries would give rise to fifteen.

[46] *See, e.g.*,Sue Konzelmann, Marc Fovargue-Davies & Gerhard Schnyder, *The Faces of Liberal Capitalism: Anglo-Saxon Banking Systems in Crisis?*, 36 Cambridge J. Econ. 495, 495, 504 (2012) (describing these jurisdictions as "the four main Anglo-Saxon economies" and explaining that "Anglo-Saxon corporate governance is typically characterised by widely dispersed equity ownership among individuals and institutions, prioritisation of shareholder interests in company law, and the protection of minority shareholder interests by securities law and regulation").

[47] *See, e.g.*, Organisation for Economic Co-operation and Development, *Gross Domestic Product: GDP, US$, Current Prices, Current PPPs, Millions*, http://stats.oecd.org/index.aspx?queryid=26646; World Bank, *GDP (current US$)*, http://data.worldbank.org/indicator/NY.GDP.MKTP.CD?order=wbapi_data_value_2009+wbapi_data_value+wbapi_data_value-last&sort=asc; World Federation of Exchanges, *2010 WFE Market Highlights* (Jan. 26, 2011), http://www.world-exchanges.org/files/file/stats%20and%20charts/2010%20WFE%20Market%20Highlights.pdf; World Federation of Exchanges, *Equity – 1.1 – Domestic Market Capitalization (USD millions)* (Jan. 2011), http://www.world-exchanges.org/statistics/ytd-monthly.

[48] *See infra* Chapter 4.B.

political theories have excessively sacrificed nuance for parsimony, developing macro-global models that may be useful in explaining, say, the ways in which the corporate governance systems of the United Kingdom or the United States diverge from the radically different system of Germany, yet provide no means of explaining the ways in which the systems of the United Kingdom and the United States diverge from each other. Ultimately I claim that the divergence among common-law countries described in the chapters that follow reveals a fundamentally different set of political dynamics to be at work in these countries, defying the pursuit of a holistic global theory.[49]

Although rejecting various assumptions that animate extant economic and political theories, the comparative theory that I develop most assuredly relies on certain assumptions itself. As a threshold matter, I make the broad assumption that "stable democratic rule" similarly requires in each of these countries that "popular demands for social protection are guaranteed some form of institutionalised access to the policy-making process."[50] In making this assumption, I build on approaches common to the political economy, social welfare, and risk management literatures. Political economist Karl Polanyi, writing in the 1940s, chronicled what he termed the "double movement" of industrial capitalism: the expansion of markets in the nineteenth and early twentieth centuries had gone hand in hand with "a network of measures and policies . . . integrated into powerful institutions designed to check the action of the market," including with respect to its social welfare impacts on the labor force.[51] In a similar manner, economic historian David Moss, writing in the 2000s, views this history through the related lens of risk management, describing distinct "phases" in the nineteenth and twentieth centuries in which the U.S. government encouraged industrial risk-taking through corporate law (notably, limited liability), and then responded to the social consequences through various social welfare structures mitigating the risks faced by labor in the new industrial landscape – a perspective from which corporate law, social welfare structures, and other regulatory fields reveal themselves to be of a piece. "Without limited liability law, bankruptcy law, government-printed money, and unemployment insurance – just to name a few pivotal risk management policies," Moss writes,

[49] *See infra* Chapter 6.A.

[50] Francis G. Castles, Australian Public Policy and Economic Vulnerability: A Comparative and Historical Perspective 2 (1988).

[51] Karl Polanyi, The Great Transformation: The Political and Economic origins of Our Time 79–80 (Beacon Press 2001) (1944). *See also* Castles, *supra* note 50, at 1 (framing his study of Australian social welfare policy by reference to Polanyi's work); James J. Rice & Michael J. Prince, Changing Politics of Canadian Social Policy 5–9 (2000) (framing their study of Canadian social welfare policy in a similar manner).

"it is doubtful that a modern industrial economy could have taken root in America."[52]

The broader dynamics of political economy and social policy examined in the work of Polanyi, Moss, and others are of course not limited to the United States, or to common-law countries for that matter. I argue, however, that this perspective helps to reveal both the differences between common-law countries and others, and the differences among common-law countries themselves. Although corporate law, labor law, and social welfare policy may affect the social risk calculus and associated politics for employees in numerous countries around the world, the manner in which they have impacted one another has differed across these various settings in ways that are both perceptible and illuminating. In saying this, I accept at least a weak version of the standard "public choice" assumption that various interest groups – including shareholders, employees, management, and other stakeholders (not to mention regulators and politicians themselves) – pursue maximization of their own utility through political processes (even if the rationality of their efforts may, at times, be open to doubt).[53] As I explore more fully in Chapters 5 and 6,[54] although social democracy may broadly correlate with stakeholder-orientation in corporate governance from a global vantage point – as Mark Roe has argued[55] – the correlation does not hold among common-law countries themselves. Put differently, although I accept that common-law countries do tend to exhibit both weaker social democracy and stronger shareholder-centrism than other countries do, my comparative analysis reveals that among common-law countries themselves, stronger shareholder-centrism and stronger social democracy actually go hand in hand. This, I suggest, indicates that although protections for minority shareholders may be a prerequisite to the emergence of equity

[52] David A. Moss, When All Else Fails: Government as the Ultimate Risk Manager 1 (Harvard University Press 2004) (2002).

[53] *See* D. Daniel Sokol, *Explaining the Importance of Public Choice for Law*, 109 Mich. L. Rev. 1029, 1037–40 (2011) (reviewing Maxwell L. Sterns & Todd J. Zywicki, Public Choice Concepts and Applications in Law (2009)). For the sake of clarity, note that "political economy" refers more broadly to economic problems faced by government. "Public choice," on the other hand, refers more specifically to the behavior of interest groups in the formation of policy. *Compare* Oxford English Dictionary Online, political, *adj.* and *n.*, S2., political economy (including "the branch of economics dealing with the economic problems of government") (3d ed. Sept. 2006, online version June 2011), *with* Oxford English Dictionary Online, public, *adj.* and *n.*, S2., public choice (including "the decision-making behaviour of politicians, voters, and interest groups in relation to government policies") (3d ed. Sept. 2007, online version June 2011). The two perspectives relate quite closely in practice, as the comparative analysis in this book demonstrates.

[54] *See infra* Chapters 5.D, 6.A.

[55] *See generally* Mark J. Roe, Political Determinants of Corporate Governance: Political Context, Corporate Impact (2003).

market-based corporate finance of the sort typically found in common-law countries, regard for the interests of employees may be a prerequisite to its consolidation and maintenance over time.

In this manner, I argue that the host of social and political variables affecting a given country's willingness to adopt and maintain structures managing social risk – not least among them, prevailing views on distributional justice – can have substantial impact on the governance of its large-scale corporate enterprises. Indeed, it is not an overstatement to say that the political foundations of shareholder power effectively lie outside corporate law itself – even among the major common-law systems so often caricatured in the comparative literature as generically and monolithically "shareholder-centric." The normative implications of this insight for the design of corporate governance regimes and social welfare regimes alike are considerable.

3 The Corporate Governance Role of Shareholders in Common-Law Jurisdictions

Aptly described as "the four main Anglo-Saxon economies,"[1] there are clearly substantial commonalities across the corporate governance systems of Australia, Canada, the United Kingdom, and the United States. In contrast with systems prevailing in Europe, for example, each exhibits relatively dispersed stock ownership, strong emphasis on shareholder interests, a unitary board structure without employee participation, and substantial "common-law" orientation relying heavily on judge-made case law.[2]

Notwithstanding these core structural and institutional similarities, however, close inspection of these "Anglo-Saxon" corporate governance systems reveals far greater divergence among them than the comparative literature typically acknowledges – notably with respect to relative degrees of shareholder orientation. U.K. shareholders in fact possess corporate governance powers, and benefit from express regard for their interests, far exceeding their U.S. counterparts. Australia and Canada, meanwhile, fall somewhere between the U.K. and U.S. extremes, though closer to the highly shareholder-centric U.K. approach.

This chapter surveys those distinctions that most clearly reflect the fundamental divergence in power and purpose among these systems, the practical and theoretical implications of which are explored more fully in the remainder of the book.

[1] Sue Konzelmann, Marc Fovargue-Davies & Gerhard Schnyder, *The Faces of Liberal Capitalism: Anglo-Saxon Banking Systems in Crisis?*, 36 CAMBRIDGE J. ECON. 495, 495 (2012).

[2] *See, e.g.*, Christopher M. Bruner, *Power and Purpose in the "Anglo-American" Corporation*, 50 VA. J. INT'L L. 579, 580–81 (2010); BRIAN R. CHEFFINS, CORPORATE OWNERSHIP AND CONTROL: BRITISH BUSINESS TRANSFORMED 4–7, 52–54 (2008); Martin Gelter, *The Dark Side of Shareholder Influence: Managerial Autonomy and Stakeholder Orientation in Comparative Corporate Governance*, 50 HARV. INT'L L.J. 129, 168–69 (2009); Konzelmann et al., *supra* note 1, at 495–96.

A. THE U.K. MODEL: STRONG SHAREHOLDERS

The United States has often been characterized as the jurisdiction "most receptive" to "the doctrine of shareholder primacy."[3] Shareholders in the United Kingdom, however, possess an arsenal of governance powers – coupled with express statutory regard for their interests – that would be the envy of shareholder activists anywhere, including the United States. Indeed, it is not an overstatement to say that U.K. company law is conceptually built on the shareholders' governance authority, of which all else – including the board's management authority – is effectively derivative.

1. Shareholders as Stewards

Shareholders of a U.K. public company – termed a "public limited company," or plc[4] – possess extraordinary power to shape the rules of corporate governance, and even the substance of corporate decision making, on a unilateral basis. The U.K. corporation's core governance document, the "constitution," includes "articles of association prescribing regulations for the company," along with various resolutions and agreements.[5] Model articles prescribed by the Secretary of State apply by default, but shareholders can unilaterally amend the articles by special resolution of a 75 percent majority,[6] giving them very direct power over the content of the corporation's core governance arrangements. The statute also gives shareholders enormous practical power to determine the composition of the board of directors. Shareholders with 5 percent voting power can demand a meeting at any time, at which by ordinary resolution of a simple majority directors can be removed without cause. Strikingly, this strong removal power applies "notwithstanding anything in any agreement" between the corporation and the director in question (although the director "is entitled to be heard on the resolution at the meeting").[7]

The removal power gives shareholders the ability to exert enormous leverage over management because, as Paul Davies explains in his leading treatise,

[3] *See, e.g.*, Antoine Rebérioux, *Does Shareholder Primacy Lead to a Decline in Managerial Accountability?*, 31 CAMBRIDGE J. ECON. 507, 507 (2007). *See also* Ruth V. Aguilera & Cynthia A. Williams, *"Law and Finance": Inaccurate, Incomplete, and Important*, 2009 BYU L. REV. 1413, 1418 (2009) (describing the United States as "the archetypical Anglo-Saxon shareholder-oriented country").

[4] In contrast with a "private limited company," or ltd, a plc may offer securities to the public, subject to the requirement that it possess a "trading certificate" and have allotted share capital of at least £50,000 (or the euro equivalent). *See* Companies Act, 2006, c. 46, §§ 4, 755–56, 761–63 (U.K.) [hereinafter U.K. Companies Act].

[5] *See id.* §§ 17–18.

[6] *See id.* §§ 19–21, 283.

[7] *See id.* §§ 168–69, 282, 303–04.

"disgruntled shareholders can say, in effect, to the directors: if you choose not to follow our views, we will by ordinary majority seek to remove you from office." This, he notes, "can be a powerful inducement" to conform to shareholder wishes – so powerful, in fact, that it almost blurs into "a power to give instructions."[8] To be sure, public threats of this nature have remained rare in the United Kingdom, but as Davies observes, "the pressure which the institutions can bring to bear privately depends in large part upon the prospect of their being able to get their way in the public meeting if the private pressures are unsuccessful."[9]

The shareholders' ability to exert pressure on management of a U.K. corporation is all that much greater in times of financial stress, when the removal power is effectively bolstered by strong preemptive rights. U.K. shareholders possess a default statutory right to participate in new share issuances on a pro rata basis.[10] Although not a form of governance authority as such, preemptive rights have functioned to augment the leverage of institutional shareholders. In essence, coordinated refusal by institutions already invested in a company to buy further shares would prove embarrassing and send a negative signal to the market, thereby improving the institutions' bargaining position in discussions with management of cash-strapped companies.[11] Although preemptive rights can be waived by the shareholders,[12] institutions are typically reluctant to do so, rendering this "a 'strong' default rule"[13] of real consequence in U.K. corporate governance.

To be sure, in the United Kingdom – as elsewhere – directors occupy a critical and mandatory position in the corporation. The Companies Act requires that a public company have at least two directors,[14] and according to the model articles for public companies, those directors are generally "responsible for the

[8] Paul L. Davies, Gower and Davies' Principles of Modern Company Law 371 (8th ed. 2008). *See also* Kenneth J. Arrow, The Limits of Organization 63–79 (1974) (exploring the relationship between accountability and control in organizational decision making).

[9] Davies, *supra* note 8, at 425.

[10] *See* U.K. Companies Act, *supra* note 4, § 561. *See also* Council Directive 77/91, art. 29, 1977 O.J. (L26/1) (EC) (requiring preemptive rights); Davies, *supra* note 8, at 835 n.35.

[11] *See* Bernard S. Black & John C. Coffee, Jr., *Hail Britannia?: Institutional Investor Behavior under Limited Regulation*, 92 Mich. L. Rev. 1997, 2034–37, 2078–79 (1994); Cheffins, *supra* note 2, at 329, 332–33. Note that U.K. institutional shareholders, unlike their U.S. counterparts, do not face substantial impediments to informal collective action. *See* John Armour, Brian R. Cheffins & David A. Skeel, Jr., *Corporate Ownership Structure and the Evolution of Bankruptcy Law: Lessons from the United Kingdom*, 55 Vand. L. Rev. 1699, 1751–52 (2002); Gelter, *supra* note 2, at 188.

[12] *See* U.K. Companies Act, *supra* note 4, §§ 568, 570–71.

[13] Davies, *supra* note 8, at 839–45.

[14] *See* U.K. Companies Act, *supra* note 4, § 154.

management of the company's business, for which purpose they may exercise all the powers of the company"[15] – an ostensibly sweeping grant of authority conveying that, in practical terms, the board of a U.K. corporation is "the most important decision-making body within the company."[16] Strikingly, however, this substantial grant of authority is followed immediately in the model articles by a reminder that shareholder power remains the true heart of the U.K. conception of the corporation: "The members [i.e. shareholders] may, by special resolution, *direct the directors* to take, or refrain from taking, specified action."[17] As a practical matter, there may be little reason to muster a 75 percent majority when threat of removal from the board requires only a simple majority, yet the very concept of shareholders directing the directors to take specified action remains illuminating as a matter of theory, reflecting the fact that shareholder power is literally the animating spirit of the U.K. corporation.[18]

Indeed, consistent with this notion of directing the directors, U.K. shareholders – particularly the large institutions that have long dominated U.K. equity markets – have actually been styled as "stewards" of the companies in which they invest.[19] Notwithstanding the substantial delegation of day-to-day management authority to the board (and through it, the officers), institutional shareholders – as the "steward" moniker implies – are not simply entitled to oversee corporate affairs and to intervene as they deem necessary, but are in fact expected to do so.[20] We will return later in this book to consider whether this expectation remains wise policy in the current environment, and whether this

[15] Companies (Model Articles) Regulations, 2008, S.I. 2008/3229, sched. 3, art. 3 (U.K.) [hereinafter U.K. Model Articles].

[16] Davies, *supra* note 8, at 365–71. For a discussion of the typical contents of public company articles, see R.C. Nolan, *The Continuing Evolution of Shareholder Governance*, 65 Cambridge L.J. 92, 115–19 (2006).

[17] U.K. Model Articles, *supra* note 15, art. 4(1) (emphasis added).

[18] Article 4(1) of the Model Articles is backstopped by a common law doctrine – preserved by the Companies Act – permitting shareholders to bind the company by unanimous consent, a power that may conceivably extend to matters allocated by the constitution to the board (although this remains unsettled). *See* Davies, *supra* note 8, at 374–75, 419–23; U.K. Companies Act, *supra* note 4, § 281(4)(a) (providing that Companies Act provisions on shareholder resolutions do not affect "any enactment or rule of law as to . . . things done otherwise than by passing a resolution"). For a historical overview of the shareholders' role in U.K. corporate governance, see generally Nolan, *supra* note 16.

[19] *See* Financial Reporting Council, The UK Stewardship Code, 2012 (U.K.). *See also* Lord Peter Mandelson, Mansion House Speech, Mar. 1, 2010, http://webarchive.nationalarchives.gov.uk/20100304014526/http://www.bis.gov.uk/mansion-house-speech; David Walker, A Review of Corporate Governance in U.K. Banks and Other Financial Industry Entities: Final Recommendations 68–89 (2009), http://webarchive.nationalarchives.gov.uk/+/http://www.hm-treasury.gov.uk/d/walker_review_261109.pdf.

[20] *See* Oxford English Dictionary Online, steward, *v.* ("To manage, administer") (2nd ed. 1989).

expectation remains realistic today in any event,[21] but for the moment, observe that this "stewardship" conception of the shareholders' role both reflects and reinforces their centrality in the U.K. corporate governance scheme.

The shareholders' substantial power to control the contents of core governance arrangements, to determine the composition of the board, and even to mandate that particular actions be taken (or not taken), are probably sufficient to demonstrate that U.K. corporate governance is extraordinarily shareholder-centric in orientation. This becomes even clearer, however – and illuminative of corporate purpose, as well – in the area of takeover regulation. Takeover regulation is of particular interest in elucidating the degree of shareholder orientation in a given corporate governance system because hostile takeovers so starkly pit the interests of shareholders, who want to accept premium bids for their stock, against those of other stakeholders such as managers and employees who fear losing their jobs, creditors who fear additional corporate debt, local communities that fear the prospect of corporate consolidation, and so on.[22] In takeover regulation – as in other areas – U.K. corporate governance places shareholders in the driver's seat, strongly favoring their interests by giving target shareholders virtually unfettered discretion to accept or reject a hostile bid.

Takeovers in the United Kingdom are regulated through a market-based structure in which institutional shareholders themselves are the dominant voices. The City Code on Takeovers and Mergers, created in 1968, is implemented and enforced by a body called the Panel on Takeovers and Mergers – an essentially private body comprised of institutions including insurers, investment companies, pensions, banks, accountants, stockbrokers, and industry representatives.[23] Although the Panel was given a statutory mandate in the Companies Act (2006) in order to comply with an EC directive requiring that a public authority be designated to oversee takeover bids,[24] the Panel nevertheless remains firmly rooted in the private sector, both in composition and in practice.[25]

[21] *See infra* Chapter 6.B.–D.

[22] *See* Bruner, *supra* note 2, at 611–46. *See also* Christopher M. Bruner, *The Enduring Ambivalence of Corporate Law*, 59 ALA. L. REV. 1385, 1408–32 (2008).

[23] *See* The Takeover Panel: About the Panel, http://www.thetakeoverpanel.org.uk/structure/about-the-panel; The Takeover Panel: Panel Membership, http://www.thetakeoverpanel.org.uk/structure/panel-membership; The Takeover Panel: The Panel on Takeovers and Mergers, http://www.thetakeoverpanel.org.uk/index.php?page_id=45.

[24] U.K. Companies Act, *supra* note 4, §§ 942–43; Council Directive 2004/25/EC, art. 4, 2004 O.J. (L 142) (EC). *See also* Marco Ventoruzzo, *Europe's Thirteenth Directive and U.S. Takeover Regulation: Regulatory Means and Political and Economic Ends*, 41 TEX. INT'L L.J. 171 (2006).

[25] *See* John Armour & David A. Skeel, Jr., *Who Writes the Rules for Hostile Takeovers, and Why? – The Peculiar Divergence of U.S. and U.K. Takeover Regulation*, 95 GEO. L.J. 1727, 1744 (2007);

The Code itself, consisting of a series of principles followed by more detailed rules, makes eminently clear that shareholders control the fate of takeover bids. The general principles require that all target shareholders be treated equally, and state that the target board "must not deny the holders of securities the opportunity to decide on the merits of the bid."[26] Rule 21.1 elaborates that the target board "must not, without the approval of the shareholders . . . take any action which may result in any offer or bona fide possible offer being frustrated or in shareholders being denied the opportunity to decide on its merits"[27] – meaning that takeover defenses such as poison pills cannot be implemented without shareholder approval.[28] Although the so-called "mandatory offer" rule – requiring that upon reaching 30 percent the bidder must make a bid for all shares – might tend to inhibit takeovers where the bidder is not interested in 100 percent ownership,[29] this rule nevertheless reinforces that the Code's principal aim is to safeguard the interests of target company shareholders.[30] Hostile takeover activity in the United Kingdom remains substantial in any event, an unsurprising outcome given the strongly shareholder-centric thrust of its takeover laws.[31]

John Birds et al., Boyle & Birds' Company Law 788–89 (6th ed. 2007). On the government's capacity to intervene in takeover regulation moving forward, see Brian E. Rosenzweig, Note, *Private versus Public Regulation: A Comparative Analysis of British and American Takeover Controls*, 18 Duke J. Comp. & Int'l L. 213, 217–20 (2007).

[26] Panel on Takeovers and Mergers, The Takeover Code General Principles 1, 3, at B1 (10th ed. 2011).

[27] *Id.* Rule 21.1(a), at I13.

[28] *See* John Armour, Simon Deakin & Suzanne J. Konzelmann, *Shareholder Primacy and the Trajectory of UK Corporate Governance*, 41 Brit. J. Indus. Rel. 531, 534 (2003); Deborah A. DeMott, *Shareholders as Principals*, *in* Key Developments in Corporate Law and Trusts Law: Essays in Honour of Professor Harold Ford 105, 118–19 (Ian Ramsey ed., 2002).

[29] *See* Panel on Takeovers and Mergers, *supra* note 26, Rule 9.1, at F1; Ventoruzzo, *supra* note 24, at 191–92, 213–14 (observing that the mandatory offer rule raises the cost of a takeover bid).

[30] *See* Panel on Takeovers and Mergers, *supra* note 26, at A1–A2; T.P. Lee, *Takeovers – the United Kingdom Experience*, *in* Takeovers, Institutional Investors, and the Modernization of Corporate Laws 192, 195, 198–200 (John H. Farrar ed., 1993).

[31] A U.K. takeover "is more likely to be hostile, and if hostile, is more likely to succeed," but U.S. takeover activity, "adjusted for the size of the economy, actually seems slightly higher." Armour & Skeel, *supra* note 25, at 1738–41. As Gelter observes, however, Armour and Skeel's data suggest a higher rate of U.K. takeover activity relative to GDP. *See* Gelter, *supra* note 2, at 151 & n.138. *See also* John C. Coates IV, *M&A Break Fees: US Litigation versus UK Regulation*, *in* Regulation versus Litigation: Perspectives from Economics and Law 239, 240, 253 n.14 (Daniel P. Kessler ed., 2011) (observing that the two countries have "a large number of bids for public companies comprising 75% of worldwide bid volume," but that there are "more hostile bids as a share of large bids in the UK").

II. Enlightened Shareholder Value

Hostile takeovers figure prominently in the comparative analysis developed later in the book precisely because they provide a unique window into the core values animating the corporate governance system. By driving a wedge between the interests of shareholders and essentially all other corporate constituencies, these transactions force a given society to clarify its priorities. Favoring target shareholders in these transactions strongly suggests that the given society feels comfortable enough addressing other constituencies' interests in other ways, whereas reluctance to do so suggests the opposite – a set of social and political dynamics to which we shall return later.[32]

In the United Kingdom, however, we are not left to infer shareholder-centrism from the rules of the corporate governance regime, because Parliament has established by statute that the defining aim of a U.K. public corporation is to advance the shareholders' interests. To be sure, the duties of a U.K. director are not unlike those familiar to lawyers from the United States and other common-law jurisdictions. U.K. directors are duty bound to act consistent with the company's constitution,[33] to pursue "the success of the company" in good faith,[34] to "exercise independent judgment,"[35] to "exercise reasonable care, skill and diligence,"[36] and generally to avoid conflicts of interest.[37] The statute states that these duties are owed "to the company" itself, which becomes significant when enforcing them,[38] a matter explored later in this chapter.[39] But with respect to what directors are actually expected to do – that is, the values and interests that are to drive their decision making – the statute makes clear that shareholders are to be first and foremost in their minds. Section 172 of the Companies Act (2006) states that a director "*must* act in the way he considers, in good faith, would be most likely to promote the success of the company *for the benefit of its members* [i.e. shareholders] as a whole."[40] Notwithstanding the statute's deference in focusing on what the director subjectively considers to be in the company's interests and in linking the obligation to the amorphous "good faith" concept, the core value to be advanced could not be more clear – directors "must" prioritize the shareholders' interests.

32 *See infra* Chapters 5–6.

33 U.K. Companies Act, *supra* note 4, § 171(a).

34 *Id.* § 172(1).

35 *Id.* § 173(1).

36 *Id.* § 174(1).

37 *Id.* §§ 175–77.

38 *Id.* § 170(1). *See also* DAVIES, *supra* note 8, at 479–80; ALAN DIGNAM & JOHN LOWRY, COMPANY LAW 301–05 (5th ed. 2009).

39 *See infra* Chapter 3.D.

40 U.K. Companies Act, *supra* note 4, § 172(1) (emphasis added). The statute elsewhere makes clear that the "members" of a corporation are its shareholders. *See id.* §§ 112–13.

This is the lens through which the remainder of § 172 must be viewed. Although the statute does require that directors "have regard" for various constituencies, including employees, suppliers, customers, and even "the community," as well as other values (including the environment, the company's ethical reputation, and "long term" consequences of their decisions), these various interests are expressly subordinated to the shareholders' interests.[41] To be sure, the fact that these other constituencies and values were included in § 172 at all reflects a spirited U.K. debate in the run-up to the Companies Act (2006) regarding the appropriate aims of corporate decision making, to which we shall return.[42] The shareholders' decisive victory has not, however, been lost on commentators.[43] Indeed, though often styled "enlightened shareholder value,"[44] it bears emphasizing that it is still "shareholder value" that the U.K. Companies Act prioritizes. Section 172 cannot be coherently read as a broader stakeholder mandate because directors are permitted to consider other interests only to the degree relevant to maximizing shareholder value. Despite the broader verbiage, § 172 is fully consistent with – and in fact exemplifies and reinforces – the shareholder-centrism of the U.K. Companies Act more generally, making explicit what emerges implicitly from examination of the core governance rules and the takeover rules of U.K. company law.

III. *Contractualism and U.K. Corporate Governance*

How and why the United Kingdom arrived at this strong form of shareholder-centrism will be investigated in some depth later in this book,[45] but it is critical to recognize from the outset another dimension of U.K. company law that further reflects the centrality of shareholders in the U.K. corporate governance system – the highly contractual nature of the U.K. corporation. According to the Companies Act (2006), the U.K. corporation – and more

[41] *See id.* § 172(1). Section 172 does, however, clarify that it "has effect subject to any enactment or rule of law requiring directors . . . to consider or act in the interests of creditors of the company." *Id.* § 172(3).

[42] *See infra* Chapter 5.A.

[43] *See, e.g.*, DAVIES, *supra* note 8, at 506–10. *See also* Tom Burns & John Paterson, *Gold Plating, Gold Standard or Base Metal? Making Sense of Narrative Reporting after Repeal of the Operating and Financial Review Regulations*, 2007 INT'L COMPANY & COM. L. REV. 247 (2007) (concluding that § 172 "represents a fairly limited modification of the *status quo*" and recounting the U.K. government's unwillingness to impose substantial narrative reporting obligations regarding other constituencies and values); U.K. Companies Act, *supra* note 4, § 417 (clarifying that the "purpose" of the limited business review included in the Companies Act is to permit shareholders to assess "how the directors have performed their duty under section 172").

[44] *See* DIGNAM & LOWRY, *supra*, note 38, at 314–16.

[45] *See infra* Chapter 5.A.

specifically, its constitution – is to be treated as a contract. Section 33 states that the constitution's provisions "bind the company and its members to the same extent as if there were covenants on the part of the company and of each member to observe those provisions."[46]

In light of the foregoing survey of U.K. corporate governance, it will be immediately clear that the constitution can be described as a contract only in a stylized sense. As § 33 itself illustrates, it is the statute that creates this contract, not the company and its shareholders. Additionally, recall that the shareholders of the company can unilaterally alter the constitution by special resolution of a 75 percent majority. In these respects, the constitution of a U.K. corporation hardly looks like a typical private contract.[47]

Nevertheless, the strong ethos of contract that pervades the U.K. conception of the corporation remains illuminating. The board's power in a U.K. corporation is effectively delegated by the shareholders, in something like the manner of a contractual delegation, through the articles. Recall that the model articles applying by default to U.K. public companies say that directors are empowered to manage the company "[s]ubject to the articles"[48] – that is, subject to the contract, the terms of which shareholders can unilaterally determine. In this respect, there would appear to be no such thing as "board power" in a U.K. corporation, if by that we mean some form of corporate governance power not ultimately grounded in the shareholders' original power. Board power in a U.K. corporation is literally and entirely derivative of a contract, if a unique one, over which the shareholders themselves possess supreme power – meaning that the shareholders are the true source of all governance power in a U.K. corporation.[49] This, for Davies, is "a point of some theoretical (even ideological) importance: the directors' authority is derived from the shareholders through a process of delegation via the articles and not from a separate and free-standing grant of authority from the State," a structure reflecting "the shareholder-centred nature of British company law."[50]

B. THE U.S. MODEL: WEAK SHAREHOLDERS

Before the backdrop of the highly shareholder-centric U.K. model – in which shareholders possess supreme governance power and shareholder wealth

[46] U.K. Companies Act, *supra* note 4, § 33(1).

[47] *See* Marc T. Moore, *Private Ordering and Public Policy: The Paradoxical Foundations of Corporate Contractarianism* 4, 34–43 (Nov. 9, 2010), http://ssrn.com/abstract=1706045 (observing the tension between the contractarian ethos of U.K. company law and "the significant presence of mandatory rules").

[48] U.K. Model Articles, *supra* note 15, art. 3.

[49] *See* Nolan, *supra* note 16, at 94–95, 120–21.

[50] Davies, *supra* note 8, at 366.

clearly represents the defining aim of the corporate enterprise – the most remarkable feature of U.S. corporate governance is its deep ambivalence regarding the role and interests of shareholders. As this section details, U.S. shareholders possess surprisingly limited capacity to intervene in corporate affairs, and their interests are not prioritized with anything approaching the clarity and consistency enjoyed by their U.K. counterparts.

I. *Shareholders as Spectators*

The defining attributes of U.S. corporate law are the shareholders' marginal role and very weak governance powers; the correlatively greater centrality and strength of the board of directors; and a long-standing, fundamental ambivalence regarding who ultimately calls the shots in circumstances where the interests of various stakeholders most clearly diverge.[51] In stark contrast with U.K. company law, U.S. corporate law "is, and will remain, deeply ambivalent . . . with respect to each of three fundamental and related issues: the locus of ultimate corporate governance authority, the intended beneficiaries of corporate production, and the relationship between corporate law and the achievement of the social good."[52]

The United States has a federal system of government with residual regulatory power defaulting to the states themselves.[53] Under the so-called internal affairs doctrine, corporate law – including the rights of shareholders – has traditionally been left to the states.[54] It is beyond question, however, that Congress possesses ample authority to federalize corporate law to the degree it likes under the broadly interpreted Commerce Clause of the U.S. Constitution.[55] Although Congress has intervened only sporadically, substantial federal regulation of aspects of corporate governance has arisen following major crises capturing national attention – some of the

[51] *See* Bruner, *supra* note 22, at 1408–32; Bruner, *supra* note 2, at 593–99; Christopher M. Bruner, *Corporate Governance Reform in a Time of Crisis*, 36 J. CORP. L. 309, 323–25 (2011).

[52] Bruner, *supra* note 22, at 1386.

[53] *See* U.S. CONST. amend. X ("The powers not delegated to the United States by the Constitution, nor prohibited by it to the States, are reserved to the States respectively, or to the people.").

[54] *See* RESTATEMENT (SECOND) OF CONFLICT OF LAWS §§ 302(2), 304 (1971); CTS Corp. v. Dynamics Corp. of Am., 481 U.S. 69, 89 (1987); Santa Fe Indus., Inc. v. Green, 430 U.S. 462, 479 (1977).

[55] *See* U.S. CONST. art. I. § 8, cl. 3 (giving Congress power to "regulate Commerce with foreign Nations, and among the several States, and with the Indian Tribes"). *See also* Leo E. Strine, Jr., *Breaking the Corporate Governance Logjam in Washington: Some Constructive Thoughts on a Responsible Path Forward*, 63 BUS. LAW. 1079, 1084 (2008) ("No substantial argument can be made that Congress does not have the constitutional authority to enact a preemptive corporate law governing publicly traded corporations operating in interstate commerce.").

most notable including the creation of federal securities regulation and the Securities and Exchange Commission (SEC) following the 1929 stock market crash and the onset of the Great Depression, and major amendments to those statutes following scandals such as the Enron meltdown and the recent financial and economic crisis.[56] The upshot is that U.S. public companies today are regulated by state corporate law and federal securities regulation.[57]

Although U.K. shareholders may reasonably be styled "stewards" of the corporations in which they invest, given the extraordinary governance powers they possess, the constraints placed upon U.S. shareholders effectively render them "spectators."[58] In the survey of U.S. corporate governance that follows I focus principally on Delaware – the jurisdiction of incorporation for most U.S. public corporations[59] – but will address other U.S. approaches that differ in illuminating ways, as well as relevant aspects of federal securities regulation.

Whereas management authority in a U.K. corporation ultimately flows from the shareholders themselves, management authority in a U.S. corporation flows from the statute, placing the board in a different position. Section 141(a) of the Delaware General Corporation Law (DGCL) states that the "business and affairs of every corporation . . . shall be managed by or under the direction of a board of directors, except as may be otherwise provided in this chapter or in its certificate of incorporation."[60] Observe that this grant of management authority appears not in the corporation's internal governance documents, but in the statute itself – a distinction that Deborah DeMott aptly suggests "reflects an architectural choice about how the law structures relationships among those who invest in corporations and those who manage them."[61] To be sure, the statute contemplates deviations from unfettered board control over day-to-day corporate affairs, just as in the United Kingdom. But such limitations must appear in the charter – the colloquial name for the articles of incorporation,

[56] *See* Christopher M. Bruner, *Managing Corporate Federalism: The Least-Bad Approach to the Shareholder Bylaw Debate*, 36 Del. J. Corp. L. 1, 26–29 (2011); Bruner, *supra* note 51, at 332–35; Marcel Kahan & Edward Rock, *Symbiotic Federalism and the Structure of Corporate Law*, 58 Vand. L. Rev. 1573, 1574–90 (2005); Mark J. Roe, *Delaware and Washington as Corporate Lawmakers*, 34 Del. J. Corp. L. 1, 7–12 (2009); Mark J. Roe, *Delaware's Competition*, 117 Harv. L. Rev. 588, 591–93 (2003); E. Norman Veasey, *What Would Madison Think? The Irony of the Twists and Turns of Federalism*, 34 Del. J. Corp. L. 35, 39–42 (2009).

[57] *See* Bruner, *supra* note 56, at 26.

[58] *See* Bruner, *supra* note 51, at 329–39.

[59] *See* State of Delaware Division of Corporations, *Why Choose Delaware as Your Corporate Home?*, http://www.corp.delaware.gov/.

[60] Del. Code Ann. tit. 8, § 141(a).

[61] Deborah A. DeMott, *Corporate Litigation in the US and UK*, 51 Am. J. Comp. L. 229, 233 (2003) (reviewing A.J. Boyle, Minority Shareholders' Remedies (2002)).

the core governance document[62] – which U.S. shareholders lack unilateral power to amend. Although Delaware shareholders possess authority to approve charter amendments, they cannot initiate them – or any other fundamental actions, for that matter. Charter amendments, mergers, sales of substantially all assets, and dissolution all require a board proposal to that effect, essentially positioning the board as a "gatekeeper."[63] The Delaware Supreme Court has accordingly described fundamental action of this sort as a "shared exercise" of the board and the shareholders.[64] From a corporate governance perspective, the upshot is that Delaware shareholders lack the straightforward means of intervening in corporate affairs that their U.K. counterparts possess – a distinction prompting Stephen Bainbridge to expressly disclaim any explanatory power for his "director primacy" theory (discussed below) beyond the United States.[65]

Although Delaware shareholders elect the board, and expansive dicta have suggested that the legitimate exercise of board authority is rooted in this mandate,[66] once directors have been elected, Delaware shareholders find it far more difficult to remove directors than U.K. shareholders do. Delaware shareholders possess default power to remove directors "with or without cause" by vote of a simple majority of shares, but the default rule reverses if the board has been staggered into multiple classes of directors. A classified board not only renders it more difficult to achieve control of the board through a proxy contest (requiring multiple annual elections to secure a majority of the board seats), but also triggers a statutory requirement that cause for early removal be demonstrated, unless the charter permits removal without cause.[67] The

[62] *See* Del. Code Ann. tit. 8, §§ 102(b)(1), 141(a). The charter generally contains a handful of mandatory terms such as the company's name and address, the nature of its business (although "any lawful act or activity" suffices), the authorized stock, and the incorporators, as well as various elective provisions – notably, a waiver of director liability to the corporation or its stockholders for breaches of the duty of care. *See id.* §§ 102(a), 102(b)(7).

[63] *See id.* §§ 242(b)(1)–(2), 251(b)–(c), 271(a), 275(a)–(b). *See also* Robert B. Thompson, *Preemption and Federalism in Corporate Governance: Protecting Shareholder Rights to Vote, Sell, and Sue*, 62 Law & Contemp. Probs. 215, 217, 234–35 (1999). *But see* Del. Code Ann. tit. 8, § 275(c) (permitting unilateral dissolution by shareholders, but only by unanimous written consent). *See also* NYSE, Inc., Listed Company Manual § 312.03(c)–(d), http://nysemanual.nyse.com/lcm (giving listed company shareholders voting rights in transactions involving issuance of common stock equaling 20 percent or more of the previous outstanding shares or voting power, and for any "issuance that will result in a change of control").

[64] *See* Omnicare, Inc. v. NCS Healthcare, Inc., 818 A.2d 914, 930 (Del. 2003).

[65] *See* Stephen M. Bainbridge, *Director Primacy* 3 n.14 (UCLA Law Sch., Law & Econ. Research Paper No. 10–06, 2010), http://papers.ssrn.com/sol3/papers.cfm?abstract_id=1615838.

[66] *See* Del. Code Ann. tit. 8, § 211(b); Blasius Indus., Inc. v. Atlas Corp., 564 A.2d 651, 659 (Del. Ch. 1988).

[67] *See* Del. Code Ann. tit. 8, §§ 141(d), (k).

	U.K.	U.S. (Delaware)
call special meetings	Y	N
remove directors without cause	Y	N (if classified)
initiate charter amendments	Y	N
approve takeover defenses	Y	N
compel board action	Y	N
preemptive rights	Y	N

Figure 3.1. Shareholders' Default Governance Powers in Public Corporations: The United Kingdom and the United States

shareholders' ability to remove directors is further undercut by their lack of default power to call special meetings, which power must be expressly provided in the charter or bylaws,[68] and by restrictive proxy and tender offer rules under federal securities regulation[69] that effectively preclude coordinated action on an informal, nonpublic basis by shareholders in U.S. public companies.

The notion of shareholders "directing the directors" in the manner contemplated by the U.K. public company model articles, meanwhile, is utterly foreign to Delaware corporate law. Indeed, it is thought that a charter provision purporting to give shareholders the power to do so would be invalid.[70] Likewise, preemptive rights of the sort provided by "strong" default to U.K. shareholders – giving institutional shareholders additional leverage over management of cash-strapped companies – are available to Delaware shareholders only if the charter grants them, which it typically does not.[71] (For the reader's convenience, the foregoing contrasts are summarized in Figure 3.1.)

Similarly – and tellingly – U.S. corporate law is far less favorable to shareholders in the area of hostile takeovers than is the U.K. approach. Unlike the

[68] *See id.* § 211(d).

[69] *See* 17 C.F.R. § 240.14a-2; 17 C.F.R. §§ 13d-1, 13d-3, 13d-5. *See also* Ruth V. Aguilera, Cynthia A. Williams, John M. Conley & Deborah E. Rupp, *Corporate Governance and Social Responsibility: A Comparative Analysis of the UK and the US*, 14 Corp. Governance: An Int'l Rev.147, 151 (2006).

[70] *See* William T. Allen, Reinier Kraakman & Guhan Subramanian, Commentaries and Cases on the Law of Business Organization 103 (2d ed. 2007); Lucian Arye Bebchuk, *The Case for Increasing Shareholder Power*, 118 Harv. L. Rev. 833, 888–90 (2005).

[71] *See* Del. Code Ann. tit. 8, § 102(b)(3); Black & Coffee, *supra* note 11, at 2079 (observing that preemptive rights "are rarely found among large U.S. firms").

market-based structure adopted in the United Kingdom, U.S. law on takeovers has largely been developed by state courts, which – in stark contrast with the clear U.K. rule in favor of shareholders – have created elaborate fiduciary duty-based tests giving target boards substantial discretion to intervene in hostile takeover bids.

In 1985, the Delaware Supreme Court handed down its seminal *Unocal* opinion, providing the conceptual foundation for the approach to hostile takeovers applicable to most U.S. public companies. In *Unocal*, the court purported to apply "enhanced" scrutiny to target board defensive tactics, because of "the omnipresent specter that a board may be acting primarily in its own interests" in opposing the bid.[72] Effectively the board is required to earn the protections of the business judgment rule – a presumption of good faith, informed business decisions[73] – by showing "reasonable grounds for believing that a danger to corporate policy and effectiveness existed because of another person's stock ownership" and that defenses responding to it were "reasonable in relation to the threat posed."[74]

It would soon become clear, however, that this nominally "enhanced" scrutiny amounted to little in practice. Later in 1985, in *Moran*, the court endorsed poison pills adopted preemptively (that is, in the absence of any "specific threat"), finding them to be a proportionate response to the general threat posed by the prevalence of coercive tender offers in the marketplace – the logic being that the board could still be dislodged through a proxy contest, after which the pill could be removed by the new board, allowing the tender offer to proceed.[75] Poison pills, commonly called "shareholder rights plans," subsequently became the most consequential defensive measure available to target boards, effectively shutting down hostile bids by threatening would-be hostile acquirers with substantial dilution should they exceed a specified ownership threshold without the target board's approval.[76]

Although *Moran* did make clear that the continuing appropriateness of a preemptively adopted pill would have to be reevaluated under *Unocal* in light of

[72] Unocal Corp. v. Mesa Petroleum Co., 493 A.2d 946, 954 (Del. 1985).

[73] *See* Aronson v. Lewis, 473 A.2d 805, 812 (Del. 1984), *overruled on other grounds by* Brehm v. Eisner, 746 A.2d 244 (Del. 2000).

[74] *Unocal*, 493 A.2d at 955. *See also* Unitrin, Inc. v. Am. Gen. Corp., 651 A.2d 1361, 1387–88 (Del. 1995) (clarifying that proportionality under *Unocal* requires that the defense be neither "coercive" nor "preclusive," and that it falls within a broad "range of reasonableness").

[75] *See* Moran v. Household Int'l, Inc., 500 A.2d 1346, 1350–54 (Del. 1985).

[76] This is accomplished by attaching rights to shares permitting all shareholders other than the would-be bidder to buy deeply discounted stock. Triggering thresholds vary, but 10–15 percent is a common range. *See* Allen et al., *supra* note 70, at 536–39.

any specific threats that might materialize,[77] the court effectively shored up target boards' capacity to fend off unwanted bids a few years later in *Paramount v. Time*. In its *Time* opinion, the court addressed "a fundamental misunderstanding of where the power of corporate governance lies" in a Delaware corporation, explaining that the board's statutory management authority renders it the board's prerogative to determine "the selection of a time frame for achievement of corporate goals."[78] This permitted Time's board to refuse to negotiate with a bidder (Paramount) making an all-cash, all-shares offer at a substantial premium – even when the board's own plan would require up to $10 billion in new debt to finance a cash tender offer by Time for its preferred strategic partner (Warner).[79]

Delaware's substantial deference regarding the adoption of defensive measures by target boards has hardly eroded in the intervening years. In its 2010 *Selectica* opinion, the Delaware Supreme Court strongly reaffirmed its traditional approach, endorsing the use of a poison pill with a 5 percent threshold to preserve the value of net operating losses in a company with no demonstrated prospect of profitability.[80] Applying *Unocal* and *Moran*, the court reiterated its long-standing view that a pill – even with a very low threshold, and in combination with a classified board – is not preclusive given the potential for a proxy contest, which the court insists would turn on "the merit of the bidder's proposal and not the magnitude of its stockholdings."[81]

II. *Ambivalence Regarding Shareholder Interests*

The fact that Delaware law marginalizes shareholder choice to this degree clearly suggests, in and of itself, that shareholder interests are not equated with corporate interests in U.S. corporate governance in the way that they are in U.K. corporate governance. Indeed, the conceptual role of shareholders in the corporate enterprise is rendered quite murky by Delaware's takeover jurisprudence, which at one moment suggests that impeding hostile takeover bids is in the shareholders' own best interests, yet the next moment suggests that impeding their ability to accept premium bids can be justified by reference to the interests of other corporate stakeholders.

77 *See Moran*, 500 A.2d at 1357.

78 Paramount Commc'ns, Inc. v. Time Inc., 571 A.2d 1140, 1154 (Del. 1990).

79 *Id.* at 1148–54.

80 *See* Versata Enter., Inc. v. Selectica, Inc., 5 A.3d 586, 588–90, 606–07 (Del. 2010). Net operating losses can reduce taxation of future income under certain circumstances. *See id.* at 589. Evidently an investment banker counseled the board that the net operating losses "were worth protecting given the possibility of a sale of Selectica or its assets." *Id.* at 600.

81 *See id.* at 599–608.

In *Time*, for example, the plaintiffs argued that, because Paramount made an all-cash, all-shares bid, there could logically be no "threat" other than "inadequate value," which the shareholders would be quintessentially well positioned to evaluate for themselves. The court, however, rejected this conclusion, endorsing the Time board's view that "Time shareholders might elect to tender into Paramount's cash offer in ignorance or a mistaken belief of the strategic benefit which a business combination with Warner might produce."[82] Put differently, the shareholders might be incapable of assessing their own interests – even when reduced to dollars and cents – such that boards are entitled, and in fact duty-bound, to protect the shareholders from themselves, substituting their own judgment of the offer's merits for the shareholders' judgment. This position, taken at face value, reflects a radically different assessment of the shareholders' capacity from that advanced in the securities disclosure context by the U.S. Supreme Court, which rejected "paternalistic withholding of accurate information" about speculative future events (e.g., ongoing merger negotiations) and the associated assumption "that investors are nitwits."[83]

There is reason to believe, however, that Delaware's purportedly dim view of the shareholders' capacities does not tell the whole story. In *Time*, the court adds that in assessing the offer, a target board may consider "the impact on 'constituencies' other than shareholders."[84] Here the court quotes its opinion in *Unocal* itself, where the court made quite explicit from the beginning of its hostile takeover jurisprudence that shareholders' interests simply are not the sole drivers of corporate law. In *Unocal*, the court stated that a target board evaluating how to respond to a hostile bid could consider "its effect on the corporate enterprise" generally, including impacts on "creditors, customers, employees, and perhaps even the community generally."[85] To be sure, the court has held that there are circumstances where directors are required to focus exclusively on the shareholders, but this so-called *Revlon* duty is triggered only in the narrow set of circumstances where a sale, a breakup, or a change of control is literally "inevitable."[86] Moreover, the target board's extraordinary discretion under *Moran* and *Time* to deploy and maintain defenses – and to decline to negotiate with a hostile bidder in favor of the board's own long-term plan – effectively renders application of *Revlon* duties entirely within the target

82 *Time*, 571 A.2d at 1152–53.

83 Basic Inc. v. Levinson, 485 U.S. 224, 234 (1988).

84 *Time*, 571 A.2d at 1153.

85 *Unocal*, 493 A.2d at 955.

86 *See* Revlon, Inc. v. MacAndrews & Forbes Holdings, Inc., 506 A.2d 173, 182 (Del. 1986). *See also* Paramount Commc'ns Inc. v. QVC Network Inc., 637 A.2d 34, 43–44 (Del. 1994) (applying this duty to "the sale of control context").

board's own control. The upshot is a decidedly ambivalent jurisprudence subordinating shareholders by reference to their own interests[87] – an awkward construct that, as I explore later in the book,[88] is more readily explicable as a rejection of strict shareholder primacy.

The marginalization of shareholders in U.S. hostile takeovers is even more emphatic in other states, a number of which (unlike Delaware) adopted so-called "constituency statutes." Indiana's corporate code, for example, includes a provision stating that a "director may, in considering the best interests of a corporation," take into account the effects of contemplated actions on various non-shareholder constituencies including "employees, suppliers, and customers of the corporation, and communities in which offices or other facilities of the corporation are located, and any other factors the director considers pertinent."[89] The statute extends this discretion to consider non-shareholder interests not only to takeovers, but to "any action," and further provides that the board "may, in its discretion, consider both the short term and long term best interests of the corporation," including the interests of the various constituencies noted above. The statute assures directors that good faith, informed approval by a majority of disinterested directors "shall conclusively be presumed to be valid."[90] Connecticut's statute is substantially similar, but applies only to fundamental transactions in public companies.[91]

It is tempting to analogize such a statute to § 172 of the U.K. Companies Act, but any resemblance is entirely superficial. Although U.K. directors may consider other constituencies' interests in corporate decision making, § 172 is crystal clear that their interests are relevant only insofar as they relate to the paramount goal of advancing the shareholders' interests. If anything, these constituency statutes more closely resemble the approach taken in Delaware hostile takeover cases such as *Unocal* and *Time*, permitting other constituencies' interests literally to trump the shareholders' interests. Indeed, the Indiana statute marginalizes shareholders even further than the Delaware case law does, effectively rejecting the *Revlon* duty to maximize the price received by shareholders in a sale, breakup, or change-of-control transaction. "Certain judicial decisions in Delaware and other jurisdictions, which might otherwise be looked to for guidance in interpreting Indiana corporate law, including" – the provision pointedly specifies – "decisions relating to potential change of control transactions that impose a different or higher degree of scrutiny on actions taken by directors in response to a proposed acquisition of control of

[87] *See* Bruner, *supra* note 22, at 1417–18; Lyman Johnson, *The Delaware Judiciary and the Meaning of Corporate Life and Corporate Law*, 68 TEX. L. REV. 865, 901–02, 909–17 (1990).

[88] *See infra* Chapter 5.B.

[89] IND. CODE § 23-1-35-1(d).

[90] *Id.* § 23-1-35-1(d), (g).

[91] *See* CONN. GEN. STAT. § 33-756(d).

the corporation, are inconsistent with the proper application of the business judgment rule under this article."[92]

In a similar spirit, although considerably more broadly, the American Law Institute's (ALI's) Principles of Corporate Governance provide that although "enhancing corporate profit and shareholder gain" should generally be the corporation's "objective," corporations may – "[e]ven if corporate profit and shareholder gain are not thereby enhanced" – weigh "ethical considerations that are reasonably regarded as appropriate to the responsible conduct of business," and "devote a reasonable amount of resources to public welfare, humanitarian, educational, and philanthropic purposes."[93] Consistent with the statutes and Delaware case law discussed above, this qualification reflects the drafters' "recognition that the corporation is a social as well as an economic institution, and accordingly that its pursuit of the economic objective must be constrained by social imperatives and may be qualified by social needs."[94] This, the drafters elaborate, includes the ability to take into account the interests of "employees, customers, suppliers, and members of the communities in which the corporation operates."[95]

The ALI approach further reflects the drafters' conclusion that U.S. case law has, over time, effectively rejected the more exclusive focus on shareholders detectable in early cases. The Michigan Supreme Court's famous 1919 decision in *Dodge v. Ford*, in particular, included strongly worded dicta to the effect that corporations are not to be run "for the merely incidental benefit of shareholders and for the primary purpose of benefiting others."[96] As an ALI reporter's note observes, however, later cases quite decidedly moved away from this position, "permit[ing] the utilization of corporate resources for public welfare, humanitarian, educational, or philanthropic purposes without requiring a showing that a direct benefit [to shareholders] is

[92] IND. CODE § 23-1-35-1(f).

[93] PRINCIPLES OF CORPORATE GOVERNANCE: ANALYSIS AND RECOMMENDATIONS § 2.01 (2005) [hereinafter ALI PRINCIPLES].

[94] *Id.* § 2.01 cmt. e.

[95] *Id.* § 2.01 cmt. f. In this light, so-called benefit corporations, were they to grow in popularity, could tend to undermine the values their proponents seek to advance. In arguing that a new business form is required to wed the pursuit of profit with the pursuit of non-shareholder interests, it is effectively conceded that shareholder interests define the aims of business corporations as they presently exist – a misstatement of current law, as explored here. As of May 2012, seven states had adopted benefit corporation statutes. *See* Mark A. Underberg, *Benefit Corporations vs. "Regular" Corporations: A Harmful Dichotomy*, HARVARD LAW SCHOOL FORUM ON CORPORATE GOVERNANCE AND FINANCIAL REGULATION, May 13, 2012, https://blogs.law.harvard.edu/corpgov/2012/05/13/benefit-corporations-vs-regular-corporations-a-harmful-dichotomy/.

[96] Dodge v. Ford Motor Co., 170 N.W. 668, 684 (Mich. 1919).

likely."[97] In addition to the highly idiosyncratic facts in *Dodge v. Ford* – involving Henry Ford's public declaration that dividends should be withheld so as to benefit employees and consumers (through expanded production at lower prices) – it should be observed that the court did explicitly accept that charitable and humanitarian expenditures could redound to the corporation's benefit, and permitted funding of a substantial long-term expansion plan before declaration of the dividend sought by the plaintiffs.[98]

Subsequent case law would seize upon these latter points, maintaining some nominal focus on shareholders while permitting corporate activity favoring other constituencies, and even society generally. In *Wrigley*, for example, an Illinois appellate court in 1968 rejected a minority shareholder's challenge of the Chicago Cubs' refusal to play night baseball games – which had already been embraced by every other major league team – apparently due to Philip Wrigley's belief that night baseball would "have a deteriorating effect upon the surrounding neighborhood." The plaintiff cited *Dodge v. Ford*, to which the court replied that eschewing night baseball could readily be squared with shareholder interests in "the long run" – for example, in preserving the park's property value and customer base by preventing deterioration of the surrounding neighborhood.[99] Meanwhile, the rare cases in recent decades expressly emphasizing the shareholders' interests have either involved highly idiosyncratic facts rivaling those of *Dodge v. Ford* itself,[100] or effectively stand for the far more modest proposition that boards are not duty-bound to favor the interests of other stakeholders over those of the shareholders.[101]

97 ALI PRINCIPLES, *supra* note 93, at § 2.01 reporter's note 2. *See also* Lynn Stout, *Why We Should Stop Teaching* Dodge v. Ford, *in* THE ICONIC CASES IN CORPORATE LAW 1 (Jonathan R. Macey ed., 2008); LYNN STOUT, THE SHAREHOLDER VALUE MYTH 25–29 (2012).

98 *See Dodge*, 170 N.W. at 683–85.

99 *See* Shlensky v. Wrigley, 237 N.E.2d 776, 777–80 (Ill. App. Ct. 1968). Wrigley, like Ford, was the controlling shareholder. *See Dodge*, 170 N.W. at 683; *Wrigley*, 237 N.E.2d at 777.

100 In his *eBay* opinion, Chancellor William Chandler rejected the use of a poison pill purportedly implemented to protect the "corporate culture" of Craigslist from the threat posed by eBay's desire to achieve control of the company. *See* eBay Domestic Holdings, Inc. v. Newmark, 16 A.3d 1, 31–35 (Del. Ch. 2010). Chandler wrote that directors are duty-bound "to promote the value of the corporation for the benefit of its stockholders," but his emphasis on the interests of shareholders appears to have been prompted by "a unique set of facts heretofore not seen in the context of a challenge to a rights plan" – specifically, a poison pill adopted by controlling shareholders of a close corporation who openly disavowed "revenue maximization," *id.* at 19–20, 30–35, idiosyncratic facts resembling those prompting the pro-shareholder language in *Dodge v. Ford*.

101 In *Katz v. Oak Industries*, Chancellor William Allen wrote that "[i]t is the obligation of directors to attempt, within the law, to maximize the long-run interests of the corporation's stockholders." This statement arose, however, in response to bondholders' argument that a proposed reorganization and recapitalization of a troubled company – including an exchange offer involving adverse amendments to their bond indentures – would impermissibly "benefit

The treatment of corporate charitable donations similarly illustrates the board's substantial discretion to favor other stakeholders without demonstrating direct benefit to shareholders. In *A.P. Smith*, the New Jersey Supreme Court in 1953 found a charitable donation to Princeton University sufficiently connected with the shareholders' interests, there being "no difficulty in sustaining, as incidental to their proper objects and in aid of the public welfare, the power of corporations to contribute corporate funds within reasonable limits in support of academic institutions." This, the court explained, could "readily be justified as being for the benefit of the corporation; indeed, if need be the matter may be viewed strictly in terms of actual survival of the corporation in a free enterprise system."[102] Today, corporate statutes routinely permit such charitable donations, as the ALI Principles suggest.[103] Delaware's statute, for example, quite broadly permits "donations for the public welfare or for charitable, scientific or educational purposes, and in time of war or other national emergency in aid thereof."[104] Strikingly, the Delaware statute places no explicit limit on this power, although courts have required that such donations remain reasonable, measured by reference to tax deductibility.[105]

U.S. ambivalence regarding the role of shareholders in corporate governance, and the degree to which their interests proxy for those of other constituencies and society generally, is further reflected in an ambiguous statement of directors' fiduciary duty of loyalty. The Delaware Supreme Court gave its classic formulation of the duty of loyalty in its 1939 *Guth v. Loft* opinion, which says that officers and directors "stand in a fiduciary relation to the corporation and its stockholders" simultaneously.[106] This ambiguous statement

Oak's common stockholders at the expense of the Holders of its debt securities." Allen's pro-shareholder statement arose in explaining that creditors' relationship with the corporation is "contractual in nature," such that this aspect of the bondholders' complaint did not "allege a cognizable legal wrong." *See* Katz v. Oak Indus., Inc., 508 A.2d 873, 875–79 (Del. Ch. 1986).

[102] A.P. Smith Mfg. Co. v. Barlow, 98 A.2d 581, 582–86 (N.J. 1953).

[103] *See* ALI Principles, *supra* note 93, at § 2.01(b)(3).

[104] Del. Code Ann. tit. 8, § 122(9).

[105] *See, e.g.*, Kahn v. Sullivan, 594 A.2d 48, 61 (Del. 1991); Theodora Holding Corp. v. Henderson, 257 A.2d 398, 405 (Del. Ch. 1969). *See also* 26 U.S.C. § 170(b)(2) (generally limiting a corporation's charitable deduction to 10 percent of taxable income); Einer Elhauge, *Sacrificing Corporate Profits in the Public Interest*, 80 N.Y.U. L. Rev. 733, 810, 836–37 (2005) (observing that average corporate donations are far below this limit).

[106] Guth v. Loft, 5 A.2d 503, 510 (Del. 1939). On the scope of the duty of loyalty and its relationship to the "good faith" concept, see generally Christopher M. Bruner, *Good Faith, State of Mind, and the Outer Boundaries of Director Liability in Corporate Law*, 41 Wake Forest L. Rev. 1131 (2006). For reflections on the degree to which management's knowledge may be imputed to the corporation, see Christopher M. Bruner, *Agency and the Ontology of the Corporation*, 69 Wash. & Lee L. Rev. 355 (2012) (comment on a student note regarding the *in pari delicto* defense to auditor malpractice liability).

of the director's duty of loyalty has recently been reiterated by the court,[107] but unfortunately remains unexplained. The core theoretical tension between more and less shareholder-centric visions of the corporation remains "bracketed" by this formulation, as Lyman Johnson suggests, permitting Delaware law to entertain multiple conceptions of corporate purpose.[108] As Chancellor William Allen observed in his 1989 *TW Services* opinion, "this particular phrase masks the most fundamental issue," namely how to reconcile long-term "corporate entity interests" with "current share value interests" – an issue that "seems inescapably to involve normative questions"[109] to which Delaware law provides no clear answers.

This core tension, apparent both in Delaware's ambivalent formulation of the duty of loyalty and in its murky case law on hostile takeovers, has once again surfaced in the area of shareholder bylaws.[110] Although Delaware shareholders lack power to initiate amendments to the charter – the core governance document – they do possess statutory authority to amend bylaws, a secondary governance document that (because of the difficulty of amending the charter) often addresses numerous aspects of corporate governance.[111] Under § 109 of the Delaware statute, the shareholders possess inalienable power to enact, amend, and repeal bylaws, but the charter may extend this power to the board as well – which often occurs at the time of formation, resulting in concurrent authority.[112] Bylaws, per the statute, "may contain any provision, not inconsistent with law or with the certificate of incorporation, relating to the business of the corporation, the conduct of its affairs, and its rights or powers or the rights or powers of its stockholders, directors, officers or employees."[113] This apparently open-ended grant of power would appear to give the shareholders substantial capacity to rewrite the rules of corporate governance, and accordingly to seize power from the board, which is precisely what activist investors have sought

[107] *See* N. Am. Catholic Educ. Programming Found., Inc. v. Gheewalla, 930 A.2d 92, 99 (Del. 2007).

[108] *See* Johnson, *supra* note 87, at 900 n.133.

[109] TW Services, Inc. v. SWT Acquisition Corp., 1989 Del. Ch. LEXIS 19, *19 n.5, *28 n.14 (Del. Ch. 1989). *See also* Johnson, *supra* note 87, at 922–25.

[110] *See generally* Bruner, *supra* note 56; Christopher M. Bruner, *Shareholder Bylaws and the Delaware Corporation*, 11 TRANSACTIONS: TENN. J. BUS. L. 67 (2009). *See also* Bruner, *supra* note 22, at 1442–48.

[111] *See* ALLEN ET AL., *supra* note 70, at 92–93.

[112] *See* DEL. CODE ANN. tit. 8, § 109(a). *See also* DAVID A. DREXLER, LEWIS S. BLACK, JR. & A. GILCHRIST SPARKS, III, DELAWARE CORPORATION LAW AND PRACTICE § 9.02 (2009); Lawrence A. Hamermesh, *Corporate Democracy and Stockholder-Adopted By-Laws: Taking Back the Street?*, 73 TUL. L. REV. 409, 467–70 (1998).

[113] DEL. CODE ANN. tit. 8, § 109(b).

to do since the 1990s.[114] By the same token, however, the board's concurrent bylaw power would appear to create the potential for "cycling amendments and counter-amendments," as shareholders adopt bylaws purporting to curtail board authority, to which the board responds by removing the offensive bylaw, and so on.[115]

Delaware's statute provides no clear guidance regarding how to reconcile inconsistent shareholder and board bylaw amendments, notwithstanding the obvious potential for such a collision. Naturally boards argue that the prohibition of bylaws "inconsistent with law" means that shareholders cannot use bylaws to undermine the board's statutory management authority. The problem, however, is that § 141 – the source of that authority – is itself limited to the extent "otherwise provided in this chapter," which might be read to include the shareholders' bylaw authority in § 109.[116] The two provisions thus give rise to a statutory conundrum that Jeffrey Gordon termed the "recursive loop."[117] There being no obvious way to prioritize these grants of power,[118] the Delaware statute creates a conceptual muddle at the heart of corporate governance. This contrasts starkly with the situation in the United Kingdom (and elsewhere, as we shall see), where the problem simply does not arise, because of the shareholders' clear unilateral authority to determine the contents of the corporation's core governance documents.[119]

The Delaware Supreme Court has begun to grapple with this problem only recently, but its nascent case law on shareholder bylaws already exhibits an uncanny resemblance to its hostile takeover case law. This is unsurprising for

[114] *See* Brett H. McDonnell, *Bylaw Reforms for Delaware's Corporation Law*, 33 Del. J. Corp. L. 651, 651–52 (2008); R. Franklin Balotti & Jesse A. Finkelstein, The Delaware Law of Corporations and Business Organizations § 1.10, at 1–18 (3d ed. 2009).

[115] Stephen M. Bainbridge, Corporate Law 16 (2d ed. 2009). *See also* DeMott, *supra* note 28, at 111; Hamermesh, *supra* note 112, at 467–75; McDonnell, *supra* note 114, at 664–65.

[116] *See* Del. Code Ann. tit. 8, §§ 109(a), 141(a).

[117] *See* Jeffrey N. Gordon, *"Just Say Never?" Poison Pills, Deadhand Pills, and Shareholder-Adopted Bylaws: An Essay for Warren Buffett*, 19 Cardozo L. Rev. 511, 546–47 (1997). *See also* John C. Coffee, Jr., *The Bylaw Battlefield: Can Institutions Change the Outcome of Corporate Control Contests?*, 51 U. Miami L. Rev. 605, 607–08 (1997); Brett H. McDonnell, *Shareholder Bylaws, Shareholder Nominations, and Poison Pills*, 3 Berkeley Bus. L.J. 205, 213–15 (2005).

[118] *See, e.g.*, Gordon, *supra* note 117, at 547; Robert B. Thompson & D. Gordon Smith, *Toward a New Theory of the Shareholder Role: "Sacred Space" in Corporate Takeovers*, 80 Tex. L. Rev. 261, 319–20 (2001). *But see* Hamermesh, *supra* note 112, at 429–33 (arguing that the limitation in § 141(a) should be read to refer solely to statutory provisions specifically addressing the board's management power); DeMott, *supra* note 28, at 110 (arguing in favor of Hamermesh's reading).

[119] *See* Bruner, *supra* note 56, at 22–23. *See also* Edward Rock, Paul Davies, Hideki Kanda & Reinier Kraakman, *Fundamental Changes*, *in* Reinier Kraakman et al., The Anatomy of Corporate Law: A Comparative and Functional Approach 183, 188–89 & n.22 (2d ed. 2009).

at least two reasons. First, aggressive use of bylaws by activist shareholders first arose in the 1990s as a response to their defeat in the 1980s takeover debate.[120] Second, shareholder bylaws carving back at board power implicate the core questions of power and purpose in a manner closely resembling that of hostile takeovers.

In its 2008 CA, *Inc.* opinion, the Delaware Supreme Court addressed two questions certified to it by the Securities and Exchange Commission (SEC) relating to a shareholder bylaw that, if enacted, would have required CA, Inc.'s board to reimburse shareholder proxy expenses under certain circumstances.[121] The shareholder in question (a public employee pension fund) sought to include the proposed bylaw in the company's proxy statement under SEC Rule 14a-8, and the SEC wanted to know whether the proposal could be rejected by management under either of two state law–based exclusions specified in the rule – first, if the proposal were not a proper subject for shareholder action under Delaware law, and second, if the bylaw would otherwise cause the company to violate Delaware law.[122]

The court acknowledged that assessing the shareholders' ability to carve back at board power through bylaw amendments is "an elusively difficult task," but ultimately cut the recursive loop in favor of the board, concluding that board authority under § 141 – "a cardinal precept of the DGCL" – prevails over § 109.[123] The court refused to take this approach to its logical extreme, however, rejecting the notion that shareholder bylaws could in no way limit board authority – a reading that would effectively render the shareholders' bylaw authority meaningless.[124] Although declining to provide a "bright line" rule, the court did distinguish between procedural and substantive bylaws, the former being permissible whereas the latter are not. In this case, the proposed bylaw represented a proper subject for shareholder action because it had "both the intent and the effect of regulating the process for electing directors."[125]

Regarding the SEC's second question, however, the court found that the bylaw, if adopted, would otherwise cause the company to violate Delaware law because it could force the board to violate its fiduciary duties by reimbursing a

[120] *See* Balotti & Finkelstein, *supra* note 114, § 1.10, at 1–18; DeMott, *supra* note 28, at 116; Gordon, *supra* note 117, at 544; McDonnell, *supra* note 117, at 209.

[121] *See* CA, Inc. v. AFSCME Emp. Pension Plan, 953 A.2d 227, 229–30 (Del. 2008). *See also* Del. Const. art. IV, § 11(8) (permitting the court to hear questions certified by the SEC).

[122] *See CA, Inc.*, 953 A.2d at 230–31. *See also* 17 C.F.R. § 240.14a-8(i)(1)-(2); Harold S. Bloomenthal & Samuel Wolff, Securities and Federal Corporate Law §§ 24.71.20–.26 (2010) (providing additional background on AFSCME's proxy-related activism).

[123] *See CA, Inc.*, 953 A.2d at 232 & n.7.

[124] *See id.* at 234.

[125] *See id.* at 234–36.

shareholder's proxy expenses in circumstances where the board itself felt that reimbursement (in any amount) would be contrary to the company's interests. Interestingly, in reaching this conclusion the court cited cases involving constraints placed on board decision making by the board itself, rejecting the argument that shareholders possess the ability to "relieve" the board of its fiduciary duties in a given area.[126] For a proxy reimbursement bylaw to be valid, the court concluded that it would have to include a fiduciary-out provision, expressly permitting refusal to reimburse expenses where the board's fiduciary duties so require.[127]

As noted above, the shareholder bylaw debate arose in the 1990s out of the shareholders' defeat in the hostile takeover debate of the 1980s, and accordingly, more aggressive use of the bylaw authority is perhaps of greatest consequence where shareholders seek to curb the use of takeover defenses. *CA, Inc.* does not directly address the fate of bylaws purporting to limit use of poison pills and other defenses, although it is difficult to imagine that such bylaws would pass muster given the court's fiduciary duty-based rationale for limiting the reach of the shareholders' authority under § 109.[128] Indeed, the bylaw debate bears a striking resemblance to the takeover debate in a number of respects – as a reflection of Delaware's traditional ambivalence regarding shareholders, in the cat-and-mouse governance dynamics involved, and in the Delaware Supreme Court's manner of bracketing the fundamental issues of power and purpose involved. In each case, board power is challenged by creative use of an under-theorized form of shareholder power; the right of shareholders unilaterally to sell their stock fueled hostile takeovers[129] just as the right of shareholders unilaterally to enact, amend, and repeal bylaws fueled later efforts to constrain board powers. In each case shareholders tested the outer reaches of the given form of authority in a manner that destabilized the existing balance of corporate governance power – and by all indication the same ambivalence

[126] *See id.* at 238–40. The court cited to Paramount Commc'ns Inc. v. QVC Network Inc., 637 A.2d 34 (Del. 1994) (invalidating a "no shop" provision in a merger agreement) and Quickturn Design Sys., Inc. v. Shapiro, 721 A.2d 1281 (Del. 1998) (invalidating a "delayed redemption" poison pill provision).

[127] *See CA, Inc.*, 953 A.2d at 240.

[128] *See* McDonnell, *supra* note 114, at 664. A case filed by Professor Lucian Bebchuk of Harvard Law School posed this question (also involving CA, Inc., although unrelated to the AFSCME case), but the Chancery Court refused on ripeness grounds to address the proposed bylaw. *See* Bebchuk v. CA, Inc., 902 A.2d 737 (Del. Ch. 2006). Ultimately the proposal was defeated, leaving the question unanswered. *See* Allen et al. *supra* note 70, at 623–25.

[129] *See* Del. Code Ann. tit. 8, § 202 (generally requiring that transfer restrictions appear in writing); Thompson & Smith, *supra* note 118, at 276 n.83 (inferring free transferability otherwise).

regarding shareholders that drove the takeover case law is now driving the court's emerging approach to shareholder bylaws.[130]

Although *CA, Inc.* sensibly distinguishes procedural and substantive bylaws, the opinion obscures as much as it clarifies. There are myriad circumstances in which it cannot be said that a given bylaw addresses purely matters of procedure as opposed to substantive decision making. As the court observes, a given bylaw's "wording, although relevant, is not dispositive of whether or not it is process-related," a distinction turning ultimately on the bylaw's "context and purpose." This effectively means that there is some underlying criterion by which we judge whether a given action falls within the shareholders' province, but we are not told what it is. The court explains that the context and purpose of the bylaw at issue in *CA, Inc.* – "promot[ing] the integrity of [the] electoral process" – renders it an appropriate subject for shareholder action because shareholders have "a legitimate and protected interest" in this area, but the metric for legitimacy of shareholder interests remains unspecified.[131] Moreover, whatever clarity the procedure-substance distinction may offer is effectively undercut by the court's fiduciary duty analysis. The court roundly rejects the argument that shareholders, as beneficiaries of the board's fiduciary duties, could "relieve the board entirely of those duties in this specific area"[132] – an approach that, if accepted, would be tantamount to forcing the court to define the parameters of the board's governance power, and effectively the corporation itself, in highly shareholder-centric terms reminiscent of U.K. shareholders' ability to "direct the directors." The court effectively evades taking such a position in the bylaw context by precisely the same means used in the takeover context – subsuming the question within the board's fiduciary duties. With hostile takeovers, the core issue of control over the success of tender offers morphs into the issue of whether the board's fiduciary duties permit such a decision to be "delegated to the stockholders."[133] With bylaws, then, the core issue of control over proxy reimbursement morphs into the issue of whether a bylaw can "relieve the board entirely of [its fiduciary] duties in this specific area."[134] In each case, resort to the board's fiduciary duties allows the Delaware Supreme Court to avoid endorsing a shareholder-centric conception of the corporation without expressly rejecting it, maintaining the ambivalent posture toward shareholders that has long characterized Delaware corporate law.

[130] *See* Bruner, *supra* note 22, at 1442–48; Bruner, *supra* note 56, at 20–24; Bruner, *supra* note 110, *at* 73–74.

[131] *See CA, Inc.*, 953 A.2d at 236–37.

[132] *Id.* at 239–40.

[133] *See* Paramount Commc'ns, Inc. v. Time Inc., 571 A.2d 1140, 1154 (Del. 1990).

[134] *CA, Inc.*, 953 A.2d at 239–40; Bruner, *supra* note 56, at 24.

		Power	
		shareholders	***board***
Purpose	***shareholders***	Shareholder Primacy	Nexus of Contracts/ Director Primacy
	stakeholders	—[135]	Team Production

Figure 3.2. Prevailing Descriptive Theories of U.S. Corporate Governance: Power and Purpose

III. Prevailing Theories of U.S. Corporate Governance

Set beside the highly shareholder-centric U.K. corporate governance system, the core doctrinal structures of U.S. corporate governance – including in Delaware – convey deep ambivalence regarding the role of shareholders, who occupy a privileged position relative to other constituencies yet lack the remarkable governance powers and exclusive emphasis on their interests enjoyed by their British counterparts (a contrast depicted in Figure 3.1).

This fundamental U.S. ambivalence is further reflected in the inability of prevailing theories of U.S. corporate governance to provide compelling descriptive accounts of the field. As I explore in this subsection, the leading descriptive theories of U.S. corporate governance all tend to emphasize either shareholder or board governance authority, and either shareholder or stakeholder orientation. Unlike in the United Kingdom, where shareholder-oriented theories have considerable descriptive power, none of the prevailing theories can accommodate U.S. corporate law's fundamental ambivalence on issues of power and purpose.[136] For the reader's convenience, I categorize the prevailing U.S. descriptive theories by reference to these core issues in Figure 3.2, and then evaluate their strengths and weaknesses more fully in the remainder of this subsection.

The "nexus of contracts" theory, widely embraced by scholars with a "law and economics" orientation, favors board power and shareholder orientation. The classic statement of this conception of the corporation is that of Frank Easterbrook and Daniel Fischel who, in their 1991 book *The Economic Structure of Corporate Law*, advanced the normative and positive claim that "corporate law *should* contain the terms people would have negotiated" in a hypothetical *ex ante* negotiation, "were the costs of negotiating at arm's length for every contingency sufficiently low," and that the law "*almost always conforms* to this

[135] Although no prevailing descriptive theory falls within the lower left quadrant of Figure 3.2, I briefly explore the potential for a normative theory to this effect below. *See infra* note 200.

[136] *See* Bruner, *supra* note 22, at 1395–1408; Bruner, *supra* note 2, at 599–603.

model."[137] Viewed in this way, the corporation is not amenable to "ownership" as such – by the shareholders or anyone else – because it amounts to nothing more than a legal nexus through which various stakeholders bargain with one another.[138] Shareholders are the primary beneficiaries of corporate activity in the nexus model, however, because rational investors with only a "residual" claim to corporate assets – that is, junior to fixed claims of employees and creditors – would demand both that they have the power to elect the board of directors and that the board (once elected) be duty-bound to advance their interests.[139] Conversely, non-shareholders with fixed claims presumably would not place such a high value on voting rights and fiduciary duties, and are therefore expected to protect themselves as best they can – notably, by negotiating for (real) contractual protections and/or by seeking regulatory protections through the political process.[140] Although the parties may decide to deviate from this default arrangement, favoring non-shareholders in corporate decision making would be legitimate only where expressly agreed upon ahead of time.[141]

By the same token, according to the nexus model shareholders have weak governance powers because rationally apathetic minority investors in large enterprises will not place a high value on the ability to directly influence corporate governance. In this light – and given the substantial heterogeneity of preferences across a public company's investor base – the efficiency benefits of centralized management are all the more attractive, and shareholders in any event retain the ability to exert some disciplinary pressure on management through the market for corporate control (arising from the potential for hostile

[137] Frank H. Easterbrook & Daniel R. Fischel, The Economic Structure of Corporate Law 15 (1991) (emphasis added). They were not, of course, the first to promote the economic analysis of corporate law. *See, e.g.*, Henry G. Manne, *The "Higher Criticism" of the Modern Corporation*, 62 Colum. L. Rev. 399, 430–32 (1962) (registering "surpris[e] that the economic factors affecting the modern corporation should have been so studiously ignored," and arguing that "[t]here is in fact no aspect of the modern corporation that does not seem peculiarly susceptible to rigorous economic analysis").

[138] *See* Stephen M. Bainbridge, *The Case for Limited Shareholder Voting Rights*, 53 UCLA L. Rev. 601, 604 (2006).

[139] *See* Easterbrook & Fischel, *supra* note 137, at 35–39, 90–93. *See also* Stephen M. Bainbridge, *Director Primacy: The Means and Ends of Corporate Governance*, 97 Nw. U. L. Rev. 547, 574–92 (2003); Henry Hansmann & Reinier Kraakman, *The End of History for Corporate Law*, 89 Geo. L.J. 440–43 (2001). On the tendency of "economically oriented scholars working in different areas" to argue that "the law should focus on the interest of a single constituency – shareholders in corporate law, creditors in bankruptcy law, and consumers in antitrust law" – see David Millon, *The Single Constituency Argument in the Economic Analysis of Business Law*, 24 Res. L. & Econ. 43 (2009).

[140] Those accepting the nexus view typically argue that other social and environmental concerns are best addressed through external regulation as well. *See* Easterbrook & Fischel, *supra* note 137, at 36–39; Bainbridge, *supra* note 139, at 587–91.

[141] *See* Easterbrook & Fischel, *supra* note 137, at 35–37.

tender offers).[142] Stephen Bainbridge takes this approach to its logical conclusion in his "director primacy" theory, characterizing the board as the very embodiment of the corporation. Building on the work of economists Kenneth Arrow and Ronald Coase on the value of centralized "fiat" in business firms,[143] Bainbridge argues that the board "can be seen as a sort of Platonic guardian – a *sui generis* body serving as the nexus for the various contracts making up the corporation and whose powers flow not from shareholders alone, but from the complete set of contracts constituting the firm."[144]

The nexus model, including Bainbridge's director primacy variant, offers a coherent explanation for the many areas of U.S. corporate law that tend to insulate board authority from shareholder interference – notably the board's sweeping statutory grant of management authority, and its gatekeeper status vis-à-vis fundamental actions such as charter amendments and mergers.[145] However, this approach cannot compellingly account for some core elements of corporate law – notably, how and when shareholders are permitted to act in furtherance of their own interests.[146] Easterbrook and Fischel argue that relatively weak shareholder voting rights are acceptable because management can be sufficiently disciplined through the market for corporate control, which depends critically on free capacity to accept hostile tender offers. The board's substantial latitude to deploy potent defenses, however, effectively undercuts this explanation for the weakness of shareholder voting rights, as they ultimately must acknowledge.[147] As Lyman Johnson observes of this concession, "[i]t is not often that halfway through a theoretical work the central thesis is undermined."[148]

[142] *See* Bainbridge, *supra* note 138, at 606–07, 613–14, 623–25; EASTERBROOK & FISCHEL, *supra* note 137, at 70–71. On the heterogeneity of shareholders' preferences, see Iman Anabtawi, *Some Skepticism about Increasing Shareholder Power*, 53 UCLA L. REV. 561, 577–93 (2006); STOUT, *supra* note 97, at 9–10, 63–94.

[143] *See, e.g.*, KENNETH J. ARROW, THE LIMITS OF ORGANIZATION (1974); R.H. Coase, *The Nature of the Firm*, 4 ECONOMICA 386 (1937).

[144] Bainbridge, *supra* note 139, at 554–60. *See also* Stephen M. Bainbridge, Unocal *at 20: Director Primacy in Corporate Takeovers*, 31 DEL. J. CORP. L. 769, 779–84 (2006).

[145] *See* Bainbridge, *supra* note 65, at 19 n.29; Bruner, *supra* note 22, at 1398.

[146] *See* Bruner, *supra* note 22, at 1398–1401.

[147] *See* EASTERBROOK & FISCHEL, *supra* note 137, at 205–06. *See also* Henry G. Manne, *Mergers and the Market for Corporate Control*, 73 J. POL. ECON. 110, 112–14 (1965) (arguing that "an active market for corporate control" alone "provides some assurance of competitive efficiency among corporate managers and thereby affords strong protection to the interests of vast numbers of small, non-controlling shareholders"); Manne, *supra* note 137, at 412–13, 420–21 (observing that this mechanism functions "only if [shareholders] remain free to sell shares when they are dissatisfied with existing corporate management").

[148] Lyman Johnson, *Individual and Collective Sovereignty in the Corporate Enterprise*, 92 COLUM. L. REV. 2215, 2245 (1992) (reviewing EASTERBROOK & FISCHEL, *supra* note 137, and ROBERT N. BELLAH ET AL., THE GOOD SOCIETY (1991)).

For Bainbridge's director primacy approach, on the other hand, the opposite problem arises – explaining the existence of any shareholder voting rights and capacity for unilateral action. Like Easterbrook and Fischel, Bainbridge relies on the market for corporate control – enabled by voting rights and free transferability of shares – to discipline management. Yet unlike Easterbrook and Fischel, Bainbridge defends the Delaware courts' acceptance of takeover defenses as a means of preserving board discretion. He essentially characterizes this construct as a "second best" means of maximizing shareholder wealth, preserving the benefits of centralized authority at the cost of takeover-inspired discipline foregone.[149] This explanation, built on the authority-versus-accountability paradigm, makes sense, however, only if one has already accepted the core legal premises of the director primacy approach – namely that boards are Platonic guardians wielding sui generis powers, and that shareholder wealth maximization represents the defining aim of the corporation.

In fact, neither premise is entirely accurate. Although boards undoubtedly enjoy enormous governance power in a Delaware corporation, the Delaware Court of Chancery has described election by shareholders as "the ideological underpinning" of board power, flatly rejecting the characterization of directors as "Platonic masters."[150] Similarly, the statute and case law alike clearly contemplate some capacity for shareholders to carve back at board power unilaterally through bylaws – which Bainbridge can only wish were "treated . . . the same way as articles of incorporation or, for that matter, virtually every other corporate action."[151] Meanwhile Delaware law remains a muddle regarding the degree to which the shareholders' interests ought to prevail over competing interests, as described above, expressly demanding exclusive focus on the shareholders only in the most limited circumstances,[152] while permitting substantial discretion under the business judgment rule to balance shareholder and non-shareholder interests.[153] Indeed, contrary to the notion that takeover defenses represent a "second best" means of advancing the shareholders' interests, Delaware case law and a number of other states' statutes make clear that boards may look past the shareholders entirely, inhibiting takeovers to

[149] *See* Bainbridge, *supra* note 144, at 827–28; Bainbridge, *supra* note 138, at 614 & n.33, 627–28 & n.74; STEPHEN M. BAINBRIDGE, THE NEW CORPORATE GOVERNANCE IN THEORY AND PRACTICE 14–15 (2008).

[150] *See* Blasius Indus., Inc. v. Atlas Corp., 564 A.2d 651, 659, 663 (Del. Ch. 1988).

[151] STEPHEN M. BAINBRIDGE, CORPORATE GOVERNANCE AFTER THE FINANCIAL CRISIS 211–12 (2012).

[152] *See* Revlon, Inc. v. MacAndrews & Forbes Holdings, Inc., 506 A.2d 173, 182 (Del. 1986); Paramount Commc'ns Inc. v. QVC Network Inc., 637 A.2d 34, 43–44 (Del. 1994).

[153] *See, e.g.*, Margaret M. Blair & Lynn A. Stout, *A Team Production Theory of Corporate Law*, 85 VA. L. REV. 247, 299–309 (1999); Bruner, *supra* note 22, at 1402, 1411–12; STOUT, *supra* note 97, at 29–31.

further the interests of other constituencies such as employees, creditors, and local communities – a point that Bainbridge effectively concedes in describing these developments as "an unfortunate change in the basic normative principles underlying corporate law."[154]

If we apply Ockham's razor, there is a far simpler explanation[155] – U.S. corporate law has never in fact adhered to the "normative principles" advanced by nexus scholars in the pure, straightforward manner asserted. We simply are not wedded to board fiat, or to shareholder wealth maximization, to the degree that nexus scholars claim.[156] Bainbridge ultimately acknowledges that "there is no unified field theory" of U.S. corporate governance, and that "pure theories of corporate governance all have problems."[157] This conclusion is inescapable, given U.S. corporate law's deep ambivalence regarding the ultimate locus of power and the beneficiaries of corporate decision making. Later, I offer an explanation of this ambivalence focusing on corporate law's interaction with other regulatory fields[158] – a larger political economy gestured toward, but not explored, by nexus theorists.[159]

The "team production" theory of U.S. corporate governance, for its part, places the board at the heart of the corporation to a degree reminiscent of the nexus of contracts approach, but adopts a very different rationale for the board's management power, arriving at strikingly different conclusions regarding the beneficiaries of corporate activity.[160] For Margaret Blair and Lynn Stout, the aim of the corporation and corporate law is to facilitate risky firm-specific investment by all the stakeholder groups whose contributions are required for complex commercial enterprises to succeed – shareholders, creditors, managers, employees, communities, and so on.[161] Blair and Stout argue that

[154] Bainbridge, *supra* note 144, at 778 n.43.

[155] *See* OXFORD ENGLISH DICTIONARY ONLINE, Ockham's razor, *n.* ("The principle that in explaining anything no more assumptions should be made than are necessary.").

[156] Nor, for that matter, is corporate law so wedded to contractual freedom as nexus scholars might like. *See* Grant M. Hayden & Matthew T. Bodie, *The Uncorporation and the Unraveling of "Nexus of Contracts" Theory*, 109 MICH. L. REV. 1127 (2011) (reviewing LARRY E. RIBSTEIN, THE RISE OF THE UNCORPORATION (2010)).

[157] Bainbridge, *supra* note 65, at 16–17; BAINBRIDGE, *supra* note 149, at 15–16 (responding to my criticisms in earlier work).

[158] *See infra* Chapter 5.B.

[159] *See, e.g.*, EASTERBROOK & FISCHEL, *supra* note 137, at 36–39; Bainbridge, *supra* note 139, at 587–91.

[160] *See* Bainbridge, *supra* note 139, at 551–52.

[161] *See* Margaret M. Blair & Lynn A. Stout, *Director Accountability and the Mediating Role of the Corporate Board*, 79 WASH. U. L.Q. 403, 418–20 (2001). Blair and Stout define "team production" as "complex productive activity that requires multiple parties to make contributions that are to some extent both team specific and unverifiable to an outside party," and which results in "nonseparable" outputs that cannot be apportioned based on the parties' relative contributions. *See id.* at 419.

the board represents a "mediating hierarch" possessing strong management authority not because this represents a more efficient means of pursuing the shareholders' interests, but in order to prevent these various stakeholder groups from exploiting one another.[162] The board constitutes a mechanism of mutual assurance among stakeholders who require reciprocal contributions, yet fear "wasteful shirking and rent-seeking" by the others – a problem resolved by entering "a 'pactum subjectionis'" through which the various corporate stakeholders "yield control over outputs and key inputs (time, intellectual skills, or financial capital) to the hierarchy" governed by the board.[163]

This conceptualization of the board's management role leads the team production theory to deviate sharply from the nexus theory with respect to corporate purpose, as Figure 3.2 illustrates. Shareholder wealth maximization cannot be the defining aim of the team production corporation because that would preclude the board from credibly committing to protect other stakeholders, undermining their willingness to make firm-specific investments. Consequently, Blair and Stout argue, directors must be "trustees for the corporation itself," favoring no particular stakeholder group over the others.[164]

The team production theory's regard for the contributions and interests of numerous constituencies would seem to lend it substantial explanatory power in precisely the areas where the nexus theory most vividly breaks down – the regulation of hostile takeovers, and more generally, the absence of a clear mandate to prioritize shareholder interests in any but the most extreme scenarios.[165] Nevertheless, there are substantial elements of corporate law for which the team production theory can provide no compelling account.[166] As David Millon observes, the "mediating hierarch" conception of the board of directors requires a stakeholder mandate, not mere discretion to show regard for their interests. "The very discretion that allows corporate boards to pay attention to nonshareholder as well as shareholder interests," Millon rightly observes, "also allows them to pursue shareholder value with relentless disregard for social costs."[167] Lacking descriptive power in this critical respect, Blair and Stout's

[162] *See* Blair & Stout, *supra* note 153, at 269–81. [163] *Id.* at 278.

[164] *Id.* at 281. *See also* Blair & Stout, *supra* note 161, at 424–25.

[165] *See* Blair & Stout, *supra* note 161, at 428–30, 434–37. *See also* Blair & Stout, *supra* note 153, at 299–309; Elhauge, *supra* note 105, at 770–76; Ian B. Lee, *Corporate Law, Profit Maximization, and the "Responsible Shareholder,"* 10 STAN. J.L. BUS. & FIN. 31, 32–38 (2005).

[166] *See* Bruner, *supra* note 22, at 1403–05.

[167] David Millon, *New Game Plan or Business as Usual? A Critique of the Team Production Model of Corporate Law*, 86 VA. L. REV. 1001, 1022 (2000). *See also* John C. Coates IV, *Measuring the Domain of Mediating Hierarchy: How Contestable Are U.S. Public Corporations?*, 24 J. CORP. L. 837, 847–48 (1999); KENT GREENFIELD, THE FAILURE OF CORPORATE LAW: FUNDAMENTAL FLAWS & PROGRESSIVE POSSIBILITIES 147–48 (2006).

conception of the board (and the corporation) at best amounts to a normative argument in favor of board independence[168] – a point readily acknowledged by "progressive" corporate law scholars who favor adoption of a stakeholder mandate as a response to the shortcomings of a corporate governance system historically placing shareholders in a favorable position vis-à-vis other constituencies.[169] Blair and Stout acknowledge that boards "remain subject to equity market pressures," and thus "have a special incentive to pay attention to shareholders' interests in making their decisions," but respond that to discharge its role as mediating hierarch, the board need merely "provide *enough* of the firm's surplus to each residual claimant to keep her in the corporate team."[170] This takes Blair and Stout only so far, however, as it assumes a surplus sufficient to satisfy all concerned – an account with nothing to say about the far more vexing circumstance in which dwindling resources inevitably pit various stakeholders' interests against one another.[171]

The marginalization of shareholders required by the team production conception of the board's role effectively leaves it with no means of explaining those aspects of corporate law that do seem to favor shareholders over other constituencies. Like the nexus theory, the team production theory offers no coherent explanation for shareholder voting rights, exercise of which generally need not involve consideration of anyone's interests other than the shareholder's own.[172] The team production theory faces even greater difficulties, however, given the privileged position that shareholders enjoy in the enforcement of management's fiduciary duties. The significance of U.S. shareholders' capacity to sue will be discussed in some detail in the concluding section of this chapter,[173] but for present purposes it suffices to observe that Delaware courts have long been reluctant to extend fiduciary protections directly to other corporate stakeholders, favoring shareholders in a manner that is clearly in tension

[168] *See* Coates, *supra* note 167, at 867; Millon, *supra* note 167, at 1023–24.

[169] *See, e.g.*, GREENFIELD, *supra* note 167, at 21–28, 134–52. *See also* Simon Deakin, *The Corporation as Commons: Rethinking Property Rights, Governance and Sustainability in the Business Enterprise*, 37 QUEEN'S L.J. 339, 367–80 (2012) (arguing that conceptualizing the corporation as a "commons" implies, among other things, a need for "multi-stakeholder governance in preference to shareholder primacy"). For an argument that corporate law already permits decision making orientation toward long-term sustainability in the interests of all stakeholders, and that short-term capital market orientation in fact represents the more pressing issue, see David Millon, *Two Models of Corporate Social Responsibility*, 46 WAKE FOREST L. REV. 523 (2011).

[170] Blair & Stout, *supra* note 161, at 435–36 (emphasis added).

[171] *See* Bruner, *supra* note 22, at 1404.

[172] *See, e.g.*, ALLEN ET AL. *supra* note 70, at 306–07 (observing that controlling shareholders owe fiduciary duties to the corporation and the minority shareholders, but that otherwise shareholders are generally entitled "to vote in their own interests").

[173] *See infra* Chapter 3.D.

with the "mediating hierarch" conception of the board. Although the traditional Delaware formulation is decidedly ambivalent in styling the corporation generally and the shareholders specifically as simultaneous beneficiaries,[174] it must be acknowledged that the shareholders – alone among the corporation's various stakeholders – are singled out. In its 2007 *Gheewalla* opinion, the Delaware Supreme Court reiterated this formulation and explained that although creditors may have standing to sue derivatively, on the corporation's behalf, if the company is insolvent (having stepped into the shareholders' shoes "as the residual beneficiaries of any increase in value"), creditors cannot sue derivatively while the company remains solvent, and never possess shareholder-like standing to sue directly for breach of fiduciary duty.[175] Blair and Stout respond that "the procedure of granting shareholders standing to sue in derivative cases is designed primarily to serve the interests of the firm as a whole," and emphasize that "any damages recovered must go into the corporation's coffers," not to the shareholders themselves.[176] Even so, however, shareholders still control the filing of derivative suits in a solvent corporation. As Millon observes, there is no reason to expect shareholders to file such a suit where a board decision uniquely harms a non-shareholder constituency – say, taking on additional debt to the detriment of existing creditors – because shareholders themselves "stand to gain nothing from the exercise."[177]

There is clearly much common ground between the foregoing theories in that they strongly emphasize the centrality of the board of directors in corporate governance and favor substantial insulation from shareholder interference. In stark contrast with the "nexus of contracts" and "team production" theories stands the "shareholder primacy" theory, so called because it places shareholders themselves at the heart of the corporation with respect to both power and purpose (see Figure 3.2). The shareholder primacy view essentially proceeds from the hotly disputed premise that shareholders "own" the corporation, accordingly conceptualizing corporate governance in straightforward principal–agent terms. Economist Milton Friedman issued the paradigmatic statement of this view in his 1970 *New York Times Magazine* article titled "The Social Responsibility of Business is to Increase Profits." Friedman argued:

> In a free-enterprise, private-property system, a corporate executive is an employe [*sic*] of the owners of the business. He has direct responsibility

[174] *See* Guth v. Loft, 5 A.2d 503, 510 (Del. 1939).

[175] *See* N. Am. Catholic Educ. Programming Found., Inc. v. Gheewalla, 930 A.2d 92, 99–103 (Del. 2007). In so doing, the court rejected the notion that creditors' interests ought to loom larger in board decision making once the corporation enters the "zone of insolvency," as the Chancery Court had previously suggested. *See* Credit Lyonnais Bank Nederland, N.V. v. Pathe Commc'ns Corp., Civ. A. No. 12150, 1991 WL 277613, at *34 & n.55 (Del. Ch. Dec. 30, 1991).

[176] Blair & Stout, *supra* note 153, at 293–95.

[177] *See* Millon, *supra* note 167, at 1013–14.

> to his employers. That responsibility is to conduct the business in accordance with their desires, which generally will be to make as much money as possible while conforming to the basic rules of the society, both those embodied in law and those embodied in ethical custom.[178]

Like nexus scholars, Friedman accepts that a corporation could be established "for an eleemosynary purpose," in which case shareholder interests would not define its aims, but insists that otherwise "the manager is the agent of the individuals who own the corporation . . . and his primary responsibility is to them."[179] Boards and officers must not favor their own conception of "'social' purposes" over the shareholders' interests, as "[t]he whole justification for permitting the corporate executive to be selected by the stockholders is that the executive is an agent serving the interests of his principal."[180]

More recently, Lucian Bebchuk has championed this approach to U.S. corporate governance, asserting that maximizing shareholder wealth constitutes the defining purpose of the corporation, and arguing for greater accountability to shareholders to minimize shirking and extraction of private benefits by management.[181] Among other things, Bebchuk has advocated robust removal powers, arguing that the assumption that shareholders can replace directors not adhering to their wishes has undergirded corporate law's deference to the board's substantive decisions, courts' willingness to countenance takeover defenses, and the board's gatekeeping role in fundamental actions more generally.[182] He likewise emphasizes expansive dicta indicating that the Delaware board's extraordinary powers are grounded in, and legitimated by, "the shareholder franchise."[183]

The shareholder primacy view championed by Friedman and Bebchuk would appear to offer quite a compelling descriptive account of the approach to corporate governance adopted in the United Kingdom where, as we have seen, shareholder power literally defines the corporation and the shareholders'

178 Milton Friedman, *A Friedman Doctrine – The Social Responsibility of Business Is to Increase Profits*, N.Y. TIMES MAG., Sept. 13, 1970, at 33.

179 *Id.* at 33. *See also* Lucian A. Bebchuk, *The Myth of the Shareholder Franchise*, 93 VA. L. REV. 675, 678 (2007); Stephen M. Bainbridge, *Executive Compensation: Who Decides?*, 83 TEX. L. REV. 1615, 1645 (2005) (reviewing LUCIAN BEBCHUK & JESSE FRIED, PAY WITHOUT PERFORMANCE: THE UNFULFILLED PROMISE OF EXECUTIVE COMPENSATION (2004)) (observing the commonality in prioritizing shareholders' interests).

180 Friedman, *supra* note 178, at 122. Note, as Bainbridge does, that regardless of whether shareholders are said to "own the firm itself" or to "own the residual claim to the corporation's assets and earnings," they "occupy a privileged position with ownership-like rights" and managers are effectively treated as "mere agents of the shareholders." *See* Bainbridge, *supra* note 139, at 563–64.

181 *See* Bebchuk, *supra* note 179, at 678–82.

182 *See id.* at 680–81.

183 *See id.* at 676 (citing Blasius Indus., Inc. v. Atlas Corp., 564 A.2d 651, 659 (Del. Ch. 1988)).

interests unquestionably represent the sole legitimate aim of corporate activity. Indeed, Bebchuk has cited the U.K. approach as a sort of ideal, constituting evidence that "shareholders' lack of power to initiate major corporate decisions is not an inevitable element of the legal structure of the modern corporation." The United States, he argues, ought to follow the United Kingdom's lead.[184] In so doing, however, it is effectively conceded that a strict shareholder primacy view cannot begin to account for the current state of U.S. corporate governance as a descriptive matter.

Friedman's more extreme version of the shareholder primacy argument, grounded in a property-based conception of the shareholders' role, is aptly described by Kent Greenfield as "crude and analytically unsound," at once reflecting "a simplistic notion of the sanctity and indivisibility of property rights" while ignoring the fact that shareholders lack the modes of direct control over corporate assets typical of an "owner" of property.[185] Bebchuk's considerably more nuanced shareholder primacy argument, grounded in the conceptual significance of board election by the shareholders, effectively concedes that – for U.S. shareholders – the franchise remains a "myth" in practical terms. Accordingly, Bebchuk's principal occupation has been the development of normative arguments aimed at transforming the myth into a reality.[186]

As to the claim that shareholder wealth maximization constitutes the proper metric of corporate decision making, the shareholder primacy view stumbles over the same obstacles that the nexus view does – the absence of any explicit duty to maximize shareholder wealth beyond limited circumstances; endorsement of substantial deviations from shareholders' interests in the critical context of hostile takeovers; additional capacity to deviate from shareholders' interests under the business judgment rule; and the ability to appeal to vague, unverifiable claims about the corporation's long-term interests in support of management strategies offering no discernible near-term benefits to shareholders.

Arguably, one U.S. state – North Dakota – bears out the shareholder primacy vision for corporate governance, but the history of the North Dakota approach and its experience to date suggest that it amounts to the exception proving the rule of U.S. ambivalence regarding shareholders. In 2007, at the behest of activist investor Carl Icahn, a decidedly shareholder-centric corporate statute for public companies was adopted by North Dakota – apparently Icahn's

[184] *See* Lucian Arye Bebchuk, *The Case for Increasing Shareholder Power*, 118 HARV. L. REV. 833, 847–50 (2005).

[185] GREENFIELD, *supra* note 167, at 43–47. *See also* Deakin, *supra* note 169, at 355–59; STOUT, *supra* note 97, at 37–38.

[186] *See* Bebchuk, *supra* note 179, at 677–79.

second choice after Vermont, where his initial campaign for such a law failed.[187] Titled the "North Dakota Publicly Traded Corporations Act,"[188] the statute (among other things) eliminates staggered boards,[189] extends proxy access and expense reimbursement to shareholders holding more than 5 percent of voting shares for at least two years,[190] requires majority voting in board elections (except where the charter permits cumulative voting),[191] gives shareholders an advisory vote on executive compensation,[192] permits shareholders to amend the charter unilaterally,[193] and substantially limits use of poison pills and other takeover defenses.[194]

This package would indeed appear quite attractive to U.S. shareholders seeking greater involvement in corporate affairs,[195] yet its passage remains a nonevent. The new act attracted literally no companies in its first two years of existence, and as of September 2011 applied to just one company – an Icahn-controlled corporation that reincorporated from Delaware in 2009.[196] The publicly filed reports of the sole company to avail itself of the new statute, American Railcar Industries, Inc., illuminate why the shareholder-centric North Dakota statute has not attracted adherents beyond Icahn himself. The proxy disclosure preceding American Railcar's vote on reincorporation explains that, due to Icahn's ability to "control most matters requiring board or shareholder approval," the company's minority shareholders "may not immediately be able to avail themselves of all of the benefits otherwise available to them under the North Dakota Corporate Law"[197] – effectively rendering the move an empty gesture. American Railcar's 2009 annual report, in the "risk factors" section,

[187] *See* Elizabeth Lopatto, *'Virgin' North Dakota Draws Billionaire Icahn in Raider Quest*, BLOOMBERG.COM (Feb. 20, 2009), http://www.bloomberg.com/apps/news?pid=newsarchive&sid=aXgfseyKwJmI.

[188] *See* N.D. CENT. CODE § 10–35–01.

[189] *See id.* § 10–35–06.

[190] *See id.* §§ 10–35–08, 10–35–10.

[191] *See id.* § 10–35–09.

[192] *See id.* § 10–35–12(5).

[193] *See id.* § 10–35–15.

[194] *See id.* §§ 10–35–22–26.

[195] *See, e.g.*, Carl Icahn, *More Rights for Shareholders in North Dakota*, ICAHNREPORT.COM (Dec. 17, 2008), http://www.icahnreport.com/report/2008/12/more-rights-for.html (describing North Dakota as "the most shareholder-friendly state in the nation").

[196] *See* American Railcar Industries, Inc., Quarterly Report (Form 10-Q), at 7, 42 (Aug. 7, 2009), http://www.sec.gov/Archives/edgar/data/1344596/000095012309032254/c89011e10vq.htm; Associated Press, *Rail Car Maker Moves Corporate Home to N.D.*, BISMARCK TRIB., July 1, 2009, at 1B; E-mail from Darcy Hurley, Administrative Staff Officer, Secretary of State Business Division, State of North Dakota (Sept. 12, 2011) (on file with the author); Lopatto, *supra* note 187; Dale Wetzel, *Icahn Company Setting Up Corporate Residence in ND*, ASSOCIATED PRESS FINANCIAL WIRE, June 11, 2009, http://www.allbusiness.com/government/government-bodies-offices-regional-local/12511376–1.html.

[197] *See* American Railcar Industries, Inc., Proxy Statement (Schedule 14A), at 43 (Apr. 30, 2009), http://www.sec.gov/Archives/edgar/data/1344596/000136231009006080/c84436def14a.htm.

added that Icahn's interests could "conflict with the interest of our other stockholders," and that it remained unclear what the North Dakota statute would amount to in practice. The law "was only recently enacted," the report explains, and "to our knowledge no other companies are yet subject to its provisions and interpretations of its likely application are scarce," resulting in a "lack of predictability [that] could be detrimental to our stockholders."[198] This presents a stark contrast with the well-developed case law in Delaware, the jurisdiction where – as Bloomberg reported in 2009 – "the publicly traded Icahn Enterprises LP remains incorporated."[199]

As the foregoing survey demonstrates, none of the prevailing theories provide a persuasive descriptive account of U.S. corporate governance, reflecting the fundamental ambivalence regarding shareholders that has long defined the field. The nexus theory overstates board power, while providing insufficient evidence to support its claim that shareholders' interests reign supreme (Figure 3.2, top right). The team production theory similarly overstates board power, while providing insufficient evidence to support its claim that the board answers to all stakeholders (Figure 3.2, bottom right). And the shareholder primacy theory offers scant evidence of shareholder centrality either as to power or as to purpose, amounting to little more than a normative argument that U.S. corporate governance ought to take a leaf out of the U.K. book (Figure 3.2, top left).[200] The next section evaluates the corporate governance systems

[198] *See* American Railcar Industries, Inc., Annual Report (Form 10-K), at 19–20 (Mar. 12, 2010), http://www.sec.gov/Archives/edgar/data/1344596/000095012310024240/c97389e10vk.htm.

[199] Lopatto, *supra* note 187. Icahn Enterprises L.P., a publicly traded master limited partnership organized in Delaware and controlled by Carl Icahn, is a diversified holding company with subsidiaries in a range of businesses. *See* Icahn Enterprises L.P., Annual Report (Form 10-K), at 1 (Mar. 8, 2011), http://www.sec.gov/Archives/edgar/data/813762/000114420411013351/v213219_10k.htm. In January 2010, Icahn Enterprises L.P. purchased a controlling stake in American Railcar from affiliates of Icahn. *See* Icahn Enterprises L.P., *supra*, at 11–12. For an argument "predicting that the North Dakota experiment will fail," see BAINBRIDGE, *supra* note 151, at 25–27.

[200] No prevailing descriptive theory of U.S. corporate governance falls squarely in the bottom left quadrant of Figure 3.2 – pairing shareholder power with stakeholder orientation. This presumably reflects the absence of an across-the-board stakeholder mandate in U.S. corporate law, coupled with the perfectly reasonable assumption that shareholders' regard for their own interests will generally render such other-regarding conduct unlikely to occur. *Cf.* Millon, *supra* note 167, at 1013 (observing that shareholders "have no legal duty" to pursue derivative suits on behalf of non-shareholders, and have no practical incentive to do so where the shareholders themselves "stand to gain nothing from the exercise").

This does not mean, however, that one could not reasonably advocate imposing stakeholder-oriented duties on shareholders themselves as a normative matter – particularly in response to pro-shareholder market trends viewed unfavorably by the advocate of such duties. For example, in response to the growth in shareholder activism in the United States, Iman Anabtawi and Lynn Stout argued in a 2008 article that activist minority shareholders who actually impact decision making ought to be subject to a fiduciary duty of loyalty in order to manage conflicts of Australia and Canada before the backdrop of these contrasting models – the U.K. approach, in which shareholders strongly dominate, and the U.S. approach, in which shareholders are substantially marginalized.[201]

C. PREDOMINANCE OF THE U.K. CORPORATE GOVERNANCE MODEL

Notwithstanding their broad similarities from a global perspective, the United Kingdom and the United States take two very different approaches to corporate governance when it comes to the appropriate role of shareholders. Later chapters explore why this fundamental divergence arose between two corporate governance systems routinely lumped together in the comparative literature, and what this divergence tells us about their future,[202] but first we turn to two additional corporate governance systems closely related to the U.K. and U.S. systems in a number of legal, economic, historical, and cultural respects – those of Australia and Canada.

of interest, particularly given the growing heterogeneity of interests across various categories of shareholders. *See* Iman Anabtawi & Lynn Stout, *Fiduciary Duties for Activist Shareholders*, 60 STAN. L. REV. 1255, 1261–62, 1274–98 (2008). *See also, e.g.*, Ashwini K. Agrawal, *Corporate Governance Objectives of Labor Union Shareholders: Evidence from Proxy Voting*, 25 REV. FIN. STUD. 187, 189 (2012) ("When a firm's unionized employees are no longer represented by the AFL-CIO, the AFL-CIO's pension funds become significantly less opposed to the firm's directors in subsequent board elections."); BAINBRIDGE, *supra* note 151, at 246–47 (arguing that "we are left mainly with union and state and local pension funds," which "are precisely the institutions most likely to use their position to self-deal or to otherwise reap private benefits not shared with other investors"). *But see* Martin Gelter, *The Pension System and the Rise of Shareholder Primacy* 34–36 (Fordham Univ. Sch. of Law Working Paper Series, 2012), http://ssrn.com/abstract=2079607 (acknowledging that "the anecdotal and empirical picture is certainly ambiguous," but arguing that "even without a full empirical assessment, it seems fair to say that union activism has to a large degree helped the cause of shareholder primacy").

Their argument is expressly normative, prompted by the perceived deficiency of the doctrinal status quo in the United States, which imposes fiduciary duties on shareholders only when they possess de facto voting control. *See* Anabtawi & Stout, *supra*, at 1268–74. It must also be emphasized that they focus solely on conflict-of-interest scenarios, expressly setting aside the question of corporate purpose. *See* Anabtawi & Stout, *supra*, at 1284. They do, however, note the absence of a shareholder wealth maximization mandate in corporate law – a theme prominent in Stout's "team production" work with Margaret Blair, in which broader fiduciary obligations are advocated – and that shareholders would, under the Anabtawi and Stout approach, remain free to vote their shares in a manner favoring the interests of non-shareholder constituencies. *See* Anabtawi & Stout, *supra*, at 1284. Thus, although their proposal does not represent the pairing of shareholder power with stakeholder orientation hypothesized here, their argument implicitly suggests that one could rationally advocate such a position.

[201] Shareholder-centric corporate governance reform efforts – pursued in the United States and the United Kingdom alike in the wake of the financial and economic crisis that emerged in 2007 – will be discussed below. *See infra* Chapter 6.D.

[202] *See infra* Chapters 5–6.

Overall, as this section demonstrates, each has adopted an approach to corporate governance more closely resembling that of the United Kingdom, empowering shareholders and favoring their interests to a far greater extent than we find in the United States. Each, however, has adopted distinct approaches – and in some cases, utterly unique doctrinal structures – that further illuminate the political and social dynamics explored later in the book.

I. Australia

Australian company law strongly resembles U.K. company law in fundamental respects, notably in that shareholders possess strong governance powers and their interests are strongly emphasized relative to those of other stakeholders.[203] To some extent this simply reflects the fact that, as a historical matter, Australian company law is quite directly rooted in U.K. company law.[204] As the leading treatise by Robert Austin and Ian Ramsay observes, although contemporary Australian company law "is less dependent upon the United Kingdom" than it once was, it nevertheless remains the case that numerous provisions of the Corporations Act 2001 "can be traced back to some pioneer legislation in the United Kingdom," such that "the expository views of courts there can be instructive."[205]

At the same time, however, Australia's federal governmental structure has required grappling with issues of federal and regional regulatory competence much like those faced in the United States (and, as we shall see, Canada). Although Australia's federal parliament possesses "trade and commerce" authority[206] superficially resembling the Commerce Clause authority widely understood to permit the U.S. Congress to regulate corporate and securities matters to the degree it likes, Australia's parliament has nonetheless been found to lack constitutional authority to regulate these matters.[207] As powers not granted to the federal parliament are reserved to the state parliaments, this

[203] *See, e.g.*, Helen Anderson, Michelle Welsh, Ian Ramsay & Peter Gahan, *The Evolution of Shareholder and Creditor Protection in Australia: An International Comparison*, 61 INT'L & COMP. L.Q. 171, 181–93 (2012).

[204] *See, e.g.*, Bernard Mees & Ian Ramsay, *Corporate Regulators in Australia (1961–2000): From Companies' Registrars to ASIC*, 22 AUSTL. J. CORP. L. 212, pt. 2 (2008); PARLIAMENTARY JOINT COMMITTEE ON CORPORATIONS AND FINANCIAL SERVICES, CORPORATE RESPONSIBILITY: MANAGING RISK AND CREATING VALUE 9 (2006) [hereinafter PJC REPORT].

[205] R.P. AUSTIN & I.M. RAMSAY, FORD'S PRINCIPLES OF CORPORATIONS LAW 2 (14th ed. 2010). *See also* Bell Group Ltd. (in liq.) v. Westpac Banking Corp. (No. 9) (2008) 70 ACSR 1, ¶¶ 4370–83 (Sup. Ct. WA) (Austl.) (tracing Australian directors' duties to their British origins).

[206] *See* Commonwealth of Australia Constitution Act, 1900 (Imp), 63 & 64 Victoria, c. 12, § 51(1) (U.K.) (compilation prepared July 25, 2003).

[207] *See* AUSTIN & RAMSAY, *supra* note 205, at 45–46.

means that only Australia's states possess the requisite constitutional authority to enact corporate and securities laws.[208] The Corporations Act 2001, to be sure, is a federal statute, but it could be placed on a sound constitutional footing only through referral – by each and every Australian state – of the regulatory capacity to enact such a law to the federal parliament, as permitted by § 51 of the Constitution Act.[209] The nature and limits of this constitutional foundation are expressly reflected in the Corporations Act, which makes amply clear that its application rests predominantly on these state-by-state referrals.[210] The principal regulatory bodies overseeing publicly traded companies in Australia are the Australian Securities and Investments Commission (ASIC), a Commonwealth body drawing its powers from this and other legislation, and the Australian Securities Exchange (ASX), effectively a "co-regulator" with ASIC "in that it prescribes standards for companies admitted to the Official List of the Exchange and reserves power to police those standards."[211]

Certain features of Australian company law do take forms closely resembling U.S. corporate law. For example, like U.S. shareholders, Australian shareholders cannot "direct the directors" as such.[212] Although Australian common law does include a "unanimous assent" doctrine – permitting shareholders to bind the company by unanimous consent – this doctrine does not extend to decisions within the board's exclusive purview.[213] Similarly, preemptive rights in Australian public companies exist only where the constitution provides for them, resembling the U.S. approach.[214] Australian company law also includes a "business judgment rule" modeled on U.S. law.[215]

[208] *See* Commonwealth of Australia Constitution Act, 1900 (Imp), 63 & 64 Victoria, c. 12, § 107 (U.K.).

[209] *See id.* § 51(xxxvii) (giving the federal parliament power to make laws regarding "matters referred ... by the Parliament or Parliaments of any State or States," but only as to referring states). *See also* AUSTIN & RAMSAY, *supra* note 205, at 43–47, 59–65; Jennifer G. Hill, *The Architecture of Corporate Governance in Australia* 1–2 (Univ. Sydney Law Sch. Legal Studies Research Paper No. 10/75, 2010), http://ssrn.com/abstract=1657810.

[210] *See Corporations Act 2001* (Cth) ss 3–5 (Austl.).

[211] *See* AUSTIN & RAMSAY, *supra* note 205, at 53–54, 68–69. ASIC implements the Financial Services Reform Act (2001), under which the ASX is licensed to operate a financial market and clearing and settlement facilities. Although the Treasurer is ultimately responsible for licensing, ASIC advises the Treasurer regarding licensing decisions and oversees licensees' compliance with law. *See* Reserve Bank of Australia, *The Australian Securities and Investments Commission*, http://www.rba.gov.au/fin-stability/reg-framework/asic.html.

[212] *See* AUSTIN & RAMSAY, *supra* note 205, at 228–29.

[213] *See id.* at 327–30.

[214] *See Corporations Act 2001*, *supra* note 210, s 254D (providing default preemption rights only for shareholders in proprietary companies); AUSTIN & RAMSAY, *supra* note 205, at 936–37.

[215] *See Corporations Act 2001*, *supra* note 210, s 180(2). *See also* Hill, *supra* note 209, at 23–24; SENATE STANDING COMMITTEE ON LEGAL AND CONSTITUTIONAL AFFAIRS, COMPANY DIRECTORS' DUTIES: REPORT ON THE SOCIAL AND FIDUCIARY DUTIES AND OBLIGATIONS OF COMPANY

	U.K.	Australia	U.S. (Delaware)
call special meetings	Y	Y	N
remove directors without cause	Y	Y	N (if classified)
initiate charter amendments	Y	Y	N
approve takeover defenses	Y	Y	N
compel board action	Y	N	N
preemptive rights	Y	N	N

Figure 3.3. Shareholders' Default Governance Powers in Public Corporations: Australia, the United Kingdom, and the United States

In terms of its core governance rules, however, the Australian system much more closely resembles the U.K. system. To facilitate the comparison, Figure 3.3 places Australia's approach to the core governance structures discussed in this chapter alongside the approaches taken in the United Kingdom and the United States. Like in the United Kingdom, a statutory distinction is drawn in Australia between "public companies" and "proprietary companies," the latter being those with fifty or fewer nonemployee shareholders that do not raise capital on public markets.[216] The core governance document, again called the "constitution," is required as a matter of company law only if the company intends to deviate from statutory default rules, but the ASX requires a constitution for listing, effectively rendering it a requirement for Australian public companies.[217] This core governance document – as in the United Kingdom – is conceptualized as a contract,[218] and the Corporations Act states that shareholders may amend it unilaterally by "special resolution" of 75 percent of shares entitled to vote.[219] The Corporations Act draws attention to the power this places in the hands of shareholders through § 141, which summarizes numerous "replaceable rules" – including core governance structures – from which corporations may deviate through contrary provisions in their constitutions.[220]

DIRECTORS 31 (1989) (Cooney Report). A statutory business judgment rule has been considered unnecessary in the United Kingdom, reflecting confidence that courts can be expected to refrain from hindsight-based second-guessing of business judgments. *See* DAVIES, *supra* note 8, at 493–94.

[216] *See Corporations Act 2001*, *supra* note 210, ss 45A(1), 112–13. *See also* AUSTIN & RAMSAY, *supra* note 205, at 164–67.

[217] *See Corporations Act 2001*, *supra* note 210, s 134; AUSTIN & RAMSAY, *supra* note 205, at 202.

[218] *See Corporations Act 2001*, *supra* note 210, s 140(1).

[219] *See id.* ss 9, 136(2).

[220] *See id.* s 141.

Australia's statute provides that the "business of a company is to be managed by or under the direction of the directors."[221] Hence, as in the United Kingdom and the United States alike, the board of directors typically constitutes the principal decision-making body in the corporation.[222] Critically, however, § 198A – the source of a board's default governance authority – is a replaceable rule, meaning that Australian shareholders possess a conceptually straightforward means of unilaterally carving back at board power, in a manner resembling the U.K. approach. Shareholders derive further governance power, then, from statutory authority to remove directors by ordinary resolution of a simple majority of shares present and voted at a meeting, a power that – like in the United Kingdom – cannot be contractually limited.[223] As Jennifer Hill concludes, threat of removal represents "an important governance device under Australian corporate law."[224]

Other corporate governance rules bolster this strong removal power. Notably, a rule on the calling of meetings even more liberal than that in the United Kingdom facilitates its use. The statute permits meetings to be called not only at the request of shareholders possessing 5 percent voting power, as in the United Kingdom, but also at the request of any one hundred shareholders – even in public companies, and regardless of how little voting power they may collectively possess.[225] Such shareholder groups can also propose a resolution for consideration at the meeting and demand that it be included in the company's notice.[226] The one-hundred shareholder rule, in particular, has spurred greater shareholder activism, notably among environmentalists and unions.[227]

[221] *See id.* s 198A(1). A public company must have at least three directors, two of whom reside in Australia. *See id.* s 201A(2).

[222] *See, e.g.*, Austin & Ramsay, *supra* note 205, at 223–24.

[223] *See Corporations Act 2001*, *supra* note 210, s 203D(1); Austin & Ramsay, *supra* note 205, at 302–03; DeMott, *supra* note 28, at 108–09, 112–13.

[224] Hill, *supra* note 209, at 16, 30–31. *See also* Jennifer Hill, *Institutional Investors and Corporate Governance in Australia*, *in* Institutional Investors and Corporate Governance 583, 598–603 (Theodor Baums, Richard M. Buxbaum & Klaus J. Hopt eds., 1994) (observing that Australian shareholder activism, including through threat of removal from the board, picked up in the early 1990s); Australian Securities & Investments Commission, Regulatory Guide 128: Collective Action by Institutional Investors (updated July 8, 1998) (providing guidance on the degree to which institutional shareholders could coordinate their actions without running afoul of various securities rules). As in the United Kingdom, the director in question has the right to "put their case to members" through a written statement and the opportunity to be heard at the meeting. *See Corporations Act 2001*, *supra* note 210, s 203D(4).

[225] *See Corporations Act 2001*, *supra* note 210, ss 249D(1), 249F (permitting shareholders with 5 percent voting power to call a meeting on their own, rather than requesting that the board do so). *See also* Anderson et al. *supra* note 203, at 189 (observing that this rule appears to be unique to Australia).

[226] *See Corporations Act 2001*, *supra* note 210, ss 249N, 249P.

[227] *See* Hill, *supra* note 209, at 35.

Effective July 2011, the so-called two strikes rule effectively amplifies the shareholders' removal power. Australia adopted a "say on pay" rule in 2005 (following the United Kingdom's lead) giving shareholders an advisory vote on executive compensation, but this mechanism came to be viewed as an insufficient constraint on pay.[228] In response, amendments to the Corporations Act adopted in June 2011 introduced new rules that ban hedging of performance-based pay[229] and trigger an automatic "spill resolution" – requiring a vote on whether the whole board ought to be put up for reelection – in the event that the statutorily required remuneration report is rejected by 25 percent of votes cast at two consecutive annual meetings (in other words, upon "two strikes").[230] Notwithstanding the substantial removal power already possessed by Australian shareholders, it has been widely recognized by proponents and opponents alike that the new "two strikes" rule will give minority shareholders substantially greater leverage, given the negative publicity that would presumably accompany even one strike, let alone the automatic spill resolution triggered by a second strike.[231] As Senator Don Farrell aptly concluded in his second reading speech on the amendment, the "two strikes" rule "will give unprecedented power to shareholders" in Australia.[232]

Australia's approach to takeover regulation, although differing from that in the United Kingdom in various respects, nevertheless resembles the U.K. approach in its fundamental focus on shareholder choice and shareholder interests. Unlike the mandatory bid approach taken in the United Kingdom,

[228] *See Corporations Act 2001*, *supra* note 210, s 250R(2)-(3). *See also* John Collett, *Shareholders to Vote on Pay Packets*, SYDNEY MORNING HERALD, May 28, 2011, http://m.smh.com.au/money/investing/shareholders-to-vote-on-pay-packets-20110527–1f8rc.html; CORPORATIONS AND MARKETS ADVISORY COMMITTEE, EXECUTIVE REMUNERATION REPORT 15, 50–53 (Apr. 2011); Cth, Parliamentary Debates, Senate, 14 June 2011, 2–3 (Don Farrell, Senator) (Austl.). The United Kingdom adopted a "say on pay" rule in 2002, and likewise found that it had little impact on compensation levels. *See* Brian R. Cheffins, *Did Corporate Governance "Fail" during the 2008 Stock Market Meltdown? The Case of the S&P 500*, 65 BUS. LAW. 1, 57 (2009). In response, a push arose in mid-2012 to render such votes binding. *See* Amy L. Goodman, *Binding Say on Pay in the UK*, HARVARD LAW SCHOOL FORUM ON CORPORATE GOVERNANCE AND FINANCIAL REGULATION, July 9, 2012, https://blogs.law.harvard.edu/corpgov/2012/07/09/binding-say-on-pay-in-the-uk/. *See also infra* Chapter 6.D.

[229] *See Corporations Amendment (Improving Accountability on Director and Executive Remuneration) Act 2011* (Cth) at 5–6 (Austl.) (s 206J).

[230] *See id.* at 13–17 (ss 250U-250Y).

[231] *See, e.g.*, Collett, *supra* note 228; Damon Kitney & Glenda Korporaal, *Report's Warning on Executive Pay Rules*, AUSTRALIAN, May 26, 2011, http://www.theaustralian.com.au/news/executive-lifestyle/reportss-warning-on-executive-pay-rules/story-e6frg9zo-1226062964816; Minter Ellison, *CAMAC Report on Executive Remuneration: Don't Change the Pitch When the Two Strikes Rule Is Coming*, LEXOLOGY, May 31, 2011, http://www.lexology.com/library/detail.aspx?g=7b75ea95-ca5e-4c0e-a5b9-d9077799133e.

[232] Cth, Parliamentary Debates, *supra* note 228, at 5.

Australian takeover regulation prohibits share acquisitions in public companies resulting in voting power between 20 and 90 percent unless the acquisition falls within one of the exceptions set forth in the statute, notably including bids meeting various statutory requirements.[233] As Hill summarizes the Australian framework, "[b]y requiring a bidder to make an offer to all shareholders before it is permitted to pass the control threshold, Australian takeover law ensures that majority and minority shareholders share equally any control premium" – an approach considered "particularly strict" relative to that of the United Kingdom, which permits the mandatory bid to follow a private control transaction.[234] Over time, however, reforms have tended toward introduction of U.K.-style flexibility, notably by shifting resolution of disputes during the pendency of a bid from the courts to a "Takeovers Panel,"[235] and by giving ASIC broad exemption powers (subject to review by the Takeovers Panel).[236]

On the issue of greatest relevance to this discussion – the shareholders' degree of freedom to accept hostile bids – Australia, like the United Kingdom, has "not proven to be hospitable terrain for poison pills," or other defenses for that matter.[237] Australian case law suggests that, although not literally prohibited, poison pills and other defenses are difficult to square with the board's fiduciary duty to act with a proper purpose.[238] Additionally, the Takeovers Panel possesses enormous discretion under the statute to "declare circumstances in relation to the affairs of a company to be unacceptable circumstances,"[239] and has clearly expressed its distaste for preclusive defenses. The Panel's guidance note on "frustrating action" – that is, action by a target board aimed at defeating a hostile bid – bluntly states that "it is shareholders who should decide on actions that may . . . inhibit the acquisition of control over their voting shares taking place in an efficient, competitive and informed market."[240] In other words, as in the United Kingdom, defenses generally require shareholder approval. The Panel elaborates that "a frustrating action may give rise to unacceptable circumstances regardless of whether it is consistent with, or

[233] *See Corporations Act 2001*, *supra* note 210, ss 606, 611. *See also* AUSTIN & RAMSAY, *supra* note 205, at 1220–23. A buyout is required once a bidder hits 90 percent voting power. *See Corporations Act 2001*, *supra* note 210, s 662A. *See also* AUSTIN & RAMSAY, *supra* note 205, at 1400.

[234] Jennifer G. Hill, *Subverting Shareholder Rights: Lessons from News Corp.'s Migration to Delaware*, 63 VAND. L. REV. 1, 24–25 (2010).

[235] *See Corporations Act 2001*, *supra* note 210, ss 659A-659C. *See also* Hill, *supra* note 234, at 25–26.

[236] *See Corporations Act 2001*, *supra* note 210, ss 655A-656B. *See also* AUSTIN & RAMSAY, *supra* note 205, at 1297–99.

[237] Hill, *supra* note 234, at 34.

[238] *See id.* at 34–35.

[239] *Corporations Act 2001*, *supra* note 210, s 657A.

[240] Takeovers Panel, Commonwealth of Australia, Guidance Note 12 – Frustrating Action 1–2 (May 6, 2011).

a breach of, directors' duties" under company law, and that "[i]t is not to the point that there is no express requirement in the law for shareholder approval of frustrating action."[241] Additionally, ASX Listing Rule 7.1 generally requires shareholder approval for non–pro rata issuances exceeding 15 percent of a company's outstanding shares,[242] a threshold presumably crossed when a poison pill is triggered.[243]

That Australian shareholders themselves consider their corporate governance regime far more favorable to their interests than the U.S. approach was vividly illustrated when News Corp. reincorporated from Australia to Delaware. As Hill observes in her detailed study of the move and its aftermath, the 2004 proposal to reincorporate "prompted a revolt by a number of institutional investors concerned that the move to Delaware would significantly diminish shareholder rights." Although moving to Delaware was said to offer better access to U.S. capital, investors nevertheless suspected that the true aim was management entrenchment, leading two institutional investor organizations (with the support of major U.K. and U.S. institutions) to initiate "a corporate governance campaign urging News Corp. to transplant certain Australian shareholder protection provisions into its prospective Delaware Charter."[244]

News Corp. did indeed agree to various protections, including (among other things) a charter provision stating that it would not delist from the ASX without majority shareholder approval, ostensibly impeding adoption of a poison pill; a charter provision prohibiting super-voting stock without majority shareholder approval; and a "board policy" to the effect that any poison pill adopted without shareholder consent would expire after a year.[245]

[241] *Id.* at 3. *See also Corporations Act 2001*, *supra* note 210, s 602 (emphasizing the centrality of shareholder interests in the Corporations Act's takeover rules); AUSTIN & RAMSAY, *supra* note 205, at 402–05, 1292–94, 1300–23, 1331–33; Hill, *supra* note 234, at 35–36. Frustrating actions that create an auction, by contrast, generally pass muster. *See* Takeovers Panel, Guidance Note 12, *supra* note 240, at 5. *See also* Takeovers Panel, Commonwealth of Australia, Guidance Note 7 – Lock-Up Devices 3, 6 (Feb. 11, 2010) (similarly permitting lock-up devices that benefit shareholders); AUSTIN & RAMSAY, *supra* note 205, at 1336–37. Note that control transactions structured as so-called schemes of arrangement – which are vetted by ASIC and a court – are not subject to the takeover rules, but similarly emphasize shareholders' interests. *See Corporations Act 2001*, *supra* note 210, ss 411, 611(17); AUSTIN & RAMSAY, *supra* note 205, 1358–59, 1370–71, 1378–80, 1385–90; Hill, *supra* note 209, at 42.

[242] *See* Australian Securities Exchange, ASX Listing Rules, Rule 7.1 (2012).

[243] *See* Hill, *supra* note 234, at 36–38.

[244] *See id.* at 3, 13–14 & n.67.

[245] *See id.* at 17–20, 27, 36–38; Australian Securities Exchange, *supra* note 242, Rule 7.1. Shareholders also sought to preserve Australia's generous rules on calling shareholder meetings and removing directors but succeeded only in getting a charter provision permitting those holding 20 percent of Class B common stock to request a meeting – an approach "more generous to shareholders than Delaware law," but "far less generous than the Australian approach." *See* Hill, *supra* note 234, at 20–22.

The aim was to maintain investor protections sufficient to induce shareholders to approve the reincorporation (as required by Australian law) – which they did, with 90 percent of shares ultimately voting in favor of reincorporation. Notwithstanding such assurances, however, the News Corp. board adopted a poison pill almost immediately following reincorporation in Delaware – a move facilitated by ASX's puzzling waiver of various listing rules (perhaps, Hill speculates, to retain News Corp.'s lucrative listing), including Rule 7.1, which generally requires shareholder approval to increase the company's outstanding equity securities by more than 15 percent. A year later, then, contrary to its stated policy, News Corp. extended the pill for two additional years without putting the extension to a shareholder vote.[246] Happily for News Corp.'s shareholders, Chancellor William Chandler ruled in the ensuing Delaware litigation that a board policy of this sort, although typically revocable, could constitute an enforceable contract in such circumstances.[247] For our purposes, however, the central point, as Hill observes, is simply that the "net result of News Corp.'s move from Australia to Delaware was an appreciable reduction in shareholder rights and an enhancement of managerial powers," reflecting the fact that Australia's approach to corporate governance much more closely resembles the strong shareholder-centrism of the United Kingdom than the approach taken in the United States.[248]

Australia further tends toward the U.K. corporate governance approach in its formulation of directors' duties. Australian directors are duty-bound to pursue "the best interests of the corporation,"[249] and like other jurisdictions, Australia has seen a lively debate in recent decades regarding how this formulation ought to be interpreted[250] – particularly in light of corporate crises with broader public interest dimensions.[251] The upshot to date, however, has strongly favored

[246] *See* Hill, *supra* note 234, at 28–30, 38–41. Public shareholders could have blocked the reincorporation because it was structured as a scheme of arrangement under Australian law, requiring class votes in which Rupert Murdoch's family voted separately. *See id.* at 15–16.

[247] *See* UniSuper Ltd. v. News Corp., No. 1699-N, 2005 WL 3529317 (Del. Ch. Dec. 20, 2005).

[248] *See* Hill, *supra* note 234, at 3, 49. *See also* Anderson et al., *supra* note 203, at 186, 190–91 (observing that Australian shareholder powers are far stronger than U.S. shareholder powers).

[249] *See Corporations Act 2001*, *supra* note 210, s 181(1).

[250] *See* Austin & Ramsay, *supra* note 205, at 385–87. *See also* Shelly Marshall & Ian Ramsay, *Shareholders and Directors' Duties: Law, Theory and Evidence* 2 (Melbourne Law Sch. Legal Studies Research Paper No. 411, 2009), http://ssrn.com/abstract=1402143.

[251] Perhaps the most notorious example in recent history involved the James Hardie Group, where asbestos-related liabilities were hived off, benefiting the shareholders to the detriment of employees and others – an approach reportedly attributable to the board's belief that it was duty-bound to favor the shareholders' interests in this manner. *See* PJC Report, *supra* note 204, at 3, 44–49. *See also* Hill, *supra* note 209, at 52–53; Marshall & Ramsay, *supra* note 250, at 3–4.

shareholders' interests. Two significant reports in 2006 assessed the degree to which boards could consider non-shareholder interests under Australian company law – one by the Parliamentary Joint Committee on Corporations and Financial Services (PJC) titled "Corporate Responsibility: Managing Risk and Creating Value," and the other by the Corporations and Markets Advisory Committee (CAMAC) titled "The Social Responsibility of Corporations."[252] Both effectively endorse an "enlightened self-interest" orientation, permitting some regard for the interests of non-shareholders as a component of a more embracing concept of the shareholders' own interests.[253]

The PJC, essentially an ASIC supervisory committee, resolved to explore the degree to which Australian boards do and/or should have "regard for the interests of stakeholders other than shareholders, and the broader community."[254] Finding existing law already "sufficiently open to allow companies to pursue a strategy of enlightened self interest" – under which "directors may consider and act upon the legitimate interests of stakeholders other than shareholders, to the extent that these interests are relevant to the corporation" – the PJC concluded that "amendment to the Corporations Act is not required."[255] The PJC's report is somewhat evasive regarding how directors ought to prioritize the interests of various stakeholders, perhaps reflecting its view that shareholders' interests and broader corporate interests "will often be contiguous," and that regard for non-shareholders will often redound to the benefit of shareholders as well.[256] The approach taken in § 172 of the U.K. Companies Act is rejected as offering "no guidance as to what form this 'regard' [for non-shareholder interests] should take," and the U.S. constituency statute approach is rejected as potentially "amount[ing] to shifting the goalposts rather than dealing with the problem."[257] The PJC concludes that Australian "[d]irectors' duties as they currently stand have a focus on increasing shareholder value," and expresses confidence that "[p]rogressive, innovative directors, in seeking to add value for their shareholders, will engage with and take account of the interests of stakeholders other than shareholders."[258]

[252] *See generally* PJC REPORT, *supra* note 204; CORPORATIONS AND MARKETS ADVISORY COMMITTEE, THE SOCIAL RESPONSIBILITY OF CORPORATIONS (2006) [hereinafter CAMAC REPORT].

[253] *See* Hill, *supra* note 209, at 52–53; Marshall & Ramsay, *supra* note 250, at 26–34.

[254] PJC REPORT, *supra* note 204, at v–vii.

[255] *Id.* at xiv, 63.

[256] *See id.* at 44, 59.

[257] *Id.* at 54–58. *See also* AUSTIN & RAMSAY, *supra* note 205, at 385–87, 394 (contrasting Australia's permissive approach with the U.K. approach and concluding that Australian directors "may implement a policy of enlightened self-interest . . . but may not be generous with company resources when there is no prospect of commercial advantage").

[258] PJC REPORT, *supra* note 204, at 59.

CAMAC, an expert committee appointed to advise the Treasury Minister,[259] was asked in 2005 to investigate whether the Corporations Act should be revised to permit or require directors to "take into account the interests of specific classes of stakeholders or the broader community when making corporate decisions."[260] Like the PJC, CAMAC concluded in its 2006 report that directors' duties were already broad enough to give directors "sufficient flexibility to take relevant interests and broader community considerations into account,"[261] similarly rejecting both the U.K. § 172 approach and the U.S. constituency statute approach.[262] In so doing, however, CAMAC more strongly emphasized the historic equation of the company's interests with those of the shareholders. Based on its review of the common law and the Corporations Act, CAMAC explained that "directors have considerable discretion concerning the interests they may take into account in corporate decision-making, provided their purpose is to act in the interests of the company as a whole, interpreted as the financial well-being of the shareholders as a general body."[263] In light of this flexibility, CAMAC suggested that "environmental or social" concerns are better addressed "through legislation targeted at the mischief in question."[264]

More recently, in its 2008 *Bell Group* opinion, the Supreme Court of Western Australia addressed the issue of corporate purpose and the nature of fiduciary duties, taking a position broadly similar to those expressed in the PJC and CAMAC reports. The court observed that "fiduciary duties are owed to the company, not to the shareholders," and that acting in the company's interests "will usually require [directors] to have close regard to how their actions will affect shareholders." Similarly, the court suggested that the shareholders' interests represent "a reflection of the interests of the company," and that

[259] *See* Corporations and Markets Advisory Committee, *About CAMAC*, http://www.camac.gov.au/camac%5Ccamac.nsf/0/7AE520F065F88121CA2572B10081C695?opendocument.

[260] CAMAC Report, *supra* note 252, at 3–4.

[261] *Id.* at 7.

[262] *See id.* at 99–102, 111–12.

[263] *Id.* at 84–96. It is interesting to consider the results of Marshall and Ramsay's survey of company directors in light of these reports. Regarding the meaning of "the best interests of the company," 55 percent thought this meant "Balancing the interests of all stakeholders," while 38.2 percent thought this meant "Interests of all stakeholders to achieve long term interests of shareholders." By the same token, however, when asked to prioritize stakeholders, 44 percent listed shareholders first while 40.4 percent listed "The Company" first. *See* Marshall & Ramsay, *supra* note 250, at 36–38. When asked to rank "Importance to You as a Director," on the other hand, employee-related concerns were rated higher than shareholder-related concerns, although they also found that the most commonly cited source of obligation to employees was "Business Imperatives." *See id.* at 41–43, 45–46. It should further be borne in mind that "75.5 per cent of respondents were from proprietary limited companies rather than public companies, and only 16.5 per cent of respondents were from listed companies." *Id.* at 35.

[264] CAMAC Report, *supra* note 252, at 96–113.

the shareholders' and the company's interests "may be seen as correlative not because the shareholders are the company but, rather, because the interests of the company and the interests of the shareholders intersect." Although not synonymous with the company's interests, "it is almost axiomatic to say that the content of the duty may (and usually will) include a consideration of the interests of shareholders."[265] Ultimately, however, the court explains that, "depending on the circumstances of the company and the nature of the power to be exercised," non-shareholder interests "might... legitimately be considered," so long as there is some long-term benefit to the company.[266] In *Bell Group*, the court concludes that the directors' duty to the company requires them to "take into account" the creditors' interests when the company approaches insolvency because, at that point, failure to do so could threaten "the very existence of the company."[267]

That shareholders ultimately control the fate of Australian public companies, however, remains clear both as a matter of accepted "best practice" in the marketplace and as a matter of Australian company law. The ASX listing rules require a listed company to disclose in its annual report "the extent to which the entity has followed the recommendations set by the ASX Corporate Governance Council during the reporting period," and to the extent that it has not, to explain why not.[268] The Council's recommendations, published as the ASX Corporate Governance Principles, indicate that a company should "consider the reasonable expectations of its stakeholders," including not only shareholders, but also "employees, customers, suppliers, creditors, consumers and the broader community in which the company operates" – but only because failing to do so "can threaten a company's reputation and the success of its business operations."[269] This "risk management" rationale for stakeholder regard contrasts sharply with the company's posture vis-à-vis shareholders, whom the company "should empower" through effective communication, access to "information about the company and corporate proposals," and ease of

[265] Bell Group Ltd. (in liq.) v. Westpac Banking Corp. (No. 9) (2008) 70 ACSR 1, ¶¶ 4389–95 (Sup. Ct. WA) (Austl.).

[266] *Id.* ¶¶ 4394–95.

[267] *Id.* ¶¶ 4398–4402, 4418, 4439, 4445. *See also* Hill, *supra* note 209, at 54; Marshall & Ramsay, *supra* note 250, at 10–11.

[268] Australian Securities Exchange, *supra* note 242, Rule 4.10.3. *See also* Austin & Ramsay, *supra* note 205, at 340–49; Hill, *supra* note 209, at 3–4.

[269] ASX Corporate Governance Council, Corporate Governance Principles and Recommendations with 2010 Amendments 33–34 (2d ed. 2010). The Council also recommends that regard for stakeholders' "reasonable expectations" be reflected in a "code of conduct." *See id.* at 22–23.

participation in shareholder meetings.[270] Put differently, companies are expected to respect and facilitate exercise of the various legal rights to participate in – and indeed control – governance of the corporation described above,[271] including unilateral power to call special meetings, remove directors, and amend the corporate constitution. Together with a takeover regime focused exclusively on their interests, Australian corporate governance remains shareholder-centric to a degree rivaling that observed in the United Kingdom, and vastly eclipsing that observed in the United States.

II. Canada

In contrast with Australia, where the shareholders' core governance powers and the heavily contractual nature of the corporation itself strongly resemble what we found in the United Kingdom, in Canada we encounter a corporate legal system more discernibly falling between the U.K. and U.S. extremes. Perhaps predictably, and for reasons more fully explored later in the book,[272] Canada has quite decidedly drawn from both U.K. and U.S. models in developing and reforming its corporate laws over recent decades, while at the same time adapting those structures – and developing new ones – in response to uniquely domestic legal and political realities. On the whole, however, Canada resembles Australia and the United Kingdom in giving shareholders strong unilateral governance powers that tend to place them at the heart of the corporate enterprise in a manner diverging from the U.S. approach.

Like Australia and the United States, Canada has a federal governmental structure, prompting contentious debates about the appropriate division of regulatory competence between national and regional authorities. Interestingly, under the Constitution Act, 1867, we encounter yet another form of federalist balance, differing from both the Australian and U.S. approaches. Whereas in the United States a broadly interpreted Commerce Clause places corporate and securities regulatory competence firmly at the federal level (even if corporate law has traditionally been left to the states as a matter of custom), and whereas in Australia a narrowly interpreted trade and commerce authority leaves these regulatory domains to the states (even if ultimately "referred" to the federal parliament), in Canada the relevant constitutional provisions have traditionally been read to provide joint federal and provincial competence in

[270] *Id.* at 31–32.

[271] Principle 6 reads: "Companies should respect the rights of shareholders and facilitate the effective exercise of those rights." *Id.* at 31.

[272] *See infra* Chapter 5.C.ii.

		Australia	Canada	U.S.
default	securities	*regional*	*regional*	national
	corporate	*regional*	*regional*/national	national
practice	securities	national	*regional*	national
	corporate	national	*regional*/national	*regional*

Figure 3.4. Allocation of Corporate and Securities Regulatory Competence: Default Constitutional Power and Current Practice

corporate law, while reserving securities law to the provinces. As Figure 3.4 reflects, no two of these countries have allocated corporate and securities regulatory competence in the same way – either as a matter of default constitutional regulatory power, or as a matter of current practice.

Section 92 of the Constitution Act, 1867 places certain matters "exclusively" within the provinces' regulatory competence, including "Incorporation of Companies with Provincial Objects."[273] The qualifier permits concurrent federal power to incorporate companies to be implied from preamble language in § 91, which grants the federal parliament authority to regulate "all Matters not coming within the Classes of Subjects by this Act assigned exclusively to the Legislatures of the Provinces"[274] – including companies that do not have "Provincial Objects." Although distinguishing these powers based on the nature of the "objects" that can be pursued at each level of government might lead one to expect a qualitative distinction in the types of enterprises that can be incorporated by the provinces and the federal government, in practice the distinction appears simply to be that federal corporations can do business across the country, whereas provincial corporations cannot (although they can acquire the right to do business in other provinces).[275]

Securities regulation, meanwhile, has traditionally been viewed as a matter of provincial law, although the issue has been hotly contested in recent years. Historically, securities regulation has been widely characterized as an expression of the provinces' power to regulate "Property and Civil Rights in the Province,"[276] the idea being that participation in the securities profession is a

[273] Constitution Act, 1867, 30 & 31 Victoria, c. 3, § 92(11) (U.K.) (consolidated with amendments).

[274] *Id.* § 91.

[275] *See* BRUCE WELLING, CORPORATE LAW IN CANADA: THE GOVERNING PRINCIPLES 9–12 (3d ed. 2006).

[276] Constitution Act, 1867, *supra* note 273, § 92(13).

matter of civil rights, and that securities trades are transactions in property.[277] Calls for a national securities regulator, however, are long-standing,[278] the principal legal argument being that the federal parliament's "exclusive" power to regulate "Trade and Commerce"[279] is broad enough to reach financial market activity that is now effectively national in scope.[280] Proponents of a national approach bemoan the fact that "Canada is the only major industrialized nation without a common securities regulator,"[281] whereas opponents – notably, the provinces of Alberta and Quebec – express suspicion that the securities regime of Ontario, the law applicable to Canada's principal capital market in Toronto, would effectively be foisted upon them as the model for a new federal law.[282] Indeed, the Court of Appeal of Alberta and the Court of Appeal of Quebec both concluded in 2011 that a proposed federal securities statute exceeded the constitutional authority of the federal parliament.[283] This, however, was ultimately a matter for the Supreme Court of Canada to

[277] *See, e.g.*, Reference re Securities Act, [2011] 3 S.C.R. 837, paras. 43–45 (Can.) [hereinafter Reference re Securities Act (Can.)]; Reference Re Power of Parliament to Regulate Securities, 2011 QCCA 591, paras. 136–58 (Can. Que. C.A.) (unofficial English translation); Reference Re Securities Act (Canada), 2011 ABCA 77, paras. 18–19 (Can. Alta.) [hereinafter Reference Re Securities Act (Alta.)].

[278] *See, e.g.*, Reference re Securities Act (Can.), *supra* note 277, paras. 11–31; CANADIAN INSTITUTE OF CHARTERED ACCOUNTANTS, STUDY GROUP ON CORPORATIONS AND SECURITIES LEGISLATION, RECOMMENDATIONS RELATING TO PROPOSALS FOR A NEW BUSINESS LAW FOR CANADA 15–1 (1972) ("As we set out in our letter of 21 November 1969 . . . we strongly support an effective central authority to qualify all securities issued in Canada.").

[279] Constitution Act, 1867, *supra* note 273, § 91(2).

[280] *See, e.g.*, Andrew Kitching, *Securities Regulation: Calls for a Single Regulator* 1–4 (PRB 08–38E) (Feb. 16, 2009); Reference Re Power of Parliament to Regulate Securities, *supra* note 277, paras. 494–527 (Dalphond, J.A., dissenting).

[281] Kitching, *supra* note 280, at 1. Note, however, that Canada is not the only "major industrialized nation" to face this issue in recent times. Indeed, Germany – which also has a federal governmental structure – "created its first federal securities regulator in 1994." JOHN W. CIOFFI, PUBLIC LAW AND PRIVATE POWER: CORPORATE GOVERNANCE REFORM IN THE AGE OF FINANCE CAPITALISM 148 (2010).

[282] *See, e.g.*, Reference Re Securities Act (Alta.), *supra* note 277, para. 12. *See also* Douglas J. Cumming & Jeffrey G. MacIntosh, *The Role of Interjurisdictional Competition in Shaping Canadian Corporate Law*, 20 INT'L REV. L. & ECON. 141, 153 (2000) (observing that national reform efforts "have foundered largely on Quebec's repeated refusals to participate," mainly due to "nationalistic concerns"); Kitching, *supra* note 280, at 5–6, 9 (observing that the Ontario Securities Commission supports national securities regulation, while Quebec's regulator opposes it and those of Alberta and British Columbia have "strong reservations"); Christopher C. Nicholls, *Civil Enforcement in Canadian Securities Law*, 9 J. CORP. L. STUD. 367, 373–74 (2009) (observing the opposition of Alberta and Quebec, provinces "with which the federal government's relationship has historically been sensitive"). *But see* Reference Re Power of Parliament to Regulate Securities, *supra* note 277, para. 508 (Dalphond, J.A., dissenting) (observing that only a national regime would position anyone outside the Ontario Securities Commission to regulate the Toronto Stock Exchange).

[283] *See* Reference Re Securities Act (Alta.), *supra* note 277, paras. 33–49; Reference Re Power of Parliament to Regulate Securities, *supra* note 277, paras. 186–222, 331–85. *See also* Nigel

decide, leading one Quebec jurist to query whether the Alberta and Quebec references were simply efforts "to score points in public opinion."[284]

Later in 2011, the Supreme Court of Canada did in fact conclude that the proposed federal statute exceeded the federal parliament's general trade and commerce authority, rejecting the claim of the federal government and Ontario (the only province supporting the federal statute) that "the securities market has been so transformed as to make the day-to-day regulation of all aspects of trading in securities a matter of national concern."[285] The court did emphasize that the federal government possesses some capacity to engage in limited securities regulation – either through a cooperative regime with the provinces, or by focusing the regime on matters beyond the regulatory capacity of individual provinces, such as management of systemic risk and data collection.[286] "[T]aken overall," however, Toronto-based securities lawyers Nigel Campbell and Doug McLeod conclude that the opinion renders it "more certain than ever that Canada's patchwork of provincial securities regulations is here to stay."[287] Meanwhile, harmonization efforts remain limited to a coordinated prospectus review program called "Passport"[288] – a system of limited utility, not least given the nonparticipation of Ontario, the jurisdiction governing the Toronto Stock Exchange.[289]

Canada's mixed system of corporate law gives those desiring to incorporate a business a number of options, just like in the United States. The impetus for a federal corporate law will be discussed later in the book, but observe for

Campbell & Doug McLeod, *Proposed Canadian National Securities Law Unconstitutional, Alberta Court Rules*, World Sec. L. Rep. (BNA) (2011).

[284] Reference Re Power of Parliament to Regulate Securities, *supra* note 277, para. 400 (Dalphond, J.A., dissenting).

[285] Reference re Securities Act (Can.), *supra* note 277, para. 117. *See also id.* paras. 1–10, 134. Although Ontario supported the federal government's position, the proposed statute was opposed by Alberta, British Columbia, Manitoba, New Brunswick, Quebec, and Saskatchewan. *Id.* paras. 32–39.

[286] *Id.* paras. 9, 103–05, 117–21, 132–33. *See also* Nigel Campbell & Doug McLeod, *Canada's Supreme Court Finds against Proposed National Securities Law, Regulator*, World Sec. L. Rep. (BNA) (2011); Bill Curry, *Supreme Court Rejects Ottawa's Bid for National Securities Regulator*, Globe & Mail Update, Dec. 22, 2011.

[287] Campbell & McLeod, *supra* note 286.

[288] *See* Canadian Securities Administrators, *About CSA: Pan-Canadian*, http://www.securities-administrators.ca/aboutcsa.aspx?id=96 (accessed Jan. 11, 2011); Canadian Securities Administrators, *About CSA: Who We Are*, http://www.securities-administrators.ca/aboutcsa.aspx?id=77 (accessed Jan. 11, 2011).

[289] *See* Taylor R. Gray, *A Corporate Geography of Canada: Insights into a Multi-Jurisdictional Model of Corporate Governance*, 41 Growth & Change 467, 475 (2010); Kitching, *supra* note 280, at 6–8; Welling, *supra* note 275, at 16 n.47. *See also* Securities Act, R.S.O. 1990, c. S.5, §§ 21(5), 21.1(4) (Can.) (consolidated to Dec. 7, 2010) [hereinafter Ontario Securities Act] (giving the Ontario Securities Commission broad authority to regulate exchanges).

the moment that Canada has not in fact seen the sort of jurisdictional competition that has preoccupied U.S. corporate legal theorists.[290] According to Corporations Canada, which administers and handles registration under the Canada Business Corporations Act (CBCA), the key advantages offered by federal incorporation are essentially technical and ministerial in nature – notably, ease of national expansion (through national name protection), and flexibility with respect to location of offices, records, and meetings.[291] This said, incorporation under the CBCA is widely thought to offer "more 'prestige,'" although precisely why remains unclear. Perhaps, as one commentator suggests, this is because of greater recognition "in the eyes of foreign business partners."[292] In any event, the rough division of labor that has evolved over recent decades is that smaller companies typically incorporate in their home province, whereas most public companies incorporate under the CBCA.[293] It bears emphasizing, however, that this serves only as a rough generalization, because industry patterns are in fact discernible. Taylor Gray has found that the vast majority of nonfederal corporations – including most companies in significant natural-resource industries such as oil and gas, and mining – are incorporated in the province where they are headquartered, and that "nearly 65 percent of Federal incorporations operate in the Finance and Products and Services categories." This pattern reinforces the notion that "Federal incorporation is perceived as a strategic asset by those operating in competitive and highly substitutable markets, both domestic and international."[294] Consistent with this view, Douglas Cumming and Jeffrey MacIntosh conclude that substantive

[290] Neither, for that matter, has the United States. *See infra* Chapter 6.D.

[291] *See* Corporations Canada, *Guide to Federal Incorporation, Chapter 1: Why Should I Incorporate?*, § 1.3, http://www.ic.gc.ca/eic/site/cd-dgc.nsf/eng/cs04841.html (last updated Aug. 12, 2011); Corporations Canada, *Frequently Asked Questions*, "What are the benefits of incorporating at the federal level?," http://www.ic.gc.ca/eic/site/cd-dgc.nsf/eng/cs02194.html (last updated July 24, 2012). For background on Corporations Canada, see Corporations Canada, *About Us*, http://www.ic.gc.ca/eic/site/cd-dgc.nsf/eng/h_cs03928.html (last updated Aug. 12, 2010).

[292] John Mackie, *Shopping for a Corporate Home in Canada*, WESTLAW BUS. CURRENTS, Feb. 9, 2011. *See also* Corporations Canada, *Guide to Federal Incorporation*, *supra* note 291, § 1.3 (suggesting that global recognition may render CBCA incorporation "a sign of distinction").

[293] *See* CHRISTOPHER C. NICHOLLS, MERGERS, ACQUISITIONS, AND OTHER CHANGES OF CORPORATE CONTROL 27 (2007). *See also* Mackie, *supra* note 292.

[294] Gray, *supra* note 289, at 480–86. Unlike other natural resource industries, "Forestry corporations demonstrate a slightly different pattern as they base their headquarters predominantly in British Columbia, yet half of them incorporate at the federal level." This may reflect an effort to draw upon both the CBCA's international prestige and British Columbia's reputation as a source of "high-quality wood sources." *Id.* at 484. For a reflection of the predominance of natural resource industries in Canadian capital markets, see TMX Group, *2010 Q2: A Capital Opportunity* (2010); TMX Group, *Understanding the Canadian Capital Markets*, http://www.tmx.com/en/listings/listing_with_us/canadian_market.html (last updated Oct. 26, 2010).

corporate law reform in Canada has been driven not by jurisdictional competition, but by uniformity concerns.[295] In a study of reincorporations they find that "inter-provincial reincorporations tend to be motivated by transaction costs considerations, whereas incorporations to the federal jurisdiction tend to be motivated by law shopping" – notably, companies with national or international operations, including many instances where "the firm felt that shareholders and the public at large viewed a federal incorporation to be superior to a provincial incorporation, even though the firm itself did not believe that this was true."[296]

In both substantive and institutional terms, Canada is aptly characterized as a "familiar stranger" to the United Kingdom and the United States. Although most provinces share historical links and common-law orientation with the other jurisdictions studied in this book, one of the largest provinces – Quebec – has a civil-law system. Likewise, although numerous aspects of its corporate and securities laws draw upon U.K. and U.S. models, Canada's system is perhaps best described as "a hybrid or amalgam of UK and US features,"[297] combined with uniquely Canadian approaches and a uniquely Canadian institutional framework.

Numerous commentators have observed the clear U.S. influence on various aspects of Canadian corporate law. For example, under the CBCA, corporations are not inherently contractual, as they are in Australia and the United Kingdom. Rather, the board of directors possesses a direct grant of power flowing from the statute itself, just as we observed in Delaware.[298] Nor can shareholders "direct the directors" in the manner that U.K. shareholders

[295] *See* Cumming & MacIntosh, *supra* note 282, at 143, 165, 179–80. Although substantial modernizing reforms enacted through the CBCA in 1975 were subsequently followed by a number of the provinces, this itself was arguably driven by uniformity concerns. *See* Douglas J. Cumming & Jeffrey G. MacIntosh, *The Rationales Underlying Reincorporations and Implications for Canadian Corporations*, 22 INT'L REV. L. & ECON. 277, 280–81, 296–97 (2002). *See also* Gray, *supra* note 289, at 488. Bruce Welling explains that the CBCA, following its adoption in 1975, "quickly became the model for most of the rest of Canada, being adopted by Manitoba, Saskatchewan, Alberta, New Brunswick, Ontario . . . , Yukon, and Newfoundland." Quebec adopted aspects of the CBCA model, while the other jurisdictions "remain anomalies." Nova Scotia and British Columbia have retained English-model registration statutes, while Prince Edward Island retained a letters patent statute. *See* WELLING, *supra* note 275, at 44–45. Events surrounding adoption of the CBCA are discussed in some detail in Chapter 5. *See infra* Chapter 5.C.ii.

[296] Cumming & MacIntosh, *supra* note 295, at 277, 293, 299–300.

[297] Nicholls, *supra* note 282, at 369–70.

[298] *See* Canada Business Corporations Act, R.S.C. 1985, c. C-44, § 102(1) [hereinafter CBCA]. *See also, e.g.*, ALLAN F. LAWRENCE ET AL., INTERIM REPORT OF THE SELECT COMMITTEE ON COMPANY LAW 57, 70 (1967) [hereinafter LAWRENCE REPORT] (observing the same of Ontario corporations); WELLING, *supra* note 275, at 60, 315.

	U.K.	Australia	Canada	U.S. (Delaware)
call special meetings	Y	Y	Y	N
remove directors without cause	Y	Y	Y	N (if classified)
initiate charter amendments	Y	Y	Y	N
approve takeover defenses	Y	Y	Y/N	N
compel board action	Y	N	N	N
preemptive rights	Y	N	N	N

Figure 3.5. Shareholders' Default Governance Powers in Public Corporations: Australia, Canada, the United Kingdom, and the United States

can.[299] This solidification of the board's management authority reflects the strong influence that U.S. jurisdictions, including Delaware and New York, exerted upon Canadian corporate law reforms in the 1960s and 1970s, a topic examined more thoroughly below.[300] Similarly, Canadian shareholders (like U.S. shareholders and Australian public company shareholders) do not possess preemptive rights unless the articles – the core governance document – grants them.[301] U.S. influence has likewise been substantial in Canadian securities regulation, which underwent fundamental reform beginning in the early 1960s.[302]

It remains the case, however, that shareholders in the typical CBCA public corporation possess substantial corporate governance rights strongly resembling those in Australia and the United Kingdom, deviating sharply from the approach that predominates in the United States. For ease of reference the Canadian governance rights discussed here are summarized in Figure 3.5, which contrasts them with the Australian, U.K., and U.S. governance rights

[299] *See* WELLING, *supra* note 275, at 298–99.

[300] *See* LAWRENCE REPORT, *supra* note 298, at iii–vii; ROBERT W. V. DICKERSON ET AL., PROPOSALS FOR A NEW BUSINESS CORPORATIONS LAW FOR CANADA, VOLUME I: COMMENTARY iv (1971) [hereinafter DICKERSON REPORT]. *See also* WELLING, *supra* note 275, at 45, 55–57; *infra* Chapter 5.C.ii.

[301] *See* CBCA, *supra* note 298, § 28(1). *See also* Nicholls, *supra* note 282, at 404 n.217 (observing that the Dickerson Report advocated the U.K. approach, but that this was not adopted in the CBCA); WELLING, *supra* note 275, at 600.

[302] *See* J.R. KIMBER ET AL., REPORT OF THE ATTORNEY GENERAL'S COMMITTEE ON SECURITIES LEGISLATION IN ONTARIO 6 (1965). *See also* PHILIP ANISMAN, TAKEOVER BID LEGISLATION IN CANADA: A COMPARATIVE ANALYSIS 5–6 (1974); James C. Baillie, *The Protection of the Investor in Ontario*, 8 CAN. PUB. ADMIN. 172, 206–10 (1965); FRANK IACOBUCCI, MARILYN L. PILKINGTON & J. ROBERT S. PRICHARD, CANADIAN BUSINESS CORPORATIONS: AN ANALYSIS OF RECENT LEGISLATIVE DEVELOPMENTS 3–4 (1977).

described previously in the chapter. Critically, Canadian shareholders can remove directors by ordinary resolution, and 5 percent voting power is sufficient to call a shareholder meeting for this purpose.[303] As Christopher Nicholls observes, this "especially potent right in Canada," closely resembling that available in the United Kingdom and contrasting sharply with Delaware, is particularly significant "when conjoined with the liberal rules for requisitioning a shareholders' meeting."[304]

Just as in Australia and the United Kingdom, Canadian shareholders also possess unilateral power to amend the articles by special resolution (which, under the CBCA, requires two-thirds of votes cast).[305] Like U.S. corporations, Canadian corporations have a secondary governance document called the "bylaws," but Canadian bylaws do not present the governance conundrum that U.S. bylaws do – because Canadian shareholders possess clear, ultimate authority to determine the bylaws' content. Although § 103 of the CBCA gives boards and shareholders concurrent authority to enact bylaws, board bylaws are expressly subject to amendment or rejection by shareholders at the next shareholders' meeting (acting by ordinary resolution, requiring a simple majority of votes cast), and in any event, bylaws cannot contradict the articles[306] – which are subject to unilateral shareholder control. Although board-enacted bylaws have effect pending amendment or rejection by the shareholders, the "cycling amendments" problem that arises in Delaware is effectively resolved by the CBCA, which says that once the shareholders have rejected a board bylaw, "no subsequent resolution of the directors to make, amend or repeal a by-law having substantially the same purpose or effect is effective until it is confirmed or confirmed as amended by the shareholders."[307]

The shareholders' governance authority is further backstopped by the unanimous shareholder agreement, which Bruce Welling describes in his leading

[303] *See* CBCA, *supra* note 298, §§ 109(1), 143(1). *See also* Barry Reiter, Directors' Duties in Canada 119–20 (4th ed. 2009) (observing that shareholders typically call meetings "when the directors do not support the proposed business and will not bring it before a meeting of the shareholders"); Welling, *supra* note 275, at 312–13, 445, 486–87. The board can call special shareholder meetings as well. *See* CBCA, *supra* note 298, § 133(2).

[304] Nicholls, *supra* note 282, at 406. The CBCA also allows 5-percent shareholders to nominate board candidates. *See* CBCA, *supra* note 298, § 137. *See also* Welling, *supra* note 275, at 455–59.

[305] *See* CBCA, *supra* note 298, §§ 2(1) (defining "special resolution"), 173. *See also* Welling, *supra* note 275, at 61–62, 490. Shareholders can also unilaterally dissolve the corporation by special resolution. *See* CBCA, *supra* note 298, § 211.

[306] *See* CBCA, *supra* note 298, §§ 2(1) (defining "ordinary resolution"), 103. *See also* Welling, *supra* note 275, at 316–17, 460–61.

[307] *See* CBCA, *supra* note 298, § 103(3)–(4).

treatise as "a statutorily authorized *coup d'etat.*" Notwithstanding their inability to "direct the directors" as U.K. shareholders can, Welling explains that "[m]ost Canadian statutes now allow the shareholders of a corporation to inhibit directors' managerial powers if all of them agree to do so in writing."[308] The CBCA expressly confirms the validity of an agreement among all shareholders "that restricts . . . the powers of the directors to manage, or supervise the management of, the business and affairs of the corporation."[309] Accordingly, the Supreme Court of Canada has described the unanimous shareholder agreement as "a corporate law hybrid, part contractual and part constitutional in nature," emphasizing its "equivalent constitutional status . . . vis-à-vis the articles."[310] To be sure, a unanimous agreement of shareholders would be effectively impossible to achieve in a widely held public company, and as with the U.K. shareholders' power to "direct the directors," there would be no practical reason to pursue this course of action in a public company when substantial leverage can be exerted by threatening to remove incumbent directors, requiring only a simple majority vote. As a matter of theory, however, the very existence of the unanimous shareholder agreement further illuminates the fundamentally shareholder-centric nature of the Canadian corporation.

Similarly, although Canadian boards have greater discretion than their Australian and U.K. counterparts to deploy defenses, Canadian takeover law ultimately favors shareholders in a manner more closely resembling their approach than that of the United States. In Canada, hostile takeovers are treated as a matter of securities regulation and, as noted above, Canadian securities reforms in recent decades have been heavily impacted by U.S. federal and state models. Yet as Nicholls observes, there are certain areas in which Canadian securities laws were "based on very different UK models" – notably, "Canadian take-over bid rules."[311] Although current Ontario takeover law is distinguishable from the U.K. approach in numerous respects, the takeover provisions of the Ontario Securities Act were originally based on the London City Code, and the "common ancestry . . . is still discernible."[312] Ontario's takeover rules turn on a 20 percent de facto control threshold, upon which a bid to all shareholders is required absent an exemption.[313] The aspects of takeover practice most likely to give rise to disputes in Canada, however, relate to defenses and deal protections.[314] Interestingly, Canada appears to fall

[308] WELLING, *supra* note 275, at 462–63.

[309] CBCA, *supra* note 298, § 146(1).

[310] *See* Duha Printers (Western) Ltd. v. Canada, [1998] 1 S.C.R. 795, paras. 66–67 (Can.).

[311] Nicholls, *supra* note 282, at 370.

[312] *See* NICHOLLS, *supra* note 293, at 81–82.

[313] *See* Ontario Securities Act, *supra* note 289, §§ 89(1), 94. *See also* NICHOLLS, *supra* note 293, at 85–87, 100–01.

[314] *See* NICHOLLS, *supra* note 293, at 170.

somewhere between the U.K. and U.S. approaches with respect to the use of defenses, in that boards possess meaningful discretion to deploy poison pills, yet their retention is heavily constrained.[315] Indeed, although poison pills are not uncommon in Canada,[316] and although Delaware has discernibly influenced Canadian takeover law,[317] Nicholls nevertheless observes a "curious" but very important divergence between the Canadian and Delaware approaches to defenses – the "just say no" approach effectively endorsed by the Delaware Supreme Court in *Paramount v. Time* has quite decidedly been rejected in Canada.[318] Canadian directors are not ultimately permitted to substitute their judgment for that of the shareholders in evaluating bids in the way that U.S. directors can.

Canadian securities regulators have effectively adopted the position advocated in Delaware in the 1980s by Chancellor Allen – rejected by the Delaware Supreme Court in its 1990 *Time* opinion – to the effect that once the success or failure of a hostile bid comes down to adequacy of price, defenses must be pulled, and the shareholders allowed to decide.[319] In 1997, the Canadian Securities Administrators promulgated National Policy 62–202 (for provincial adoption), the notice for which indicates that takeover regulation "should leave the shareholders of the target company free to make a fully informed decision," and that regulators would take action to address defenses "likely to deny or limit severely the ability of shareholders to respond to a take-over bid or to a competing bid."[320] Just as in the United Kingdom, the policy confirms that the "primary objective of the take-over bid provisions of Canadian securities legislation is the protection of the bona fide interests of the shareholders of the target company." Although the administrators "appreciate that defensive tactics . . . may be taken by a board of directors of a target company in a genuine attempt to obtain a better bid," they state flatly that defenses "likely to deny or limit severely the ability of the shareholders to respond to a take-over bid or a competing bid may result in action by the Canadian securities regulatory authorities." The policy does not technically require prior

[315] *See* Reiter, *supra* note 303, at 326–29.

[316] *See* Jeffrey G. MacIntosh, *Institutional Shareholders and Corporate Governance in Canada*, 26 Can. Bus. L.J. 145, 171 (1995–96); Reiter, *supra* note 303, at 327 n.16.

[317] *See* Nicholls, *supra* note 293, at 185.

[318] *See id.* at 190–91.

[319] *See id.* at 202–07. *See also* Reiter, *supra* note 303, at 328–29; Paramount Commc'ns, Inc. v. Time Inc., 571 A.2d 1140, 1152–53 (Del. 1990) (rejecting the approach taken by Chancellor Allen in City Capital Associates v. Interco, Inc., 551 A.2d 787 (Del. Ch. 1988) "as not in keeping with a proper *Unocal* analysis").

[320] Ontario Securities Commission, Notice of National Policy 62–202 and Rescission of National Policy Statement No. 38: Take-Over Bids – Defensive Tactics (July 4, 1997).

shareholder approval of defenses, but states that such approval would "allay such concerns."[321]

Although this policy "does not have the force of law," Nicholls explains that "it is nevertheless an important guide to the manner in which securities regulators are likely to exercise their public interest discretion."[322] And critically, as Barry Reiter notes, it "applies notwithstanding that the target's board of directors' actions may be in accordance with their corporate fiduciary duties."[323] Reiter indicates that the Ontario Securities Commission "has consistently intervened to terminate [poison pills] after the target has had sufficient time to find a better offer," typically considering "a period of 42 to 50 days from the date when the offer is announced to be a reasonable one."[324] Listed companies, however, face additional restrictions on the preemptive adoption of poison pills. The Toronto Stock Exchange listing rules state that poison pills "adopted at a time when the listed issuer is not aware of any specific take-over bid" must generally be "ratified by the security holders of the listed issuer at a meeting held within six months following the adoption of the poison pill." Should the shareholders decline to ratify it, the pill "must be immediately cancelled."[325]

Canadian takeover law fundamentally favors the shareholders by giving them the last word on the success or failure of a hostile bid – again, regardless of what corporate law might have to say about the fiduciary duties of target boards. Recent developments in the context of negotiated (i.e., "friendly") deals, however, have raised at least a theoretical possibility of conflict between these fundamentally shareholder-centric securities rules and a strand of Canadian corporate law that appears more favorably inclined toward the interests of other stakeholders. Although core aspects of the Canadian corporate governance structure are strongly shareholder-centric, as described above – notably, the shareholders' unilateral power to call meetings, remove directors by ordinary resolution, and control the content of the corporation's articles (and thus its bylaws as well) – there are aspects of Canadian corporate law that

[321] Ontario Securities Commission, National Policy 62–202: Take-Over Bids – Defensive Tactics, ¶¶ 2–3, 6 (Aug. 4, 1997).

[322] NICHOLLS, *supra* note 293, at 202.

[323] REITER, *supra* note 303, at 328.

[324] *Id.* at 329.

[325] Toronto Stock Exchange Company Manual, § 636(a), http://tmx.complinet.com/en/tsx_manual.html. Any such intervention can be appealed to the Ontario Securities Commission, and likewise the Exchange defers to the Commission with respect to defenses adopted following announcement of a takeover bid. *See id.* §§ 634(b), 636(c), 642. *See also* Ontario Securities Act, *supra* note 289, §§ 21.6–21.7 (permitting exchange rules to "impose additional requirements" not contravening the Act, and providing for Commission review of exchange decisions).

gesture toward a broader conception of corporate purpose. It was long assumed that Canadian courts would follow Delaware's *Revlon* approach to negotiated deals – requiring that boards maximize the price received by shareholders in the company's sale, breakup, or change of control[326] – but the application of *Revlon* duties has been expressly rejected in Canada.[327] This development relates closely to the availability in Canada of a form of transaction called an "arrangement," which has increasingly been used to facilitate negotiated corporate deals, as well as a broad "oppression" remedy. Consequently, one must account for these additional facets of Canadian corporate law and practice in order to assess the significance of this trend in the case law and its potential impact on the degree of shareholder-centrism otherwise exhibited by Canadian governance and takeover rules.

In essence, the alternative transactional form called an "arrangement"[328] permits the corporation to go to a court for preemptive approval of any of a number of fundamental actions, an approach that the statute permits "[w]here it is not practicable" to proceed under the standard statutory procedure for the given type of action.[329] This requirement has been interpreted quite liberally, however, to permit use of the arrangement process where the alternative is merely "inconvenient or less advantageous."[330] Nicholls explains that the arrangement does indeed offer distinct advantages over traditional transactional forms in complex negotiated deals – notably, the ability to collapse multistep transactions into a single step, and the enhanced legal certainty gained through preapproval by a court, giving the parties "great comfort that their transaction cannot subsequently be impugned."[331]

[326] *See, e.g.*, CW Shareholdings Inc. v. WIC Western International Communications Ltd. (1998), 39 O.R. 3d 755, paras. 40–43, 56–57 (Can. Ont. Ct. J. Gen. Div.). *See also* NICHOLLS, *supra* note 293, at 187–96.

[327] *See* BCE Inc. v. 1976 Debentureholders, [2008] 3 S.C.R. 560, paras. 85–87 (Can.). *See also* Nicholas Dietrich, *Revlon Redux: Reconciling the BCE Case in Change of Control Transactions – Is Lyondell the Better Way?*, 10 BUS. L. INT'L 218, 224–26 (2009).

[328] *See* CBCA, *supra* note 298, § 192. Other fundamental transactions include amalgamations (effectively mergers) and sales of substantially all assets. *See id.* §§ 181–83, 189(3)–(9).

[329] *See id.* § 192(1)–(3). Actions that can be pursued through an arrangement include amending the articles, amalgamations, divisions, sales of substantially all assets, exchange offers, going-private transactions, liquidation and dissolution, and "any combination of the foregoing." *See id.* § 192(1).

[330] *See* Corporations Canada, Policy of the Director Concerning Arrangements under Section 192 of the *Canada Business Corporations Act*, ¶ 2.06 (Policy Statement 15.1) (Jan. 4, 2010). *See also* NICHOLLS, *supra* note 293, at 75.

[331] NICHOLLS, *supra* note 293, at 72. The United Kingdom has a similar procedure, but it is not widely used, while "the United States has no counterpart." *See* John Armour, Bernard Black, Brian R. Cheffins & Richard Nolan, *Private Enforcement of Corporate Law: An Empirical*

In *Re BCE, Inc.*, creditors objected to a leveraged buyout organized as an arrangement, arguing that the transaction amounted to oppression under CBCA § 241, and that the transaction should not have been approved under CBCA § 192 because it was unfair to them.[332] Section 241 creates a broad oppression remedy available to "any security holder, creditor, director or officer" who has been subjected to corporate conduct that "is oppressive or unfairly prejudicial to or that unfairly disregards [their] interests."[333] In providing an oppression remedy to non-shareholder security holders – and expressly to creditors – the statute effectively required the courts to grapple with the issue of corporate purpose in *BCE* to assess whether the creditors' interests had been subordinated to those of the shareholders in an impermissible manner. As a threshold matter, the Supreme Court of Canada explains in its 2008 opinion that the directors' duty of loyalty is owed to "the corporation" – not to the shareholders or any other stakeholder group – and that the board may focus on the corporation's "long-term interests" as opposed to "short-term profit or share value." In pursuit of "the best interests of the corporation," the court elaborates, "directors may look to the interests of, *inter alia*, shareholders, employees, creditors, consumers, governments and the environment to inform their decisions."[334] The court adds that other "remedial" provisions of the CBCA are open to non-shareholder stakeholders as well, notably derivative suits and the court approval requirements for arrangements.[335] With respect to the oppression remedy, the court explains that the shareholders' interests must be balanced with the "reasonable expectations" of other stakeholders, such that the *Revlon* approach – requiring single-minded focus on maximizing the price received by shareholders – could not be adopted.[336] Similarly, the court explains that although the § 192 arrangement process "was initially conceived as permitting and has principally been used to permit useful restructuring while protecting

Comparison of the UK and US, 6 J. EMPIRICAL LEGAL STUD. 687, 719–20 (2009). On Australian schemes of arrangement, see AUSTIN & RAMSAY, *supra* note 205, at 1355–91.

332 *See* BCE Inc. v. 1976 Debentureholders, [2008] 3 S.C.R. 560, paras. 1–22 (Can.).

333 *See* CBCA, *supra* note 298, § 241(1)–(2). By contrast, Australia and the United Kingdom effectively limit this form of remedy to shareholders. *See* AUSTIN & RAMSAY, *supra* note 205, at 766–74 (describing the Australian oppression remedy); DAVIES, *supra* note 8, at 681–84 (describing the U.K. remedy for "unfairly prejudicial" conduct). Some U.S. jurisdictions – notably, Massachusetts – provide special oppression remedies for minority shareholders, but Delaware is not among them. *See* ROBERT A. RAGAZZO & DOUGLAS K. MOLL, CLOSELY HELD BUSINESS ORGANIZATIONS: CASES, MATERIALS, AND PROBLEMS 565–603, 617–28 (2006).

334 *See BCE Inc.*, 3 S.C.R. 560, paras. 37–40. *See also* CBCA, *supra* note 298, § 122(1)(a) (requiring director and officer loyalty to "the best interests of the corporation"); Duha Printers (Western) Ltd. v. Canada, [1998] 1 S.C.R. 795, para. 61 (Can.).

335 *See BCE Inc.*, 3 S.C.R. 560, paras. 41–48. *See also* CBCA, *supra* note 298, §§ 192, 239.

336 *See BCE Inc.*, 3 S.C.R. 560, paras. 56–64; 81–88. *See also* REITER, *supra* note 303, at 49–51.

minority shareholders against adverse effects, the goal of ensuring a fair balance between different constituencies applies with equal force when considering the interests of non-shareholder security holders."[337]

Notwithstanding the broad stakeholder-orientation that the court ascribes to the formulation of the duty of loyalty and these various "remedial" provisions of the statute, however, in *BCE* the Supreme Court of Canada arrives at an outcome highly favorable to shareholders, effectively blunting the potential for these structures to overcome the strong shareholder-centric skew of the corporate governance and takeover rules described above. In assessing what the "reasonable expectations" of creditors include, and what "fair" regard to their interests requires, the court focuses narrowly on the contracts they negotiated. "In determining whether a stakeholder expectation is reasonable," the court explains, it "may consider whether the claimant could have taken steps to protect itself against the prejudice it claims to have suffered."[338] This principle effectively undermines the ability of sophisticated institutional creditors to claim oppression when a leveraged buyout impairs the value of their investments. The court emphasizes that "leveraged buyouts of this kind are not unusual or unforeseeable," and that "trust indentures can include change of control and credit rating covenants where those protections have been negotiated." The board had no duty to the creditors beyond ensuring that "the contractual terms of the debentures would be honoured," and given the court's conclusion that a buyout was "inevitable" to maintain the company's success, the creditors could not show that their interests had been unfairly disregarded.[339] Likewise, the challenge based on § 192 failed because absent "extraordinary circumstances," the arrangement approval process protects "legal rights," not "economic interests" – the upshot being that no special protection is available where "a group whose legal rights are left intact faces a reduction in the trading value of its securities."[340] Although § 192 "clearly contemplates the participation of security holders in certain situations," this does not ordinarily include those whose legal rights remain unaffected by the deal. In *BCE*, "[t]he investment and the return contracted for remain intact," and given the foreseeability of a leveraged buyout and the court's acceptance that "the continuance of the corporation required acceptance of an arrangement that would entail increased debt and debt guarantees by Bell Canada," there was no error in the trial judge's acceptance of the arrangement as "fair and reasonable."[341]

337 *BCE Inc.*, 3 S.C.R. 560, para. 129.
338 *Id.* para. 78.
339 *Id.* paras. 95–114.
340 *Id.* paras. 130–35.
341 *Id.* paras. 131, 156–65. The court observes that all three bids received "were leveraged, involving a substantial increase in Bell Canada's debt." *Id.* para. 106.

Reactions of regulators, practitioners, and scholars alike illustrate the degree to which the outcome in *BCE* constrains the stakeholder-oriented potential of the CBCA, effectively redounding to the benefit of shareholders. In a policy statement detailing what companies can do to avoid regulatory intervention, Corporations Canada observes that § 192 arrangements can alter the rights of all "security holders," including creditors, and that the proponent of the deal bears the burden of demonstrating that it is "fair from the perspective of the security holder constituencies whose rights are affected," effectively requiring a broad fairness opinion.[342] It is also suggested that, although § 192 itself "does not require security holder approval as a pre-condition to a court order approving an arrangement," Corporations Canada takes the position that all "affected" security holders should be permitted to vote on the plan.[343] At the same time, however, the policy statement adds that it is really "legal rights" that matter most in determining whose approval is required – and that for debt security holders, "the trust indenture or other contractual instrument creating such securities should ordinarily be determinative absent extraordinary circumstances."[344] Although the court's focus on the apparent necessity of a leveraged deal and the reasonableness of the board's decision under the circumstances suggest that the analysis might be more complex if a lower-priced bid were to include stakeholder-friendly terms,[345] *BCE* makes amply clear that boards ordinarily cannot be expected to reject shareholder value-maximizing deals simply because doing so could hurt the economic interests of debt security holders who failed to negotiate contractual protections.[346] Indeed, Anita Anand argues that "BCE was a relatively healthy corporation and the proposed arrangement was not necessary for its continued existence," suggesting that the court embraced "a broad understanding of necessity" highly deferential to the board's assessment of the company's prospects.[347] As Nicholas Dietrich concludes, "the Supreme Court of Canada, notwithstanding the complicated analytical framework, constructs, prongs and factors associated with each of the oppression and arrangement challenges, appeared to condone target directors

[342] *See* Corporations Canada, Policy Statement 15.1, *supra* note 330, ¶¶ 1.03, 2.05, 4.01–4.05.

[343] *See id.* ¶¶ 3.06, 3.09. *See also* Anita I. Anand, *Flexibility vs. Certainty: The Law Relating to Arrangements after* BCE, 48 CAN. BUS. L.J. 174, 176, 183 (2009) (observing that who votes on an arrangement is up to the board, the constraint being the need to persuade the court that the deal is fair).

[344] Corporations Canada, Policy Statement 15.1, *supra* note 330, ¶ 3.09. *See also* Anand, *supra* note 343, at 184–85.

[345] *See* Dietrich, *supra* note 327, at 235, 238.

[346] *See BCE Inc.*, 3 S.C.R. 560, paras. 162–63. *See also* Anand, *supra* note 343, at 185.

[347] Anand, *supra* note 343, at 182–83. *See also* P.M. Vasudev, *Stakeholders in the Canada Business Corporations Act: An Appraisal and Some Proposals* 37 (2011), http://ssrn.com/abstract=1874264.

employing *Revlon* and progeny-like process in a change of control transaction." The upshot appears to be that boards need only "observe all of the window dressing and . . . mouth the appropriate platitudes in minutes of meetings and bid documents, of considering debenture-holder interests in a fair manner," a gesture requiring "little more than an acknowledgment to honour contractual commitments."[348]

Regardless of the shareholder-centric outcome in *BCE*, however, the oppression remedy, in particular, creates the potential for broader stakeholder orientation to take root in Canada[349] – which could raise potentially thorny issues where the interests and expectations of other stakeholders are impacted by the decidedly shareholder-centric structures described above. Although the CBCA oppression provision was initially aimed at protection of minority shareholders[350] – and although in practice minority shareholders in closely held companies have fared better than others using it[351] – the remedy is clearly phrased in a manner permitting protection of the interests of non-shareholders. The critical term "complainant" could not be defined more broadly, including anyone "who, in the discretion of a court, is a proper person to make an application"[352] – which itself remains undefined, but presumably could include even non–security holders such as employees. The potential for the oppression remedy to promote non-shareholder interests would seem to be reinforced by the fact that the CBCA does not define the "best interests of the corporation," a move that the Dickerson Committee suggested would "seem to leave the way free . . . for the courts to escape from the constraints of what has somewhat charitably been described as the 'anachronistic' view that has developed in the English courts" – that is, strict shareholder primacy.[353]

To date, employees have not benefited from the potential breadth of the oppression remedy (or other similar remedies for that matter). Stephanie Ben-Ishai and Poonam Puri, in their empirical study of oppression cases from 1995 to 2001, found that "[f]reestanding employees had no success in qualifying as complainants under the discretionary category in section 238," and that even when they qualified by virtue of shareholder status, they had just

[348] Dietrich, *supra* note 327, at 238.

[349] *See* Vasudev, *supra* note 347, at 13–14.

[350] *See, e.g.*, *BCE Inc.*, 3 S.C.R. 560, para. 129; DICKERSON REPORT, *supra* note 300, at 160. *See also* Stephanie Ben-Ishai & Poonam Puri, *The Canadian Oppression Remedy Judicially Considered: 1995–2001*, 30 QUEEN'S L.J. 79, 92 (2004).

[351] *See* Ben-Ishai & Puri, *supra* note 350, at 81, 91–102 (analyzing seventy-one cases between 1995 and 2001); Vasudev, *supra* note 347, at 17–18.

[352] *See* CBCA, *supra* note 298, § 238.

[353] DICKERSON REPORT, *supra* note 300, at 82. *See also* Vasudev, *supra* note 347, at 12; *infra* Chapter 5.C.ii (discussing the Dickerson Committee's role in Canadian corporate law reform).

a 2 percent success rate.[354] The Ontario Superior Court of Justice's 2007 decision in *Air Canada Pilots Ass'n.* illuminates the degree to which employees remain overlooked as a class of potential oppression complainants, both with respect to the framing of the employees' complaint in the case and in terms of the judicial response. Rather than pursuing complainant status as employees, the pilots characterized themselves as unsecured creditors by reference to wage and pension obligations, which they argued the company would be unable to pay if certain shareholder distributions were permitted. The court rejected this characterization, however, concluding that the pilots were creditors only "in the ephemeral sense of being employees receiving wages from time to time," and emphasizing that no "breach of contract" or "breaches of the employment relationship" were pled.[355] The implication is at once that employee status, as such, would not suffice, and that even if it did, the employees should expect nothing beyond the protections negotiated in their contracts or provided by labor and employment law.[356]

In any event, the potential for stakeholder-centric analysis through one legal lens to contradict shareholder-centric analysis through another raises an interesting question of priorities. The issues involved in such a collision would be particularly complex in the context of hostile takeovers, given that for a typical Canadian public company, claims of oppression and breach of fiduciary duty would be matters of federal corporate law whereas the conduct of a tender offer and the target board's response to it would be matters of provincial takeover law. Indeed, notwithstanding that takeovers have substantially been left to provincial securities regulators, there has long been evidence that courts could arrive at very different conclusions if called upon to assess these transactions by reference to fiduciary duties. Indeed, although little Canadian case law addressed the issue of corporate purpose prior to the last decade, at least one case – *Teck Corp. Ltd. v. Millar* – suggested that target boards could consider the interests of non-shareholders in responding to a hostile takeover without necessarily breaching their fiduciary duties.[357] The British Columbia Supreme Court, in its 1972 opinion, accepted that "it would be a breach of their duty for directors to disregard entirely the interests of a company's shareholders in order to confer a benefit on its employees," but continued that showing "a

[354] *See* Ben-Ishai & Puri, *supra* note 350, at 102–03.

[355] *See* Air Canada Pilots Ass'n v. Air Canada Ace Aviation Holdings Inc., [2007] O.J. No. 89, paras. 1–13, 75–90 (Can. Ont. Super. Ct. J.).

[356] *Cf.* Vasudev, *supra* note 347, at 25–30 (arguing that the court's analysis reflects a "contractarian" approach).

[357] *See* Ian B. Lee, Peoples Department Stores v. Wise *and the "Best Interests of the Corporation,"* 41 CAN. BUS. L.J. 212, 213–15 (2005).

decent respect for other interests lying beyond those of the company's shareholders" would not "leave directors open to the charge that they have failed in their fiduciary duty to the company."[358] Ultimately this was not at issue because the target board was found to be "acting in the best interests of the general body of shareholders,"[359] and for decades the court's expansive dicta went essentially un-cited.[360] In its 2004 *Peoples* opinion, however, the Supreme Court of Canada looked to *Teck* in distinguishing the interests of the company from those of particular stakeholder groups, citing the case in support of the assertion that "courts have long recognized that various other factors may be relevant in determining what directors should consider in soundly managing with a view to the best interests of the corporation"[361] – a broad statement of corporate purpose in turn cited in *BCE*.[362]

Building a stakeholder-oriented conception of corporate purpose on a single British Columbia case from the early 1970s, while effectively ignoring widespread Canadian reliance on the shareholder-centric English conception of the company, has been questioned by pro-shareholder and pro-stakeholder scholars alike.[363] Regardless of the quality of the legal analyses in *Peoples* and *BCE*, however, these decisions clearly reflect a pro-stakeholder strand of Canadian corporate law, the potential for which has been implicit in the CBCA's remedial provisions since its adoption in 1975, and which appears difficult to reconcile with the pro-shareholder governance rules and provincial takeover rules described above. Although the practical outcome in *BCE* strongly favored shareholders, the theoretical potential for conflict would nevertheless appear quite real in the context of hostile takeovers – an area in which the interests of shareholders and other stakeholders sharply conflict, and which implicates multiple federal and provincial legal regimes that may well incline in opposite directions when it comes to the conduct of target boards. As Jeffrey MacIntosh observed in the wake of *BCE*, "[t]he purpose of the takeover bid provisions in securities legislation is the 'protection of the bona fide interests of

[358] Teck Corp. Ltd. v. Millar (1973), 33 D.L.R. 3d 288, 314 (Can. B.C. S.C.).

[359] *Id.* at 329–30.

[360] *See* Lee, *supra* note 357, at 214–15.

[361] *See* Peoples Dept. Stores Inc. v. Wise, [2004] 3 S.C.R. 461, paras. 41–43 (Can.).

[362] *See* BCE Inc. v. 1976 Debentureholders, [2008] 3 S.C.R. 560, para. 39 (Can.).

[363] *Compare* Lee, *supra* note 357, at 213–20 (favoring the outcome in *Peoples* while lamenting the court's "unconvincing analysis" of the case law and its failure to address the normative arguments against shareholder primacy), *with* Jeffrey G. MacIntosh, BCE *and the Peoples' Corporate Law: Learning to Live on Quicksand*, 48 Can. Bus. L.J. 255, 257–58 (2009) (arguing that the *Peoples* opinion "ignores a vast English and Canadian jurisprudence accepting shareholder primacy"). *See also* Edward Iacobucci, *Indeterminacy and the Canadian Supreme Court's Approach to Corporate Fiduciary Duties*, 48 Can. Bus. L.J. 232, 233–41 (2009); Jacob S. Ziegel, *The Peoples Judgment and the Supreme Court's Role in Private Law Cases*, 41 Can. Bus. L.J. 236, 237–38 (2005).

the shareholders of the offeree company,'" and regulators "have made it clear that in responding to a hostile takeover bid, they expect directors of the target company to maximize *shareholder* value." Following *BCE*, however, it would seem that "directors must now choose. Either they satisfy the requirements of corporate law, or they satisfy the requirements of securities law. They cannot do both."[364]

If we set aside Canada's core governance rules – which strongly militate in the shareholders' favor in any event – the degree of shareholder-centrism will presumably be impacted by how this collision between fiduciary duties under corporate law and takeover rules under securities regulation (should it in fact arise) plays out in practice and in the courts. Although the case law provides some limited guidance, drawing clear lines between the respective domains of corporate law and securities regulation in Canada has presented challenges. In *Danier Leather Inc.*, the Supreme Court of Canada rejected the argument that business judgment rule protection should extend to sales forecasts included in prospectuses, explaining that "while forecasting is a matter of business judgment, disclosure is a matter of legal obligation." The business judgment rule "should not be used to qualify or undermine the duty of disclosure," such that "the disclosure requirements under the [Ontario Securities] Act are not to be subordinated to the exercise of business judgment."[365] Conversely, however, in *Magna International*, disclosure had a real impact on the adequacy of approval of an arrangement under corporate law. The Ontario Securities Commission forced additional disclosures before a recapitalization (abandoning a dual class structure) pursued as an arrangement under the Ontario Business Corporations Act could be put to a shareholder vote, and the Ontario Superior Court of Justice emphasized that "[t]he outcome of the vote of informed shareholders, acting in their self-interest, is in itself a very significant indicator as to whether or not a plan of arrangement is fair and reasonable" – an analysis predicated on the adequacy of disclosures made.[366]

Matters become more complex, however, where a single domain of activity implicates both corporate and securities law. For example, in *Multiple Access Limited*, the Supreme Court of Canada observed (quoting Jacob Ziegel) that securities regulation "has a double character,"[367] and declined to find that, for a CBCA corporation traded on the Toronto Stock Exchange, insider trading rules under Ontario securities law were rendered inoperative because of

[364] MacIntosh, *supra* note 363, at 270–71. *See also* Iacobucci, *supra* note 363, at 248.
[365] Kerr v. Danier Leather Inc., [2007] 3 S.C.R. 331, paras. 53–55 (Can.).
[366] Magna International Inc. (Re), [2010] O.J. No. 3791, paras. 7–30, 55–57 (Can. Ont. Super. Ct. J. Div. Ct.).
[367] *See* Multiple Access Ltd. v. McCutcheon, [1982] 2 S.C.R. 161, 181 (Can.).

those contained in the CBCA. The court explained that "[m]ere duplication without actual conflict or contradiction is not sufficient to invoke the doctrine of paramountcy and render otherwise provincial legislation inoperative." Rather, "actual conflict in operation" would have to be shown, "as where one enactment says 'yes' and the other says 'no'" – a condition not met as between the insider trading rules of Ontario securities regulation and federal corporate law.[368]

Like insider trading, takeovers implicate both corporate law and securities regulation,[369] yet unlike the rules at issue in *Multiple Access Limited*, the potential for yes/no conflict as between the takeover rules of Ontario securities regulation and the demands of fiduciary duties under federal corporate law would appear quite real with respect to the conduct of target boards. Prior to *BCE*, the potential for a conflict of the sort described by MacIntosh remained latent because – notwithstanding stakeholder-oriented dicta in *Teck Corp. Ltd. v. Millar* – it was widely assumed that the shareholders' "reasonable expectations" for purposes of the CBCA oppression remedy and their rights under provincial takeover law were broadly compatible. For example, in its 1998 opinion in *CW Shareholdings Inc.*, the Ontario Court of Justice stated that the CBCA oppression remedy was available to a bidder in a hostile takeover in its capacity as a shareholder, and that "the reasonable expectations of the shareholders as a group is that the target company's directors and management will take appropriate steps to maximize shareholder value"[370] – a formulation consistent with the takeover rules' prioritization of target shareholder interests. Following *BCE*, however, the two regulatory fields arguably approach the target boards' duties differently, in that the strength of the shareholders' "reasonable expectations" that their interests be prioritized has been weakened, perhaps creating the sort of yes/no contradiction that *Multiple Access Limited* suggested could support a finding of federal paramountcy. On the other hand, "the clear distinction between directors' fiduciary duties, which are directed to the corporation, and the securities regulators' public interest jurisdiction, which is directed to the well-being of the capital markets and the interests of participants in those markets," suggests that *BCE* need not necessarily impede provincial securities regulators' emphasis of target shareholders' interests.[371]

Viewed in this light, the degree to which Canada maintains a shareholder-centric approach to takeovers may depend heavily on where takeover disputes

[368] *See id.* at 169, 184–91.

[369] *See, e.g.*, CW Shareholdings Inc. v. WIC Western International Communications Ltd. (1998), 39 O.R. 3d 755, paras. 101–05 (Can. Ont. Ct. J. Gen. Div.); *Multiple Access*, 2 S.C.R. at 179.

[370] *See CW Shareholdings*, 39 O.R. 3d 755, paras. 101–03.

[371] Ralph Shay, *Take-Over Defenses and Directors' Fiduciary Duties – Can National Policy 62–202 and the* BCE *Decision Live Side by Side?*, Sec. L. Newsl., Dec. 2009.

arise – before securities regulators, or in the courts. The likelihood appears to be that they will tend to arise in the former rather than the latter, which will institutionally favor the shareholders' interests. As noted above, Canadian disputes regarding the use of takeover defenses have tended to "come before provincial securities commissions rather than the courts."[372] And despite some early equivocating, the Ontario Securities Commission appears to have arrived at the view that it is not subject to *BCE* in its review of takeover defenses, confirming "its traditional view . . . that it is generally time for a [poison pill] to go when it has served its purpose by facilitating an auction."[373]

Although the strand of Canadian corporate law leading to the Supreme Court of Canada's *BCE* decision clearly reflects an ambivalence regarding shareholders and their interests not unlike that observed in the United States,[374] Canada's corporate governance system remains considerably more shareholder-centric on the whole. Notwithstanding stakeholder-oriented statements of corporate purpose in *Peoples* and *BCE*, and the availability of the oppression remedy to non-shareholders (or at least creditors), Canada's corporate governance rules lean decidedly in the shareholders' favor by giving them strong powers to call meetings, remove directors, and amend the articles, closely resembling the approaches taken in Australia and the United Kingdom. And notwithstanding the greater latitude of Canadian boards to deploy takeover defenses such as poison pills unilaterally, provincial securities law nevertheless constrain their retention, limiting their use to the facilitation of auctions redounding to the target shareholders' interests – an approach to which the Ontario Securities Commission remains committed notwithstanding *BCE*. The upshot is a corporate governance system that, although less shareholder-centric than the Australian and U.K. systems, nevertheless resembles them more closely than it does the U.S. system.

D. SHAREHOLDER LAWSUITS AND CORPORATE GOVERNANCE

As the overview of the Australian, Canadian, U.K., and U.S. corporate governance systems provided in this chapter illustrates, the governance powers possessed by U.S. shareholders are vastly eclipsed by those available to their

[372] NICHOLLS, *supra* note 293, at 202.

[373] Jeff Barnes et al., *Canada: OSC Rejects Deference to Target Boards in Poison Pill Decisions*, MONDAQ BUS. BRIEFING, Jan. 18, 2011.

[374] *Cf.* Lee, *supra* note 357, at 213–20 (arguing that "the question whether the 'interests of the corporation' are reducible to the interests of the shareholders was not the subject of authoritative case law in Canada prior to *Peoples*," and that "in light of the sparseness and inconclusiveness of the prior case law . . . the court's omission to take seriously the normative aspect of the question is to be regretted").

counterparts elsewhere in the common-law world. One area in which U.S. shareholders' capacity for meaningful action exceeds that available to shareholders in these other countries, however, is their far greater practical ability to sue for breaches of fiduciary duty and securities disclosure violations.[375] This naturally prompts one to ask whether the greater capacity of U.S. shareholders to sue substantially closes the gap in shareholder orientation identified in the foregoing analysis.[376] In this final section of the chapter, I conclude that the gap remains quite substantial.

Several aspects of U.K. company law and civil litigation render it far more difficult for U.K. shareholders to bring suit than their U.S. counterparts. As a matter of company law, the fact that directors' duties are owed to the company alone, restrictive derivative standing rules, and the subjective nature of the duty to pursue the shareholders' interests largely undermine the ability of aggrieved shareholders to pursue directors and officers in court.[377] More generally, "the U.K.'s 'loser pays' fees rule" tends to "discourage representative litigation,"[378] inhibiting the aggregation of shareholders' claims into a single suit with a potential payoff sufficient to render the action economically worthwhile. Conversely, "in the United States, the circumstances under which shareholders can bring a direct action against directors are broader and the rules governing derivative actions are more lenient." Similarly, takeovers in the United States are heavily litigated, unlike in the United Kingdom, where

375 *See, e.g.*, Armour et al., *supra* note 331; Elizabeth Boros, *Public and Private Enforcement of Disclosure Breaches in Australia*, 9 J. CORP. L. STUD. 409, 429–33 (2009); James D. Cox & Randall S. Thomas, *Mapping the American Shareholder Litigation Experience: A Survey of Empirical Studies of the Enforcement of the U.S. Securities Law* 2 (Vanderbilt Univ. Law Sch. Law & Econ., Research Paper No. 09–10, 2009; Duke Univ. Law Sch. Pub. Law & Legal Theory, Research Paper No. 246, 2009), http://ssrn.com/abstract=1370508; Eilís Ferran, *Are US-Style Investor Suits Coming to the UK?*, 9 J. CORP. L. STUD. 315, 339–40 (2009); Jennifer G. Hill, *The Rising Tension between Shareholder and Director Power in the Common Law World*, 18 CORP. GOVERNANCE: AN INT'L REV. 344, 348 (2010).

376 *Compare* Brian Cheffins, A *Response to Christopher Bruner*, OPINIO JURIS (Apr. 14, 2010), http://opiniojuris.org/2010/04/14/a-response-to-christopher-bruner-by-brian-cheffins/ (arguing that it may) *with* Christopher M. Bruner, *A Response to Brian Cheffins*, OPINIO JURIS (Apr. 14, 2010), http://opiniojuris.org/2010/04/14/a-response-to-brian-cheffins/ (arguing that it does not). *See also* Bruner, *supra* note 2, at 609–10.

377 *See* BIRDS ET AL., *supra* note 25, at 674–677; DAVIES, *supra* note 8, at 480–82, 507–12, 614–27; DeMott, *supra* note 61, at 229–31; DIGNAM & LOWRY, *supra* note 38 at 187–90, 301–03, 312.

378 Armour et al., *supra* note 331, at 692. *See also* Letter from Jonathan Taylor, Managing Director, Financial Services and Stability, HM Treasury, United Kingdom, to Elizabeth M. Murphy, Secretary, Securities and Exchange Commission (Feb. 11, 2011), at 3, http://www.sec.gov/comments/4–617/4617–4.pdf; Letter from John Davidson, Chair, GC100 Group, to Elizabeth M. Murphy, Secretary, Securities and Exchange Commission (Feb. 18, 2011), at 3, http://www.sec.gov/comments/4–617/4617–5.pdf (observing that "'[l]oser pays' rules are prevalent" outside the United States).

the City Code on Takeovers and Mergers "largely precludes civil litigation concerning takeover bids."[379] More generally, the United States is globally perceived as uniquely favoring civil litigation, maintaining various rules and procedures giving "entrepreneurial attorneys" strong economic incentives to identify and facilitate the filing of potential corporate and securities suits on behalf of shareholders.[380] Chief among them are a fees rule generally requiring each side to bear its own litigation costs; so-called contingency fee arrangements, under which plaintiffs' attorneys bear the costs of litigation but receive a substantial percentage of any recovery; "opt-out" class actions; and relaxation of the traditional common-law fraud requirements, notably in the form of a "fraud on the market" theory permitting shareholders alleging securities fraud to substitute reliance on the integrity of public trading prices for actual reliance on the alleged misstatements.[381]

Although Australia and Canada have facilitated shareholder suits to a greater extent than the United Kingdom has, there nevertheless remains a strong reluctance in these countries to go so far as the United States has historically. For example, Australia has sought to facilitate shareholder class actions over recent decades through the development of "independent funding organizations that enable class plaintiffs to deal with the 'loser pays' cost rules that exist in Australia," as well as through use of "opt-out" class actions.[382] Nevertheless, Australia has remained reluctant to permit juries to hear "complex business

[379] Armour et al., *supra* note 331, at 692–96.

[380] *See id.* at 692. *See also* Rob Bauer & Robin Braun, *Misdeeds Matter: Long-Term Stock Price Performance after the Filing of Class-Action Lawsuits*, 66 Fin. Analysts J. 74, 89 (2010); Davidson, *supra* note 378, at 3; Michael Klausner, *Are Securities Class Actions "Supplemental" to SEC Enforcement? An Empirical Analysis* 10 (Feb. 23, 2010) (manuscript on file with author); Michael Klausner, *Personal Liability of Officers in US Securities Class Actions*, 9 J. Corp. L. Stud. 349, 349–58 (2009).

[381] See Armour et al., *supra* note 331, at 692; Davidson, *supra* note 378, at 2–3; Klausner, *Personal Liability of Officers*, *supra* note 380, at 353 (observing that contingency fees typically range from 25 to 33 percent in securities class actions); Taylor, *supra* note 378, at 2–3. For an influential discussion of the "fraud on the market" theory of reliance, see Basic Inc. v. Levinson, 485 U.S. 224, 243–49 (1988) (describing this theory as a presumption supported by empirical work indicating that market prices typically reflect "most publicly available information," a presumption that can be overcome by "[a]ny showing that severs the link between the alleged misrepresentation and either the price received (or paid) by the plaintiff, or his decision to trade at a fair market price").

[382] *See* Australian Government Submission to the Study on Extraterritorial Private Rights of Action (Feb. 18, 2011), at 10, http://www.sec.gov/comments/4-617/4617-34.pdf. *See also* DeMott, *supra* note 61, at 230 (observing that derivative actions in Australia and other countries "are less encumbered by preliminary obstacles" than in the United Kingdom). On the emergence of litigation-funding organizations in Australia and the United Kingdom, see generally George R. Barker, *Third Party Litigation Funding in Australia and Europe* (ANU Coll. of Law Ctr. for Law & Econ. Working Paper No. 2, 2011), http://ssrn.com/abstract=2034625 (concluding that "[w]hile

cases" or to award U.S.-style punitive damages,[383] and likewise has rejected the "fraud on the market" theory of reliance in securities fraud cases.[384] It should be added that, as in the United Kingdom, Australia's Corporations Act 2001 includes a provision permitting a court, "in any civil proceeding . . . for negligence, default, breach of trust or breach of duty," to decide that a director's or officer's liability "ought fairly to be excused . . . on such terms as the court thinks fit" where that individual "has acted honestly."[385] That such a provision could further insulate corporate decision makers from threat of suit by investors is vividly illustrated by *Re Welfab Engineers Ltd.*, a 1990 U.K. decision in which directors who accepted a lower bid for the company's assets in order to save the struggling business and employees' jobs were found not to have violated their fiduciary duties. The final paragraph of the opinion pointedly adds that even if a breach of duty had been found, the court "would consider that the [directors] had acted honestly and reasonably and ought fairly to be excused from liability."[386]

Canada likewise has sought to liberalize shareholder litigation, while resisting the perceived excesses of the U.S. litigation landscape. Nicholls, writing in 2009, observes that "both public and private securities law enforcement have been less vigorous in Canada than in the US,"[387] and he identifies a number of impediments to shareholder litigation applicable to corporate law and securities regulation alike. Factors inhibiting such suits in Canada have historically included the lack of statutory civil liability for securities misrepresentations and "the practical difficulty" of pursuing them through traditional common-law negligence or fraud claims; rejection of the "fraud on the market" theory of reliance; the "slow development of effective class action legislation" in Canada;

the legal environment in these jurisdictions has become more accommodating . . . ongoing uncertainty about the legal rules . . . may still be hindering its further development").

383 *See* Australian Government Submission to the Study on Extraterritorial Private Rights of Action, *supra* note 382, at 6. *See also* Renee M. Jones & Michelle Welsh, *Toward a Public Enforcement Model for Directors' Duty of Oversight*, 45 VAND. J. TRANSNAT'L L. 343, 380 (2012) ("In the United States, directors' duties are enforced principally through private litigation. In Australia, private enforcement against outside directors plays an insignificant role, but ASIC enjoys broad enforcement authority.").

384 *See* Boros, *supra* note 375, at 429–33.

385 *Corporations Act 2001*, *supra* note 210, s 1318(1). *See also* AUSTIN & RAMSAY, *supra* note 205, at 473–75. The U.K. provision, interestingly, requires that the individual have "acted honestly *and reasonably*." *See* Companies Act, 2006, c. 46, § 1157(1) (U.K.) (emphasis added). Austin and Ramsay suggest that although the Australian provision solely requires honesty, "[w]hether a director has exercised care could be relevant to the court's exercise of discretion" in loyalty cases. AUSTIN & RAMSAY, *supra* note 205, at 473.

386 Re Welfab Engineers Ltd. [1990] B.C.C. 600, 600–04. *See also* DIGNAM & LOWRY, *supra* note 38, at 351–52.

387 Nicholls, *supra* note 282, at 383.

the "loser pays" rule and "resistance" toward contingency fee arrangements; and fear of "strike suits" filed only for their settlement value, coupled with the "widespread perception in Canada . . . that the US securities law system is overly litigious."[388] Over recent years Canada has created a new civil liability regime for securities disclosure violations, has liberalized class actions generally, and has eased restrictions on the use of contingency fee arrangements, yet tempers these moves with others intended "to exorcise the spectre of American strike suits" – notably, proportionate liability rules, a leave requirement, liability caps, and perhaps most significantly, retention of the loser-pays rule.[389] To be sure, the availability of "a broad, multi-purpose investor remedy" in the form of the corporate law oppression remedy may relieve pressure from the securities regime to take more concerted steps to facilitate private enforcement through civil suits.[390] But the pervasive and powerful impact of "the usual rule that costs follow the result" has not been lost on the Supreme Court of Canada, which remarked in its 2007 *Danier Leather Inc.* opinion that "protracted litigation has become the sport of kings in the sense that only kings or equivalent can afford it. Those who inflict it on others in the hope of significant personal gain and fail can generally expect adverse cost consequences."[391]

There is certainly intuitive appeal to the notion that greater capacity to sue in the United States might focus boards more intently on the shareholders' interests.[392] Although I doubt, for the reasons explained below, that it substantially narrows the gap in shareholder orientation, it must be acknowledged that it is inevitably a matter of speculation because of the difficulty of studying how the shareholders' capacity to sue affects board conduct. As James Cox and Randall Thomas observe in their review of studies on U.S. securities litigation, it is exceptionally difficult to establish the deterrent value of shareholder suits because we cannot know "the level of precautionary measures . . . that would not be there but for the present looming threat" of suit. "Just how much additional protection" the fear of suit inspires "is at best speculative and indeterminate and, hence, beyond the empiricists' reach."[393] Similarly, demonstrating

[388] *Id.* at 384, 389, 391.

[389] *See id.* at 370–403 (describing the influential Ontario reforms). *See also* MacIntosh, *supra* note 316, at 176–77 (observing that institutional minority shareholders "have increasingly spearheaded judicial challenges to corporate conduct").

[390] *See* Nicholls, *supra* note 282, at 405.

[391] Kerr v. Danier Leather Inc., [2007] 3 S.C.R. 331, paras. 63, 70 (Can.).

[392] *Cf.* DeMott, *supra* note 61, at 234 (suggesting that "Delaware's historical pattern of relatively greater receptivity to derivative litigation could be explained by the predictable need for devices to constrain the greater degree of unilateral discretion invested in directors," and that the converse may be true in the United Kingdom).

[393] Cox & Thomas, *supra* note 375, at 20. *See also* Bruner, *supra* note 2, at 609–10; Bruner, *supra* note 376; Roberta Romano, *The Shareholder Suit: Litigation without Foundation?*, 7

that shareholder suits actually lead to improved corporate governance "may prove very difficult."[394] Indeed, the inherent challenges involved with empirically studying the deterrent value of litigation in the corporate governance context are presumably heightened by the fact that shareholders are not the only corporate constituency who might sue. For example, the *Revlon* case establishing the Delaware board's duty to maximize return to shareholders in a sale, breakup, or change of control was itself prompted by the target board's preference for a deal in which part of the value received would go toward supporting the value of previously issued notes – a preference reflecting the board's fear of suit by the noteholders, who naturally disliked the leveraged structure of the deal.[395]

In any event, it is clear that shareholder governance powers in Australia, Canada, and the United Kingdom vastly eclipse those available in the United States, and others have suggested that this may explain the limited appeal of U.S.-style litigation in those countries. Eilís Ferran, for example, observes that "the [U.K.] investor community is dominated by sophisticated institutions that are accustomed to exerting influence via informal, reputational and market mechanisms underpinned by governance rights conferred by company law," and speculates that they accordingly may not "regard private litigation as an important control tool."[396] Similarly, Nicholls suggests that "the greater efficacy of corporate law shareholder rights may explain the less litigious Canadian securities law environment" – notably, the shareholders' strong powers to call meetings and remove directors, and "the discipline exerted by

J. L. ECON. & ORG. 55, 84–85 (1991). Tom Baker and Sean Griffith, in an intriguing study focusing on the role of directors' and officers' (D&O) insurers, conclude that policies covering shareholder litigation are priced "according to the risk posed by each corporate insured," and that insurers "make a detailed inquiry into the corporate governance practices of the prospective insured." Tom Baker & Sean Griffith, *Predicting Corporate Governance Risk: Evidence from the Directors' and Officers' Liability Insurance Market*, 74 U. CHI. L. REV. 487, 489 (2007). They acknowledge, however, that "[t]here is, of course, ample reason to doubt that this theoretical ideal" actually deters conduct that hurts shareholders – notably because "D&O expenses may not be large enough to change corporate behavior." *Id.* at 533–37.

394 *See* Cox & Thomas, *supra* note 375, at 38. *See also* Andrew S. Gold, *A Decision Theory Approach to the Business Judgment Rule: Reflections on* Disney, *Good Faith, and Judicial Uncertainty*, 66 MD. L. REV. 398, 453 & n.333 (2007). Eliezer Fich and Anil Shivdasani, for example, find "a dramatic decline in the other directorships held by . . . outside directors" of companies facing U.S. securities fraud class actions, but cannot determine conclusively whether this represents a reputational penalty, a choice by outside directors to reduce their overall liability exposure, or endogenous factors. Eliezer M. Fich & Anil Shivdasani, *Financial Fraud, Director Reputation, and Shareholder Wealth*, 86 J. FIN. ECON. 306, 307–08 (2007).

395 *See* Revlon, Inc. v. MacAndrews & Forbes Holdings, Inc., 506 A.2d 173, 178–79, 182–83 (Del. 1986).

396 Ferran, *supra* note 375, at 342–44.

the market for corporate control" because of the constraints placed on the use of poison pills.[397]

That shareholder litigation might hold considerably less appeal in an environment characterized by strong shareholder governance rights is broadly consistent with the little empirical work done in this area. John Armour, Bernard Black, Brian Cheffins, and Richard Nolan, in a 2009 study thought to be "the first comparative quantitative analysis of the private enforcement of corporate law," evaluated "hand-collected data sets from the United Kingdom and the United States, on the number and outcome of lawsuits brought against directors of publicly traded companies under corporate law."[398] Predictably, they conclude that "private enforcement of corporate law, through lawsuits against directors of publicly traded companies, is indeed more common in the United States than in the United Kingdom," yet that "[e]ven in the United States, directors face risk from private litigants less than is commonly imagined."[399] The annual chance of a director of an NYSE- or NASDAQ-listed company facing a corporate lawsuit generating a judicial decision was found to be just 1.1 percent, and the total number of cases found over a seven-year period in which inside or outside directors in public companies had to make out-of-pocket payments amounted to just 3 and 1, respectively.[400] This may help explain why U.K. (or Australian or Canadian) shareholders might rationally decline to exert themselves to gain broader access to courts, notably where those shareholders are diversified institutions that may consider themselves just as likely to bear the costs of such litigation indirectly – via indemnification and insurance – as to benefit from it.[401]

[397] Nicholls, *supra* note 282, at 404–06.

[398] Armour et al., *supra* note 331, at 689.

[399] *Id.* at 690.

[400] *See id.* at 706, 709–10.

[401] *See* Bauer & Braun, *supra* note 380, at 78, 83, 89 (finding "a consistent decline in stock price on the filing of a class-action lawsuit," and that aside from insider trading cases, "[o]n average, shareholder litigation does not seem to pay off in terms of stock price recovery"); Bruner, *supra* note 376. *See also* Armour et al., *supra* note 331, at 701–03 (discussing prior literature establishing that "settlements are reasonably common . . . and settlements are paid principally by D&O insurance"); Ferran, *supra* note 375, at 340 (suggesting that the restrictive civil liability rules in the United Kingdom reflect the view that shareholder litigation in the United States is "wastefully circular"); Nicholls, *supra* note 282, at 368 (observing that shareholder suits "may have the perverse effect of punishing other equally innocent shareholders of the same corporation"). *But see* Simon Deakin, *What Directors Do (and Fail to Do): Some Comparative Notes on Board Structure and Corporate Governance*, 55 N.Y.L. Sch. L. Rev. 525, 534–35 (2010/11) (observing that although litigation against company directors "remains a very rare event" in the United Kingdom, over the last decade "there is a growing perception of an increased litigation risk").

Michael Klausner, in the first empirical study of its kind, similarly found that officers rarely make out-of-pocket payments in U.S. securities class actions. His investigation of all such

Armour et al. investigate various "substitutes for private enforcement" in the United Kingdom, observing in particular that the Takeover Code "imposes tighter constraints on directors than directors' fiduciary duties under corporate law," while "[s]hareholder governance rights . . . also likely serve as a substitute for formal civil enforcement." They rightly suggest that "the United Kingdom has stronger corporate law than the United States, in ways that let shareholders protect themselves without the need to file lawsuits."[402] It is important to observe, however, that the nature of Armour et al.'s core comparative question differs fundamentally from that posed here. Whereas I look first to the stronger shareholder governance powers available in other countries and then ask whether the greater capacity of U.S. shareholders to sue closes the gap in overall shareholder orientation, Armour et al. look first to the greater capacity of U.S. shareholders to sue and then ask whether stronger shareholder governance powers, among other things, might represent "substitutes" supporting "strong securities markets" by other means.[403] Ultimately they decline to adopt a firm conclusion, observing the potential for "other factors" to constrain

actions filed between 2000 and 2003 – of which there were 756 in total – found that 256 were "dismissed or voluntarily dropped," while 437 settled and 44 remained pending as of 2009. Of the three cases that went to trial, two ultimately settled, and one resulted in a default judgment. Of the 409 settlements for which the source of payments could be determined, just 27 (i.e., 6 percent) included payments by individual officers. Interestingly, he also found that those suits paralleled by SEC actions were far less likely to be dismissed, and that "among class actions that settled with no payment by any officer, a large majority of parallel SEC actions resulted in substantial sanctions for the officers involved." Klausner, *Personal Liability of Officers*, *supra* note 380, at 351, 358–65. *See also* Michael Klausner & Jason Hegland, *How Protective Is D&O Insurance in Securities Class Actions? – Part I*, XXIII PROF. LIABILITY UNDERWRITING SOC'Y J. (REPRINT) (Feb. 2010); Michael Klausner & Jason Hegland, *When Are Securities Class Actions Dismissed, When Do They Settle, and for How Much? – Part II*, XXIII PROF. LIABILITY UNDERWRITING SOC'Y J. (REPRINT) (Mar. 2010); Romano, *supra* note 393, at 84–85. *But see* Fich & Shivdasani, *supra* note 394, at 308 (arguing that "outside directors of firms accused of fraud bear a financial penalty" in the form of reduced directorships). Although these results do not necessarily mean that securities class actions are not cost-justified, over recent decades courts and Congress alike have sought to carve back at private securities litigation, including through more demanding pleading standards. *See* STEPHEN J. CHOI & A.C. PRITCHARD, SECURITIES REGULATION: CASES AND ANALYSIS 246–48 (2d ed. 2008); CIOFFI, *supra* note 281, at 104–08.

402 Armour et al., *supra* note 331, at 717–21. *See also* Nicholls, *supra* note 282, at 404 n.217 (observing that "the shareholder rights identified by the authors . . . are precisely the rights that Canadian shareholders also enjoy, with the possible exception of pre-emption rights"); Edward Walker-Arnott, *Company Law, Corporate Governance and the Banking Crisis*, INT'L CORP. RESCUE (Special Issue) 3, 5 & n.17 (2010) (observing that although the Companies Act does not address the board's collective responsibilities and thus "does not, in terms, provide any remedy for breach," the shareholders' removal power "enables the removal of all the directors at a stroke").

403 *See* Armour et al. *supra* note 331, at 711.

directors, but describe their potential substitutability as "plausible"[404] – a position broadly compatible with those taken by governments, including those of Australia and the United Kingdom, that have voiced strong opposition to extraterritorial private rights of action in U.S. courts (largely because of concerns over excessive litigation and strike suits) while emphasizing the adequacy of their own strategies to protect investors.[405]

To return to the question posed here: does the greater capacity of U.S. shareholders to sue substantially close the gap in shareholder orientation identified in the foregoing analysis? Notwithstanding the difficulty of assessing the matter empirically, there remains good reason to conclude that a substantial gap in shareholder orientation remains. Aside from corporate governance powers and capacity to sue, it is important to consider another important metric of shareholder-centrism: explicit statements of corporate purpose. If greater capacity to sue were truly intended to substitute for strong shareholder governance powers, constituting an equivalent means of focusing directors' minds on the shareholders' interests, then we might expect to find similarly strong expressions of commitment to shareholders in the articulation of directors' duties. Yet, the divergence between the express shareholder-centrism of the U.K. Companies Act and the ambivalent formulation of directors' fiduciary duties in Delaware is every bit as stark as the divergence between the shareholders' governance powers in the two jurisdictions.[406]

Moreover, even where governance powers and the formulation of duties diverge less starkly from the U.S. approach, there are indications that institutional shareholders – professional investors with real money on the line – do not consider the United States to be equally committed to shareholders' interests. Recall, for example, the events surrounding News Corp.'s reincorporation from Australia to Delaware – for our purposes, an illuminating natural

[404] *See id.* at 721.

[405] *See generally* Taylor, *supra* note 378 (responding, on behalf of the U.K. Government, to the SEC's study on extraterritorial private rights of action); Australian Government Submission to the Study on Extraterritorial Private Rights of Action, *supra* note 382. *See also* Davidson, *supra* note 378; Letter from Jonathan Faull, Director General, Internal Market and Services, European Commission, to Mary L. Schapiro, Chairman, Securities and Exchange Commission (Feb. 22, 2011), http://www.sec.gov/comments/4–617/4617–49.pdf; Jones & Welsh, *supra* note 383, at 379–90; Letter from Prof. Dr. Ruediger von Rosen, President, Deutsches Aktieninstitut to Elizabeth M. Murphy, Secretary, Securities and Exchange Commission (Feb. 18, 2011), http://www.sec.gov/comments/4–617/4617–52.pdf; Letter from White & Case LLP to Elizabeth M. Murphy, Secretary, Securities and Exchange Commission (Feb. 17, 2011), http://www.sec.gov/comments/4–617/4617–3.pdf; Walker-Arnott, *supra* note 402, at 5–7; Yin Wilczek, *U.K. Government, Foreign Groups Urge SEC to Keep to* Morrison *in Private Rights Study*, Sec. L. Daily (BNA) (Feb. 23, 2011).

[406] *See* Bruner, *supra* note 376.

experiment requiring institutional investors in an Australian corporation to assess the consistency of the Australian and U.S. corporate governance regimes with their own interests. As Hill recounts, "the original 2004 reincorporation proposal prompted a revolt by a number of institutional investors concerned that the move to Delaware would significantly diminish shareholder rights," and it was only following "concessions preserving existing shareholder rights under Australian corporate law" that shareholders approved the reincorporation.[407] Tellingly, opponents of the proposal "claimed that Delaware law provided less protection for minority shareholders than Australian corporate law," and Australian, U.K., and U.S. institutions alike contributed to the effort, ultimately resulting in wide-ranging concessions relating to "securities exchange listing rules, super-voting shares, shareholder meetings and voting, takeovers, and best practice principles."[408] These investors had every reason to focus on their own respective bottom-lines, and their protests suggest that they did not view capacity to engage in U.S.-style *ex post* litigation as offering protection of their interests equivalent to the *ex ante* governance powers that would be lost in the move from Australia to Delaware.

To be sure, the investors' interests were in fact protected by the Delaware Court of Chancery – which found that a "board policy" to put poison pill extensions to a shareholder vote could be made irrevocable, and accordingly rejected News Corp.'s motion to dismiss[409] – but Chancellor Chandler's *UniSuper Ltd.* opinion makes amply clear that the outcome was driven entirely by the shareholders' foresight in negotiating for the importation of special protections rather than anything substantively intrinsic to Delaware law. Although "a contract to adopt and keep in place a [board] resolution (or a policy) that others justifiably rely upon to their detriment... may be enforceable," Chandler granted News Corp.'s motion to dismiss with respect to the breach of fiduciary duty claim, finding the complaint "bereft of any facts that suggest a violation of the duty of loyalty."[410] Ironically, the true takeaway from *UniSuper Ltd.* may be that the greater capacity to litigate in Delaware cannot be expected to provide shareholder protection equivalent to the governance powers found in other common-law countries unless shareholders take the extraordinary step of synthetically grafting foreign governance powers onto Delaware law by contract. Of course, minority shareholders will normally lack the leverage

[407] Hill, *supra* note 234, at 3–7.

[408] *See id.* at 12–29 & n.67.

[409] *See* UniSuper Ltd. v. News Corp., No. 1699-N, 2005 WL 3529317 (Del. Ch. Dec. 20, 2005).

[410] *Id.* at *5, *9–*10. The promissory estoppel claim likewise survived the motion to dismiss while the claims of fraud and negligent misrepresentation did not. *See id.* at *8–*9.

to negotiate this, absent unusual circumstances such as those in *UniSuper Ltd.*[411]

Given the substantial divergence in shareholder orientation between the United States and the other common-law countries examined in this book – a divergence that does not appear to have been substantially diminished by the greater capacity of U.S. shareholders to engage in *ex post* litigation – the natural question becomes why such a divergence would have arisen among their otherwise similar corporate governance systems. In Part II of the book I turn to this question, arguing that the answer effectively lies beyond corporate law itself. In each of these countries, the degree of shareholder-centrism exhibited by the corporate governance system has been conditioned by other regulatory domains and social structures affecting the social welfare and interests of other corporate stakeholders, notably employees. As the following chapters explore, the broader political economy in each of these countries has demonstrably impacted the corporate governance system's regard for shareholders in fundamental ways that have received little attention in the extant comparative literature.

[411] *Cf.* Hill, *supra* note 234, at 50 (observing that "if Delaware law fails to recognize concessions provided to shareholders in exchange for their support of reincorporation proposals, shareholders of foreign companies may be deterred from approving reincorporation in Delaware in the future"); *UniSuper Ltd.*, 2005 WL 3529317 at *1 (observing that concessions were negotiated in the shadow of the public shareholders' ability because of their voting rights under Australian law "to prevent the reorganization").

PART II

A POLITICAL THEORY OF CORPORATE GOVERNANCE IN THE COMMON-LAW WORLD

4 Comparative Theories of Corporate Governance

The methodological discussion in Chapter 2 explored the twin challenge of strict functionalism and contextualism, suggesting that comparative scholarship must effectively steer a middle course, at once avoiding the excessive abstraction of the former approach and the excessive contingency of the latter. The comparative scholar must endeavor to balance these competing intellectual tendencies, positing commonality sufficient to permit meaningful comparison while grappling with the significant impact of distinctive histories, cultures, and legal contexts. The impossibility of doing so in a manner that fully captures the reality of each country's legal system counsels a heavy dose of methodological humility; the aim of the work must be to "fail better," as Legrand puts it – to illuminate these legal systems by reference to one another, while remaining conscious of the contingency of the exercise and acknowledging its inevitable limitations. This, I suggested, requires transparency regarding the assumptions one is willing to make in order to facilitate cross-border comparison, and close scrutiny of the nature and defensibility of claims advanced based on the comparative analysis provided.

In the following chapters I explore why the otherwise similar corporate governance systems of Australia, Canada, the United Kingdom, and the United States diverge in terms of their relative degrees of shareholder orientation – a divergence that I argue can be explained only by placing each country's corporate governance system in its broader social and political context. In preparation for that discussion, however, I first return to the methodological discussion initiated above to assess the strengths and weaknesses of extant economic and political theories of comparative corporate governance, specifying the critical respects in which my own approach builds on them, and deviates from them, as the case may be.

A. ECONOMICS

The allure of functionalism is largely the allure of the grand simplifying assumption. By assuming that all jurisdictions struggle to solve the same problems – or at least very similar problems – functionalism facilitates coherent descriptive comparison of legal systems, and even normative evaluation of the varying solutions they develop. This move, however, inevitably sacrifices nuance for parsimony, as contextualist scholars have emphasized. Historical, cultural, social, and political drivers of a given country's legal system are effectively airbrushed out of the picture to achieve the predicate universality.

The comparative corporate literature building on the "law and economics" movement exemplifies this tendency, bringing the economist's penchant for grand simplifying assumptions to bear on the analysis of corporate governance systems.[1] Although comparative corporate work in the past may have "focused on the differences that exist between national legal rules governing corporate activity," the more recent wave of scholarship in this area has emphasized "the similarities between major jurisdictions."[2] This trend directly reflects the growing prominence of the law and economics movement, proponents of which typically characterize the corporation as a purely private endeavor defined the world over by the challenge of managing "agency costs" – notably those arising from misalignment of shareholder and management interests and incentives.[3] As Klaus Hopt rightly observes, "the principal-agent problem," generally focusing on "how company law can make the board more responsive to shareholder interests," has loomed large in "company law reform initiatives in all industrialized countries," reflecting the growing influence of the law and economics movement in comparative corporate governance.[4]

The Anatomy of Corporate Law illustrates these trends, practically purporting by its title to make a science of comparative corporate law. Hopt, one of its coauthors, candidly describes the book as "tak[ing] a strongly functional

[1] *See* Klaus J. Hopt, *Comparative Company Law, in* THE OXFORD HANDBOOK OF COMPARATIVE LAW 1161, 1184–86 (Mathias Reimann & Reinhard Zimmermann eds., 2006).

[2] ALAN DIGNAM & MICHAEL GALANIS, THE GLOBALIZATION OF CORPORATE GOVERNANCE 53 (2009). *See also* David A. Skeel, Jr., *Corporate Anatomy Lessons*, 113 YALE L.J. 1519, 1520–21 (2004).

[3] *See, e.g.*, FRANK H. EASTERBROOK & DANIEL R. FISCHEL, THE ECONOMIC STRUCTURE OF CORPORATE LAW 14–15 (1991); Michael C. Jensen & William H. Meckling, *Theory of the Firm: Managerial Behavior, Agency Costs and Ownership Structure*, 3 J. FIN. ECON. 305 (1976).

[4] Hopt, *supra* note 1, at 1166, 1172, 1184–86. *See also* Simon Deakin, *The Corporation as Commons: Rethinking Property Rights, Governance and Sustainability in the Business Enterprise*, 37 QUEEN'S L.J. 339, 344 (2012); Martin Gelter, *The Dark Side of Shareholder Influence: Managerial Autonomy and Stakeholder Orientation in Comparative Corporate Governance*, 50 HARV. INT'L L.J. 129, 129–30 (2009).

approach" in that it "is more interested in finding out why there is so much uniformity of company law than in analysing or even merely describing the many divergences."[5] *The Anatomy* reflects "collaboration among nine authors from six countries," and takes an expressly "functional" approach in "highlight[ing] the economic logic of corporate law." The preface elaborates that the book "is predicated on the idea of a field of corporate – or company – law, with problems and legal strategies that, at a mid-level of abstraction at least, are independent of the laws of specific jurisdictions."[6] The core problem, then, is described as "reducing the scope for value-reducing forms of opportunism among different constituencies" – in other words, agency costs, which may arise between managers and shareholders, among shareholders, and between shareholders and other stakeholders.[7]

Other scholars, meanwhile, although less methodologically self-aware, are equally committed to an implicit functionalist approach built on agency-cost analysis. Lucian Bebchuk, for example, bases his "case for increasing [U.S.] shareholder power" in part on the greater powers of U.K. shareholders. Notably, he emphasizes U.K. shareholders' ability to direct the directors, to unilaterally amend the charter, to remove directors without cause, and to determine the outcome of hostile bids, which collectively demonstrate that U.S. "shareholders' lack of power to initiate major corporate decisions is not an inevitable element of the legal structure of the modern corporation." His argument that the United States should similarly empower shareholders, however, rests on the assumption that U.S. corporate governance should apply the same shareholder-centric policy metric that U.K. corporate governance does in determining the balance of power between boards and shareholders.[8]

In both instances, the authors (either explicitly or implicitly) treat agency costs as the core problem faced in all jurisdictions, and accordingly style their respective corporate governance systems as differing institutional responses to it – an approach that, as discussed in Chapter 2, reflects an implicit convergence bias. Bebchuk, although not addressing issues of comparative methodology, quite clearly favors U.S. convergence toward the U.K. approach, which he presents as the superior means of achieving the purportedly shared goal

[5] Hopt, *supra* note 1, at 1185–86. *See also* Skeel, *supra* note 2, at 1521–22.

[6] Reinier Kraakman, *Preface*, *in* REINIER KRAAKMAN ET AL., THE ANATOMY OF CORPORATE LAW: A COMPARATIVE AND FUNCTIONAL APPROACH vii (2d ed. 2009). In addition to Hopt and Kraakman, the other authors are John Armour, Paul Davies, Luca Enriques, Henry Hansmann, Gerard Hertig, Hideki Kanda, and Edward Rock.

[7] John Armour, Henry Hansmann & Reinier Kraakman, *What Is Corporate Law?*, *in* THE ANATOMY OF CORPORATE LAW, *supra* note 6, at 1, 2.

[8] Lucian Arye Bebchuk, *The Case for Increasing Shareholder Power*, 118 HARV. L. REV. 833, 847–50, 908–13 (2005).

of maximizing benefit to shareholders. *The Anatomy*, for its part, disclaims any normative position on the optimal structure for a corporate governance system, and likewise disclaims any normative position on the optimal degree of shareholder orientation,[9] although the authors' descriptive emphasis of similarity nevertheless implicitly points in the direction of convergence. Indeed, the point of the book is to reveal "the underlying uniformity of the corporate form" across the jurisdictions investigated.[10] To be sure, the authors "do not believe that *every* aspect of corporate law is economically rational, still less that any particular corporate law is optimal."[11] Yet, defining the field of corporate law from the outset as being about a single universal problem – minimizing agency costs – would appear to go further than forecasting convergence, suggesting that major corporate governance systems in fact have already converged on a single regulatory goal.

As with all functionalist comparative scholarship, evaluating economically oriented theories of corporate governance requires examining the degree to which they in fact identify a true common problem. As we have seen, even the staunchest advocates of the functionalist approach to comparative law express misgivings about how to react when purportedly straightforward comparisons break down. Recall, for example, that notwithstanding their high degree of confidence that functional equivalents can be found among virtually any legal systems, Zweigert and Kötz ultimately acknowledge that one may sometimes have to "rethink the original question" in increasingly abstract terms to achieve comparability of function. This, however, may ultimately bleed into highly contextual study of a nation's history, culture, and politics – for example, where the "solution [in a given jurisdiction] is provided by custom or social practice," or where "there is something about the structure of the foreign society which makes the adoption of a legal solution unnecessary."[12] This, however, is simply tantamount to conceding that the functionalist assumption of a common *legal* problem will not always remain tenable – and, correlatively, that a given country's unique history, culture, and politics will reveal the outer boundaries of the functionalist's explanatory domain.

The authors of *The Anatomy*, to their credit, are careful to cabin their claims. In the second edition they acknowledge "the very real differences across jurisdictions," advancing the more modest argument that the similarities are "at

[9] *See* Armour et al., *supra* note 7, at 5, 29.

[10] *See id.* at 1. *The Anatomy* focuses on "six 'core' jurisdictions: France, Germany, Italy, Japan, the UK, and the U.S." Kraakman, *supra* note 6, at vii.

[11] Kraakman, *supra* note 6, at vii.

[12] *See* Konrad Zweigert & Hein Kötz, Introduction to Comparative Law 34–35 (Tony Weir trans., 3d ed. 1998).

least as impressive." Specifically, they emphasize five "basic legal characteristics of the business corporation" across the jurisdictions they investigate, including "legal personality, limited liability, transferable shares, delegated management under a board structure, and investor ownership."[13] Like the authors of *The Anatomy* – and presumably most scholars of comparative corporate governance – I am prepared to assume that these attributes do in fact typify the world's major corporate legal systems, and I readily acknowledge the value of exploring such similarities.[14] Yet, it must be recognized that this hardly represents the "mid-level of abstraction" claimed; it is a very high level of abstraction indeed, leaving such enormous room for variation across corporate governance systems, and over time, that we can readily expect history, culture, and politics to intrude upon the analysis in precisely the way that Zweigert and Kötz concede they must.

In the previous chapter I have catalogued substantial differences among a set of corporate legal systems often said to be among the most similar of any in the world, including vast divergences in the degree to which shareholders are empowered to advance their own interests, and even the degree to which their interests are embraced as defining goals of corporate law. Given the depth and fundamental nature of these divergences, it is no surprise that *The Anatomy* operates at the level of abstraction that it does. Correlatively, it is no surprise that the authors ultimately acknowledge the relevance of history, culture, and politics in explaining divergences beyond the reach of their framework. The second edition of *The Anatomy* entertains the possibility that some divergences across countries may constitute "historical, cultural, or political artifacts driven by distributional rather than functional concerns"[15] – an eminently sensible inquiry, yet one that lies entirely beyond the functionalist methodology and associated assumptions motivating the project. To acknowledge the inevitability of this inquiry is effectively to concede the necessity of a political theory of comparative corporate governance to explain the sorts of divergences that I explore in this book.

[13] *See* Armour et al., *supra* note 7, at 1–16.

[14] *Cf.* Katharina Pistor, *The Standardization of Law and Its Effect on Developing Economies*, 50 Am. J. Comp. L. 97, 126–27 (2002) (arguing that "developing countries and emerging markets" would benefit from a menu of "alternative legal solutions found in living legal systems," facilitating development of "solutions that are adequate and potentially effective given the institutional constraints their country faces"). *See also* Daniel Berkowitz, Katharina Pistor & Jean-Francois Richard, *Economic Development, Legality, and the Transplant Effect*, 47 Eur. Econ. Rev. 165 (2003).

[15] *See* John Armour, Henry Hansmann & Reinier Kraakman, *Agency Problems and Legal Strategies*, *in* The Anatomy of Corporate Law, *supra* note 6, at 35, 51.

B. POLITICS

Referring generically to history, culture, and politics does not, in itself, substantially advance the ball in explaining divergence and change in corporate governance – principally because the intensive focus on context that such inquiry invites threatens to subsume the analysis in jurisdictional idiosyncrasy. The challenge, again, is to balance abstraction with context, and a number of approaches have arisen in recent years that offer various ways of tackling this challenge. I group them here under the general rubric of "political" theories.

In this section I canvas a number of prominent political theories of comparative corporate governance, exploring their strengths and weaknesses. As we shall see, a more overtly political approach to comparative corporate governance requires engaging with the growing literature on how and why share ownership has dispersed, particularly in the United Kingdom and the United States. Although distinct from the issue of shareholder orientation, the issue of share dispersal is nevertheless closely related, in that protection of minority shareholder interests has increasingly been identified as a factor contributing to the dispersal of shares and the development of vibrant capital markets.

Although I argue that none of the extant political theories offers a compelling explanation for the divergence in shareholder orientation among common-law jurisdictions, they all advance important insights regarding the role of history, culture, and politics in the development of corporate governance systems. As I discuss in the final section of this chapter, my own approach builds upon these contributions in various respects.

1. "Law Matters"

In an influential series of articles in the late 1990s and early 2000s, Rafael La Porta, Florencio Lopez-de-Silanes, Andrei Shleifer, and Robert W. Vishny advanced the claim that the degree of ownership dispersal depends upon legal protections for minority shareholders, the degree of which in turn depends upon the general orientation of the legal system in a given country.[16] These four economists, often referred to as "LLSV," more specifically argued that common-law legal systems provide better minority shareholder protections

[16] *See generally* Rafael La Porta et al., *Legal Determinants of External Finance*, 52 J. FIN. 1131 (1997); Rafael La Porta et al., *Law and Finance*, 106 J. POL. ECON. 1113 (1998); Rafael La Porta, Florencio Lopez-de-Silanes & Andrei Shleifer, *Corporate Ownership around the World*, 54 J. FIN. 471 (1999); Rafael La Porta et al., *Investor Protection and Corporate Governance*, 58 J. FIN. ECON. 3 (2000).

than civil-law legal systems do,[17] a divergence they attribute to the state's "relatively greater role in regulating business in civil law countries" and the role of common-law courts in "protect[ing] private property against the crown."[18] By a sort of transitive property, then, LLSV argued that the emergence of dispersed ownership in some countries and the persistence of concentrated ownership in others was literally "a consequence" of common-law or civil-law orientation, respectively[19] – an approach now widely known as the "law matters" theory.[20]

A significant weakness of this "law matters" theory is its inability to account for the chronology of share dispersal in the two quintessential dispersed ownership systems – the United Kingdom and the United States. Careful historical analyses have demonstrated that, in each case, share ownership dispersed in the first instance due to minority shareholder protections developed by private intermediaries in the marketplace – notably, financial firms and stock exchanges – and that these protections only later received public recognition in law.[21] As John Coffee explains, "[l]egal reforms are enacted at the behest of a motivated constituency that will be protected . . . by the proposed reforms," and obviously such a constituency "must first arise before it can become an effective lobbying force and an instrument of legal change."[22]

Similarly, the "law matters" theory cannot explain relative levels of shareholder protection and share dispersal across common-law countries, or within a given country over time. Australia, for example, offers substantially stronger shareholder protections than the United States does, yet Australian share ownership nevertheless remains more concentrated[23] – a divergence the "law

[17] *See generally* La Porta et al., *Legal Determinants of External Finance*, *supra* note 16.

[18] *See* La Porta et al., *Investor Protection and Corporate Governance*, *supra* note 16, at 12.

[19] *See* La Porta, Lopez-de-Silanes & Shleifer, *supra* note 16, at 511–12.

[20] *See, e.g.*, John Armour, Brian R. Cheffins & David A. Skeel, Jr., *Corporate Ownership Structure and the Evolution of Bankruptcy Law: Lessons from the United Kingdom*, 55 VAND. L. REV. 1699, 1713 (2002); Brian R. Cheffins, *Does Law Matter? The Separation of Ownership and Control in the United Kingdom*, 30 J. LEGAL STUD. 459, 462 (2001).

[21] On the dispersal of share ownership in the United Kingdom, see Cheffins, *supra* note 20, at 466–76; Brian R. Cheffins, *Law as Bedrock: The Foundations of an Economy Dominated by Widely Held Public Companies*, 23 OXFORD J. LEGAL STUD. 1, 12–14 (2003); John C. Coffee, Jr., *The Rise of Dispersed Ownership: The Roles of Law and the State in the Separation of Ownership and Control*, 111 YALE L.J. 1, 39–44 (2001). On dispersal in the United States, see Cheffins, *Law as Bedrock*, *supra*, at 7–12; Coffee, *supra*, at 25–39.

[22] Coffee, *supra* note 21, at 7.

[23] *See* Helen Anderson, Michelle Welsh, Ian Ramsay & Peter Gahan, *The Evolution of Shareholder and Creditor Protection in Australia: An International Comparison*, 61 INT'L & COMP. L.Q. 171, 175–77, 185–87 (2012). *See also* Jennifer G. Hill, *The Rising Tension between Shareholder and Director Power in the Common Law World*, 18 CORP. GOVERNANCE: AN INT'L REV. 344, 345 (2010).

matters" theory cannot explain. More generally, the fixed historical fact of a country's association with a given legal family offers no means of explaining why a given country's corporate governance system would remain stable, or evolve, over time. Characterizing a regulatory field so complex and dynamic as corporate governance by reference to "a single political act in a distant past," as Peter Gourevitch and James Shinn explain, permits "no account of why and when [subsequent] laws are passed or enforced," let alone why and when those laws might later change. "Interpretations based on legal tradition," they observe, "seem to leave countries trapped in their founding moment."[24] Although one might readily accept that common-law and civil-law systems do in fact exhibit detectable differences in approaches to corporate governance – a topic addressed later in the book – such generic historical associations cannot themselves account for the sorts of divergences in shareholder orientation (either at a point in time, or over time) observed within the common-law world.[25]

By the same token, it should be noted that arguments based on the historical origins of a body of law within a given legal system suffer the same inability to explain persistence versus change over time. For example, L.C.B. Gower observed (in 1956) that "the modern English business corporation has evolved from the unincorporated partnership, based on mutual agreement," whereas modern U.S. corporations statutes evolved from the early nineteenth-century practice of legislative chartering – the upshot being that "modern American corporation law owes less to partnership and contractual principles than does the British."[26] This would seem to illuminate the greater power and centrality of contemporary U.K. shareholders (relative to their U.S. counterparts) through the implicit bridging of past and present encoded within the term

[24] Peter Alexis Gourevitch & James J. Shinn, Political Power and Corporate Control: The New Global Politics of Corporate Governance 86–87 (2005). *See also* Marco Pagano & Paolo Volpin, *The Political Economy of Finance*, 17 Oxford Rev. Econ. Pol'y 502, 504–06, 517 (2001); Raghuram G. Rajan & Luigi Zingales, *The Great Reversals: The Politics of Financial Development in the Twentieth Century*, 69 J. Fin. Econ. 5, 7 (2003). For example, Rajan and Zingales argue that common-law financial markets were not better developed than their civil-law counterparts prior to World War II. *See* Rajan & Zingales, *supra*, at 14–15, 42–43. *See also* Marco Pagano & Paolo F. Volpin, *The Political Economy of Corporate Governance*, 95 Am. Econ. Rev. 1005, 1006 (2005).

[25] *See infra* Chapter 6.A. Notwithstanding its descriptive shortcomings, however, it must be acknowledged that LLSV's framework has had substantial impact upon development initiatives. *See* Ruth V. Aguilera & Cynthia A. Williams, *"Law and Finance": Inaccurate, Incomplete, and Important*, 2009 BYU L. Rev. 1413, 1424–34 (2009).

[26] Gower attributes reference to "company" law in the United Kingdom, versus "corporate" law in the United States, to this divergence. *See* L.C.B. Gower, *Some Contrasts between British and American Corporation Law*, 69 Harv. L. Rev. 1369, 1371–72 (1956).

"path dependence."[27] It must be recognized, however, that this terminology at best describes the phenomenon of empirically observed persistence. Setting aside the fact that relative degrees of shareholder orientation have in fact changed considerably over time in the countries investigated here – dynamics explored at some length below[28] – Adrian Kay rightly emphasizes that "the concept of path dependency does not *per se* provide necessary or sufficient conditions to understand or explain that which it labels: path dependent processes, even when identified, require theorizing."[29]

To be clear, I do not intend to suggest that past policy choices cannot constrain subsequent policy choices – clearly they can.[30] The point is rather that the concept of path dependence does not itself illuminate the mechanism by which some policies endure while others evolve. As Paul Pierson explains, "[i]t is not the past per se but the unfolding of processes over time that is theoretically central."[31] Much like common-law versus civil-law orientation, the differing historical roots of U.K. company law and U.S. corporate law represent, from today's perspective, fixed historical facts that cannot themselves explain persistence or change in the relative degrees of shareholder orientation exhibited by these corporate governance systems.

II. *Social Democracy*

In light of these shortcomings, others have sought to develop theories of comparative corporate governance engaging with societal politics more directly, perhaps the most important such effort being Mark Roe's "social democracy" theory. Broadly speaking, Roe associates the persistence of concentrated share ownership with left-leaning social democratic politics, and dispersal of share ownership with right-leaning rejection of social democracy. Roe describes "social democracies" as "nations committed to private property but whose governments play a large role in the economy, emphasize distributional considerations, and favor employees over capital-owners when the two conflict,"[32] and the logic of his argument is straightforward. "Social democracies press

[27] *See, e.g.*, Hill, *supra* note 23, at 348 (characterizing the historical divergence observed by Gower as "an interesting example of path dependence in operation").

[28] *See infra* Chapters 5–7.

[29] Adrian Kay, *A Critique of the Use of Path Dependency in Policy Studies*, 83 PUB. ADMIN. 553, 554 (2005). *See also* James Mahoney, *Path Dependence in Historical Sociology*, 29 THEORY & SOC'Y 507, 507 (2000).

[30] *See* Kay, *supra* note 29, at 556–58; Mahoney, *supra* note 29, at 510–12; Paul Pierson, *Increasing Returns, Path Dependence, and the Study of Politics*, 94 AM. POL. SCI. J. 251, 252 (2000).

[31] Pierson, *supra* note 30, at 264.

[32] *See* MARK J. ROE, POLITICAL DETERMINANTS OF CORPORATE GOVERNANCE: POLITICAL CONTEXT, CORPORATE IMPACT 24 (2003).

managers to stabilize employment, [and] to forgo some profit-maximizing but risky opportunities for the firm," driving a wedge between the managers' and the shareholders' incentives and thereby rendering minority shareholdings unattractive to investors. Roe argues that "when we line up the world's richest nations on a left-right political continuum and then line them up on a close-to-diffuse ownership continuum, the two correlate powerfully." Much like LLSV's binary model turning on common-law versus civil-law orientation, then, Roe posits two equilibria – one with "weakly competitive markets fitting with social democratic politics and concentrated ownership," and another with "fiercely competitive markets, conservative almost *laissez-faire* politics, and diffuse ownership" – perhaps most vividly illustrated by the comparison between continental Europe and the United States, respectively.[33] In Germany, for example, concentrated ownership goes hand in hand with codetermination rules placing employees on the boards of large companies, consistent with the claim that strongly emphasizing labor interests undermines dispersal of share ownership by rendering management less directly answerable to shareholders. Conversely, in the United States, where the more fragmented financial landscape defused social democracy "by removing the visible targets" of such a movement, "norms like shareholder-wealth maximization flourished more easily than they otherwise would have," facilitating share dispersal.[34]

This Europe–U.S. comparison would seem to offer strong evidence in favor of the claimed association of left-leaning politics with concentration and stakeholder orientation, and right-leaning politics with dispersal and shareholder orientation – but Roe's theory encounters serious challenges when the comparative analysis focuses within the common-law world. The United Kingdom poses the most glaring problem for Roe, as the best evidence indicates that U.K. share ownership substantially dispersed during a period when social democracy prevailed, contradicting the claimed impact of left-leaning politics.[35] Unlike in the United States, where it is widely accepted that dispersal had occurred by the 1930s,[36] in the United Kingdom the timing is less clear. Roe acknowledges

33 *Id.* at 2–6, 16–17. *See also* Peter A. Gourevitch, *The Politics of Corporate Governance Regulation*, 112 YALE L.J. 1829, 1842, 1855 (2003) (reviewing Roe's book and observing its resemblance to the two equilibria posited by the "Varieties of Capitalism" literature discussed in this chapter).

34 *See* ROE, *supra* note 32, at 71–82, 104–05 (emphasis removed).

35 *See* BRIAN R. CHEFFINS, CORPORATE OWNERSHIP AND CONTROL: BRITISH BUSINESS TRANSFORMED 46–51 (2008).

36 *See, e.g.*, ADOLPH A. BERLE, JR. & GARDINER C. MEANS, THE MODERN CORPORATION AND PRIVATE PROPERTY 47–65 (1932); Brian R. Cheffins, *Corporate Law and Ownership Structure: A Darwinian Link?*, 25 U. NEW S. WALES L.J. 346, 347–48 (2002); Coffee, *supra* note 21, at 24–25. Although it has recently been argued that "most public corporations in the United States have large-percentage shareholders," and that "ownership concentration of U.S. corporations is similar to the ownership concentration of corporations elsewhere," these conclusions largely reflect the use of a low threshold of 5 percent share ownership and inclusion of small public

that "[t]he United Kingdom would seem the hardest case for the political theory" due to its long postwar period of social democracy, yet argues that "Britain's revolution from the right in 1979" upon Margaret Thatcher's election rendered "the fully public diffusely owned firm much more viable than it had been during Britain's social democratic era." In essence, the claim is that ownership fully dispersed only "when Britain moved rightward" in the 1980s.[37] However, although various historians have dated U.K. dispersal from as early as the 1950s to as late as the 1980s,[38] Brian Cheffins's comprehensive review of the available data concludes that by the 1970s concentrated ownership "had become the exception to the rule in large UK companies."[39] Although the later dispersal of U.K. shareholdings undoubtedly holds important comparative implications – helping to explain, for example, why the United Kingdom long resisted U.S.-style double taxation of corporate profits[40] – it does not lend support to Roe's comparative theory of corporate governance, because the

companies. *Compare* Clifford G. Holderness, *The Myth of Diffuse Ownership in the United States*, 22 REV. FIN. STUD. 1377, 1379–82, 1392–95 (2009), *with* Brian R. Cheffins & Steven A. Bank, *Is Berle and Means Really a Myth?*, 83 BUS. HIST. REV. 443, 458, 463–474 (2009).

[37] *See* ROE, *supra* note 32, at 98–103.

[38] *See* Brian R. Cheffins, *Law, Economics and the UK's System of Corporate Governance: Lessons from History*, 1 J. CORP. L. STUD. 71, 80–84 (2001). *See also* CHEFFINS, *supra* note 35, at 11–17 (reviewing various studies and observing "an unfortunate data gap" in the 1950s and 1960s).

[39] *See* CHEFFINS, *supra* note 35, at 11–17, 303–07. Interestingly, the argument that concentrated share ownership persisted as of the mid-1970s appears to have reflected use of a low threshold of 5 percent share ownership, *id.* at 306, much like recent claims to this effect in the United States. *See also* Brian R. Cheffins, *Putting Britain on the Roe Map: The Emergence of the Berle-Means Corporation in the United Kingdom, in* CORPORATE GOVERNANCE REGIMES: CONVERGENCE AND DIVERSITY 147, 160–63 (Joseph A. McCahery et al. eds. 2002). By the same token, it should be observed that Thatcher-era welfare cuts, although quite substantial, did not target core programs such as the National Health Service. *See infra* Chapter 5.A.

[40] *See* STEVEN A. BANK, ANGLO-AMERICAN CORPORATE TAXATION: TRACING THE COMMON ROOTS OF DIVERGENT APPROACHES 142–87 (2011). Bank suggests that the differing pace of share dispersal in the United Kingdom and the United States helps explain their divergent views on entity-level taxation in the early twentieth century, although he warns against overgeneralization:

> In the UK... where large corporations were often controlled by families or individual shareholders, tax measures often favored shareholders. During periods of concern about excessive distributions, though, tax measures were targeted at wealthy shareholders who were suspected of draining the corporate coffers at the expense of both labor and the economic community at large. By contrast, in the USA, where large corporations were often controlled by managers, tax measures often served to protect the corporation from the high graduated marginal rates applicable to individuals. During periods of concern about excessive retentions, though, tax measures were targeted at the entity level to limit the ability of managers to drain the corporate coffers at the expense of shareholders and the economic community at large.

Id. at 181–82. On the potential for convergence of U.K. and U.S. approaches to corporate taxation, see *id.* at 223–49.

dispersal of U.K. shareholdings was substantially complete prior to the shift away from social democracy in British politics.

More generally, although Roe's theory would seem to explain the position of any one of the common-law countries examined in this book vis-à-vis the radically different approaches taken in continental Europe, it cannot explain the positions of the common-law countries vis-à-vis each other. For example, the United Kingdom, which (as we have seen) is far more shareholder-centric than the United States, is also more left-leaning in its domestic politics. An *Economist*-commissioned poll of U.K. and U.S. views on various "social, political and economic matters" conducted in March 2008 found that "Britons tend to have more left-wing views than Americans," with "left" defined to mean "a big-state, secular, socially liberal, internationalist and green outlook."[41] More recently, the *New York Times* similarly observed in April 2011 that the British Conservative Party's tolerance of a 50 percent tax rate on the wealthy "suggest[s] that even Europe's most conservative party is markedly to the left of the mainstream Republican position in the United States, and in some ways is more liberal than the position Mr. Obama has taken."[42] As discussed in the next chapter, Australia and Canada, like the United Kingdom, have similarly demonstrated greater commitment to social democracy while exhibiting stronger shareholder-centrism in their corporate governance systems – none of which would be predicted by Roe's theory. Moreover, Roe cannot account for the fact that, notwithstanding their higher levels of shareholder-centrism, Australia, Canada, and the United Kingdom all exhibit higher levels of share concentration than the United States does.[43] These apparent anomalies

[41] *Anglo-Saxon Attitudes*, ECONOMIST, Mar. 29, 2008, at 71.

[42] Landon Thomas Jr., *Pain of British Fiscal Cuts Could Inform U.S. Debate*, N.Y. TIMES, Apr. 14, 2011, http://www.nytimes.com/2011/04/15/business/global/15iht-pound15.html.

[43] Gourevitch and Shinn report that, although just 15 percent of listed companies in the United States have a 20-percent blockholder, the levels of concentration are 23.6 percent in the United Kingdom, and 27.5 percent in Australia and Canada. *See* GOUREVITCH & SHINN, *supra* note 24, at 16–20. On share concentration in Australia, see generally Geof Stapledon, *Share Ownership and Control in Listed Australian Companies* (Apr. 1999), http://ssrn.com/abstract=164129. *See also* Anderson et al., *supra* note 23, at 191-92; Brian R. Cheffins, *Corporate Governance Convergence: Lessons from Australia*, 16 TRANSNAT'L LAW. 13, 21 (2002); Alan Dignam, *The Role of Competition in Determining Corporate Governance Outcomes: Lessons from Australia's Corporate Governance System*, 68 MOD. L. REV. 765, 769–71 (2005); Jennifer G. Hill, *The Architecture of Corporate Governance in Australia* 2 (Univ. Sydney Law Sch. Legal Studies Research Paper No. 10/75, 2010), http://ssrn.com/abstract=1657810; Jennifer G. Hill, Ronald W. Masulis & Randall S. Thomas, *Comparing CEO Employment Contract Provisions: Differences between Australia and the United States*, 64 VAND. L. REV. 559, 561 (2011). On share concentration in Canada, see Brian R. Cheffins, *Current Trends in Corporate Governance: Going from London to Milan via Toronto*, 10 DUKE J. COMP. & INT'L L. 5, 36 (1999); Jeffrey G. MacIntosh, *Institutional Shareholders and Corporate Governance in Canada*, 26 CAN. BUS. L.J.

strongly suggest that a different approach is required to explain the impact of social democracy, and politics generally, on corporate governance and capital markets within the common-law world.

III. Institutions

Recall Coffee's observation that legal rules favoring minority shareholders in the United Kingdom and the United States actually emerged after share ownership had already substantially dispersed, suggesting that a sufficiently motivated and powerful constituency "must first arise before it can become an effective lobbying force and an instrument of legal change."[44] Consistent with this insight, some have focused their attention on discerning how and why institutional shareholders, in particular, rose to prominence, and the impact they have had on the degree of shareholder-centrism exhibited by various corporate governance systems – a particularly promising approach in the United Kingdom and the United States, where events unfolded quite differently in this regard. In the United States, populist New Deal–era banking and securities laws long inhibited the growth of U.S. financial institutions,[45] and institutional shareholders achieved their current prominence only in the 1990s, by which time laws restricting the size and geographic scope of financial institutions had substantially unwound.[46] In the United Kingdom, on the other hand, investor composition "changed radically" in the years following World War II "as retail investors became persistent net sellers of equity" and "[p]ension funds and insurance companies largely filled the gap."[47] As John Armour and David

145, 149, 155–58 (1995–96); Randall K. Morck, Michael Percy, Gloria Y. Tian & Bernard Yeung, *The Rise and Fall of the Widely Held Firm: A History of Corporate Ownership in Canada*, *in* A History of Corporate Governance around the World: Family Business Groups to Professional Managers 65, 98–102, 110 (Randall K. Morck ed., 2005).

44 Coffee, *supra* note 21, at 7.

45 *See generally* Mark J. Roe, Strong Managers, Weak Owners: The Political Roots of American Corporate Finance (1994).

46 *See* John Armour & David A. Skeel, Jr., *Who Writes the Rules for Hostile Takeovers, and Why? – The Peculiar Divergence of U.S. and U.K. Takeover Regulation*, 95 Geo. L.J. 1727, 1767 (2007); Christopher M. Bruner, *The Enduring Ambivalence of Corporate Law*, 59 Ala. L. Rev. 1385, 1432–35 (2008); Christopher M. Bruner, *Corporate Governance Reform in a Time of Crisis*, 36 J. Corp. L. 309, 312–13 (2011).

47 Cheffins, *supra* note 35, at 87. *See also* Armour & Skeel, *supra* note 46, at 1768–69. John Armour and Jeffrey Gordon argue that a U.S. distrust of financial institutions resulted in use of the "retail investor as its regulatory heuristic," leading to regulatory emphasis on disclosure and "aggressive enforcement," but weak governance powers. The U.K. facilitation of institutional investment, meanwhile, led to stronger governance powers but less regulatory reliance on disclosure. *See* John Armour & Jeffrey N. Gordon, The Berle-Means Corporation in the 21st Century 3–4 (2008) (unpublished manuscript) (on file with the author).

Skeel explain, this was essentially "an unintended consequence of various legislative measures that had the effect of actively promoting [institutional] ownership of stock" – most significantly, the differential between individual income tax rates, which remained very high until Thatcher's election, and the more favorable tax treatment of institutions such as insurance companies, which were taxed at a lower rate, and pension funds, which remained exempt from taxes on investment income until 1997.[48] Family blockholders facing high dividend, income, and estate tax rates in the postwar years had strong incentives to sell their stock, and the institutions stepped forward as ready buyers.[49]

Armour and Skeel compellingly argue that U.K. institutions' early rise to prominence figured centrally in the coalescence of a strongly shareholder-centric U.K. takeover regime. Unlike in the United States, where the fragmentation of finance largely undercut the potential for market-based self-regulation, leaving takeovers to state courts where boards benefitted from "a structural bias in favor of the directors,"[50] in the United Kingdom the prominence of the institutions encouraged reliance on the market to police itself – an approach leaving institutional shareholders well-placed to advance their own interests. "In a range of different contexts," Armour and Skeel observe, dominant U.K. institutions "have been active either in lobbying regulators or in seeding market norms," and given their "clear interest in rules that maximize expected gains to shareholders, it is not surprising that the emergence of a pro-shareholder approach to takeover regulation coincided with the emergence of institutional investors as a significant force in British share ownership."[51] From this perspective, they argue, "the regulatory mode" in each country would appear to be "the largely unintended consequence of regulation designed to achieve other objectives."[52]

I have no fundamental problem with this argument, so far as it goes. In fact, I broadly accept it, and agree that there must be room for serendipity in any plausible account of the evolution of corporate governance. Nevertheless, Armour and Skeel's institutional approach provides an incomplete account, leaving many questions unanswered. For example, the early rise to prominence of institutional shareholders helps illuminate the emergence of strongly pro-shareholder political forces, as they suggest, yet cannot illuminate

[48] *See* Armour & Skeel, *supra* note 46, at 1768–69. *See also* CHEFFINS, *supra* note 35, at 341–49.

[49] *See* CHEFFINS, *supra* note 35, at 323–28, 344–46. *See also* Ruth V. Aguilera, Cynthia A. Williams, John M. Conley & Deborah E. Rupp, *Corporate Governance and Social Responsibility: A Comparative Analysis of the UK and the US*, 14 CORP. GOVERNANCE: AN INT'L REV.147, 149–51 (2006) (contrasting the dominance of insurers and pensions in the United Kingdom with the dominance of mutual funds and investment advisors in the United States).

[50] *See* Armour & Skeel, *supra* note 46, at 1781–84.

[51] *See id.* at 1756–64, 1771–72.

[52] *See id.* at 1784.

the absence of countervailing forces sufficient to overcome (or substantially blunt) pro-shareholder efforts. Put differently, the emergence of a strongly pro-shareholder takeover regime requires not only a pro-shareholder impetus, but broad political acceptability of the pro-shareholder agenda. Likewise, such a regime – once created – can be expected to endure only if it remains broadly compatible with prevailing social views, politics, and related regulatory structures.[53] As Roe observes, "[b]efore a nation can produce, it must achieve social peace," a goal requiring different things of corporate governance in different countries at different times.[54] Should the corporate governance system fall out of sync with the prevailing politics – even if only because of changes in the political or regulatory background conditions – then we can expect some degree of "backlash" against the corporate governance system itself. "Corporate structures," Roe insightfully concludes, are "resolved continually, not sequentially, with some packages more stable than others."[55] As Gourevitch and Shinn add, "[a]nything that shapes wealth, opportunities, stability, and corruption is sure to attract the concerns of the powerful and provoke the anxiety of the weak." Predictably, then, all have "a stake in the corporate governance system" and "an interest in how it is structured."[56]

The upshot is that one cannot fully explain the emergence or persistence of shareholder-centric corporate governance structures solely by reference to pro-shareholder forces. As the events described in the next chapter vividly illustrate, varying degrees of shareholder-centrism in the common-law world have as much – and possibly more – to do with the range of political forces and regulatory regimes that condition the interests and incentives of other corporate stakeholders and political constituencies.

IV. *"Varieties of Capitalism" and Institutional Complementarities*

Like Roe, others have investigated how corporate governance might relate to external regulatory domains and the interests of other stakeholders. Whereas Roe focuses on how external regulation may impede the emergence of shareholder-centrism, arguing that social democracy undermines incentives to unwind controlling equity stakes, the "Varieties of Capitalism," or VOC,

[53] *See* Peter A. Hall & David Soskice, *An Introduction to Varieties of Capitalism, in* VARIETIES OF CAPITALISM: THE INSTITUTIONAL FOUNDATIONS OF COMPARATIVE ADVANTAGE 1, 13–14 (Peter A. Hall & David Soskice eds., 2001).

[54] ROE, *supra* note 32, at 1.

[55] *Id.* at 120. *See also* Peter A. Hall & Kathleen Thelen, *Institutional Change in Varieties of Capitalism*, 7 SOCIO-ECON. REV. 7, 11–15 (2009).

[56] GOUREVITCH & SHINN, *supra* note 24, at 3.

literature focuses more broadly on the complementarity of certain regulatory approaches across differing domestic legal domains in solving social problems. VOC places corporate governance within the larger context of various "spheres in which firms must develop relationships to resolve coordination problems central to their core competencies," including industrial relations, vocational training, relations with other firms (such as customers and suppliers), and coordination with and among employees.[57] Scholars associated with VOC strongly emphasize the significance of "institutional complementarities" among institutions from these differing spheres of the political economy – effectively synergistic relationships where "the presence (or efficiency) of one [institution] increases the returns from (or efficiency of) the other" – and suggest that "nations with a particular type of coordination in one sphere of the economy should tend to develop complementary practices in other spheres as well."[58] Ultimately they argue that such complementarities can foster "comparative institutional advantage" of one sort or another at the firm level, the idea being that "the institutional structure of a particular political economy provides firms with advantages for engaging in specific types of activities there."[59]

The VOC approach, much like the "law matters" theory and Roe's social democracy theory, posits two equilibria through which countries manage coordination problems across spheres of the political economy and derive comparative institutional advantages through their complementarities – so-called coordinated market economies, or CMEs, and so-called liberal market economies, or LMEs. In a CME, such as Germany, companies typically rely on cooperative "non-market" coordination mechanisms to incentivize stable, long-term, firm-specific investment. In an LME, such as the United States, companies typically rely on "competitive" market-based exchanges, favoring shareholders' interests and labor market flexibility.[60] This framework offers the great strength of acknowledging how policies pursued in various regulatory domains can synergistically reinforce one another, illustrating that none of these domains can be fully understood in isolation.

Like the "law matters" theory and Roe's social democracy theory, however, VOC's pursuit of a single, holistic global theory leads it to lump together

[57] Hall & Soskice, *supra* note 53, at 6–7.

[58] *Id.* at 17–18.

[59] *Id.* at 37.

[60] *Id.* at 8–10, 17–33. *See also* PEPPER D. CULPEPPER, QUIET POLITICS AND BUSINESS POWER: CORPORATE CONTROL IN EUROPE AND JAPAN 35–36 (2011) (observing that Australia, Canada, Ireland, the United Kingdom, and the United States – the countries with "the most active markets for corporate control" among those considered – also exhibit the least "patient capital," just as "the varieties of capitalism suggests that they would"); Gourevitch, *supra* note 33, at 1842 (observing that the two equilibria posited by Roe resemble those posited by VOC); Hall & Thelen, *supra* note 55, at 9–11.

common-law countries that, as we have already seen, differ markedly from one another in fundamental respects. Australia, Canada, the United Kingdom, and the United States are, as one would predict based on the foregoing description, all categorized as LMEs.[61] This categorization would appear to offer substantial explanatory power at the global level, as the stylized comparison of Germany and the United States suggests.[62] Much like Roe's theory, however, VOC's binary distinction between CMEs and LMEs can explain the position of any of the common-law countries vis-à-vis the radically different system of Germany, yet provides no clear means of explaining the positions of the common-law countries vis-à-vis each other.

To be sure, Peter Hall and David Soskice – in their introduction to their well-known VOC volume – acknowledge that they deal in "broad differences," that "there will be additional variation in corporate strategies inside all economies in keeping with differences in the resource endowments and market settings of individual firms," and that "the relevant institutions [may] depend heavily on statutes or regulations promulgated by national states, as do many institutions in the financial arena and labor market."[63] Generalizations, however, remain difficult to resist – as when LMEs are broadly described as "tolerant of . . . the hostile takeovers that become a prospect when the market valuation of a firm declines." They rightly clarify that "[t]he relevant contrast is with CMEs,"[64] implicitly acknowledging that such generalizations offer no insight into the markedly divergent levels of comfort with hostile takeovers among the common-law countries themselves. As with Roe's social democracy theory, this strongly suggests that a more nuanced approach is required to explain how various regulatory approaches across the political economy interact – and more specifically, how they affect corporate governance and capital markets – within the common-law world.

Alan Dignam and Michael Galanis offer a potential refinement of the VOC approach, building on the concept of institutional complementarities and the LME/CME distinction while emphasizing the VOC literature's failure to address transnational variables impacting corporate governance. They agree that "institutions, especially formal ones, are often shaped so as to be compatible and often reinforce each other," and that "the nature of the corporate governance system is shaped by the institutional environment in which it operates," leading them to take a broad view of the spheres of regulation relevant to a study of corporate governance – including not only corporate law and the financial system, but also industrial relations and "the government

[61] *See* Hall & Soskice, *supra* note 53, at 19–20.
[62] *See id.* at 21–33.
[63] *See id.* at 15–16.
[64] *See id.* at 27–29.

demand function."[65] They criticize VOC, however, for focusing excessively on "national institutional structures," arguing that the comparative institutional advantages of LMEs and CMEs may be heavily impacted by transnational economic and financial forces.[66]

Much like the "law matters" theory, Roe's social democracy theory, and the VOC literature, Dignam and Galanis posit two equilibria. Specifically, they contrast the "outsider shareholder model" embraced by the United Kingdom and the United States – based on "a market-based financial system with powerful institutional shareholders enhancing stock market efficiency, on flexible labour markets and on a strict competition policy regime that prevents managers from forming inter-corporate alliances to insulate themselves from market disciplines" – with the "insider model" embraced by Germany, which permits "enhanced managerial discretion" based on "a financial system that enhances long-term commitment between financial and productive capital, an industrial relations system that facilitates labour market internalization by providing formal and informal mechanisms for cooperation and conflict resolution between employers and employees, and a competition policy regime that allows inter-firm cooperation." Each, they argue, has historically constituted a "workable" combination of regulatory structures and strategies.[67]

Dignam and Galanis rightly emphasize the significance of institutional complementarities between corporate governance and other domestic regulatory domains, while highlighting important transnational factors not effectively addressed by the VOC literature. Ultimately, however, a similarly rigid binary distinction, coupled with the centrality of macroeconomic shock in their account of the evolution of U.K. and U.S. corporate governance, renders their approach unable to account for the substantial divergences in shareholder governance powers across common-law countries. Dignam and Galanis argue that from the interwar years through the 1950s the United Kingdom and the United States "moved deeper into the insider paradigm" as their governments' economic roles expanded and labor power increased. Both countries, they contend, later began the transition to "outsider" systems – requiring "a core managerial focus on shareholders" – only following the economic shocks of the 1970s and 1980s, by which time "labour and government were significantly reduced as an influence on managerial discretion."[68] Critically, however, Dignam and Galanis offer no explanation for the enormous divergence in

[65] *See* Dignam & Galanis, *supra* note 2, at 51–53.

[66] *See id.* at 160–61, 224–25.

[67] *See id.* at 86–88.

[68] *See id.* at 224–25, 262. *See also* John W. Cioffi, Public Law and Private Power: Corporate Governance Reform in the Age of Finance Capitalism 26 (2010).

hostile takeover regulation; they offer no account of the coalescence of a strongly shareholder-centric regime in the United Kingdom before the relevant period of macroeconomic shock and, conversely, the coalescence of a strongly stakeholder-centric regime in the United States well after its onset – both of which stand in tension with the claim that the two countries similarly adopted pro-shareholder "outsider" systems in the 1980s.[69] They suggest that U.S. case law and statutes permitting wide latitude in the use of takeover defenses merely "raise the price necessary to succeed in a bid rather than necessarily defeat a bid," ignoring Delaware's de facto embrace of the "just say no" defense in *Paramount v. Time*. Similarly, in characterizing such moves as "managers' defenses," they ignore the interests of employees and other stakeholders who share managers' strong preference for stability in this context, as well as the range of political factors that led to these developments.[70]

Dignam and Galanis do cite these post-1980 decisions and statutes as indicating that "US corporate law has been somewhat anti-shareholder in its tendency,"[71] but of course this tends to contradict their core historical claims. Similarly, they do ultimately concede that U.K. shareholders' long-standing removal right indicates that U.K. company law is "arguably more shareholder oriented" than is U.S. corporate law[72] – a position reflecting the fundamental shareholder-centrism widely ascribed to U.K. corporate governance. Indeed, Dignam suggests in his treatise (with John Lowry) that the U.K. shareholders' unilateral ability to amend the constitution and to remove directors without cause – both of which long predate the purportedly operative crises – "place the shareholders at the centre of the corporate power structure."[73] This view, shared by other authorities on U.K. company law,[74] casts further doubt on the ability of the Dignam-Galanis framework to explain the sorts of divergences across common-law countries explored here.

69 *Compare* Dignam & Galanis, *supra* note 2, at 219–20 (describing the emergence of the City Code in the 1960s and its "central guiding principle of shareholder decision making") *with* 232–34 (acknowledging that "Delaware courts favoured managers' defences during a bid" in their 1980s takeover jurisprudence).

70 *See id.* at 233–34.

71 *See id.* at 243–44.

72 *See id.* at 244–45.

73 *See* Alan Dignam & John Lowry, Company Law 7–8 (5th ed. 2009). *See also* Paul L. Davies, Gower and Davies' Principles of Modern Company Law 389 (8th ed. 2008) (dating the shareholders' strong removal right to the Companies Act 1948); Malleson v. National Insurance and Guarantee Corp. [1894] 1 Ch. 200 (citing the shareholders' power under the Companies Act 1862 to amend the articles "by passing a special resolution").

74 *See, e.g.*, Davies, *supra* note 73, at 63, 74–76, 371 (explaining that the shareholders' power to control the constitution's content makes them "the ultimate source of managerial authority," and that their removal right creates "a powerful inducement to the directors to follow the line of action preferred by the shareholders").

To be clear, I fully agree with Dignam and Galanis that institutional complementarities across regulatory domains are critical to understanding corporate governance systems, and broadly accept that macroeconomic shocks can destabilize hitherto "workable" equilibria, prompting corporate governance systems to evolve in response. Their binary structure positing just two equilibria, however, leaves Dignam and Galanis – much like the "law matters" theory, Roe's social democracy theory, and the VOC literature – unable to explain substantial divergences across corporate governance systems inhabiting a single category within their framework. Although it is undoubtedly true that, in the 1970s and 1980s, both the United Kingdom and the United States shifted rightward in their politics, carved back at welfare state protections, and saw institutional investors achieve greater dominance in capital markets,[75] it is also the case that U.K. shareholders' corporate governance powers were substantially strengthened during the left-leaning decades prior to Thatcher's election, that U.S. shareholders' powers were expressly limited during the right-leaning years following Ronald Reagan's election, and that U.K. shareholders' powers have vastly exceeded those possessed by their U.S. counterparts throughout.

As I will argue in the next chapter, the crises of the 1970s and 1980s – and the rightward shift in prevailing politics conventionally mapped onto this historical period – do in fact contribute to an explanation of the varying degrees of shareholder-centrism in common-law countries. I argue, however, that it is precisely the differences in the respective political and regulatory background conditions prevailing in the United Kingdom and the United States that most compellingly explain the U.K. shift in favor of shareholders, which occurred during a left-leaning social democratic period, and the U.S. shift in favor of stakeholders, which occurred during a right-leaning period heavily infused with antiwelfare rhetoric. Simply put, in the former scenario, external stakeholder protections were sufficiently strong to deflect stakeholder-oriented political pressures from the corporate governance system, whereas in the latter scenario they were not.

V. *Coalitions*

As Peter Hall and Kathleen Thelen observe, "questions have been raised about the adequacy of the varieties-of-capitalism perspective for understanding institutional change," principally reflecting the view that the LME/CME distinction is "overly static." They rightly acknowledge, however, that "a promising literature in comparative political economy is beginning to link institutional

[75] *See* DIGNAM & GALANIS, *supra* note 2, at 246–61.

analysis to coalitional analysis" as a means of explaining how and why corporate governance systems evolve over time.[76] Perhaps the most influential effort in this vein has been that of Peter Gourevitch and James Shinn.

Building on the strengths of the VOC literature – particularly the concept of institutional complementarity[77] – Gourevitch and Shinn posit a broader and considerably more nuanced range of potential equilibria through the dynamics of coalition formation. Specifically, they examine how corporate governance and ownership structures are impacted by the varying preferences of three groups of corporate stakeholders – managers, shareholders, and employees – and the manner in which coalitions among them are formed. This move represents a substantial advance over the law and economics approach, which as they observe, "focuses on owners and managers" while ignoring employees – "largely because the labor contract is assumed to be complete." As Gourevitch and Shinn rightly emphasize, all three stakeholder groups can, and do, bring their varying preferences to bear on politics and lawmaking, and they join forces in various ways depending on the nature of the issue and the prevailing background conditions.[78]

In their 2005 book, *Political Power and Corporate Control*, Gourevitch and Shinn explore three forms of "cleavages," as they call them, each of which results in one of the three stakeholder groups being isolated against the others – "class conflict" isolates employees against shareholders and managers, whereas "sectoral" isolates shareholders against employees and managers, and "property and voice" isolates managers against shareholders and employees.[79] That these stakeholder groups could form differing coalitions toward differing ends at various times is hardly surprising, given the complexity of each group's interests and preferences. "Owners and managers ally to contain workers' demands on wages and job security; workers and managers combine to secure employment and stable wages in the firm; and workers and owners combine to contain managerial agency costs and preserve the security of their investments and pensions, and even jobs."[80] By positing three forms of coalition-driven "cleavages," and then evaluating potential win–loss scenarios in each case, Gourevitch and Shinn posit six potential equilibria.[81]

Merging the VOC concept of institutional complementarity with this attention to coalition formation represents a substantial advance over other approaches, permitting considerably more nuanced and compelling analyses

[76] *See* Hall & Thelen, *supra* note 55, at 8, 25.
[77] *See* Gourevitch & Shinn, *supra* note 24, at 11, 53.
[78] *See id.* at 8–9.
[79] *See id.* at 59–62.
[80] *See id.* at 8.
[81] *See id.* at 60 (summarizing these equilibria in tabular format).

of stability and change in corporate governance systems.[82] I myself take up these tools in the political analyses presented in the remainder of this book. The manner in which Gourevitch and Shinn categorize various countries within their schema, however, proves overly rigid, limiting the explanatory power of their approach with respect to the divergences observed across common-law countries.

The United Kingdom and the United States are, once again, lumped together, explored by Gourevitch and Shinn through the conceptual lens of "property and voice," emphasizing the isolation of managers against shareholders and employees whose interests increasingly correlate through growing pension fund investment.[83] To be sure, Gourevitch and Shinn recognize that the two countries differ markedly in the corporate governance powers made available to shareholders, acknowledging that "[t]he United Kingdom has more vigorous markets for control, shareholder rights . . . , codes of corporate responsibility on financial and social standards, and active financial intermediaries who press managers." They argue, however, that the greater success of U.K. institutional shareholders reflects the fact that "[t]he United Kingdom is more majoritarian," permitting quicker and more decisive policy shifts. "At the same time," they suggest, "Britain's structures encourage aggregation toward public goods, toward a more general bargain and the common goals," in contrast with the more cumbersome and fragmented U.S. federal structure, "which gives plenty of space to particularistic interests."[84]

Although I broadly agree that issues of federalism have loomed large in the development of U.S. corporate governance (as well as Australian and Canadian corporate governance, for that matter),[85] and although I further agree that the relative alignment of employee interests with those of other stakeholders is critical to understanding numerous corporate governance developments in recent decades, Gourevitch and Shinn's approach cannot explain a number of key divergences among common-law countries. They describe the U.S. legal response to hostile takeovers principally as a manifestation of management entrenchment, devoting little attention to the management–labor coalition that fueled antitakeover laws and associated case law in the 1980s.[86] This is doubly odd, given that their coalition-based approach would seem to offer a

[82] *Cf.* Peter A. Hall, *Historical Institutionalism in Rationalist and Sociological Perspective, in* EXPLAINING INSTITUTIONAL CHANGE: AMBIGUITY, AGENCY, AND POWER 204, 206–16 (James Mahoney & Kathleen Thelen eds., 2010) (similarly emphasizing institutional complementarities and coalition formation in developing an account of institutional stability and change).

[83] *See* GOUREVITCH & SHINN, *supra* note 24, at 61–62, 223–25.

[84] *See id.* at 259–62.

[85] *See infra* Chapter 5.B.-C.

[86] *See* GOUREVITCH & SHINN, *supra* note 24, at 250–54. *See also* Hall, *supra* note 82, at 211–12 (observing that various actors may enter a coalition for differing reasons).

particularly useful framework for understanding the relevant history, and given their own observation elsewhere that employees and shareholders "part company on the rules for takeovers" because of the employees' strong preference for giving managers "latitude to factor in the consequences on employment," regardless of the shareholder wealth impacts.[87] Similarly, the emphasis they place on the United Kingdom's strongly majoritarian parliamentary system leaves unexplored the extent to which shareholder-centric corporate governance structures took shape during the left-leaning decades following World War II, when the U.K. government was (among other things) busy constructing an elaborate welfare state – a development that one would expect to impact the preferences and interests of employees in substantial ways.

The potential for employees to align with management in opposition to perceived hostile interests of shareholders, as well as the impact of social welfare structures on the coalescence of any such coalition, receive sustained attention in the next chapter. For the moment, however, it suffices to suggest that Gourevitch and Shinn may be predisposed to view the U.S. response to hostile takeovers predominantly as a reflection of management entrenchment, and the success of U.K. shareholders predominantly as a reflection of parliamentary lawmaking, because both resistance to hostile takeovers and the construction of a welfare state are phenomena that they associate with successful alignment of managers and employees against shareholders. This, they predict, should result in corporatism and blockholding[88] – a prediction that is clearly not borne out by the United Kingdom or the United States in the relevant periods.

Although Gourevitch and Shinn make a considerable contribution in emphasizing the political dynamics of coalition formation, ultimately their theory exhibits a weakness common to all the political theories explored thus far – the inability to explain fundamental divergences among common-law countries themselves.

[87] Gourevitch & Shinn, *supra* note 24, at 222–23. *See also* Pagano & Volpin, *The Political Economy of Finance*, *supra* note 24, at 506, 510; Marco Pagano & Paolo F. Volpin, *Managers, Workers, and Corporate Control*, 60 J. Fin. 841 (2005).

[88] *See* Gourevitch & Shinn, *supra* note 24, at 149. *See also* Pagano & Volpin, *The Political Economy of Finance*, *supra* note 24, at 508–10. Marco Pagano and Paolo Volpin encounter a similar problem in categorizing various "Anglo-Saxon" political systems as "majoritarian," which they predict should produce "strong shareholder protection and weak employment protection." *See* Pagano & Volpin, *The Political Economy of Corporate Governance*, *supra* note 24, at 1007, 1018–20, 1027. Although this permits globally accurate generalizations regarding how common-law systems differ from others, it provides no means of distinguishing between these common-law systems themselves. Indeed, as we shall see, the United States in fact provides weaker shareholder protections *and* weaker employment protections than other common-law countries, defying their prediction. *See infra* Chapter 5.A.-C.

VI. *Political Parties and Political Salience*

An alternative approach places political *parties* at the heart of the action. John Cioffi and Martin Höpner have argued that, across a striking range of countries, "center-left parties and politicians have often been instrumental proponents of [pro-shareholder corporate governance] reform, while conservative parties and politicians have typically resisted reform and defended the interests of incumbent managers."[89] In the United States, for example, they point to the Sarbanes-Oxley Act of 2002, the passage of which they characterize as "Democrats us[ing] the post-bubble scandals and the collapse of share prices to attack a deeply conservative and pro-manager Republican leadership and as a well-placed appeal to middle-class voters in a country where mass shareholding was well established."[90] This account, they argue, stands in tension with the VOC literature's emphasis on "self-reinforcing institutional complementarities," and contradicts Roe's claim that "shareholder protections weaken . . . with the political strength of the labor movement and social democratic parties."[91] Likewise, they suggest, such developments cannot be attributed to a "transparency coalition" of employees and shareholders under Gourevitch and Shinn's schema "because shareholding remained undeveloped in our European cases and codetermination is far stronger in Germany than elsewhere."[92] Cioffi and Höpner concede that union pension funds "have long been the most activist investors in [U.S.] corporate governance," and acknowledge that they remain "closely tied to their founding unions and the AFL-CIO, which . . . remain core contributors and voting constituencies of the Democratic Party," but argue that labor unions and their pension funds have not played decisive roles in bringing about corporate governance reform in recent decades.[93] Rather, they argue, shareholder-centric reforms arose from the center-left because the center-right was constrained by strong political and class ties with managers, whereas the center-left was "induced . . . to embrace corporate governance reform" as a means of improving their "electoral competitiveness" – notably by articulating an agenda that would simultaneously "cast it as a force of economic modernization, resonate with centrist middle-class voters, and still appeal to a left-wing and working-class electoral base." In

[89] John W. Cioffi & Martin Höpner, *The Political Paradox of Finance Capitalism: Interests, Preferences, and Center-Left Party Politics in Corporate Governance Reform*, 34 Pol. & Soc'y 463, 464 (2006). Cioffi and Höpner investigate the United States, Germany, France, and Italy. In subsequent work focusing on the United States and Germany, Cioffi similarly emphasizes the role of center-left parties. *See* Cioffi, *supra* note 68, at 8–10, 36–37, 235–36.

[90] Cioffi & Höpner, *supra* note 89, at 484. *See also* Cioffi, *supra* note 68, at 108–21.

[91] Cioffi & Höpner, *supra* note 89, at 465.

[92] *Id.* at 501 n.99.

[93] *Id.* at 484, 501 n.99.

this light, Democrats could capitalize on "an increase in shareholding among the public and the looming importance of securities market investments as a component of national retirement and pensions systems," which "gave the center-left an opportunity to fashion a corporate governance agenda consistent with more traditional anti-elite and pro-welfare state political appeals."[94]

Cioffi and Höpner cast considerable light on an underappreciated aspect of recent corporate governance reforms, but their strong emphasis on the role of political parties, as such, in shareholder-centric corporate governance reforms provides no clear means of explaining the core divergences in power and purpose among common-law countries discussed here. Aside from the fact that the study aims to explore commonalities in party politics across various countries, the selection of countries (Germany, France, Italy, and the United States) implicitly encourages generalizations about Anglo-American corporate governance and finance of the sort described above by focusing on one common-law country as "the archetype of modern finance capitalism."[95] In a similar spirit, Cioffi's more recent work comparing U.S. and German corporate governance reforms encourages generalizations about "the Anglo-American governance model"[96] and broad contrasts between continental stakeholder-centrism and U.S. shareholder-centrism.[97] In neither case are the substantial divergences with respect to shareholder power and purpose among common-law countries themselves the subject of sustained examination.

More critically, however, Cioffi and Höpner's association of right-leaning parties with managers and left-leaning parties with shareholders proves overly rigid when one takes a longer historical view. Although the Republican party may well have "much closer ties to business interests and corporate managers in terms of both policy orientation and electoral support than do the Democrats"[98] as a general matter, Republicans have supported strongly pro-shareholder positions vociferously opposed by managers at critical points in the development of U.S. corporate governance – notably the Reagan administration's support of an unfettered market for corporate control, a partisan inconsistency acknowledged by Cioffi in later work.[99] Cioffi and Höpner's account offers no explanation for the formation of the U.S. takeover regime in

[94] *Id.* at 484–90. *See also* Martin Gelter, *The Pension System and the Rise of Shareholder Primacy* 4–5, 29–30 (Fordham Univ. Sch. of Law Working Paper Series, 2012), http://ssrn.com/abstract=2079607.

[95] Cioffi & Höpner, *supra* note 89, at 480.

[96] *See* Cioffi, *supra* note 68, at 4.

[97] *See id.* at 240.

[98] Cioffi & Höpner, *supra* note 89, at 486–87.

[99] *See* Cioffi, *supra* note 68, at 87 (observing "the largely pro-takeover Reagan administration and SEC" of the 1980s). *See also* Culpepper, *supra* note 60, at 15 ("Among partisan theorists, there is . . . disagreement over whether we should expect political challenges to passive markets for corporate control to come from parties of the *right* or from parties of the *left*.").

the 1980s, perhaps reflecting the fact that fundamental aspects of state corporate law, conditioned by the complex federalist balance of the U.S. corporate governance system, do not lend themselves to straightforward analysis through the lens of national party politics to the degree that issues of federal securities regulation do.[100] Indeed, as Cioffi observes in his recent study of U.S. and German corporate governance reforms since the 1990s, "[s]ecurities law and disclosure regulation have undergone the most pronounced pro-shareholder reforms," while "company law has experienced more limited change," eliciting "intense political conflict over the substance and extent of reform."[101]

To be sure, their emphasis of the Democrats' appeal to middle class voters in the wake of the corporate meltdowns of the early 2000s through development of an agenda speaking at once to their investment and social welfare–related goals and concerns is a compelling one, and strongly resonates with the account I offer later in this book of shareholder-centric reforms following the recent financial crisis. Ultimately, however, I conclude that the interests and incentives of employees, in particular, offer greater explanatory power than party politics, rendering shareholder-centric reforms in the wake of Enron, as well as those following the recent financial crisis, fully consistent with the politics that drove the adoption of a stakeholder-centric takeover regime in the 1980s. Just as a perceived shareholder-based threat to workers' interests led to an employee-manager coalition to restrain takeovers in the 1980s, perceived manager-based threats to workers' interests led to employee-shareholder coalitions to constrain managerial recklessness in the 2000s.[102] Truly operative here, politically, are the interests of middle class workers, which have been substantially impacted by the relative strength of extra-corporate stakeholder protections, notably social welfare protections. As the next chapter explores, although protections of the sort that have deflected political pressure from the corporate governance system in other countries – permitting shareholder-centrism to flourish to a greater extent than it has in the United States – may broadly be associated with left-leaning politics, neither social welfare-oriented programs nor shareholder-centrism in corporate governance uniformly map

[100] *Cf.* Cioffi & Höpner, *supra* note 89, at 480–84 (identifying the takeover battles of the 1980s as background for analysis of securities regulatory reforms since the 1990s).

[101] CIOFFI, *supra* note 68, at 12.

[102] *See infra* Chapter 6.D. *See also* Gerhard Schnyder, *Revisiting the Party Paradox of Finance Capitalism: Social Democratic Preferences and Corporate Governance Reforms in Switzerland, Sweden, and the Netherlands*, 44 COMP. POL. STUD. 184 (2011) (similarly questioning the ability of Cioffi and Höpner's "party paradox" thesis to explain reform efforts in the Netherlands and Sweden, where "a broad coalition uniting center-right and center-left parties opposed – with considerable success – proshareholder reforms," and arguing that "the historical role of labor . . . is critical in the formation of center-left preferences").

onto the left–right divide in so clean a manner as Cioffi and Höpner's approach would presumably predict.

Recognizing the difficulty of mapping corporate governance initiatives onto a strict left–right party spectrum, Pepper Culpepper has offered an alternative view of the role of partisan politics. In his study of hostile takeover regulation in France, Germany, Japan, and the Netherlands, Culpepper acknowledges that if "the policy salience of a corporate governance issue becomes high and stays high," then "the role of political parties, and the differences between parties of the left and the right, . . . become[s] important" – a dynamic exemplified in the United States by the heated debate in recent decades over executive compensation.[103] He argues, however, that corporate governance normally remains a matter of "low political salience," a condition favoring managers better able to pursue their interests behind the scenes than other constituencies are. Specifically, he argues that "organized managers typically prevail in political conflicts over corporate control because those issues are of little immediate interest to most voters," permitting the managers' superior lobbying capabilities to work unopposed.[104] This mode of "quiet politics" is all the more effective, Culpepper argues, when a given matter is addressed through "informal" institutions, where opposing viewpoints are more easily marginalized and politicians need only be persuaded not to intervene.[105]

Although the notion that low-versus-high political salience and informal-versus-formal rulemaking could systematically affect the role of party politics in corporate governance reform has strong intuitive appeal, Culpepper's application of this framework to the development of rules governing hostile takeovers would appear to be flatly contradicted by the United Kingdom and the United States alike. Culpepper concludes, following analyses of reform efforts in France, Germany, Japan, and the Netherlands, that managers "tend to dominate" when a matter of low political salience is governed by an informal regime, while at the other extreme – a matter of high political salience governed by a formal regime – the "arena of struggle is the parliament as well as the court of public opinion, as parties battle to secure support in the electorate to be able to pass their preferred laws."[106] This schema would naturally lead one to predict that U.K. takeover regulation – which took shape through an informal regime in a context of relatively lower political salience – should strongly favor managers, whereas U.S. takeover regulation – which took shape through formal law in a context of relatively higher political salience – should not. The reality, however, as we have seen, is precisely the opposite. The formal

[103] CULPEPPER, *supra* note 60, at 145–47.
[104] *Id.* at 4.
[105] *Id.* at 55.
[106] *Id.* at 181.

U.S. approach strongly favors managers, notwithstanding the intense glare of state and federal politics that attended its development, and the informal U.K. approach strongly favors shareholders, contradicting the claim that managers systematically prevail in backroom settings involving "quiet politics."

It would appear that neither strict left–right party politics, nor the political salience of the issues in question, are sufficient to explain the divergence among common-law corporate governance systems explored here. This, I argue, requires more direct attention to how the various corporate constituencies themselves conceptualize and pursue their interests in varying circumstances.

VII. *Extra-Corporate Stakeholder Protections*

We have already observed that economically oriented theorists argue for exclusive orientation of corporate decision making toward the shareholders' interests based in part on the claim that other stakeholders are sufficiently well positioned to negotiate contractual protection and to lobby for regulatory protection. Although this claim reflects at least an implicit recognition of a broader balance or equilibrium to be struck across forces internal and external to corporate law, nexus scholars nevertheless routinely fail to grapple with the complex ways in which shareholder-centric corporate governance structures interact with external stakeholder protections, typically assuming that the latter can be addressed completely independently of the corporate governance system itself.[107] As Gourevitch and Shinn observe, employees are the most glaring omission from this law and economics–based corporate governance equation. "They are often left out of models of corporate governance, largely because the labor contract is assumed to be complete" – an assumption that remains "contestable" in its own right, and that "does not at any rate fully cover the power of employees or the need for management and owners to have a well-functioning workforce."[108]

[107] *See, e.g.*, FRANK H. EASTERBROOK & DANIEL R. FISCHEL, THE ECONOMIC STRUCTURE OF CORPORATE LAW 38 (1991) ("We do not address optimal ways to deal with pollution, bribery, plant closings, and other decisions that have effects on people who may not participate in the corporate contract."); Henry Hansmann & Reinier Kraakman, *The End of History for Corporate Law*, 89 GEO. L.J. 439, 449 (2001) (assuming that the interests of non-shareholders "can generally be given substantial protection by contract and regulation"). On this tendency, see John Parkinson, *Corporate Governance: The Company Law Review and Questions of 'Scope,'* 8 HUME PAPERS ON PUB. POL'Y 29, 43–44 (2000).

[108] GOUREVITCH & SHINN, *supra* note 24, at 8. *See also* David Millon, *Default Rules, Wealth Distribution, and Corporate Law Reform: Employment at Will versus Job Security*, 146 U. PA. L. REV. 975, 987–89 (1998).

The reality is that regulatory structures internal and external to corporate governance respond to one another in a dynamic process – and as I will argue in the remainder of this book, it is only by reference to their interaction that varying degrees of shareholder-centrism in common-law corporate governance systems can be understood. In this light, my argument dovetails with a growing comparative corporate governance literature focusing on the relationship between shareholder-centric corporate laws and extra-corporate stakeholder protections. Martin Gelter, for example, argues that "stronger shareholder influence" – defined broadly to include structural power possessed through blockholding – "implies a greater risk of expropriation for stakeholders, such as employees," and that countries have managed this problem in various ways that respond to their share ownership structures.[109] In Europe, where blockholding remains widespread, the substantial risk of expropriation faced by employees has been addressed through stakeholder-friendly directors' duties, employee governance powers (including through board representation, as in Germany), and employment laws that make it "difficult and costly to lay off workers."[110] In the United States, where shares are highly dispersed, employee vulnerability has been addressed through broad managerial discretion to deviate from the shareholders' interests to accommodate those of other constituencies.[111] Meanwhile the United Kingdom – where stock ownership is highly dispersed, but less so than in the United States – falls in the middle, exhibiting intermediate levels of shareholder influence (with stronger shareholder governance rights than in the United States but fewer blockholders than in Europe) and intermediate levels of employment protections as well.[112]

In dispersed and concentrated ownership systems alike, Gelter argues, stakeholder-centric rules took shape in response to preexisting ownership structures and associated levels of shareholder influence.[113] It is a compelling argument, and appears well-founded if one focuses on employment protections, the form of stakeholder protection of interest to Gelter. Taking into account a broader array of stakeholder protections, however, renders the picture considerably more complex, and in fact tends to suggest that the effects of external regulation upon corporate governance in the common-law world differ systematically from what one observes elsewhere.

Gelter rightly notes that stakeholder-friendly employment protections chronologically follow the prevailing concentrated ownership structure in

[109] Gelter, *supra* note 4, at 144.

[110] *Id.* at 168–76. *See also* Marianna Belloc & Ugo Pagano, *Co-Evolution of Politics and Corporate Governance*, 29 Int'l Rev. L. & Econ. 106 (2009).

[111] *See* Gelter, *supra* note 4, at 148–54.

[112] *See id.* at 186–93.

[113] *See id.* at 181–93.

Europe as a matter of course, for the simple reason that blockholding, "the international norm," represents "the primeval state of any corporate governance system." Insofar as businesses begin their lives with concentrated stock ownership and go public only later, if at all, "it is not the persistence of concentrated ownership, but rather its unraveling in the United States and the United Kingdom that calls for an explanation."[114] On this score, I argue, a more embracing concept of relevant stakeholder protections reveals that shareholder-centric structures in the United Kingdom and the United States – as well as in Australia and Canada – have in fact coevolved in tandem with extra-corporate protections for employees. Indeed, strong welfare state structures largely predated the emergence of the strong shareholder-centric corporate governance rules that we found in Australia, Canada, and the United Kingdom, and conversely there is evidence that the absence of strong welfare state structures has loomed large in the rejection of strong-form shareholder-centrism in the United States. To this extent, welfare state structures of the sort investigated in the next chapter, unlike the employment protections upon which Gelter focuses, could aptly be characterized as a form of what David Millon calls "precontractual" state action – state action outside the corporate governance system that conditions how various stakeholders, including employees, formulate their interests and bring them to bear upon public corporations.[115] Welfare state structures, I argue, are not simply reactions to static, preexisting corporate governance systems and capital market structures. They in fact represent a crucial element of the explanation for how common-law corporate governance systems came to take the forms they have – including their disparate degrees of shareholder-centrism.

C. TOWARD A POLITICAL THEORY OF CORPORATE GOVERNANCE IN THE COMMON-LAW WORLD

In developing the comparative theory that follows, I part ways – to greater or lesser extents – with all of the foregoing economic and political theories. I reject the functionalist assumptions underlying contemporary economic theories of corporate governance, permitting assessment of the degree to which the substantial divergences in power and purpose among these common-law legal systems reflect not differing degrees of success by some universal

[114] *Id.* at 182. *See also* Lucian Arye Bebchuk & Mark J. Roe, *A Theory of Path Dependence in Corporate Ownership and Governance*, 52 STAN. L. REV. 127, 139–53 (1999) (discussing potential explanations for "structure-driven path dependence").

[115] *See* Millon, *supra* note 108, at 990–92 (describing employment at will as a "precontractual" default rule that conditions potential contractual outcomes).

policy metric, but rather differences in what each society expects corporate governance – and public corporations – to achieve. Put differently, I explore the degree to which regulatory divergences reflect variation in the social needs and problems that each society aims to manage through its corporate governance system, an inquiry requiring sustained attention to historical, cultural, and political context. Taking as my independent variable the broader prevailing politics of social welfare – a dynamic set of processes that constantly evolves as society and the economy evolve – permits a much more nuanced exploration of why divergences have emerged among these otherwise similar corporate governance systems, how corporate governance has changed over time in each country, and how these systems may develop in the future. At the same time, I believe that focusing the analysis on a specific set of political forces and issues – those concerning the welfare state and related structures impacting social welfare protections available to non-shareholders – offers substantial explanatory power while avoiding excessive contingency.

My theory builds on the foregoing political theories in important respects. First and foremost, these theories all demonstrate the centrality of politics in the formation of corporate governance systems, emphasizing that these systems cannot be understood in isolation from larger social dynamics and other forms of regulation affecting relationships among stakeholders in the corporation. The recognition of institutional complementarity across regulatory systems – a concept figuring centrally, in one way or another, in the VOC literature as well as the theories developed by Roe, Dignam and Galanis, Gourevitch and Shinn, and Gelter – likewise figures centrally in my theory, as does coalitional analysis of the sort advanced by Gourevitch and Shinn.

I part ways with each of these political theories, however, in arguing that the manner in which external regulatory structures interact with the corporate governance system may change fundamentally as ownership disperses, as it has to varying degrees across the common-law countries studied here. This effectively amounts to a rejection of the possibility for a holistic global theory of corporate governance, an implicit aspiration of many of the political theories discussed in the previous section. Indeed, my approach suggests that the resulting modes of interaction among various regulatory structures in common-law countries may defy conventional understandings of left–right political preferences within any single domain. In the following chapter I argue that, unlike in the highly concentrated ownership systems prevailing elsewhere – where left-leaning, stakeholder-oriented regulatory structures may well correlate with weaker shareholder orientation in corporate governance (as Roe suggests) – in countries where substantial ownership dispersal has occurred, the correlation may actually reverse. Whereas stronger left-leaning social welfare policies and legal structures appear to have freed up U.K. corporate governance to focus intently on shareholders without precipitating political backlash in favor of employees and other stakeholders, the opposite has occurred in the United States, where weaker social welfare policies and legal structures have tended to inhibit strongly shareholder-centric corporate governance rules. Similar dynamics, I argue, have conditioned the evolution of corporate governance in Australia and Canada, which have higher degrees of share ownership concentration yet are still relatively dispersed by global standards. These countries exhibit social welfare–corporate governance equilibria more closely resembling that found in the United Kingdom, although in these cases the balances struck reflect other dynamics that help illuminate the outer boundaries of my theory's explanatory power – notably the impact of influential foreign regulatory models, as well as idiosyncrasies of national history, culture, and politics.

5 Shareholders, Stakeholders, and Social Welfare Policy

The foregoing chapters describe the divergence among Australia, Canada, the United Kingdom, and the United States in terms of the relative degrees of shareholder-centrism exhibited by their corporate governance systems, and argue that prevailing economic and political theories of comparative corporate governance offer no compelling explanation for this divergence. In this chapter I explore the social welfare models adopted in each country and evaluate their interaction with, and impact upon, the development of their respective corporate governance systems.

Specifically, I argue that stronger social welfare protections in the United Kingdom have permitted the U.K. corporate governance system to focus more intently on shareholders without precipitating political backlash, contrasting starkly with the United States, where weaker social welfare protections have inhibited U.S. corporate governance from doing the same. I then turn to Australia and Canada, arguing that the equilibrium struck in each country broadly resembles that struck in the United Kingdom, while acknowledging and exploring unique aspects of the Australian and Canadian experiences that further support – and reveal the limits of – my social welfare–based approach, as the case may be.

A. THE U.K. MODEL: STATE-BASED SOCIAL WELFARE POLICY

The United Kingdom and the United States clearly have much in common – indeed, they "arguably have more in common than any other pair of developed economies."[1] Yet, as we have seen, the two countries take radically different

[1] *See* John Armour & David A. Skeel, Jr., *Who Writes the Rules for Hostile Takeovers, and Why? – The Peculiar Divergence of U.S. and U.K. Takeover Regulation*, 95 Geo. L.J. 1727, 1751 (2007). *See also* Bernard S. Black & John C. Coffee, Jr., *Hail Britannia?: Institutional Investor Behavior under Limited Regulation*, 92 Mich. L. Rev. 1997, 2001 (1994); Brian R. Cheffins, *Does Law*

approaches to the role of shareholders in corporate governance. As we shall see, they also differ radically in their prevailing politics and social welfare landscapes[2] – a regulatory divergence with substantial, although largely unexplored, consequences for corporate governance itself.

Based solely on the prioritization of shareholders' interests over those of other corporate stakeholders, one might be inclined to predict that U.K. politics are more right-leaning. After all, shareholder-centrism, as a normative matter, is typically associated with the strong market orientation of the political right.[3] The reality, however, is quite the opposite as between the United Kingdom and the United States; to the degree they differ, the British tend to be more left-leaning than Americans are. The *Economist* poll discussed in Chapter 4 suggests that "the differences between the two countries look more striking than the similarities," and specifically that "Britons tend to have more left-wing views than Americans, . . . often by a surprising margin."[4]

How do we reconcile the United Kingdom's more left-leaning politics with the City of London's success in cultivating a free-market ethos and relatively hands-off, self-regulatory approach to finance and corporate governance – an approach that, as we have seen, has strongly redounded to the benefit of shareholders? In a discussion of the popularity of the U.K. National Health Service – providing free health care at the point of service for all since 1948 – the *Economist* addresses this apparent contradiction, concluding:

> Britons are an incoherent lot. Convinced of their Anglo-Saxon tightfistedness, left-wing politicians have felt obliged to moderate or camouflage their egalitarian urges. Free-marketeers, meanwhile, moan that the British are at bottom soggy socialists. Both are right: British voters are willing to tolerate greater inequalities than many Europeans, but are stubbornly attached to a few totems of communitarianism.[5]

Matter? The Separation of Ownership and Control in the United Kingdom, 30 J. LEGAL STUD. 459, 460 (2001).

[2] *See* Christopher M. Bruner, *Power and Purpose in the "Anglo-American" Corporation*, 50 VA. J. INT'L L. 579, 621–43 (2010).

[3] *See, e.g.*, David Millon, *Default Rules, Wealth Distribution, and Corporate Law Reform: Employment at Will versus Job Security*, 146 U. PA. L. REV. 975, 976–79 (1998) (contrasting the "progressive" views of "communitarian" corporate scholars with the "contractarian" view that "improving the welfare of nonshareholders would amount to interference with private ordering"); MARK J. ROE, POLITICAL DETERMINANTS OF CORPORATE GOVERNANCE: POLITICAL CONTEXT, CORPORATE IMPACT 2–3 (2003) (associating shareholder-centrism with deviation from social democracy).

[4] *See Anglo-Saxon Attitudes*, ECONOMIST, Mar. 29, 2008, at 71. For the full survey results, see ANGLO-SAXON ATTITUDES: A SURVEY OF BRITISH AND AMERICAN VIEWS OF THE WORLD (2008) (commissioned by the *Economist* and conducted by YouGov in the United Kingdom and Polimetrix in the United States).

[5] *Bagehot: The Shock of the Old*, ECONOMIST, July 5, 2008, at 70.

This blend of free-market ethos and communitarianism in U.K. politics strikes many as paradoxical, even contradictory. In this section I argue, however, that in terms of corporate governance, these facets of U.K. politics in fact reinforce one another. Understanding precisely how they mutually contributed to the emergence of what is probably the most shareholder-centric corporate governance system in the world requires delving into the complex array of political forces at work in British society in the decades following World War II.

The origins of the U.K. welfare state lie in the Liberal government of the early decades of the twentieth century.[6] The introduction of "old-age pensions, health and national insurance, school meals, the supervision and control of 'mental deficiencies', maternity and child welfare, public housing and the various employment benefits after 1919," were part of a broad-based effort not only to address "social need," but also "to appease, supervise and control an increasingly militant working class."[7] The Labour Party – created in 1900 by disaffected "working people, trade unionists and socialists" – rose to prominence following the split of the Liberal Party in 1916, achieving its first government in 1924,[8] and the vast expansion of U.K. social welfare programs since the 1940s is largely associated with the Labour Party, although it is perhaps more accurately described as reflecting a leftward shift across the spectrum of British politics. Welfare state expansion largely responded to the economic difficulties experienced during the interwar decades and what one observer, looking back in 1949, would describe as the "craving for stability [that] dominated British public life" – a tendency bridging the political left and right, with both Labour and Conservative parties "increasingly accept[ing] the idea that the state had to provide jobs and comforts when business could not."[9] As Brian Cheffins explains, the Conservative Party "captured the middle ground of British politics by adopting sufficiently left-wing policies to ensure swing voters did not defect to Labour" during the interwar years,[10] and postwar programs adopted by the 1945–1951 Labour government – including development of the National Health Service – were based largely on plans initiated by Winston Churchill's coalition government.[11]

[6] *See* Brian R. Cheffins, Corporate Ownership and Control: British Business Transformed 47 (2008); Number10.gov.uk, *Past Prime Ministers*, http://www.number10.gov.uk/history-and-tour/past-prime-ministers/ (noting Liberal Party power from 1905 to 1922).

[7] John Clarke et al., *The Construction of the British Welfare State*, 1945–1975, *in* Comparing Welfare States 29, 32, 39 (Allan Cochrane et al. eds., 2d ed. 2001).

[8] *See* The Labour Party, *History of the Labour Party*, http://www.labour.org.uk/history_of_the_labour_party.

[9] Richard H. Fry, *Appraisal of Britain's Welfare State*, N.Y. Times, Sept. 25, 1949, at SM12.

[10] Cheffins, *supra* note 6, at 48.

[11] *See* Fry, *supra* note 9, at SM12, 50. *See also* Number10.gov.uk, *supra* note 6; Clarke et al., *supra* note 7, at 34.

Richard Fry, financial and industrial editor of the *Manchester Guardian*, in a 1949 article for the *New York Times* describing the postwar U.K. welfare state, emphasized the universality and cradle-to-grave nature of the programs offered:

> Today the Englishman is offered – in return for his taxes, local rates, and national insurance contribution – a wide range of benefits: free education; medical attention, including medicines, spectacles and the now-famous false teeth; family allowances for each child except the first; free milk for school children; a fixed weekly payment in times of sickness or unemployment – as a right, not as charity; a pension in old age, and a funeral free of charge.[12]

Perhaps no element of Fry's account would have struck U.S. readers of the late 1940s (or today, for that matter) as more distinctively foreign than universal, state-based medical care. The National Health Service (NHS) was founded in 1948, and continues to provide health care "free at the point of use for anyone who is resident in the UK." Although it has "grown to become the world's largest publicly funded health service," it remains "funded centrally from national taxation" and administered through regionally managed services that "remain similar in most respects and continue to be talked about as belonging to a single, unified system."[13] The Labour Party to this day touts the NHS, in particular, as one of its signal achievements,[14] and it remains highly regarded across the political spectrum.[15] British political strategist John McTernan, writing in April 2011, observed that "NHS satisfaction is at an all-time high, according to surveys," adding that the British public "love the NHS. It is Britain's secular religion."[16]

Notwithstanding that the Labour Party ruled for just about half the period, the leftward shift in social attitudes reflected in creation of the NHS and expansion of the welfare state would effectively define British politics for the three decades following the end of World War II until Margaret Thatcher's election in 1979.[17] The fact that the government took on "the role of primary provider"

[12] Fry, *supra* note 9, at SM50.

[13] National Health Service (UK), *About the NHS*, http://www.nhs.uk/NHSEngland/thenhs/about/Pages/overview.aspx.

[14] *See* The Labour Party, *supra* note 8.

[15] *See Bagehot: The Shock of the Old*, *supra* note 5.

[16] John McTernan, *If David Cameron Fails on the NHS He Will Lose the Next General Election*, TELEGRAPH BLOG (Apr. 14, 2011), http://blogs.telegraph.co.uk/news/johnmcternan1/100083688/if-david-cameron-fails-on-the-nhs-he-will-lose-the-next-election/. *See also* Landon Thomas Jr., *Pain of British Fiscal Cuts Could Inform U.S. Debate*, N.Y. TIMES, Apr. 14, 2011, http://www.nytimes.com/2011/04/15/business/global/15iht-pound15.html (observing that "icons like the National Health Service [had] largely been spared" in post-crisis spending cuts).

[17] The Labour Party ruled from 1945 to 1951 (Attlee), 1964 to 1970 and 1974 to 1976 (Wilson), and 1976 to 1979 (Callaghan). *See* Number10.gov.uk, *supra* note 6.

in education and health care is thought to have "reflected Labourist commitments to greater egalitarianism" more generally.[18] As Cheffins observes, examination of governing party platforms suggests that the United Kingdom in fact "had a left-wing government all but three years" during this period. Indeed, the United Kingdom largely pursued a corporatist "tripartite orientation to economic policy-making as post-World War II British governments liaised constantly with unions and provided representatives of the UK business community with ample opportunity to confer with civil servants and politicians."[19]

Interestingly, the wave of hostile takeovers that arose in the United Kingdom in the 1950s was itself partly a consequence of Labour-sponsored amendments to the Companies Act closely coinciding in time with expansion of the British welfare state. As Leslie Hannah explains, "takeover bids contesting the views of incumbent directors were virtually unknown before 1950," among other things due to "the inadequacy of the information possessed by shareholders about the asset and profit position of their companies" at the time.[20] The Companies Act 1948, however, passed by the postwar Labour government, required far more elaborate financial reporting, facilitating the investigation of potential takeover targets.[21] At the same time, the 1948 amendments granted shareholders clear power to remove directors without cause by ordinary resolution of a simple majority, permitting would-be acquirers to achieve substantial governance power through open-market share purchases.[22]

Lord Lionel Cohen, who chaired the committee generating the recommendations embodied in the 1948 amendments, observed that the committee was initially appointed by the Board of Trade in 1943 – under Churchill, a Conservative – as "the Government was beginning to think of the brave

[18] *See* Clarke et al., *supra* note 7, at 44–45.

[19] CHEFFINS, *supra* note 6, at 49–50. *See also* TOM HADDEN, COMPANY LAW AND CAPITALISM 439 (2d ed. 1977); Michael Blanden, *The City Regulations on Mergers and Takeovers, in* READINGS ON MERGERS AND TAKEOVERS 199, 215–16 (J.M. Samuels ed., 1972); Alan Dignam & Michael Galanis, *Corporate Governance and the Importance of Macroeconomic Context*, 28 OXFORD J. LEGAL STUD. 201, at pt. 3.C. (2008); ALAN DIGNAM & MICHAEL GALANIS, THE GLOBALIZATION OF CORPORATE GOVERNANCE 214–21 (2009).

[20] LESLIE HANNAH, THE RISE OF THE CORPORATE ECONOMY: THE BRITISH EXPERIENCE 149 (1976).

[21] *See* Brian R. Cheffins, *Mergers and the Evolution of Patterns of Corporate Ownership and Control: The British Experience*, 46 BUS. HIST. 256, 270 (2004); Andrew Johnston, *Takeover Regulation: Historical and Theoretical Perspectives on the City Code*, 66 CAMBRIDGE L.J. 422, 427 (2007).

[22] *See* CHEFFINS, *supra* note 6, at 363. Paul Davies observes that prior to the 1948 amendments the shareholders' power to remove directors "depended, as with their appointment powers, on the provisions of the articles." *See* PAUL L. DAVIES, GOWER AND DAVIES' PRINCIPLES OF MODERN COMPANY LAW 389–90 (8th ed. 2008).

new world which they desired to see come into being when the war ended." The committee was made "as representative as possible," Cohen explained, including "Members of Parliament from both parties, accountants, lawyers, business men and trade unionists." He further observed that the committee's 1945 report (generally referred to as the Cohen Report) was "unanimous," and that most of its recommendations were adopted in 1947 – under Atlee's Labour government – taking effect in the Companies Act 1948.[23]

Looking back on the amendments, in a 1957 lecture Lord Cohen would explain that "the limited company" was not viewed as incompatible with the "increasingly socialistic" bent of postwar Labour policies.[24] The Cohen Report itself took the position that "the fullest practicable disclosure of information concerning the activities of companies will lessen . . . opportunities [for abuses by insiders] and accord with a wakening social consciousness"[25] – aims to which the committee evidently thought more rigorous disclosure requirements and facilitation of board removal would contribute.[26] In his 1957 lecture, then, Lord Cohen appears to recognize that these developments contributed to the rise of hostile takeovers, an "interesting subject-matter" to which the Board of Trade had turned its investigation powers (themselves products of the 1948 amendments) in the intervening years. In particular, he recounts an attempt by investor Harold Samuel "to acquire control" of the Berkeley Hotel in 1953 through open-market purchases of stock in Savoy Hotel Ltd. (which owned the Berkeley) – there being "an active market in the shares of that company" – in order to convert the Berkeley to commercial offices, and the efforts of incumbent management to prevent this from occurring.[27] Essentially the Savoy board arranged for the Berkeley to be sold to an entity controlled by the Savoy pension fund's trustees – including the chairman of Savoy's board – and then leased back to Savoy in a deal requiring that the premises be used as a hotel.[28] This defensive tactic led to two reports by Board of Trade inspectors, the second of which in 1954 was of "distinct

[23] Lionel Cohen, One Hundred Years of Limited Liability Companies in England, Lecture at the Hebrew University of Jerusalem (Hebrew Univ. of Jerusalem Lionel Cohen Lectures, 3d Series, Jan. 1957), at 27. *See also* Number10.gov.uk, *supra* note 6.

[24] *See* Cohen, *supra* note 23, at 43. *See also* E. Merrick Dodd, Book Review, 58 HARV. L. REV. 1258, 1265 (1945) (reviewing REPORT OF THE COMMITTEE ON COMPANY LAW AMENDMENT (1945)) (observing that the Board of Trade President who appointed the committee in 1943 became Chancellor of the Exchequer under the subsequent Labour government).

[25] REPORT OF THE COMMITTEE ON COMPANY LAW AMENDMENT ¶ 5 (1945) [hereinafter COHEN REPORT].

[26] *See id.* ¶¶ 5–7, 124, 130. *See also* Cohen, *supra* note 23, at 24–28, 36–37; Dodd, *supra* note 24, at 1258–59.

[27] *See* Cohen, *supra* note 23, at 40–41. *See also* Armour & Skeel, *supra* note 1, at 1756–58.

[28] *See* Armour & Skeel, *supra* note 1, at 1757.

interest to company lawyers," as it "expressed the opinion that the ingenious scheme devised by the [Savoy] Board would not hold water," regardless of their good faith belief that their actions were in the company's long-term best interests.[29]

Although Cohen does not discuss the Savoy battle at any length, his account of how the board "with the advice of counsel devised an ingenious scheme to prevent" Samuel from securing control[30] suggests that Cohen tended to view such defensive action as an improper end-run around the investor protections and shareholder powers recommended by the Cohen Report and adopted by the Companies Act 1948. Through much of the 1950s, however, the U.K. business, financial, and legal establishment remained unsure what to make of hostile tender offers and defensive responses. On the one hand, takeover bids extended directly to shareholders were viewed dimly, as Charles Clore's successful bid for J. Sears in early 1953 demonstrated. Clore realized that valuation based on dividend yields would not reflect the full value of a company such as Sears, with undervalued commercial properties – which Clore exploited by going straight to the shareholders themselves, a move "considered very sharp practice [that] came as an enormous shock for the company's management and the City establishment in general."[31] The Savoy battle later that year, on the other hand, demonstrated that defenses undercutting the shareholders' ability to accept such deals freely appeared equally suspect – "the financial press disliked directors who seemed to regard their own retention as inseparable from the interests of the company."[32] As a legal matter, however, the Board of Trade's opinion rejecting the Savoy directors' defensive maneuver resolved little. Although the report was written by "a leading company law barrister," it "lacked the binding force of a court judgment." Indeed, as John Armour and David Skeel observe, "the Savoy board had taken advice from another leading barrister to the effect that their scheme was perfectly lawful. Direct precedents on the point were non-existent."[33]

The matter ultimately came to a head in 1958 with the battle for British Aluminium, the board of which attempted to ensure a deal with its favored bidder, Alcoa, by issuing shares to Alcoa amounting to one-third of British

[29] *See* Cohen, *supra* note 23, at 41.

[30] *See id.* at 40–41.

[31] *See* Armour & Skeel, *supra* note 1, at 1756–57.

[32] ALEXANDER JOHNSTON, THE CITY TAKE-OVER CODE 12 (1980).

[33] *See* Armour & Skeel, *supra* note 1, at 1757–58. *See also* Cohen, *supra* note 23, at 41 (observing the Savoy board's reliance on "the advice of counsel," and the Board of Trade report's reliance on a 1920 court decision holding invalid a board's issuance of stock "with the avowed purpose of affecting voting majorities").

Aluminium's stock – a move that was publicly acknowledged only once the rival bidder, Tube Investments, decided to put a direct offer to the shareholders anyway. The British Aluminium board's defensive tactic "provoked widespread calls for takeover regulation," and the following year the Bank of England "secretly invited a committee comprised of trade groups representing merchant banks, institutional investors, the largest commercial banks, and the London Stock Exchange to devise a code of conduct to regulate takeover bids." This resulted in the so-called Notes on Amalgamation of British Businesses, which resolved the confusion over takeover defenses as a matter of principle by establishing that the fate of hostile takeover bids should be left to the shareholders.[34] Although the Notes were widely disregarded – not least because of the lack of an effective enforcement mechanism – the core principle of shareholder control was confirmed, and in fact reinforced, through the creation of the City Code in 1968.[35] While retaining the self-regulatory approach of the Notes, the City Code was paired with the City Panel, bringing an enforcement capability that "piggybacked" on that of the Panel's various constituents, notably the London Stock Exchange's power to sanction listed companies, the Board of Trade's power to sanction securities dealers, and the trade associations' power to sanction their members.[36] The self-regulatory approach was, of course, only reinforced by the relative proximity and homogeneity of "the City" – London's financial district – populated by "repeat players" highly dependent on reciprocal relationships and reputational capital.[37]

That London's financial establishment would favor self-regulation emphasizing their own interests – and resist the perceived excesses of the U.S. securities regulatory approach – is entirely predictable. The notion of a legislative solution "appalled the City and practitioners in this field. It conjured up a ponderous bureaucracy with all the least attractive features of the then US Securities and Exchange Commission."[38] As Tom Hadden, writing in

[34] *See* Armour & Skeel, *supra* note 1, at 1757–59. For background on prominent British takeover attempts of the 1950s, see JOHNSTON, *supra* note 32, at 8–18.

[35] *See supra* Chapter 3.A.

[36] *See* Armour & Skeel, *supra* note 1, at 1759–63. *See also* HADDEN, *supra* note 19, at 374–78; Johnston, *supra* note 21, at 432–36.

[37] *See* Armour & Skeel, *supra* note 1, at 1771–72. *See also* Blanden, *supra* note 19, at 199–212; Caroline Bradley, *Transatlantic Misunderstandings: Corporate Law and Societies*, 53 U. MIAMI L. REV. 269, 299–300 (1999); *Square Mile's Sheriff*, FIN. WORLD ONLINE (Mar. 2008), https://www.financialworld.co.uk/Archive/2008/2008_03mar/Features/the_takeover_panel/13916-print.cfm.

[38] *See* T.P. Lee, *Takeovers – the United Kingdom Experience*, *in* TAKEOVERS, INSTITUTIONAL INVESTORS, AND THE MODERNIZATION OF CORPORATE LAWS 192, 192 (John H. Farrar ed., 1993). *See also* Ruth V. Aguilera, *Corporate Governance and Director Accountability: An Institutional Comparative Perspective*, 16 BRIT. J. MGMT. S39, S43 (2005) (contrasting U.K. reliance on "soft regulation" of corporate governance with U.S. reliance on "legislation enforceable in the court system").

1977, observed, the "British securities market, unlike the American, is very highly centralized," such that "[m]any of the functions of the SEC in America can . . . be effectively carried out in Britain by the Stock Exchange authorities and the City Panel without formal statutory authority."[39] Although beyond the scope of this book, it should be observed that this divergence in securities regulatory style closely parallels that between U.K. and U.S. approaches to financial accounting, the former traditionally favoring flexible standards and the latter favoring prescriptive rules.[40]

In light of the general association of shareholder-centrism with free market-oriented, right-leaning political attitudes, however, it is far from obvious why a starkly shareholder-centric approach to takeover regulation would have emerged and remained stable in the left-leaning political environment of postwar Britain. Indeed, it is quite remarkable that these shareholder-centric structures were reaffirmed and reinforced under the 1964–1970 Labour government of Prime Minister Harold Wilson.[41] Much like they would in the United States, hostile takeovers brought the core issues of corporate power and purpose to the forefront of British politics, tempting U.K. shareholders to accept premium bids that, if successful, could conceivably impose substantial costs on other constituencies including management, employees, creditors, and local communities. As Sir Alexander Johnston, a member of the City Panel, observed in 1980, defensive measures by target boards "raised in an acute form the questions – who was ultimately in charge of a company and whose interests should be safeguarded?"[42] The Labour Party's acceptance – and even facilitation – of so shareholder-centric a response to these core issues requires some political explanation.

As a 1978 parliamentary review of monopolies and mergers policy observed, "[p]olicies of successive Governments towards mergers have been based on the assumption that the great majority of mergers are desirable or at least not against the public interest."[43] James Foreman-Peck and Leslie Hannah explain

[39] HADDEN, *supra* note 19, at 361. *See also* Blanden, *supra* note 19, at 212, 216; JOHNSTON, *supra* note 32, at 21, 170–78.

[40] *See* David Alexander & Eva Jermakowicz, *A True and Fair View of the Principles/Rules Debate*, 42 ABACUS 132, 133–34 (2006). For additional background, see Alexander & Jermakowicz, *supra*; Timothy S. Doupnik & Stephen B. Salter, *An Empirical Test of a Judgmental International Classification of Financial Reporting Practices*, 24 J. INT'L BUS. STUD. 41 (1993); C.W. Nobes, *A Judgmental International Classification of Financial Reporting Practices*, 10 J. BUS. FIN. & ACCT. 1 (1983); *True and Fair*, ECONOMIST, Sept. 22, 2008, http://www.economist.com/node/12284475/print (adapted from TIM HINDLE, THE ECONOMIST GUIDE TO MANAGEMENT IDEAS AND GURUS (2008)).

[41] *See* Number10.gov.uk, *supra* note 6.

[42] *See* JOHNSTON, *supra* note 32, at Preface, 13.

[43] SECRETARY OF STATE FOR PRICES AND CONSUMER PROTECTION, A REVIEW OF MONOPOLIES AND MERGERS POLICY: A CONSULTATIVE DOCUMENT, 1978, Cm. 7198, at 97 (U.K.) [hereinafter REVIEW OF MONOPOLIES AND MERGERS POLICY].

that "[g]overnment policy and public opinion until the 1980s were still prone to conclude that Britain needed to become more like the United States in the scale of its industrial businesses."[44] This gave rise to a widely shared predisposition toward mergers and acquisitions creating larger British businesses. Indeed, throughout the 1950s and 1960s the U.K. government was "directly active in the promotion of mergers," a policy that was, "despite differences of approach and emphasis, broadly bipartisan."[45] Prime Minister Wilson himself credited mergers in the 1960s for bringing the United Kingdom "kicking and screaming into the twentieth century,"[46] and hostile bidders accordingly came to be viewed as agents of change, rationalization, and increased competitiveness.[47]

Indeed, Labour's own position on takeovers evolved considerably over this period as party leaders sought to reconcile potentially conflicting priorities regarding employment stability and industrial competitiveness. Johnston observes of their response to the "intensive take-over activity" of 1953 and 1954 that "Labour Party spokesmen disliked the large tax-free profits made by successful bidders at a time when capital gains were not taxed," as well as "the coach and four that was driven through a policy of dividend restraint during and after bid contests," which they believed "impeded capital investment."[48] Indeed, Roy Jenkins in 1954 introduced a motion "That this House deplores recent manifestations of the technique of take-over bids in so far as they have put large, untaxed capital profits into the hands of certain individuals and seriously undermined the policy of dividend restraint," calling for a governmental inquiry.[49]

By the end of the decade, Labour concerns regarding the social impact of takeovers remained substantial. Wilson, as shadow chancellor, criticized the Conservative government of Harold MacMillan in a 1959 House of Commons debate in terms reflecting the shareholder/stakeholder conflict that takeovers inevitably raise. "Just as shareholders are becoming more and more avid for quick gains," Wilson charged, "so the Government regard any quick capital

[44] James Foreman-Peck & Leslie Hannah, *Britain: From Economic Liberalism to Socialism – And Back?*, *in* EUROPEAN INDUSTRIAL POLICY: THE TWENTIETH-CENTURY EXPERIENCE 18, 44 (James Foreman-Peck & Giovanni Frederico eds., 1999). *See also* CHEFFINS, *supra* note 6, at 360–61.

[45] HANNAH, *supra* note 20, at 171. *See also* R. Goodman, *Taming and Controlling Power*, *in* READINGS ON MERGERS AND TAKEOVERS, *supra* note 19, at 218, 219.

[46] *See* WILLIAM DAVIS, MERGER MANIA 2 (1970) (quoting Wilson).

[47] *See* CHEFFINS, *supra* note 6, at 365–66.

[48] JOHNSTON, *supra* note 32, at 10–11. *See also* Helen Callaghan, *Insiders, Outsiders and the Politics of Corporate Governance: How Ownership Shapes Party Positions in Britain, Germany, and France*, 42 COMP. POL. STUD. 733, 744–45 (2009).

[49] DAVIS, *supra* note 46, at 6.

gains as good business, to be encouraged whatever the production realities." He asked how the government could "appeal for wage restraint in the payment of a job honestly and well done, while millions of pounds can be made in this effortless manner by a section which does no work at all," concluding that "[t]hese people 'toil not, neither do they spin' yet their gains are out of all proportion to any services they render to that industry."[50] This attitude toward takeovers clearly animates the Labour Party's 1959 Manifesto, which – in its opening paragraphs – illustrates "the contrast between the extremes of wealth and poverty" by reference to takeovers, on the one hand, and a flagging social safety net, on the other. "The business man with a tax-free expense account, the speculator with tax-free capital gains, and the retiring company director with a tax-free redundancy payment due to a take-over bid" have "never had it so good," while "the sick, the disabled and the old have continually seen the value of state benefits and small savings whittled away by rising prices."[51] Naturally enough, then, the Labour Party in 1959 sought "a statutory body to regulate takeovers,"[52] while calling in its Manifesto for increased funding of the National Health Service and broader "extension of the Welfare State."[53]

Over the course of the 1960s, however, Labour's position softened – and then ultimately reversed entirely – as Party leaders reassessed the capacity of takeovers to improve British competitiveness, and the capacity of the welfare state to buffer the social costs.[54] The Labour Party's 1964 Manifesto reflects continued hostility toward takeovers, promising to "[g]ive teeth to the Monopolies Commission" and "control take-over bids and mergers," while continuing to deride the "present situation where the largest gains are made, not through hard work but through the untaxed rewards of passive ownership of Stock Exchange speculation." At the same time, it called for "a charter of rights for all employees" including "compensation for loss of job or disturbance" and "half-pay maintenance during any period of sickness and unemployment," as well as "retraining for adult workers" and "full transferability of pension

[50] *See* Callaghan, *supra* note 48, at 745 (quoting Wilson).

[51] Labour Party [U.K.], Britain Belongs to You: The Labour Party's Policy for Consideration by the British People (1959), http://politicsresources.net/area/uk/man/lab59.htm [hereinafter 1959 Labour Manifesto].

[52] *See* Johnston, *supra* note 21, at 432.

[53] *See* 1959 Labour Manifesto, *supra* note 51.

[54] Helen Callaghan has argued that, with respect to U.K. corporate governance, the left/right political divide "from the 1950s until the arrival of Tony Blair . . . was a straightforward battle between capital and labor," with Labour attacking the shareholder-centric takeover regime supported by Conservatives. *See* Callaghan, *supra* note 48, at 734. She cites Wilson's strong antitakeover position in the 1950s in support of this argument, but does not grapple with how the Labour Party actually approached takeover regulation (and mergers more generally) once in power in the 1960s. *See id.* at 744–46.

entitlements" – all of which would naturally be of keen interest to employees fearing job loss following a takeover. The 1964 Manifesto at the same time argued that the National Health Service – "among the foremost achievements of the 1945–50 Labour Government" – had "been starved of resources," and promises more generally that "Labour will reconstruct our social security system."[55] By 1966, however – just two years into Wilson's Labour government – Labour's Manifesto included no mention whatever of takeovers. Like the 1964 Manifesto, the 1966 Manifesto reflects continued Labour commitment to welfare state programs, but places this in the context of a broader "National Plan" with the "central aim . . . to accelerate industrial expansion without undermining our social priorities."[56] This required not merely scaling back Labour's attacks on takeovers and industrial concentration more generally, but in fact a commitment to facilitating them through creation of the Industrial Reorganisation Corporation (IRC), which aimed to "stimulate rationalisation, modernisation and expansion in those fields where British industry at present seems unable to compete with the giant firms of the U.S. and Europe."[57] That this would effectively require a pro-takeover policy (of a sort) was clear. As Douglas Hague and Geoffrey Wilkinson explain, the means by which the IRC was to facilitate rationalization of British industry included not only mergers of equals and "re-grouping" of existing corporate groups, but also "the formation of groups through leading companies taking over smaller ones."[58]

The tension with Labour's call for greater oversight of takeovers by the Monopolies Commission[59] would appear considerable, but in practice there was no overt conflict between these goals. U.K. competition regulation at the time was "modest" in comparison with U.S. antitrust regulation, reflecting the view of "ministers of both parties who, in general, felt that the majority of mergers produced real economic benefits."[60] Indeed, it is critical to observe

[55] Labour Party [U.K.], The New Britain (1964), http://politicsresources.net/area/uk/man/lab64.htm.

[56] Labour Party [U.K.], Time For Decision (1966), http://politicsresources.net/area/uk/man/lab66.htm [hereinafter 1966 Labour Manifesto]. *See also* Clarke et al., *supra* note 7, at 44, 57.

[57] 1966 Labour Manifesto, *supra* note 56. *See also* Clarke et al., *supra* note 7, at 44; Davis, *supra* note 46, at 10–11; Douglas Hague & Geoffrey Wilkinson, The IRC – An Experiment in Industrial Intervention 3–5 (1983); Review of Monopolies and Mergers Policy, *supra* note 43, at 20.

[58] *See* Hague & Wilkinson, *supra* note 57, at 14.

[59] *See* 1966 Labour Manifesto, *supra* note 56 (promising "a vigorous anti-monopoly policy in fields where market powers are abused").

[60] *See* Hannah, *supra* note 20, at 176. *See also* Review of Monopolies and Mergers Policy, *supra* note 43, at 17, 97–99.

that both the IRC – built to promote merger and takeover activity – and the Monopolies Commission – built to contain it – were in fact used as means of market intervention, permitting the Labour government to coordinate such transactions by reference to Labour leaders' perceptions of the public interest.[61] The IRC's exceptionally broad mandate – to "promote or assist the reorganisation or development of any industry"[62] – gave the entity enormous discretion to engage in direct market activity, and in practice when the IRC took an interest in a given transaction, the matter simply would not be referred to the Monopolies Commission.[63]

Despite recognition of the "need to reassure businessmen that the IRC was not an instrument of the Labour Government which would be used to force them, for political reasons, to do things which they did not want to do,"[64] the IRC – together with high government officials, including Prime Minister Wilson – did in fact make controversial interventions in high-profile corporate transactions. Indeed, the Labour government effectively determined the outcome of the January 1968 merger between Leyland Motors and British Motor Holdings,[65] as well as the June 1968 takeover of Cambridge Instrument by George Kent.[66] In this regard, it should be noted that the City Panel – created that year to reinforce market-based self-regulation of takeovers – had what one Panel member described as "a good working relationship" with the IRC, facilitating the IRC's intervention in the Cambridge Instrument takeover through issuance of a press release stating that the Panel "has authorized IRC to say that in its view the IRC has conformed to the [City] Code."[67]

Although it may be difficult to imagine today, judged by reference to the U.K. political spectrum of the 1960s, the IRC – strongly supported by Prime Minister Wilson himself[68] – may have actually appeared to be a relatively moderate approach to improving British industrial competitiveness. William Davis observes that although conservatives naturally favored leaving the market for corporate control to itself, "left-wing MPs thought the IRC was a feeble alternative to what they considered to be the real solution – an extension of

[61] *See* Hannah, *supra* note 20, at 179–80; Johnston, *supra* note 32, at 31. *See also* 1966 Labour Manifesto, *supra* note 56 (observing that the IRC would allow the Labour government "to apply social priorities, giving preference to industrial investment and to a better regional balance").

[62] *See* Hague & Wilkinson, *supra* note 57, at 22 (quoting § 2(1) of the Industrial Reorganisation Act of 1966). *See also* Davis, *supra* note 46, at 145–46.

[63] *See* Davis, *supra* note 46, at 131.

[64] Hague & Wilkinson, *supra* note 57, at 27.

[65] *See* Davis, *supra* note 46, at 94–109; Hague & Wilkinson, *supra* note 57, at 119–33.

[66] *See* Davis, *supra* note 46, at 136–39; Hague & Wilkinson, *supra* note 57, at 72–90.

[67] *See* Johnston, *supra* note 32, at 138.

[68] *See* Hague & Wilkinson, *supra* note 57, at 24.

public ownership."[69] While presiding over what was arguably "the period of the greatest social and industrial change" for twentieth-century Britain, it has been observed of Wilson himself that he in fact "hovered between moderate left and moderate right throughout the late 1950s and into the 1960s," with many of his more left-leaning Labour colleagues suspecting that "Wilson was really a right-winger at heart."[70] Nevertheless, the Conservative Party deeply disliked the form of direct government intervention in the marketplace that the IRC pursued – and in fact embodied – which presumably drove its decision to eliminate the IRC upon its return to power in 1970.[71]

In any event, the key question remains how the 1964–1970 Labour government became so comfortable with the potential employment impacts of takeover activity, even coming to favor corporate control transactions threatening substantial negative consequences for Labour's core political constituency. The answer is that Labour leaders not only believed that the right mergers would maximize stable job opportunities, but also that external regulatory structures could buffer the downside risks for employees. Notwithstanding their negative reaction to hostile takeovers in the 1950s and early 1960s, Hannah explains that "earlier fears of Labour leaders that mergers and rationalization created unemployment had now given way to a feeling that larger (and, it was hoped, more productive) units would in the long run be better for employment." He elaborates that although "[i]t was, of course, recognized that there would be unemployment problems following mergers, . . . these were now felt to be problems of a transitional phase," and that the "social costs faced by unemployed workers were also more broadly shared as a result of the redundancy payments scheme initiated by Labour."[72] Recall, for example, Labour's 1966 Manifesto, which abandoned criticism of takeovers, focusing rather on the benefits of modernization and rationalization of British industry through the IRC. The Manifesto also reminds voters that "the purpose of our Redundancy Payments Act [1965], which brings lump sum compensation, related to service, to those affected by redundancy," was to "[e]ase the transition from one job to another."[73] This legislation bolstered protections under the Contract

[69] DAVIS, *supra* note 46, at 132.

[70] *See* Geoffrey Goodman, *Harold Wilson: Leading Labour Beyond Pipe Dreams*, GUARDIAN, May 25, 1995, at 14.

[71] *See* HAGUE & WILKINSON, *supra* note 57, at 3, 80–81.

[72] HANNAH, *supra* note 20, at 172 & n.26. *See also* Michael Bennett, *Interpreting Unfair Dismissal and Redundancy Payments Law: The Judicial Reluctance to Disapprove Employer Decisions to Dismiss*, 23 STATUTE L. REV. 135, 136–37 (2002); DAVIS, *supra* note 46, at 2–3; Martin Gelter, *The Dark Side of Shareholder Influence: Managerial Autonomy and Stakeholder Orientation in Comparative Corporate Governance*, 50 HARV. INT'L L.J. 129, 190 (2009).

[73] 1966 LABOUR MANIFESTO, *supra* note 56 (emphasis removed).

of Employment Act 1963 (which imposed minimum notice periods to protect non-union workers lacking collective bargaining capacity),[74] and remains effective today.[75] Recall further that the 1966 Manifesto presents this reform amidst a number of safety nets – including social security, health, and other welfare services – that together represent "what the responsible citizen wishes for himself and his family." These "social priorities," then, are to be balanced against "accelerate[d] industrial expansion" in pursuit of a holistic "National Plan."[76]

Structures such as the redundancy payments scheme – and welfare state programs more generally – effectively shore up a perceived deficiency of corporate law in terms of protections afforded to non-shareholder employees, vividly illustrating that social welfare policy, labor law, and corporate law can represent alternative strategies for safeguarding employee interests.[77] Although it was long accepted that expenditures for the benefit of employees were permissible so long as they were somehow connected with pursuit of the company's best interests – "cakes and ale . . . for the benefit of the company," as Bowen L.J. famously put it in 1883 in *Hutton v. West Cork Railway Company*[78] – subsequent case law clearly established the limits of this approach. In his 1962 decision in *Parke v. Daily News Ltd.*, Plowman J. concluded that the proceeds of the sale of a business could not be directed to employees because, in light of the company's demise, it could not plausibly be said that doing so benefited the company in any straightforward sense. Plowman explains that although the

[74] *See* Bennett, *supra* note 72, at 136.

[75] *See* Directgov, *Entitlement to Redundancy Pay*, http://www.direct.gov.uk/en/Employment/RedundancyAndLeavingYourJob/Redundancy/DG_10029836. *See also* Directgov, *Calculating Your Redundancy Pay*, http://www.direct.gov.uk/en/Employment/RedundancyAndLeavingYourJob/Redundancy/DG_174330; Directgov, *Your Rights if Your Employer Is Insolvent*, http://www.direct.gov.uk/en/Employment/Employees/Pay/DG_10026695.

[76] 1966 Labour Manifesto, *supra* note 56.

[77] *See, e.g.*, Matthew T. Bodie, *Employees and the Boundaries of the Corporation, in* Research Handbook on the Economics of Corporate Law 85, 97–99 (Claire A. Hill & Brett H. McDonnell eds., 2012) ("Corporate law has definitively separated employees from the governance of the firm. . . . In order to balance out the employment relationship, the power that the firm has taken unto itself to better coordinate joint production must be mitigated through specific substantive protections that apply only to employees."); Simon Deakin, *The Corporation as Commons: Rethinking Property Rights, Governance and Sustainability in the Business Enterprise*, 37 Queen's L.J. 339, 361–66 (2012) ("The law structures the business enterprise through devices which complement the operation of company law, in particular through employment law and the law of enterprise liability."). *Cf.* Lynn Stout, The Shareholder Value Myth 84–85 (2012) (arguing that greater shareholder-centrism and correlatively "less ability to lock in corporate capital in a fashion that protects stakeholders" helps explain "why U.K. public companies concentrate in finance and commodities extraction," industries requiring little "firm-specific investment").

[78] *See* Hutton v. W. Cork Ry. Co., [1883] 23 Ch. D. 654, 672–73.

notion that a board of directors is "entitled to take into account the interests of the employees, irrespective of any consequential benefit to the company, is one which may be widely held," nevertheless "no authority to support that proposition as a proposition of law was cited to me; I know of none, and in my judgment such is not the law." Plowman additionally clarified that "the benefit of the company meant the benefit of the shareholders as a general body."[79] It is against the background of this case law – and particularly the 1962 *Parke* decision – that passage of the Redundancy Payments Act just three years later must be assessed. H.A.J. Ford, assessing these developments from the comparative perspective (in his 1974 treatise on Australian company law), emphasized this nexus between company law and extra-corporate stakeholder protections, observing that *Parke* left "little scope . . . for the board of a company which is going out of business to make voluntary provision for employees," and that the "solution to this problem" in the United Kingdom was to be found "in the enactment of redundancy compensation laws of application to employers generally," rather than in company law.[80]

Interestingly, commentators have identified responses within U.K. company law as well, including statutory authority to pay some regard to employee interests,[81] and a statutory mechanism permitting payments to employees when a business is sold or closes down.[82] In reality, both of these company law responses remain fundamentally quite shareholder-centric – the former permitting regard for employee interests only when benefiting the shareholders, and the latter requiring shareholder consent before any such payment to employees may be made. For present purposes, however, the point is simply that corporate law, on the one hand, and labor law and social welfare policy, on the other, offer alternative means of addressing the very same employee vulnerabilities.[83] As Raghuram Rajan and Luigi Zingales suggest, "insurance

79 *See* Parke v. Daily News Ltd. [1962] Ch. 927, 962–63.

80 *See* H.A.J. Ford, Principles of Company Law 90 (1974).

81 *See* R. Baxt, An Introduction to Company Law 215–16 (2d ed. 1982); Davies, *supra* note 22, at 518–19; Alan Dignam & John Lowry, Company Law 248 (5th ed. 2009); Companies Act, 2006, c. 46, § 172(1)(b) (U.K.). *See also* Companies Act, 1980, ch. 22, § 46 (U.K.); Companies Act 1985, ch. 6, § 309 (U.K.).

82 *See* Baxt, *supra* note 81, at 216 n.18; Davies, *supra* note 22, at 166–67; Dignam & Lowry, *supra* note 81, at 248; Companies Act, 2006, c. 46, § 247 (U.K.). *See also* Companies Act, 1980, ch. 22, § 74 (U.K.); Companies Act 1985, ch. 6, § 719 (U.K.).

83 Interestingly, U.K. union leaders appear not to have pursued direct board representation, fearing that they would lack substantive power yet appear to employees "to have 'sold out' to management." *See* Hadden, *supra* note 19, at 446–47. *Cf.* Sanford M. Jacoby, *Corporate Governance and Employees in the United States, in* Corporate Governance and Labour Management: An International Comparison 33, 50–51 (Howard Gospel & Andrew Pendleton eds., 2005) (observing the AFL-CIO's fear in the U.S. context that seeking board representation would

schemes that will soften the impact of economic adversity on individuals will help ward off an anti-market reaction,"[84] a political dynamic clearly at work in the formation of the United Kingdom's corporate governance system. As Hannah emphasizes in the conclusion of his 1976 study of the "corporate economy" in the United Kingdom, "corporations exercise a pervasive influence not only on economic but on political and social life," such that "considerations of political and social welfare have always been important in public assessment of modern industrial tendencies" – a sensibility exemplified by the Labour Party's response to increased corporate concentration.[85] In the end, a shareholder-centric corporate governance regime – giving shareholders unilateral power over some of the most important decisions in a public company – could be accepted as politically stable and even beneficial by the political left, so long as external protections were available to address the needs and vulnerabilities of other constituencies, ensuring broader social stability.

Martin Gelter observes that labor legislation such as that discussed earlier in this section "finally arriv[ed] during the 1960s and 1970s," and that "shareholder influence was pervasive before these came into existence" – a sequence potentially suggesting that "employment legislation brought U.K. corporate governance into balance."[86] However, although the Redundancy Payments Act of 1965 may well respond to case law perceived to be excessively skewed toward the shareholders' interests, it should also be observed that it predates by three years the Labour government's reinforcement of an extremely shareholder-centric takeover regime through the creation of the City Code and the City Panel. Moreover, by the 1960s, the National Health Service (like other state-based social welfare structures) had itself been in place for decades, helping to defuse what might otherwise have been among the most pressing concerns for British employees confronting the prospect of redundancy – a set of dynamics vividly illustrated in the U.S. context when a wave of hostile takeovers hit in the 1980s.[87] The extra-corporate stakeholder protections described

"require loosening of the labour law's strictures on employer involvement in representation activities"). Although U.K. unions' strength has waned since the 1950s and 1960s, employment law protections have improved. *See* Beth Ahlering & Simon Deakin, *Labor Regulation, Corporate Governance, and Legal Origin: A Case of Institutional Complementarity?*, 41 LAW & SOC'Y REV. 865, 884 (2007); John Armour, Simon Deakin & Suzanne J. Konzelmann, *Shareholder Primacy and the Trajectory of UK Corporate Governance*, 41 BRIT. J. INDUS. REL. 531, 541 (2003); Gelter, *supra* note 72, at 191–92.

[84] Raghuram G. Rajan & Luigi Zingales, *The Great Reversals: The Politics of Financial Development in the Twentieth Century*, 69 J. FIN. ECON. 5, 45 (2003).

[85] *See* HANNAH, *supra* note 20, at 197–98.

[86] *See* Gelter, *supra* note 72, at 190–91.

[87] *See infra* Chapter 5.B.

above shed substantial light on how Harold Wilson – the Labour leader who condemned takeovers as incompatible with the interests of employees in the 1950s – could, as Prime Minister in the 1960s, accept and reinforce a mode of takeover regulation permitting shareholders alone to call the shots without regard to any interests other than their own. While Wilson threatened statutory regulation as a last resort,[88] shareholder-centric self-regulation nevertheless survived and flourished under a Labour government confident that employee vulnerability could be mitigated by other regulatory structures.

Although it could hardly be said that the welfare state flourished in the period of Conservative Party rule following Margaret Thatcher's election in 1979,[89] for purposes of our inquiry what is most remarkable about the 1980s and 1990s is that the British welfare state endured consistent ruling party hostility as well as it did. During this period "a principal concern was to reduce the role of the state in the provision of welfare," motivating "a sustained ideological campaign which placed a heavy burden of blame on the welfare state for causing economic and moral decline."[90] Under Thatcher, the U.K. government also aimed to weaken trade unions and privatize industry.[91] Nevertheless, core aspects of the welfare state remained quite resilient. To be sure, the availability and amount of benefits were reduced and the labor market was substantially deregulated, bringing about "a sharp deterioration in the welfare rights of a substantial section of the population."[92] In light of this, it would presumably be "reasonable to expect evidence of a shrinking welfare state or declining public spending on welfare" during the 1980s and 1990s – yet this did not occur. Indeed, U.K. welfare expenditures remained "remarkably stable" between 1973 and 1996, demonstrating that "'welfare policy successfully weathered an economic hurricane in the mid 1970s and an ideological blizzard in the 1980s.'"[93] John Clarke, Mary Langan, and Fiona Williams attribute the staying power of the U.K. welfare state to "bureaucratic and professional inertia within the state," combined with demographic changes – notably, growth in the elderly and unemployed populations. At the same time, it must be acknowledged that "some welfare programmes far[ed]

[88] *See* Johnston, *supra* note 32, at 49–50; Lee, *supra* note 38, at 192. *See also* Blanden, *supra* note 19, at 205; Johnston, *supra* note 21, at 442.

[89] Margaret Thatcher (1979–1990) was immediately succeeded by John Major (1990–1997). *See* Number10.gov.uk, *supra* note 6.

[90] John Clarke et al., *Remaking Welfare: The British Welfare Regime in the 1980s and 1990s*, *in* Comparing Welfare States, *supra* note 7, at 71, 73.

[91] *See* Dignam & Galanis, *supra* note 19, at 235–41; Monica Prasad, The Politics of Free Markets: The Rise of Neoliberal Economic Policies in Britain, France, Germany, and the United States 121–35, 146–47, 155–56 (2006).

[92] *See* Clarke et al., *supra* note 90, at 79–80.

[93] *See id.* at 76–77 (quoting J. Le Grand).

better than others" in this period, with social security, health care, and "personal social services" benefitting at the expense of education and housing.[94] As Monica Prasad explains, Thatcher's conservative government in fact "failed to reduce spending as a share of national income or significantly alter any of the major programs." Indeed, when a 1982 report of the Central Policy Review Staff proposing (among other things) to privatize health insurance leaked to the press, "Thatcher was forced to promise that the government would not introduce any of the proposals in the paper,"[95] prompting her to declare that "the National Health Service is safe in our hands."[96] The upshot is that, notwithstanding the ideological challenges faced during the 1980s and 1990s, the British welfare state was not remotely dismantled to the degree one might have predicted. Despite effective "withdrawal from much direct provision of services, particularly in the field of social care," as of 2001 it could be said that "the [British] state remains the dominant provider of education, healthcare and income maintenance."[97]

Tolerance for shareholder-centrism among the British left – which returned to power with Tony Blair's election in 1997[98] – had not waned by the turn of the millennium, when an in-depth review of company law was undertaken. Under Blair's centrist "New Labour" government,[99] a Steering Group created by the Department of Trade and Industry was charged (among other things) with evaluating "the proper scope of company law, that is, whose interests it should be designed to serve and the legal means by which it should do so."[100] In other words, the Steering Group was to reexamine how the core issues of power and purpose ought to be addressed in U.K. company law. In its February 1999 consultation document the Steering Group established a descriptive baseline for this inquiry, presenting preexisting directors' duties as fundamentally shareholder-centric in nature (even citing to Frank Easterbrook and Daniel Fischel's work) and explaining that permitting directors to prioritize the interests of other constituencies would require a change in the law.[101] The principal goal of the reform effort was to maximize "competitiveness and efficient creation of wealth and other benefits for all participants in the enterprise," although secondary goals were to "minimise the negative impacts

[94] *See id.* at 76–79.

[95] *See* PRASAD, *supra* note 91, at 136–38.

[96] *See id.* at 138 (quoting Thatcher).

[97] *See* Clarke et al., *supra* note 90, at 103.

[98] *See* Number10.gov.uk, *supra* note 6.

[99] *See* Clarke et al., *supra* note 90, at 98–99; *Who Killed New Labour?*, ECONOMIST, Sept. 18, 2008, at 37; PETER ALEXIS GOUREVITCH & JAMES J. SHINN, POLITICAL POWER AND CORPORATE CONTROL: THE NEW GLOBAL POLITICS OF CORPORATE GOVERNANCE 262 (2005).

[100] COMPANY LAW REVIEW STEERING GROUP, MODERN COMPANY LAW FOR A COMPETITIVE ECONOMY: THE STRATEGIC FRAMEWORK 33 (1999) [hereinafter STRATEGIC FRAMEWORK].

[101] *See id.* at 34–46.

of corporate activity on participants and to maximise welfare more widely." Accordingly, the Steering Group had to decide from the outset whether U.K. company law ought to retain the shareholder-centric formulation of directors' duties or adopt what it termed the "Pluralist" approach, requiring directors to orient corporate decision making toward the aggregate benefit of all stakeholders in a manner resembling the team production approach.[102]

To be sure, the Steering Group acknowledges the diversity of views on corporate purpose in the United Kingdom, implicitly reflecting the fact that enthusiasm for strict shareholder-centrism is far from universal in British society.[103] Indeed, pro-employee corporate governance initiatives garnered substantial support at various times in recent history – although none succeeded in eroding the fundamental shareholder-centrism of U.K. company law to a substantial degree. The *Report of the Committee of Inquiry on Industrial Democracy*[104] – typically called the "Bullock Report" after its chair, Lord Alan Bullock – even proposed in 1977 that large U.K. companies be required to include substantial employee representation on their boards of directors.[105] The Bullock Report clearly acknowledged the long-standing shareholder-centrism of U.K. company law, observing that "[t]he ultimate control of the company is seen in law as residing with its owners or shareholders," and that the board's duty to act in "the best interests of the company" had been "narrowly interpreted by the Courts to mean the best interests of the shareholders."[106] The fact that the Bullock Report failed to displace shareholders from their central position in U.K. company law has been attributed, with some force, to opposition by

[102] *See id.* at 36–39.

[103] *See id.* at 36 ("The principal arguments which are advanced for change are that the present scheme of the law fails adequately to recognise that businesses normally best generate wealth where participants operate harmoniously as teams and that managers should recognise the wider interests of the community in their activities."). *Cf.* Ruth V. Aguilera, Cynthia A. Williams, John M. Conley & Deborah E. Rupp, *Corporate Governance and Social Responsibility: A Comparative Analysis of the UK and the US*, 14 CORP. GOVERNANCE: AN INT'L REV. 147, 151–56 (2006) (describing evidence suggesting that issues of corporate social responsibility are more widely discussed by the press and institutional investors in the United Kingdom than in the United States).

[104] LORD ALAN BULLOCK ET AL., REPORT OF THE COMMITTEE OF INQUIRY ON INDUSTRIAL DEMOCRACY (1977) [hereinafter BULLOCK REPORT].

[105] For concise summaries of proposals advanced in the Bullock Report, see HADDEN, *supra* note 19, at 458–59; Otto Kahn-Freund, *Industrial Democracy*, 6 INDUS. L.J. 65, 65–69 (1977).

[106] BULLOCK REPORT, *supra* note 104, at 59–62. Interestingly, the Bullock Report contrasts the stark shareholder-centrism of U.K. company law with corporate law in the United States, where "the shareholders do not enjoy the sole right to decide certain fundamental issues of corporate structure or policy." *Id.* at 82.

City institutions, employers, and the Thatcher government alike,[107] and may also reflect concerns that the objective of corporate decision making would be rendered insufficiently clear if strict shareholder-centrism were abandoned.[108] At the same time, however, it is critical to observe that unions themselves were hardly uniform in their support of the Bullock Report's proposals, many fearing that employee board representation might tend to undermine efforts to secure gains through arms'-length collective bargaining.[109] In any event, by the turn of the new millennium the Bullock Report's "emphasis . . . on the principle of trade union representation on company boards [had] long been discarded."[110]

Employee interests would, to be sure, come to be recognized in the Companies Act, though not to any substantial effect. The Bullock Report approvingly cited proposals earlier in the 1970s to amend the Companies Act to permit, or even require, boards to show regard for employee interests, and argued that such regard should be required "whether employee representatives are put on the board or not."[111] In 1980, then, the Companies Act was amended to state that "[t]he matters to which the directors of a company are to have regard in the performance of their functions shall include the interests of the company's

[107] *See* Andrew Gamble & Gavin Kelly, *Shareholder Value and the Stakeholder Debate in the UK*, 9 CORP. GOVERNANCE: AN INT'L REV. 110, 112 (2001) (observing that the Thatcher government "was not interested in reorganising the way in which companies were run"); HADDEN, *supra* note 19, at 459 (observing that "the minority report . . . effectively representing the Confederation of British Industry, recommended a much more flexible and gradual implementation of any [such] requirement," and that "[i]t seems unlikely that any government will seek to press through the package recommended by the majority in the face of concerted opposition from employers"); James Moher, *Democracy in the Workplace – The Bullock Report Revisited* (July 9, 2010), http://www.historyandpolicy.org/forums/union/meeting_090710.html (report on a joint meeting of the History and Policy Trade Union Forum and the Centre for Contemporary British History) (summarizing the view of Lord David Lea, a member of the Bullock Committee, that "City interests were totally opposed to any dilution of boardroom control or of the primacy of shareholder value," and that "employers were hostile to having any worker representation on their boards" as well).

[108] *Compare* Kahn-Freund, *supra* note 105, at 77 (arguing that "employee representatives on a board . . . [would be] exposed to a conflict of duties which is simply insoluble") *with* Paul Davies & Wedderburn of Charlton, *The Land of Industrial Democracy*, 6 INDUS. L.J. 197, 201–02 (1977) (arguing that Kahn-Freund overstates the clarity of "profit maximisation" as a corporate objective, that "[t]here is consequently vested in such managements an element of discretion in the setting of corporate goals," and that "[o]ne of the main purposes of employee representation on the board is . . . to secure effective influence for the employees in the exercise of that discretion").

[109] *See* Gamble & Kelly, *supra* note 107, at 112; Moher, *supra* note 107 (reporting Lord David Lea's view to this effect).

[110] Gamble & Kelly, *supra* note 107, at 115.

[111] BULLOCK REPORT, *supra* note 104, at 62, 84.

employees in general as well as the interests of its members."[112] This provision would seem to have given the Bullock Committee its fallback – a mandate that directors "have regard" for employees – but in practice the provision proved to be of little consequence, not least due to the fact that employees could not enforce it.[113] As Simon Deakin and Giles Slinger would observe in 1997, the provision "simply stipulates that the employees' interests are to be taken into account" – the provision "does not stipulate that at any point employees' interests should take priority," a reality "reaffirmed in the few cases in which it has been discussed since its first appearance in 1980."[114] Neither was the provision "interpreted as standing in the way of the principle of board neutrality" in a takeover, "nor as diluting the specific obligations that boards have under the Takeover Code to ensure that objective financial advice is provided to shareholders on the merits to the bid."[115] Indeed, by the time the company law reform Steering Group turned to the matter in 1999, the provision appeared to be more trouble than it was worth, prompting a call to clarify U.K. law's "true character" with regard to corporate purpose.[116]

The Steering Group concluded that a "broader objective" than shareholder wealth maximization could "dangerously distract management into a political balancing style at the expense of economic growth and international competitiveness," rejecting the Pluralist position outright. Non-shareholders' interests, the Steering Group explained, "are best made good by changes in other areas of the law and public policy."[117] The Steering Group preferred the approach it termed "Enlightened Shareholder Value," preserving shareholder wealth maximization as "the ultimate objective of companies" while acknowledging other stakeholders' interests to the degree relevant to that objective.[118] This approach was in fact adopted in § 172 of the Companies Act 2006, which, as we have seen, requires directors to focus on the shareholders' interests "and in doing so [to] have regard" for other stakeholders, the environment,

[112] Companies Act, 1980, ch. 22, § 46(1) (U.K.). *See also* Companies Act 1985, ch. 6, § 309 (U.K.).

[113] *See* D.D. Prentice, *A Company and Its Employees: The Companies Act 1980*, 10 Indus. L.J. 1, 4 (1981). *See also* Simon Deakin & Giles Slinger, *Hostile Takeovers, Corporate Law, and the Theory of the Firm*, 24 J. Law & Soc'y 124, 135 (1997) (observing the same of § 309 of the Companies Act 1985).

[114] Deakin & Slinger, *supra* note 113, at 135.

[115] Armour et al., *supra* note 83, at 537.

[116] *See* Strategic Framework, *supra* note 100, at 41.

[117] *See id.* at 44.

[118] *See id.* at 37–39. *See also* Company Law Review Steering Group, Modern Company Law for a Competitive Economy: Completing the Structure 33–34 (2000) [hereinafter Completing the Structure]; Company Law Review Steering Group, Modern Company Law For a Competitive Economy: Developing the Framework 10–11 (2000) [hereinafter Developing the Framework].

and the long-term consequences of their decisions.[119] Although some viewed this approach as "a classic piece of New Labour triangulation" and a "half way house" between shareholder-oriented and stakeholder-oriented conceptions of the company,[120] § 172 is more widely and accurately recognized as a continuation of the preexisting shareholder-centric law, placing shareholders' interests at the heart of the corporate enterprise and requiring by negative implication that stakeholder interests be set aside except to the degree relevant to the pursuit of shareholder wealth.[121]

This commitment to shareholder-centrism clearly pervades the Steering Group's assessment of the shareholders' governance powers as well. For example, the Steering Group in 1999 recognized the stark divergence between the shareholder-centric U.K. approach to takeovers and the U.S. approach, which it fairly characterizes as resembling the "Pluralist" conception.[122] In its March 2000 document, then, the Steering Group concedes that "the evidence on the impact of takeovers is mixed," but nevertheless takes the position that "contested takeovers are on balance beneficial and also have important disciplinary effects," concluding that "we see no grounds for using company law to inhibit the takeover market."[123] Likewise, in its November 2000 document, the Steering Group reiterated, "[w]e remain of the view that changes to company law to inhibit hostile takeovers, for example by enabling the directors of target companies to take action that would have the effect of frustrating a bid (without shareholder consent), would weaken an important source of managerial accountability."[124]

More generally, the Steering Group approvingly cited "evidence of a large number of cases in recent years in which substantial shareholders, mainly insurance companies and fund managers, had been able to assert major influence on under-performing companies." Although "many of these cases . . . were never publicised and the evidence remains confidential," they report having seen "evidence of 50 cases between 1989 and 1999 of major intervention by institutional investors . . . in the management of listed companies,"

[119] Companies Act, 2006, c. 46, § 172(1) (U.K.).

[120] *See* Giles Richardson & Serle Court, *The Companies Act 2006, Directors' Duties and the Onset of Insolvency*, 23 TOLLEY'S INSOLVENCY L. & PRAC. 138 (2007).

[121] *See, e.g.*, DAVIES, *supra* note 22, at 507–08; DIGNAM & LOWRY, *supra* note 81, at 389; Robert Goddard, *Directors' Duties*, 12 EDIN. L. REV. 468, 471 (2008); Andrew Keay, *Tackling the Issue of the Corporate Objective: An Analysis of the United Kingdom's "Enlightened Shareholder Value Approach,"* 29 SYDNEY L. REV. 577, 604–10 (2007); John Parkinson, *Corporate Governance: The Company Law Review and Questions of 'Scope,'* 8 HUME PAPERS ON PUB. POL'Y 29, 32–33 (2000).

[122] *See* STRATEGIC FRAMEWORK, *supra* note 100, at 47–48.

[123] *See* DEVELOPING THE FRAMEWORK, *supra* note 118, at 81.

[124] *See* COMPLETING THE STRUCTURE, *supra* note 118, at 75.

which "often involved the removal of executives or boards," in addition to "a further 86 more minor cases of governance intervention in that period." The Steering Group "found this evidence impressive, if somewhat anecdotal," and concluded that "we do not regard it as supporting a case for a radical reappraisal of the governance system"[125] – a conclusion reflected in the Companies Act 2006 itself, which if anything only underscores the dominance of shareholders. As we have seen, this development is fully consistent with the larger postwar trajectory of U.K. company law, in which Labour-inspired reinforcement of shareholder-centric corporate governance rules occurs within a broader political economy safeguarding the interests of Labour's core constituency through extra-corporate social welfare programs.

B. THE U.S. MODEL: EMPLOYER-BASED SOCIAL WELFARE POLICY

Events could not have unfolded more differently in the United States – particularly in the area of takeover regulation, where the traditional U.S. ambivalence toward shareholders, and divergence from the express shareholder-centrism of U.K. corporate governance, are most clearly on display.[126] The core issues of takeover regulation – including the use of defenses by target management – were worked out in the United Kingdom between 1959, when the Bank of England spearheaded the Notes on Amalgamation of British Businesses, and 1968, when the City Code and City Panel took shape. In the United States the Williams Act likewise took effect in 1968, regulating U.S. tender offers for the first time – but this federal securities statute did not directly address the use of defenses, focusing rather on procedural mechanics of timing and disclosure while remaining agnostic on the social costs and benefits of takeovers. U.S. rules on the use of defenses would develop decades later, in the 1980s, following a wave of leveraged hostile tender offers.[127]

[125] Developing the Framework, *supra* note 118, at 78 & n.94. The Steering Group's conclusion is consistent with that of Bernard Black and John Coffee, who observe that, although public governance challenges are rare, U.K. institutions do "act behind closed doors," negotiating for desired outcomes before the omnipresent threat that recalcitrant directors will be removed. *See* Black & Coffee, *supra* note 1, at 2002, 2028–29, 2035–37, 2041–42. Andrew Pendleton and Howard Gospel add that this "facilitates rapid and decisive action by investors when firms are in distress," potentially involving "drastic adjustments at labour's expense." *See* Andrew Pendleton & Howard Gospel, *Markets and Relationships: Finance, Governance, and Labour in the United Kingdom, in* Corporate Governance and Labour Management: An International Comparison, *supra* note 83, at 1, 76–81.

[126] *See* Bruner, *supra* note 2, at 635–43.

[127] *See* William T. Allen, Reinier Kraakman & Guhan Subramanian, Commentaries and Cases on the Law of Business Organization 443–44, 525–28 (2d ed. 2007); Lyman Johnson & David Millon, *Misreading the Williams Act*, 87 Mich. L. Rev. 1862, 1889–1909 (1989).

	U.K.	U.S.
time period	1960s	1980s
prevailing politics	left	right
social welfare system	welfare state	"employee welfare state"
takeover regulation	self-regulation	state courts/legislatures
regulatory emphasis	shareholders	stakeholders

Figure 5.1. U.K. and U.S. Hostile Takeover Regulation: Political and Social Context

The upshot is that U.K. and U.S. takeover regulation took shape in radically different political circumstances (summarized in Figure 5.1). Whereas the shareholder-centric U.K. regime took shape during the left-leaning Labour administration of Harold Wilson, the stakeholder-centric U.S. regime took shape during the right-leaning Republican administration of Ronald Reagan, who strongly opposed governmental intrusions in the marketplace and broadly favored takeovers.[128] To be sure, U.S. takeover regulation – and particularly the use of defenses – has predominantly been a matter of state law, but the fact that a regime effectively built to constrain takeovers out of regard for non-shareholders should have emerged on the watch of the pro-market, pro-takeover Reagan administration remains every bit as remarkable as a starkly shareholder-centric regime receiving the support and promotion of the U.K. Labour Party. Neither would be predicted by Roe's social democracy theory, which associates stakeholder-centric policies with left-leaning social democracy and shareholder-centric policies with right-leaning rejection of social democracy.[129] Just as the foregoing section argued that the presence of left-leaning, state-based social welfare programs substantially facilitated the coalescence of shareholder-centric corporate governance in the United Kingdom, this section will argue that the weakness of the social safety net has tended to undermine shareholder-centric corporate governance in the United States, a dynamic most vividly illustrated by the emergence of stakeholder-centric takeover laws.

In stark contrast with the United Kingdom's postwar reliance on state-based social welfare structures, the United States has relied primarily on large

[128] *See* Mark J. Roe, Strong Managers, Weak Owners: The Political Roots of American Corporate Finance 156 (1994); Mark J. Roe, *Delaware's Competition*, 117 Harv. L. Rev. 588, 627–28 (2003); Mark J. Roe, *Delaware's Politics*, 118 Harv. L. Rev. 2491, 2510 (2005). *See also* Ronald Reagan Presidential Library, *The Reagan Presidency*, http://www.reagan.utexas.edu/archives/reference/pressketch.html; White House, *Ronald Reagan*, http://www.whitehouse.gov/about/presidents/ronaldreagan.

[129] *See supra* Chapter 4.B.ii.

corporate employers to be "primarily responsible for workers' social welfare," including "health insurance, pensions, unemployment insurance (in the form of severance pay, and job security and income guarantees), disability insurance, and life insurance," as well as required contributions to various state-run programs "on a per-worker or experience-rated basis."[130] This "elaborate web of legally enforceable contracts, implicit agreements, background legal norms, and discrete public regulatory and insurance systems" – termed the "employee welfare state" by David Charny – effectively aims to provide income, health, and retirement protections that workers in other developed countries often receive through government programs.[131] As Charny explains, although the employee welfare state "provided fairly comprehensive social insurance protections" to U.S. workers from the 1920s through the 1960s, elements not taking the form of enforceable legal rights – typically referred to as "implicit contracts" – have proven difficult to maintain in times of crisis. Hostile takeovers, in particular, have substantially destabilized the relationships among corporate stakeholders that historically sustained this uniquely American approach to social welfare policy.[132] In the 1970s and 1980s, Charny observes, companies "threatened with takeover by acquirers that would breach implicit commitments" often themselves "dispensed with the need to maintain their reputations for reliability among United States workers."[133]

To be sure, there are areas in which the U.K. and U.S. approaches to social welfare do not radically differ, including their similar reliance on private pensions.[134] Likewise neither country's labor laws provide particularly

[130] David Charny, *The Employee Welfare State in Transition*, 74 TEX. L. REV. 1601, 1601 (1996). *See also* John Clarke, *US Welfare: Variations on the Liberal Regime*, *in* COMPARING WELFARE STATES, *supra* note 7, at 113, 114–16; Jacoby, *supra* note 83, at 37–39; Toni Johnson, *Healthcare Costs and U.S. Competitiveness* (Council on Foreign Relations, updated Mar. 26, 2012), http://www.cfr.org/publication/13325/; Orly Lobel, *The Four Pillars of Work Law*, 104 MICH. L. REV. 1539, 1542–43 (2006) (reviewing RAYMOND HOGLER, EMPLOYMENT RELATIONS IN THE UNITED STATES: LAW, POLICY, AND PRACTICE (2004) and KATHERINE V.W. STONE, FROM WIDGETS TO DIGITS: EMPLOYMENT REGULATION FOR THE CHANGING WORKPLACE (2004)).

[131] Charny, *supra* note 130, at 1606. *See also* Sanford Levinson, *The Welfare State*, *in* A COMPANION TO PHILOSOPHY OF LAW AND LEGAL THEORY 553, 555 (Dennis Patterson ed., 1996).

[132] *See* Charny, *supra* note 130, at 1601–20. *See also* Julia Contreras & Orly Lobel, *Wal-martization and the Fair Share Health Care Acts*, 19 St. THOMAS L. REV. 105, 111–12 (2006); Matthew Dolan, *Obama Seeks Concessions from UAW Retirees*, WALL ST. J., Mar. 31, 2009, at A4; Jacoby, *supra* note 83, at 35–42; Lobel, *supra* note 130, at 1542–49. On implicit contracts, see Andrei Shleifer & Lawrence H. Summers, *Breach of Trust in Hostile Takeovers*, *in* CORPORATE TAKEOVERS: CAUSES AND CONSEQUENCES (Alan J. Auerbach ed., 1988).

[133] Charny, *supra* note 130, at 1613.

[134] *See* CHEFFINS, *supra* note 6, at 348; Simon Deakin, *Workers, Finance and Democracy*, *in* THE FUTURE OF LABOUR LAW 79, 89–94 (Catherine Barnard et al. eds., 2004) (describing the decline of state-based pension benefits in the United Kingdom); Martin Gelter, *The Pension*

strong protections in the takeover context[135] – although as between the two, U.S. employment protections generally are weaker than U.K. protections.[136] Health care is another matter, however, the patchwork of state-based and private programs in the United States falling far short of the universal coverage taken for granted in the United Kingdom. "Medicare" provides health insurance for those aged 65 or older (and certain disabled and end-stage renal patients);[137] "Medicaid" provides health insurance for the very poor;[138] the Children's Health Insurance Program – or "CHIP" – offers expanded coverage for uninsured children;[139] and the Department of Veterans Affairs administers a health program for veterans.[140] As T.R. Reid has observed, the prevailing global models of health care provision "should be fairly easy for Americans to understand because we have elements of all of them in our fragmented national health care apparatus. When it comes to treating veterans, we're Britain or Cuba. For Americans over the age of 65 on Medicare, we're Canada. For working Americans who get insurance on the job, we're Germany." Meanwhile, for the uninsured, "the United States is Cambodia or Burkina Faso or rural India, with access to a doctor available if you can pay the bill out-of-pocket at the time of treatment or if you're sick enough to be admitted to the emergency ward at the public hospital."[141]

System and the Rise of Shareholder Primacy 41 (Fordham Univ. Sch. of Law Working Paper Series, 2012), http://ssrn.com/abstract=2079607 (observing similar reliance on private, defined contribution pensions in the two countries).

135 *See* Simon Deakin et al., *Implicit Contracts, Takeovers, and Corporate Governance: In the Shadow of the City Code* 12 (ESRC Ctr. for Bus. Research, Univ. of Cambridge, Working Paper 254, 2002), http://ideas.repec.org/p/cbr/cbrwps/wp254.html.

136 *See* Margarita Estevez-Abe et al., *Social Protection and the Formation of Skills: A Reinterpretation of the Welfare State, in* VARIETIES OF CAPITALISM: THE INSTITUTIONAL FOUNDATIONS OF COMPARATIVE ADVANTAGE 145, 163–73 (Peter A. Hall & David Soskice eds., 2001); Gelter, *supra* note 72, at 170, 189–190. *Cf.* GOUREVITCH & SHINN, *supra* note 99, at 153–54 (reporting higher "corporatism" in the United Kingdom than in the United States); Pendleton & Gospel, *supra* note 125, at 68 (reporting substantial "income inequality" in both countries, but that "[t]his is most marked of all in the United States").

137 *See* Centers for Medicare & Medicaid Services, *Medicare Program – General Information*, https://www.cms.gov/medicare/Medicare-General-Information/MedicareGenInfo/.

138 *See* Medicaid.gov, *Eligibility*, http://www.medicaid.gov/Medicaid-CHIP-Program-Information/By-Topics/Eligibility/Eligibility.html.

139 *See* Medicaid.gov, *Children's Health Insurance Program*, http://www.medicaid.gov/CHIP/CHIP-Program-Information.html.

140 *See* United States Department of Veterans Affairs, *Health Benefits: Veteran Eligibility*, http://www.va.gov/healthbenefits/apply/veterans.asp.

141 T.R. Reid, *Health Care Systems – The Four Basic Models*, FRONTLINE (Apr. 15, 2008), http://www.pbs.org/wgbh/pages/frontline/sickaroundtheworld/countries/models.html. *See also* Timothy Stolzfus Jost, *Why Can't We Do What They Do? National Health Reform Abroad*, 32 J.L. MED. & ETHICS 433, 433–35 (2004) (describing the implementation of Germany's social

As in corporate law, there is a complex federalism dimension to U.S. health care regulation – states have historically regulated health care through their police power and role as *parens patriae*, while Congress possesses broad capacity to legislate in this area pursuant to its taxing/spending and interstate commerce authority. In practice, however, the federal government often acts through conditional grants to states, as with Medicare and Medicaid.[142] The potential for recent reforms to expand coverage is discussed below,[143] but historically the medical profession and the insurance industry have strongly opposed comprehensive state-based health insurance programs in the United States.[144] The consequence is that – in stark contrast with the United Kingdom, where the highly regarded National Health Service provides access to health care for all British residents – the United States relies heavily on a costly employer-based system achieving poor outcomes on a number of key metrics while leaving tens of millions of Americans with no health coverage of any kind.[145] According to OECD data, "the United States spends two-and-a-half times more than the OECD average, and yet ranks with Turkey and Mexico as the only OECD countries without universal health coverage."[146] As health

insurance–based coverage through "non-profit organizations, which are accountable to their members (and their members' employers)").

[142] *See* Lawrence O. Gostin, Public Health Law: Power, Duty, Restraint 77–110 (2d ed. 2008). *See also* U.S. Const. art. I, § 8, cls. 1, 3.

[143] *See infra* Chapter 6.D.

[144] *See* Clarke, *supra* note 130, at 123, 138–139; Jost, *supra* note 141, at 438–39.

[145] *See* Contreras & Lobel, *supra* note 132, at 108–12; Karen Davis, Cathy Schoen & Kristof Stremikis, Mirror, Mirror on the Wall: How the Performance of the U.S. Health Care System Compares Internationally (2010 update); Jost, *supra* note 141, at 435–37; Press Release, U.S. Census Bureau, Household Income Rises, Poverty Rate Unchanged, Number of Uninsured Down (Aug. 26, 2008), http://www.census.gov/Press-Release/www/releases/archives/income_wealth/012528.html (reporting 45.7 million people without health insurance as of 2007).

[146] Johnson, *supra* note 130. *See also Expensive Health Care Is Not Always the Best Healthcare, Says OECD's Health at a Glance*, Org. for Econ. Co-operation and Dev. (Dec. 8, 2009), http://www.oecd.org/document/23/0,3343,en_2649_37407_44216846_1_1_1_1,00.html; Suzanne Mettler, The Submerged State, How Invisible Government Policies Undermine American Democracy 98 (2011); Mark Pearson, Head, Health Division, OECD, *Disparities in Health Expenditure across OECD Countries: Why Does the United States Spend So Much More than Other Countries?* (Written Statement to Senate Special Committee on Aging) (Sept. 30, 2009). According to the OECD, aggregate "social expenditure" in the United States – including both public and private expenditure – exceeds that in Australia, Canada, and the United Kingdom. *See* Organisation for Economic Co-operation and Development, *Social Policies and Data: Social Expenditure Database (SOCX)*, http://www.oecd.org/els/socialpoliciesanddata/socialexpendituredatabasesocx.htm#socx_data (reporting "Public and private social expenditure in percentage of GDP in 2007"). *See also* Willem Adema & Maxime Ladaique, *How Expensive Is the Welfare State?* (OECD Social, Employment and Migration Working Papers No. 92, 2009); Mettler, *supra*, at 121–23.

law scholar Timothy Jost sums it up, "no other developed country relies on private insurance . . . to provide primary coverage for its population" – for the simple reason that it "cannot cover everyone."[147]

In this light, it is unsurprising that stakeholder-oriented responses to hostile takeovers in the 1980s would have been expressly linked to concerns about employee vulnerability in the face of limited state-based social welfare protections. The preamble to a 1987 antitakeover statute in North Carolina, for example, noted the "increasing frequency" of hostile takeovers, that "such activity can be highly disruptive to communities" because of the ensuing "high unemployment and erosion of the State and local economy and tax base," and that "these corporations provide their North Carolina employees with health, retirement and other benefits."[148] These concerns were particularly pressing in the 1980s, when social welfare programs were scaled back in a manner resembling that in the United Kingdom.[149] As John Clarke observes, "[b]y 1983, 58 per cent of Americans were covered by employment-based schemes," and "[e]conomic uncertainty in the 1980s and 1990s led to many more American citizens becoming anxious about the security of their healthcare arrangements." Given widespread dependence on employer-provided health insurance, "widespread job losses . . . threatened both the insurance arrangements and the citizens' sense of health security."[150] Indeed, "a three-nation survey of how Americans, Canadians, and Britons viewed the performance of their health care systems" published in *Health Affairs* in 1989 found that "Americans expressed the greatest degree of dissatisfaction" and, strikingly, that "only Americans were so dissatisfied that they would consider adopting the type of health system found in another country."[151] As Robert Blendon and his coauthors would conclude a year later, this appeared to have little to do with "the quality of health services available," reflecting rather "the

[147] Jost, *supra* note 141, at 433.

[148] David Millon, *State Takeover Laws: A Rebirth of Corporation Law?*, 45 WASH. & LEE L. REV. 903, 922–24 (1988) (quoting 1987 N.C. Sess. Laws ch. 124). *See also* Lyman Johnson, *State Takeover Statutes: Constitutionality, Community, and Heresy*, 45 WASH. & LEE L. REV. 1051, 1053–54 (1988); Lyman Johnson, *The Delaware Judiciary and the Meaning of Corporate Life and Corporate Law*, 68 TEX. L. REV. 865, 909–10 (1990); Johnson & Millon, *supra* note 127, at 1878–82; Lyman Johnson & David Millon, *Missing the Point about State Takeover Statutes*, 87 MICH. L. REV. 846, 848–53 (1989); ROE, *supra* note 128, at 152–53.

[149] *See* Clarke, *supra* note 130, at 125–34; PRASAD, *supra* note 91, at 82–87.

[150] Clarke, *supra* note 130, at 137.

[151] Robert J. Blendon et al., *Satisfaction with Health Systems in Ten Nations*, HEALTH AFFAIRS, Summer 1990, at 185, 185 (citing R.J. Blendon & H. Taylor, *Views on Health Care: Public Opinion in Three Nations*, HEALTH AFFAIRS, Spring 1989, at 149). "The majority of the public (61 percent) stated they would prefer the Canadian system of national health insurance . . . to the current U.S. system." *Id.*

interaction between our sharply rising health care costs and the inadequate financial protection provided by our health insurance system," relying as it did (and does) on "individual employers."[152] In this environment, hostile takeovers were widely perceived as threatening the uniquely American "employee welfare state" that Charny describes, precipitating legislative and judicial responses that British observers would later characterize – correctly – as "pluralistic" in orientation.[153]

Although Delaware, the legal home for most U.S. public companies, was not among those states adopting constituency statutes, its takeover case law nevertheless bears the imprint of the social dynamics prompting statutory responses elsewhere. *Unocal*, the 1985 decision in which the Delaware Supreme Court established the framework for evaluating takeover defenses, states that in determining how to respond to a hostile bid, the target board may legitimately consider "the nature of the takeover bid and its effect on the corporate enterprise," including "the impact on 'constituencies' other than shareholders (i.e., creditors, customers, employees, and perhaps even the community generally)."[154] The scare quotes around the word "constituencies" presumably represent a nod to the emergence of constituency statutes elsewhere, which aim to accomplish much the same thing. The court did hold in *Revlon* that once the sale, breakup, or change of control of the corporation is "inevitable" – for example, "when an auction among active bidders is in progress" – the board must focus on "maximization of the company's value . . . for the stockholders' benefit."[155] The narrow scope of this duty to maximize short-term value, however, was amply driven home in *Paramount v. Time*, where the court clarified that "absent a limited set of circumstances as defined under *Revlon*, a board of directors . . . is not under any *per se* duty to maximize shareholder value in the short term, even in the context of a takeover." Indeed, the court cited to the "constituencies" language from *Unocal* in support of its conclusion that the board could simply refuse to negotiate in the face of an all-cash, all-shares, premium bid.[156]

[152] *Id.* at 190–92.

[153] *See* STRATEGIC FRAMEWORK, *supra* note 100, at 48. I focus on the perception of such a threat because the empirical evidence regarding the impacts of hostile takeovers is in fact mixed. *See, e.g.*, Charny, *supra* note 130, at 1629; Deakin et al., *supra* note 135, at 14–15; Jacoby, *supra* note 83, at 36; DALE A. OESTERLE, THE LAW OF MERGERS AND ACQUISITIONS 660–61 (3d ed. 2005); Pendleton & Gospel, *supra* note 125, at 67–68. Nevertheless, it is the perception that drives the politics, and the perception of a threat to employee welfare was clearly quite real.

[154] Unocal Corp. v. Mesa Petroleum Co., 493 A.2d 946, 955 (Del. 1985).

[155] Revlon, Inc. v. MacAndrews & Forbes Holdings, Inc., 506 A.2d 173, 182 (Del. 1986). *See also* Paramount Commc'ns Inc. v. QVC Network Inc., 637 A.2d 34, 43–44 (Del. 1994) (applying this duty to "the sale of control context").

[156] Paramount Commc'ns, Inc. v. Time Inc., 571 A.2d 1140, 1150, 1152–53 (Del. 1990).

That it would be judicial opinions addressing such core matters of corporate law is not surprising in Delaware, a jurisdiction where – aside from a business combination statute aptly described as being "fairly mild as anti-takeover statutes go"[157] – the legislature has consistently refused to weigh in on such matters. Delaware judges themselves have remarked on the "legislative vacuum" this creates in the area of hostile takeovers, rendering it "unavoidable that the [adjudication] process for developing those legal rules will involve policy choices." For lack of a clear policy in the statute itself, "the judicial task unavoidably (and awkwardly) acquires legislative characteristics."[158] Former Delaware Chancellor William Allen, Vice Chancellor (now Justice) Jack Jacobs, and Vice Chancellor (now Chancellor) Leo Strine, in a 2002 law review article, recognize that the Delaware statute does not straightforwardly endorse a shareholder-centric or stakeholder-centric conception of corporate purpose, but candidly concede that "[j]udges presented with takeover cases are unavoidably aware that the interests of more than stockholders are usually at stake," and express "uncertainty" regarding whether a shareholder-centric approach to takeovers would "best facilitate the maximization of societal wealth." They elaborate: "it is credibly arguable that an approach that locates these decisions in the hands of directors" may effectively balance shareholder and stakeholder interests[159] – an approach flatly rejected in the U.K. company law review process.[160]

To be sure, various market dynamics have tended to advance the interests of U.S. shareholders over recent decades, not least being the rise of institutional shareholders.[161] This naturally introduces a powerful and sophisticated pro-shareholder constituency into the U.S. context resembling that present in the U.K. context decades earlier.[162] Greater capital mobility has, at the same time,

[157] Allen et al., *supra* note 127, at 609 n.59. *See also* Del. Code Ann. tit. 8, § 203 (prohibiting "business combinations" with 15 percent shareholders for three years, subject to various exceptions).

[158] William T. Allen, Jack B. Jacobs & Leo E. Strine, Jr., *The Great Takeover Debate: A Meditation on Bridging the Conceptual Divide*, 69 U. Chi. L. Rev. 1067, 1068–70 (2002). *See also* Johnson, *The Delaware Judiciary and the Meaning of Corporate Life and Corporate Law*, *supra* note 148, at 886–91 (similarly discussing Delaware's "legislative public-law vacuum" in this area); Roe, *supra* note 128, at 160–61 (observing that "the key move" in the state-level response to hostile takeovers was endorsement of the poison pill by courts, tending to obscure the political dimensions of the issue).

[159] *See* Allen et al., *supra* note 158, at 1074–89.

[160] *See* Completing the Structure, *supra* note 118, at 34; Developing the Framework, *supra* note 118, at 14; Strategic Framework, *supra* note 100, at 44. *See also* Companies Act, 2006, c. 46, § 172 (U.K.).

[161] *See* Christopher M. Bruner, *The Enduring Ambivalence of Corporate Law*, 59 Ala. L. Rev. 1385, 1432–35 (2008).

[162] *See id.* at 1439–42. *See also* Christopher M. Bruner, *Corporate Governance Reform in a Time of Crisis*, 36 J. Corp. L. 309, 334–35 & n.160 (2011).

augmented the capacity of shareholders (notably institutions) to vote with their feet,[163] while a 1993 amendment to the U.S. Internal Revenue Code has strongly skewed executive compensation toward equity-based pay. The Code now provides that only the first $1 million of pay for public company executives is deductible, but critically, the limit does not apply to performance-based pay – the result being not the intended reduction in overall executive compensation, but an explosion in compensation linked to the value of the corporation's stock.[164] The finance literature tends to suggest that increased alignment of managers' interests with those of shareholders, including through equity-based pay, does in fact result in a greater managerial appetite for risk, as shareholders generally prefer[165] – an issue pertinent to the financial crisis and subsequent regulatory responses, to which we shall return later in the book.[166] For the moment, however, it is sufficient to observe that the increasing dominance of institutional investors, the increasing mobility of capital, and the explosion of equity-based executive pay all presumably tend to focus U.S. managers' minds more intently on shareholders' interests than would have been the case in the 1980s.

Nevertheless, recent events tend to suggest that the social dynamics driving the response to hostile takeovers in the 1980s have remained powerful political forces in the new millennium. Gallup surveys conducted in early 2003, for example, found that although Americans, Canadians, and Britons did not differ markedly in their perceptions of "the *quality* of medical care in their country," Americans expressed far greater dissatisfaction regarding "the availability of affordable healthcare" – results leading Rick Blizzard, Gallup's health care editor, to observe that "this dichotomy seems to support the hypothesis that private healthcare encourages high-quality standards, but may be a barrier to access and affordability."[167] Interestingly, as Blizzard would observe in 2004, although a "somewhat higher percentage of Americans rate the quality of

[163] *See, e.g.*, William T. Allen, *Our Schizophrenic Conception of the Business Corporation*, 14 CARDOZO L. REV. 261, 279 (1992); DIGNAM & GALANIS, *supra* note 19, at 103–107; Rajan & Zingales, *supra* note 84.

[164] 26 U.S.C. § 162(m). *See also* Sanjai Bhagat & Roberta Romano, *Reforming Executive Compensation: Focusing and Committing to the Long-Term*, 26 YALE J. ON REG. 359, 365 (2009); Jennifer G. Hill, Ronald W. Masulis & Randall S. Thomas, *Comparing CEO Employment Contract Provisions: Differences between Australia and the United States*, 64 VAND. L. REV. 559, 573, 595–96 (2011); Frederick Tung, *Pay for Banker Performance: Structuring Executive Compensation for Risk Regulation*, 105 NW. U. L. REV. 1205, 1216–18 & n.55 (2011).

[165] *See* Bruner, *supra* note 162, at 316–17 (discussing this literature).

[166] *See infra* Chapter 6.D.

[167] "In Great Britain, satisfaction with *access* to affordable healthcare (43%) is consistent with satisfaction with *quality* (42%). In Canada, satisfaction with access to affordable healthcare

healthcare they receive as 'excellent' (33%) than do either Britons (27%) or Canadians (24%)," 38 percent of Americans said "they would like to replace the current, private U.S. healthcare system with a government-run system similar to that in Canada and Great Britain," whereas just 21 percent of Britons and 13 percent of Canadians favored the opposite move. This divergence, Blizzard suggested, had less to do with quality than with costs and "[p]erceived inequality."[168]

These dynamics were vividly illustrated when Walmart, the United States' largest private employer as of 2006, sought to boost shareholder returns by "shifting health care costs to both their employees and to the taxpayers" who fund limited state health care programs – a move prompting states to respond with legislation aimed at pushing those costs back onto Walmart.[169] Although these legislative efforts failed due to federal preemption, Walmart nevertheless improved its employee health benefits in response to "a vast range of campaigns and litigation against the corporation."[170] Julia Contreras and Orly Lobel rightly conclude of this episode that Walmart's problems stemmed from its failure to acknowledge and respect the social and political equilibrium that Charny termed the "employee welfare state" by excessively subordinating the interests of employees and taxpayers to those of Walmart's shareholders.[171]

Broader concerns regarding the social impacts of takeovers have even played out in the presidential political arena. For example, Mitt Romney, a private equity investor turned politician, was dogged throughout his run for the 2012 Republican presidential nomination by claims that the buyout profits placing him "among the wealthiest candidates ever to run for president" came at the expense of target company employees who lost their jobs.[172] Strikingly, these attacks would come from the left and right alike,[173] reflecting concerns

(57%) is slightly higher than satisfaction with quality (52%). But the most dramatic variation . . . occurs in the United States, where only 25% are satisfied with the availability of affordable healthcare, but 48% are satisfied with quality." Rick Blizzard, *Healthcare System Ratings: U.S., Great Britain, Canada*, GALLUP (Mar. 25, 2003), http://www.gallup.com/poll/8056/healthcare-system-ratings-us-great-britain-canada.aspx.

[168] Rick Blizzard, *Greener on the Other Side? Universal vs. Private Healthcare*, GALLUP (Jan. 20, 2004), http://www.gallup.com/poll/10339/greener-other-side-universal-vs-private-healthcare.aspx.

[169] *See* Contreras & Lobel, *supra* note 132, at 105–17.

[170] *See id.* at 121–34.

[171] *See id.* at 111–13, 134–35. *See also* Ceci Connolly, *At Wal-Mart, a Health-Care Turnaround*, WASH. POST, Feb. 13, 2009, at A01.

[172] Nicholas Confessore et al., *Buyout Profits Keep Flowing to Romney*, N.Y. TIMES, Dec. 18, 2011. *See also* Mark Maremont, *Romney at Bain: Big Gains, Some Busts*, WALL ST. J., Jan. 9, 2012.

[173] *Compare* Confessore et al., *supra* note 172 (reporting that "Democrats have already made layoffs at Bain companies during Mr. Romney's tenure at the firm a centerpiece of their attacks

regarding the social desirability of corporate takeovers strongly resonating with those raised in the 1980s. Indeed, a labor-backed group called "Americans for Change" even ran "an ad campaign comparing Mr. Romney to Gordon Gekko, the marauding buyout king portrayed in the movie 'Wall Street'"[174] – a tactic vividly illustrating that the social concerns associated with the 1980s takeover wave remained politically consequential decades later in the run-up to the 2012 election. As President Barack Obama himself told the press of private equity, "their priority is to maximize profits, and that is not always going to be good for communities or businesses or workers." He pointedly continued that, as President, "[y]our job is to think about those workers who get laid off."[175] As we shall see, these social dynamics also figured centrally in regulatory responses to the recent financial crisis – both in corporate governance and in social welfare policy.[176]

C. PREDOMINANCE OF THE U.K. SOCIAL WELFARE MODEL

As the foregoing discussion demonstrates, the United Kingdom and the United States – for all their similarities – have struck radically different social and political equilibria in responding to the interests of non-shareholder constituencies in public corporations. In this section I argue that Australia and Canada have adopted social welfare models and struck larger social and political equilibria broadly resembling those in the United Kingdom, and that they have done so for broadly similar reasons – even if each has arrived there by its own path because of unique legal, economic, historical, and cultural factors.

1. Australia

We noted earlier that whereas neither the United Kingdom nor the United States offers strong employment or unemployment protections by global standards, if anything U.K. protections exceed U.S. protections. The same is broadly true of Australia, which similarly falls near the bottom of the scale in global terms but offers stronger protections than the United Kingdom and the United States alike (if only marginally so).[177]

on him") *with* Maremont, *supra* note 172 (reporting that primary rivals Rick Perry and Newt Gingrich both criticized Romney for profiting from layoffs).

[174] Confessore et al., *supra* note 172.

[175] *See* John Cassidy, *Obama Doubles Down on Bain Capital Attacks*, NEW YORKER, May 21, 2012, http://www.newyorker.com/online/blogs/johncassidy/2012/05/obama-doubles-down-on-bain-attacks.html (quoting President Obama). *See also* Jim Rutenberg & Jeff Zeleny, *Bain Attacks Make Inroads for President*, N.Y. TIMES, July 1, 2012, http://www.nytimes.com/2012/07/01/us/politics/bain-attacks-make-inroads-for-president.html?pagewanted=all.

[176] *See infra* Chapter 6.D.

[177] *See* Estevez-Abe et al., *supra* note 136, at 163–73.

Like the United Kingdom, however, Australia differs enormously from the United States in at least one critical form of social welfare protection – health care. Australia's "Medicare" system is a "universal health care system" aiming to provide Australian residents with "affordable, accessible and high quality health care," reflecting a commitment to social equity much like that in the United Kingdom. Australia's Medicare system "was established based on the understanding that all Australians should contribute to the cost of health care according to their ability to pay," and accordingly the program provides "free treatment as a public . . . patient in a public hospital" and "free or subsidised treatment by medical practitioners including general practitioners, specialists, participating optometrists or dentists."[178] Those holding Medicare cards are also eligible for the Pharmaceutical Benefits Scheme, under which "the government subsidises the cost of medicine for most conditions," with minimal co-payments.[179] Public hospitals are funded by the Commonwealth and the states, while states administer them, reflecting a complex federalism balance not unlike that in the United States. Although there is no express federal constitutional power to run public hospitals directly, it remains conceivable that states could refer their own power, or that other more general constitutional powers could be read broadly to permit the federal government to do so. In any event, it is clearly established that the Commonwealth's authority to tax and then make transfers to states with conditions attached in fact gives the federal government substantial regulatory power in this area.[180]

Looking no further than this, it would appear that Australia has struck upon a social–political equilibrium strongly resembling that in the United Kingdom, and sharply contrasting with that in the United States – strong shareholder powers and decision-making orientation within corporate law, and strong social welfare protections available to employees outside corporate law. The reality in Australia is considerably more complex than this static comparison would

[178] Government of Western Australia Department of Health, *Medicare*, http://www.health.wa.gov.au/services/detail.cfm?Unit_ID=2467. *See also* Amanda Biggs, *Medicare – Background Brief*, at "How Medicare Works" and "Eligibility," updated Oct. 29, 2004, http://www.aph.gov.au/About_Parliament/Parliamentary_Departments/Parliamentary_Library/Publications_Archive/archive/Medicare.

[179] Pharmaceutical Benefits Scheme, *PBS – Brief Overview*, http://www.pbs.gov.au/info/about-the-pbs.

[180] *See generally* Sharon Scully, *Does the Commonwealth Have Constitutional Power to Take Over the Administration of Public Hospitals?* (Parliament of Australia Research Paper No. 36 2008–09, 2009), http://www.aph.gov.au/About_Parliament/Parliamentary_Departments/Parliamentary_Library/pubs/rp/rp0809/09rp36. *See also* SENATE SELECT COMMITTEE ON MEDICARE, MEDICARE – HEALTHCARE OR WELFARE? 5–6 (Oct. 2003); *See* Commonwealth of Australia Constitution Act, 1900 (Imp), 63 & 64 Victoria, c. 12, §§ 81, 96 (U.K.) (compilation prepared July 25, 2003) (permitting federal taxation "for the purposes of the Commonwealth" and grants to states "on such terms and conditions as the Parliament thinks fit").

suggest, however, because unlike in the United Kingdom, it cannot be said that strong state-based social welfare protections predate the modernization of Australian corporate law. Social welfare policy has in fact impacted Australian corporate governance in striking ways, but their interaction has unfolded in a different manner largely because of unique approaches to social welfare that Australia has taken at various points in its history. I delve into that history here, and then pick up the story again later in the book.[181]

Up through the 1960s, Australian labor policy and social welfare policy were based on what political scientist Francis Castles has described as the "wage-earners' welfare state." Castles emphasizes the manner in which balances are struck across regulatory domains, observing that "[p]olicies are both designed and experienced in a context which is constituted by the total package," and can achieve different goals depending on the broader policy context they inhabit. Notably, state-based programs do not represent the sole means of delivering social welfare protections, which can also be provided through full employment policies – even though the latter "will not appear under any public expenditure category."[182] We have already seen this dynamic at work in the United States, and it actually figured quite centrally in Australia for much of the twentieth century as well. For several decades, Australian labor policy and social welfare policy were deeply intertwined with policies aimed at preserving a high level of stable employment, including protective tariffs; national, industry-based wage arbitration; and discriminatory immigration policies.[183] The idea was to protect domestic industry and domestic labor alike from foreign competition, and the upshot from a social welfare perspective was that a stable "living wage" would permit workers to accumulate savings sufficient to weather short-term periods of unemployment and illness (in the latter case bolstered by private insurance) – effectively meaning that state-based protections needed only to address matters not reached by the labor market, such as old-age pensions and workers' compensation. As Castles explains, this approach focused "almost exclusively on the working population and [its] dependents – it provided a *wage-earners' welfare state*, not one of which all citizens were members by right."[184]

This approach appears to have remained broadly politically stable well into the postwar period. Unlike in Europe, Australia's Labor Party ruled for just

[181] *See infra* Chapter 6.B.

[182] FRANCIS G. CASTLES, AUSTRALIAN PUBLIC POLICY AND ECONOMIC VULNERABILITY: A COMPARATIVE AND HISTORICAL PERSPECTIVE 5 (1988).

[183] *See id.* at 91–102, 135–52. *See also* Richard Mitchell, Peter Gahan, Andrew Stewart, Sean Cooney & Shelley Marshall, *The Evolution of Labour Law in Australia: Measuring the Change*, 23 AUSTL. J. LAB. L. *23–*25 (2010) (Lexis pagination).

[184] *See* CASTLES, *supra* note 182, at 102–04, 157.

sixteen years between 1910 and 1970, yet as a political matter tariffs and wage arbitration appealed to the right as a less "socialistic" alternative to "Labor proposals to amend the constitutional provisions relating to the economic powers of the Commonwealth [and] to institute a national health service, both of which the conservative parties fought tooth and nail." At the same time, the wage-earners' welfare state was broadly acceptable to unions, which was important because even though Labor won few elections in this period, they averaged over 40 percent of the federal vote.[185] Although in 1960 just two advanced countries spent less of their national product on welfare (Japan and the United States), there was little political pressure in Australia to increase welfare spending because of the combination of low unemployment and wage arbitration.[186] As Castles and John Uhr explain, "[h]igh minimum wages" left Australia with "relatively few 'working poor,'" and "the functioning of the wages system made for a considerable equality of condition. . . . Combined with full employment and an extremely high level of private home ownership, Australia could and did see itself in the early post-war decades as a 'lucky country', in which the condition of those who remained poor would also improve as the economy continued to prosper."[187] Indexing of wage awards to the consumer price index was abandoned in 1953, but "the implications of the change were masked for more than a decade by Australia's growing prosperity."[188]

Although in global terms Australia resembles the other common-law countries more closely than it does the corporatism pursued in Europe,[189] the wage-earners' welfare state of the postwar decades nevertheless differs starkly from the approaches to labor policy and social welfare policy taken elsewhere in the common-law world.[190] So when – and why – did Australia move away from this employment-based approach in favor of a more state-based approach? The political forces and processes at work were very complex, but Castles dates the beginning of this transition to the late 1960s and early 1970s,

[185] *See id.* at 140–43.

[186] *See id.* at 14–18.

[187] Francis G. Castles & John Uhr, *Australia: Federal Constraints and Institutional Innovations*, *in* FEDERALISM AND THE WELFARE STATE: NEW WORLD AND EUROPEAN EXPERIENCES 51, 80 (Herbert Obinger, Stephan Leibfried & Francis G. Castles eds., 2005). *See also* GØSTA ESPING-ANDERSEN, SOCIAL FOUNDATIONS OF POSTINDUSTRIAL ECONOMIES 89–90 (1999).

[188] *See* CASTLES, *supra* note 182, at 144–45.

[189] *See* Meredith Jones & Richard Mitchell, *Legal Origins, Legal Families and the Regulation of Labour in Australia*, *in* VARIETIES OF CAPITALISM, CORPORATE GOVERNANCE AND EMPLOYEES 60, 83, 86 (Shelley Marshall, Richard Mitchell & Ian Ramsay eds., 2008); RICHARD MITCHELL ET AL., LAW, CORPORATE GOVERNANCE AND PARTNERSHIPS AT WORK: A STUDY OF AUSTRALIAN REGULATORY STYLE AND BUSINESS PRACTICE 51–55 (2011).

[190] *See* Jones & Mitchell, *supra* note 189, at 64–65, 84–86; MITCHELL ET AL., *supra* note 189, at 45–50. It is worth observing that if anything it more closely resembles the U.S. approach described by Charny as an "employee welfare state," at least in the sense that employment relationships constituted the principal means of advancing social welfare goals.

when the conditions underwriting exclusive reliance on the wage-earners' welfare state began to erode. Notably, unemployment spiked following the first oil shock,[191] and the Labor Party – led by Gough Whitlam – seized on an opportunity to differentiate itself from the right-leaning Liberal Party and Country Party by advocating more egalitarian social policies.[192] In his famous "It's Time" speech, delivered at the Blacktown Civic Centre in Sydney in November 1972, Whitlam emphasized education spending, pensions, health care, and social insurance, blasting "the Liberals' health insurance system" as the "most notorious single instance of unequal sharing."[193]

Although in retrospect there is certainly an "irony" in Australia's Labor Party turning to egalitarian state-based social welfare policy almost precisely when such policies would become most difficult to finance, "offering all citizens fair access to the good fortunes of the lucky country just at the point when the luck had begun to run out,"[194] as a political matter this shift in Labor Party policy clearly responded to a core instability in the wage-earners' welfare state – its inability to respond effectively to the needs of the nonworking population in a time of growing unemployment.[195] This core tension – the political demand for state-based welfare coinciding with diminishing capacity to pay for it – would in turn give rise to a period of substantial instability in Australian social welfare provision that would last for over twenty years, from the 1970s through at least the mid-1990s.[196]

Although the Pharmaceutical Benefits Scheme "began as a limited scheme in 1949, with free medicines for pensioners" and certain medicines free to others,[197] the more comprehensive Australian approach to health care would take shape much later. Health economist Richard Scotton recalled (in 2000) that, in June 1967, he and John Deeble, research fellows at the University of Melbourne, were approached by Gough Whitlam, Federal Opposition Leader, who "asked us to put our ideas on paper" regarding the shortcomings of the existing Australian medical system. "[T]he voluntary health insurance schemes enacted by the Menzies Government," Scotton explains, "represented a typically Australian compromise between government and private arrangements," and although they "served their purpose for a period," they nevertheless "fell

[191] *See* Castles, *supra* note 182, at 21–23.

[192] *See id.* at 19–21, 149–50. Castles further observes that a mining boom and stronger manufacturing sector rendered the case for protective tariffs less compelling. *See id.* at 148.

[193] Gough Whitlam, It's Time for Leadership, Nov. 13, 1972 (address at the Blacktown Civic Centre).

[194] *See* Castles, *supra* note 182, at 21.

[195] *See id.* at 156–57.

[196] *Cf. id.* at 151 (observing the "far greater policy volatility of Australia from the early 1970s onwards").

[197] Pharmaceutical Benefits Scheme, *supra* note 179.

progressively short of meeting coverage and other equity goals." In May 1968, Scotton and Deeble "produced a short paper titled A *scheme of universal insurance*" that "bears a striking resemblance to the present Medicare program." Indeed, Whitlam apparently "offered it as de facto Labor Party policy" several weeks later, and "about a year later the scheme was formally accepted by Labor's Federal Conference as party policy." Although Labor fell short in the October 1969 election, in Scotton's estimation these moves "brought national health insurance to the centre of the political stage."[198]

While the Liberal-Country Party coalition[199] "attempted to buttress voluntary insurance," the 1972 election of Whitlam's Labor Party led to a "bitter battle" over the future of Australian health care. The Labor Party pressed ahead with its "Medibank" program, which was ultimately enacted in August 1974 over stiff opposition from the Australian Medical Association. The precursor to the current Medicare system, Medibank took effect in July 1975 and within nine months "registered and issued health insurance cards to 90% of the Australian population."[200]

Castles describes Medibank's creation as "the realisation of a 30-year old labour movement dream."[201] The program's structure would vacillate dramatically for decades, however, in an "on/off sequence" between greater universality and public orientation on the one hand, and greater individualism and private orientation on the other.[202] Malcolm Fraser, who "famously promised, contrary to the views of many of his [Liberal] colleagues, to 'maintain Medibank'" during the 1975 election, nevertheless oversaw a move back toward private health insurance.[203] "Medibank Private" was established in 1976 "to promote competition in the industry,"[204] and ultimately "[b]udgetary considerations, combined with pressure on the Fraser Government to produce policies more favourable to private providers and insurers, resulted in 1981 in a decision to abolish universal coverage and revert to pre-Medibank arrangements." As of

198 *See* Richard B. Scotton, *Medibank: From Conception to Delivery and Beyond*, 173 MED. J. AUSTL. 9–11 (2000), at "The Historical Context" and "The Making of Medibank."

199 The coalition was led by John Gorton of the Liberal Party, who served as Prime Minister from 1968 to 1971. *See* National Archives of Australia, *Australia's Prime Ministers*, http://primeministers.naa.gov.au/primeministers/; Scotton, *supra* note 198.

200 *See* Scotton, *supra* note 198, at "The Making of Medibank." *See also* Biggs, *supra* note 178, at "History."

201 CASTLES, *supra* note 182, at 20.

202 *See* Stephen R. Leeder & Ian A. McAuley, *The Future of Medicare and Health Service Financing*, 173 MED. J. AUSTL. 48 (2000). *See also* Anne-Marie Boxall, *Reforming Australia's Health System, Again*, 192 MED. J. AUSTL. 528, 530 (2010).

203 *See* Scotton, *supra* note 198, at "From Medibank to Medicare."

204 *See* Medibank Private, *History*, http://www.medibank.com.au/About-Us/Corporate-Information/History.aspx.

September 1981, free care "would be available only to pensioners qualifying for health cards, sickness beneficiaries and people meeting stringent means tests," while others "were not entitled to any medical benefits for private treatment or to free treatment at public hospitals."[205] This naturally "creat[ed] more demand for private health insurance," and Medibank Private "claimed the top spot as the largest health insurance organisation in Australia" as of October 1981.[206] As Scotton explains, however, "[t]he outcomes of the abandonment of universal coverage were so unsatisfactory that, in February 1982, the Labor Party ... resumed its commitment to a universal program," which took the name "Medicare" under the Hawke Labor Government elected in 1983. By Scotton's reckoning, "Medicare helped the Labor Party to a substantial election victory," and legislation passed in late 1983 permitted Medicare to take effect in 1984, "differ[ing] from the original Medibank program only in matters of detail."[207]

Following the election of the Hawke government, a hybrid social welfare approach began to take shape, effectively combining public and private attributes. Although Medicare was restored, the government remained cautious about welfare spending generally, introducing means testing in other areas such as old-age pensions and the family allowance.[208] The system of wage arbitration was reinvigorated by the 1983 negotiation of an "accord" between the Hawke Labor government and the Australian Council of Trade Unions – including "proposals for prices control, orderly wage bargaining, the protection of living standards for wage earners, improvements in the social wage, and active intervention to promote full employment and greater investment" – but employers' skepticism toward the arrangement, coupled with "serious deterioration in Australia's external trading conditions from 1985 onwards, gradually led to a downgrading of the social wage and interventionist components of the package."[209] Brian Cheffins observes that "[i]n the 1980s, the Australian Settlement was unraveling but remained influential,"[210] indicating that this was a time of flux and transition. Labor scholars have documented a gradual shift since the 1980s toward less specification of core terms of the employment

[205] *See* Scotton, *supra* note 198, at "From Medibank to Medicare." *See also* Biggs, *supra* note 178, at "History"; Boxall, *supra* note 202, at 528–29; CASTLES, *supra* note 182, at 26–27.

[206] *See* Medibank Private, *supra* note 204.

[207] *See* Scotton, *supra* note 198, at "From Medibank to Medicare." *See also* Biggs, *supra* note 178, at "History"; Boxall, *supra* note 202, at at 529; CASTLES, *supra* note 182, at 27–28. For additional background on the early history of Australian national health insurance, see SENATE SELECT COMMITTEE ON MEDICARE, *supra* note 180, at 6–8.

[208] *See* CASTLES, *supra* note 182, at 27–28.

[209] *See id.* at 28–29.

[210] Brian R. Cheffins, *Corporate Governance Convergence: Lessons from Australia*, 16 TRANSNAT'L LAW. 13, 28 (2002).

relationship through the wage arbitration system, and correlatively greater leeway for employers and employees to negotiate firm-specific deals, bringing Australia more into line with approaches taken in other common-law countries.[211] As Meredith Jones and Richard Mitchell observe, a "pattern of wage system fragmentation has continued to grow as the enterprise bargaining system has developed and the award system has either been reduced to the role of a safety net... or has been entirely displaced in individual enterprises by agreements."[212]

Over the same period, however, the deep conflict regarding national health insurance that marked the 1970s and early 1980s gradually gave way to grudging acceptance of its existence by the political right. Although "alternative schemes" were proposed on multiple occasions following the Hawke government's resurrection of Medicare, the Liberal Party ultimately declared support for the program in its successful 1996 campaign – an "affirmation" that, as Scotton put it, "marked the final stage of universal health insurance becoming settled policy in Australia."[213] Although John Howard, as a shadow treasurer in the early 1980s, argued that if Australia "could put aside the introduction of Medicare" it could "save three or four hundred million dollars in one hit," in the 1996 election he promised that "a future Coalition Government will not be eroding the safety net that underpins our social security system." He offered "a number of ironclad guarantees," notably that they would "not force Australian workers off awards," and that they would "retain Medicare."[214] Today, Medibank Private is owned by the government – its sole shareholder – and although the Howard government announced in 2006 that it planned to sell its shares in a public offering if reelected, the Rudd and Gillard Labor governments elected in 2007 and 2010 respectively have said that they will maintain government ownership.[215] The upshot is a public–private balance in Australian health care that – although perhaps blurry at the margin[216] – remains broadly politically

[211] *See* Mitchell et al., *supra* note 189, at 55–65. *See also* Jones & Mitchell, *supra* note 189, at 75–77; Richard Mitchell, Anthony O'Donnell & Ian Ramsay, Shareholder Value and Employee Interests: Intersections between Corporate Governance, Corporate Law and Labour Law 33–37 (Research Report, Univ. Melbourne Ctr. for Corp. L. & Sec. Regulation, Univ. Melbourne Ctr. for Emp't & Labour Relations L., 2005).

[212] Jones & Mitchell, *supra* note 189, at 76.

[213] *See* Scotton, *supra* note 198, at "From Medibank to Medicare."

[214] Nick Grimm, *Looking Back Over Medicare's History*, World Today (May 7, 2003), http://www.abc.net.au/worldtoday/content/2003/s849092.htm (quoting Howard).

[215] *See* Medibank Private, *supra* note 204. *See also* National Archives of Australia, *supra* note 199.

[216] *See, e.g.*, Boxall, *supra* note 202, at 530 (observing that "Australia's private insurance scheme functions sometimes as a replacement for the public scheme... and sometimes as a top-up," and arguing that the "lack of clarity about [its] role... has created tensions between the two schemes"); Leeder & McAuley, *supra* note 202 (arguing that "[t]he debate should not be

stable. Although 45 percent of Australians had private insurance as of 2010,[217] Medicare's "public satisfaction" rating stood at 96 percent.[218]

It bears emphasizing that this steady progression from a predominantly employer-based "wage-earners' welfare state" through the 1960s, which more closely resembles the U.S. approach, to a more state-based social welfare system in recent decades, which more closely resembles the U.K. approach, clearly reflects the ascendance of the Australian left. This is perhaps most vividly reflected in the strong divergence between the left-leaning Labor Party and the right-leaning Liberal Party and Country Party on issues relating to national health insurance (at least until election of the Howard government in 1996). Indeed, it must be recalled that the push for national health insurance was, from the beginning, part of a broader Labor Party effort to differentiate itself through more egalitarian social policies. Bill Hayden's Second Reading Speech for the Health Insurance Bill 1973 describes Medibank's purpose as being to provide the "most equitable and efficient means of providing health insurance coverage for all Australians." Likewise, following the Hawke government's rejection of the Fraser government's privatization plan, the return to the original Medibank concept in 1983 (through Medicare) was described in Neil Blewett's Second Reading Speech as "a major social reform" restoring "a health insurance system that is simple, fair and affordable" and reaffirming that universal coverage is "desirable from an equity point of view."[219] Although Labor held power for just three of thirty-four years from 1949 to 1983 – those three years being the window in which Medibank was created under Whitlam – Labor held power for twenty of the thirty-nine years from 1972 to 2011. Moreover, eleven of the remaining years – those of the conservative Howard government – represent a period in which the Liberal Party no longer formally opposed Medicare's existence.[220] Although approval ratings for Medicare stood at a bare majority of 52 percent following its (re)introduction in 1984, it is now firmly established as "a very popular government program and public support has been high."[221] Overall this history indicates a broad leftward

between private and public insurance, but between insurance and the market"). On competing notions of universality in health care and concerns regarding increasing reliance on private insurance, see SENATE SELECT COMMITTEE ON MEDICARE, *supra* note 180, at 64–65, 88–89.

[217] *See* Boxall, *supra* note 202, at 530.

[218] *See* Medicare Australia, *Medicare Australia Annual Report 2009–2010: Medicare Australia Overview*, http://www.dhs.gov.au/publications-policies-and-plans/annual-reports/medicare/0910/chapter01/04.html [hereinafter Medicare Australia Overview].

[219] *See* Biggs, *supra* note 178, at "History" (quoting Hayden and Blewett).

[220] *See* National Archives of Australia, *supra* note 199.

[221] *See* Biggs, *supra* note 178, at "Key Statistics." *See also* Medicare Australia Overview, *supra* note 218; Medicare Australia, *Medicare Australia Annual Report 2009–2010: Customer Service and*

shift – certainly vis-à-vis the United States, where the medical system today more closely resembles that advocated by the conservative Fraser government, an approach roundly rejected by the Australian public in 1982 and 1983.

How does this social welfare history relate to the emergence of modern Australian corporate law? Although Australia appears to have arrived at a social and political balance broadly resembling that in the United Kingdom, as a threshold matter the relationship between social welfare policy and corporate law is more complex in Australia, at least insofar as a well-established state-based social welfare system was not a background condition to the modernization of Australian corporate law. The colonial corporate laws adopted in the nineteenth century "followed almost word for word the English model," reflecting the fact that they were enacted principally "to accommodate the needs of English businesses who wished to set up subsidiaries in Australia or alternatively to register as 'foreign' corporations."[222] As Rob McQueen vividly suggests, little substantive evolution would occur in the century following their enactment. "The *Uniform Companies Acts* of 1961–1962," he writes, "would have been quite recognisable to a time travelling legal practitioner from the English home counties of 1862," and reform efforts through the early 1990s would largely remain preoccupied with creating national administrative and regulatory structures rather than updating the substantive law itself. Indeed, dramatic substantive revisions appear to have been avoided during this period to minimize potential objections to enactment of federal corporate legislation.[223] More substantive statutory reform efforts – including in the areas of directors' duties, shareholders' rights, and takeover regulation – would develop substantial momentum only in the mid-1990s, the most consequential result being the Corporations Act 2001, which constitutes the foundation of current Australian company law.[224]

Australia's long-standing tendency to rely on U.K. legislative models and case law should not, however, be overstated.[225] Indeed, Australia has deviated from the U.K. approach in critical areas of corporate governance at various

Partnerships – Stakeholder Consultation, http://www.dhs.gov.au/publications-policies-and-plans/annual-reports/medicare/0910/chapter06/05.html; Medicare Australia, *Medicare Australia Annual Report 2009–2010: Measuring Our Performance*, http://www.dhs.gov.au/publications-policies-and-plans/annual-reports/medicare/0910/chapter01/09.html.

222 Rob McQueen, *An Examination of Australian Corporate Law and Regulation 1901–1961*, 15 U. New S. Wales L.J. 1, 6–7 (1992).

223 *See id.* at 3–4, 24–28. *See also* R.P. Austin & I.M. Ramsay, Ford's Principles of Corporations Law 43–46 (14th ed. 2010).

224 *See* Austin & Ramsay, *supra* note 223, at 1, 46–47.

225 *Cf. id.* at 1–2 (acknowledging this historical reliance while observing that "[p]resent-day company law in Australia is less dependent upon the United Kingdom").

points in recent decades, reflecting not only the differing administrative and regulatory challenges posed by its federal governmental structure, but also the differing role and significance of corporate law in Australia's unique political economy. Once again takeovers provide a particularly illuminating window on these dynamics – indeed, the evolution of Australian takeover regulation maps quite coherently onto the evolution of social welfare provision discussed above. Hostile takeovers became a salient issue for Australia in the 1970s, takeovers having been rare before the 1950s, and "mostly friendly affairs" in the 1950s and 1960s.[226] Although rules requiring greater information for investors were adopted in 1970, it remained unclear how much autonomy target boards ought to possess in responding to hostile bids.[227] Defensive tactics were evaluated by courts through a fiduciary duty-based analysis of whether such action was taken for a "proper purpose," an approach that would seem to require a strong focus on shareholders' interests in takeovers – because whether board action was taken for a "proper purpose" was, like in the United Kingdom, assessed by reference to the best interests of the company, which were in turn understood to mean the best interests of the shareholders as a whole.[228] By the late 1970s, however, and into the 1980s – the very period of greatest instability in terms of social welfare provision – concerns were being raised by prominent politicians, scholars, and market actors alike regarding the social impacts of takeovers, particularly with respect to employees.

Frank Walker, the Attorney-General of New South Wales, argued in 1979 that "the costs of protecting employees should be capable of absorption into the take-over process. The contribution of employees may not be as tangible as share scrip, but undoubtedly makes up the assets and the profits of a going concern and they deserve corresponding protection under the law."[229] Gareth Evans, the Attorney-General of Australia, likewise took the position in 1983 that "statements of present intention" regarding target company employees "hardly add up to firm protection." He suggested that "[i]t may be that we should consider including employees as another party whose interests should be expressly protected," adding that regulators and courts should "at the very

[226] *See* MITCHELL ET AL., *supra* note 189, at 34–35; MITCHELL ET AL., *supra* note 211, at 22–23.

[227] *See* MITCHELL ET AL., *supra* note 211, at 16, 22–23.

[228] *See* Deborah A. DeMott, *Shareholders as Principals*, *in* KEY DEVELOPMENTS IN CORPORATE LAW AND TRUSTS LAW: ESSAYS IN HONOUR OF PROFESSOR HAROLD FORD 105, 118–20 (Ian Ramsey ed., 2002); MITCHELL ET AL. *supra* note 211, at 16, 22–23. *See also* BAXT, *supra* note 81, at 215–17; FORD, *supra* note 80, at 90, 338–43; H.A.J. FORD, PRINCIPLES OF COMPANY LAW 390–92, 553–55 (4th ed. 1986).

[229] *See* Gareth Evans, An Overview of Some Key Issues Relation to Takeovers 1, 12 (address at Takeovers & Mergers: The New Experience, Institute of Chartered Accountants in Australia, New South Wales Branch, Oct. 27, 1983) (quoting Walker).

least . . . be required to have regard" for employee interests.[230] In 1986, Henry Bosch, Chairman of the National Companies and Securities Commission (NCSC), observed the "dramatic surge in the number and size of takeovers in the U.S.A., the U.K. and Canada, as well as Australia," and the "remarkable increase in public concern about takeovers," signaling openness to the possibility of giving boards greater latitude to employ takeover defenses. "We could permit the issue of non-voting shares," he suggested, "or allow wider discretion in the use of Articles of Association as defensive barriers," both of which "would remove regulations that restrain defending boards."[231] Dr. David Round of the University of Adelaide, coauthor of an NCSC-sponsored study on takeovers, similarly argued in 1986 that "mergers must be evaluated in terms of their overall long-run social costs and social benefits, and not just from the point of view of the managers of the firms involved, or even just from the point of view of the shareholders."[232] Likewise in 1986 Jim Kennan, Attorney-General of Victoria, observed that "the purpose of all this [takeover] regulation as it affects consumers and employees as well as investors is often overlooked," and argued that Australia should "consider very carefully the interests of employees and consumers and, above all, the national economic interests" in developing takeover regulation.[233] Merchant banker Graeme Samuel, Chairman of Macquarie Bank, found himself asking "whether changing social attitudes are not now demanding that, consistent with their obligations to take account of shareholders' interests, directors should take a longer term view and act to also protect the interests of other stakeholders who are vital to the future generation of shareholders' wealth – employees, customers, suppliers and the like."[234]

[230] *Id.* at 13.

[231] Henry Bosch, NCSC Viewpoint on Regulation of Takeover Bids 1, 1, 13–14 (address at Takeovers, Centre for Commercial Law and Applied Legal Research, Faculty of Law, Monash University, Apr. 28, 1986).

[232] David Round, Economic Evidence: The Need to Regulate Takeover Bids 15, 25 (address at Takeovers, Centre for Commercial Law and Applied Legal Research, Faculty of Law, Monash University, Apr. 28, 1986) (emphasis removed).

[233] Jim Kennan, Regulation of Takeover Bids: Legislative Initiative Past and Future 80, 84, 87 (address at Takeovers, Centre for Commercial Law and Applied Legal Research, Faculty of Law, Monash University, Apr. 28, 1986). Kennan cites an article in *The Age* discussing the position of employees at BHP, the target of a widely followed takeover bid that Kennan suggests "really elevate[d] the impact of takeovers on employees into an issue for public debate." *See id.* at 84. *See also* Anne Coombs, *In the Trenches at BHP*, AGE GOOD WEEKEND, Apr. 25, 1986, at 14 (article cited by Kennan).

[234] Graeme Samuel, Regulation and the Vesting of Discretions in the NCSC 97, 118 (address at Takeovers, Centre for Commercial Law and Applied Legal Research, Faculty of Law, Monash University, Apr. 28, 1986). *See also* Mr Graeme Samuel AC, http://www.monash.edu.au/alumni/find/profiles/prominent-alumni//graeme-samuel.html.

Concerns such as these ultimately prompted broader calls for Australian corporate law to move away from its exclusive focus on shareholders and permit greater regard for employees and other stakeholders. In 1989, the Senate Standing Committee on Legal and Constitutional Affairs was charged with a mandate to investigate "the social and fiduciary duties and responsibilities of company directors," and produced a report on this subject known as the Cooney Report (for its Chairman, Barney Cooney).[235] The report recognizes that Australian society "wants ethical conduct, with due regard being given to the rights of shareholders, employees, creditors and consumers, and to the environment," but rejects expansion of directors' duties as a means of achieving this, for reasons that appear largely consistent with the rationale accepted in the United Kingdom. The report explains that under Australian corporate law, directors pursuing the best interests of the company are "required first and foremost to give regard to the shareholders' interests," whereas "others such as employees" are deemed "extrinsic" to the corporation, with any duties owed to them being "not in the nature of the corporation itself but in the nature of its traffic with those other entities."[236] The Committee concludes that company law should remain focused on matters "intrinsic" to the corporation – notably, the shareholders – and that "[w]here there is a need to govern the relationship between companies and things external to them, this is more appropriately done in separate legislation."[237] The readers' attention is directed to legislation focusing on "the welfare of workers, of consumers, of competitors, of the environment," and observes that Australia's unique adjunct to state-based welfare, the wage arbitration system, further diminishes the rationale for corporate law to require regard for employee interests. "Because the corporations which they control are bound by comprehensive awards and determinations," the Cooney Report explains, "Australian company directors are compelled by law, extrinsic to company law, to take into account a wide range of worker entitlements."[238] Although the Committee does recommend clarifying that employees' interests "may be taken into account" in managing the company for the shareholders – essentially the enlightened shareholder value concept discussed previously – the call for broader directors' duties is rejected.[239]

It is telling in itself that the Cooney Report's rejection of a stakeholder mandate in 1989 is substantially rooted in confidence that external regulation – including what remained of Australia's unique wage-earners' welfare

[235] *See* Senate Standing Committee on Legal and Constitutional Affairs, Company Directors' Duties: Report on the Social and Fiduciary Duties and Obligations of Company Directors iii, 1 (1989) [hereinafter Cooney Report].

[236] *Id.* at 7–8, 83.

[237] *Id.* at 18.

[238] *Id.* at 11, 23, 86.

[239] *See id.* at 90, 95–97.

state – could, in theory, ensure that employees' and other stakeholders' interests would be adequately addressed. At the same time, however, in light of the flux and instability in social welfare provision discussed previously – and notwithstanding the formally shareholder-centric nature of "proper purpose" analysis – it is unsurprising that courts evaluating concrete takeover disputes in the 1980s adopted a posture that, in practice, gave target boards some capacity to resist hostile bids.[240] In *Pine Vale Investments Ltd v. East Ltd*, for example, a bidder representing about 26 percent of a public company's shares made a "partial" offer to purchase additional shares that would have taken its stake to about 42 percent, "thereby conferring control of the company." The target board responded with a share offer – ostensibly aimed at financing expansion, but with the "effect" of "alter[ing] both the number and market value of the issued share capital of the company" and thereby "affect[ing] the assumptions on which the takeover offer was made." The bidder got an injunction restraining the share offer and argued that the board's conduct constituted a breach of duty because it was in fact intended to defeat the bid. The Supreme Court of Queensland, however, in its 1983 opinion, found the proposed expansion to be "commercially justifiable," and found no breach of duty resulting from its impact on the hostile bid. Taking an approach strikingly similar to the one that would take shape in Delaware, the Queensland court explained that determining whether the board had acted for a proper purpose required focusing on "the substantial object the accomplishment of which formed the real ground of the board's action." In this case, the board's conduct passed muster because the court was satisfied that the "real ground of the board's action was not the frustration of the take-over offer but the desire to take advantage of a genuine commercially favourable opportunity," a conclusion apparently bolstered by the fact that the form of the transaction was "consistent with past policy of the board that heavy borrowing should be avoided." Strikingly, neither the timing of the board's conduct nor its "preclusive effect" rendered it improper.[241] The court's emphasis on consistency with past practice resonates strongly with the highly deferential approach that the Delaware Supreme Court would take in its 1990 *Paramount v. Time* opinion,[242] and the Queensland court arguably seems willing to go even further than Delaware would in favor of board discretion to resist hostile bids with "preclusive" defenses.[243]

[240] *See* DeMott, *supra* note 228, at 119–20.

[241] *See* Pine Vale Invs. Ltd. v. East Ltd. & East Ltd. & ANOR (1983) 8 ACLR 199 (Austl. Sup. Ct. Qld).

[242] *See* Paramount Commc'ns, Inc. v. Time Inc., 571 A.2d 1140, 1154 (Del. 1990).

[243] *See* Unitrin, Inc. v. Am. Gen. Corp., 651 A.2d 1361, 1387–88 (Del. 1995) (explaining that "preclusive" defenses do not meet the *Unocal* proportionality test). It must be acknowledged,

The 1989 opinion of the Supreme Court of New South Wales in *Darvall v. North Sydney Brick & Tile Co Ltd* provides a similarly vivid illustration of the latitude afforded Australian target boards to deploy takeover defenses during this period. A shareholder made a bid to buy all outstanding shares of North Sydney Brick & Tile at a substantial premium, in response to which the target board concluded that the bid undervalued the company's net assets, based principally on a "revaluation" of certain real estate. The board then approved a series of transactions that apparently rested on a "quid pro quo" – Lanceley, the managing director, would make a higher offer to the shareholders, which would be financed on a nonrecourse basis by Chase Corporation Ltd, evidently in exchange for a commitment to enter a joint venture with Chase to develop the real estate. The court below found a breach of fiduciary duty by Lanceley in failing to disclose the facts surrounding this quid pro quo to the board, yet "concluded that the other directors of the company were ignorant of the private gain which the managing director stood to make out of the arrangement," and thus that "the relevant decision of the directors were made bona fide and in the best interests of the company as a whole," rendering them "immune from disturbance." On appeal, the proper purpose analysis was applied in a manner highly deferential to the target board, once again resembling the Delaware approach. Mahoney JA explained that although a board cannot act for the purpose of entrenching itself, "[i]n some circumstances, it will be proper for a company to concern itself with those who take its shares on transfer," and that the board could legitimately act to generate alternatives to a takeover bid. In this case, Mahoney concluded, the board's "substantial purpose" was to generate a better alternative for shareholders, to "demonstrate to shareholders that it was not in their interests to accept the plaintiff's offer, and to advance the commercial interests of the company." As in *Pine Vale*, the fact that the timing of the board's action was driven by the bid was not conclusive. Clarke JA agreed, citing (among other cases) to the Queensland court's opinion in *Pine Vale* and the British Columbia court's opinion in *Teck Corporation Ltd v. Millar*, and taking the position that although the target board's latitude may be more limited with respect to share issuances, "the bald proposition that it is improper to take action to defeat a takeover offer is too widely stated to constitute a legal principle."[244]

To be sure, Mahoney did acknowledge the difficulty "in determining what, in the context of a takeover situation, may legitimately be done for the good

of course, that the defense employed in *Pine Vale* would not be considered "preclusive" in Delaware, where even a preemptive poison pill is not considered preclusive as long as a proxy contest remains viable. *See id.* at 1387.

[244] Darvall v. N. Sydney Brick & Tile Co. Ltd. & ORS (1989) 15 ACLR 230 (Austl. Sup. Ct. N.S.W.).

of the company as a whole."[245] Even as of the mid-1990s, as Jennifer Hill observed, "[t]he law in Australia concerning the duties of directors in the face of hostile takeovers is less than clear." Notwithstanding the theoretical shareholder-orientation of "proper purpose" analysis, Hill rightly noted that "a number of more recent cases in the takeover context support[ed] a broader focus for directors' duties and the company's interests" (including *Pine Vale* and *Darvall*), creating an Australian takeover jurisprudence that appeared "functionally equivalent" to U.S. constituency statutes.[246] At the same time, it was widely understood that latitude to deploy defenses was reinforced by the capacity to resort to "tactical" litigation – notably, seeking an injunction against a bid based on an alleged disclosure violation, which could function as a delaying tactic to buy time for development of defensive strategies.[247]

Hill concluded that, as of 1995, "Australian law [was] in a state of flux" regarding directors' duties in target companies,[248] and the parallel she draws with U.S. constituency statutes is an illuminating one. Indeed, it is effectively impossible to square these developments with the formal shareholder orientation of the traditional corporate law doctrine that Australia inherited from the United Kingdom – a tension illustrated in successive volumes of the leading Australian treatise, which reflect an increasingly strained effort to read U.S. and Australian takeover developments through the lens of strict U.K.-style shareholder-centrism. For example, the 1990 edition of *Ford's Principles of Company Law* includes a discussion of Delaware's takeover jurisprudence that emphasizes the auction duty in *Revlon* while ignoring entirely the stakeholder language in *Unocal*. This effectively allows the U.S. approach to be presented as more shareholder-centric than the one taken by the New South Wales court in *Darvall*, where "[t]here is no assertion of a duty to auction the company."[249] The 1992 edition reiterates this characterization, notwithstanding the obvious tension with the Delaware Supreme Court's 1990 decision in *Paramount v. Time*. The brief discussion of this decision ignores the Delaware Supreme Court's reiteration of the stakeholder language in *Unocal*, although

245 *Id.*

246 Jennifer Hill, *At the Frontiers of Labour Law and Corporate Law: Enterprise Bargaining, Corporations and Employees*, 23 FED. L. REV. 204, 216 (1995). *See also* Margaret Taylor, Duty to Act in Good Faith in the Best Interests of the Company 22 (paper presented at Directors Duties, University of New South Wales Faculty of Law Continuing Legal Education, Mar. 10, 2005).

247 *See* Bruce Dyer & Marie McDonald, *Why Was the Takeovers Panel Established*, *in* THE TAKEOVERS PANEL AND TAKEOVERS REGULATION IN AUSTRALIA 80, 85–86 (Ian Ramsay ed., 2010). *See also Darvall*, 15 ACLR 230 (Kirby P recognizing the tactical use of litigation and observing that a takeover panel could address disputes more quickly than courts).

248 Hill, *supra* note 246, at 216.

249 *See* H.A.J. FORD & R.P. AUSTIN, PRINCIPLES OF COMPANY LAW 646–47, 721 (5th ed. 1990).

it does observe that permitting the target board to maintain defenses in pursuit of its own strategic plan for the company effectively "narrowed the scope of the 'auction' duty... established in *Revlon*," rendering the decision "a retreat by the Delaware Supreme Court from the shareholder protection aspects of both *Revlon* and *Unocal*."[250] The 1995 edition, then, simply notes *Revlon* while dropping discussion of the more problematic *Unocal* and *Paramount v. Time* decisions entirely,[251] implicitly reflecting the impossibility of squaring these takeover developments with strict shareholder-centrism.

Today, as explored earlier in the book, the Australian approach to takeovers is virtually as shareholder-centric as the U.K. approach. It is critical to observe, however, that this dates only to 2000, when the Takeovers Panel displaced courts as the primary tribunal for disputes regarding pending takeover bids – a move in part aimed at curbing "tactical" litigation that had helped impede bids in the 1980s and 1990s.[252] This, of course, follows the coalescence of a more settled approach to social welfare and broad acceptance of a substantial state role – notably in health care – rendering the Takeovers Panels' rejection of fiduciary duty–based analysis (in favor of a far more shareholder-centric focus on the effects of defensive tactics) considerably less politically sensitive than such a move would have been in prior decades.[253] Indeed, to step back, Australia would appear to have moved from a form of social and political equilibrium resembling that of the United States to one resembling that of the United Kingdom. Although hostile takeovers would not arise until later, Australia adhered to an employer-based approach to social welfare through the 1960s that resembled the U.S. approach to the extent that social welfare protections were largely job-linked – an approach that remained broadly stable in a period of economic prosperity and low unemployment. In the 1970s,

[250] *See* H.A.J. FORD & R.P. AUSTIN, FORD'S PRINCIPLES OF COMPANY LAW 476–77, 703–04 (6th ed. 1992).

[251] *See* H.A.J. FORD & R.P. AUSTIN, FORD & AUSTIN'S PRINCIPLES OF CORPORATIONS LAW 274–75 (7th ed. 1995).

[252] *See, e.g.*, Jennifer G. Hill, *Takeovers, Poison Pills and Protectionism in Comparative Corporate Governance, in* FESTSCHRIFT FÜR KLAUS J. HOPT ZUM 70. GEBURTSTAG AM 24. AUGUST 2010 UNTERNEHMEN, MARKT UND VERANTWORTUNG 795, 803–04 (Stefan Grundmann et al. eds., 2010); Dyer & McDonald, *supra* note 247, at 85–89; MITCHELL ET AL., *supra* note 211, at 22–23; Luke Nottage, *Corporate Governance and M&A in Australia: An Overview for Assessing Japan and the "Americanisation" Thesis* 25–26 (Sydney Law School Legal Studies Research Paper No. 08/28, Mar. 2008); Ian Ramsay, *The Takeovers Panel: A Review, in* THE TAKEOVERS PANEL AND TAKEOVERS REGULATION IN AUSTRALIA, *supra* note 247, at 1, 7, 15, 23–24.

[253] *Cf.* Takeovers Panel, Commonwealth of Australia, Panel Publishes Final Guidance on Frustrating Action 2–3 (June 16, 2003), http://takeovers.gov.au/content/DisplayDoc.aspx?doc=media_releases/2003/059.htm&pageID=&Year=2003 (noting that some preferred the fiduciary duty-based approach, but rejecting this in favor of the effect-based approach and noting that there was "support for it in the London City Code").

	1950s-1960s	1970s-1990s	1990s-2000s
social welfare system	"wage-earners' welfare state"	public/private flux	welfare state
social welfare stability	stable	unstable	stable
emphasis of takeover regulation	n/a	stakeholders	shareholders

Figure 5.2. Australia's Social Safety Net and Takeover Regulation

1980s, and 1990s, then, Australian courts responded to the advent of hostile takeovers in a manner resembling that in the United States – giving managers substantial latitude to deploy defenses – in part because moves toward state-based social welfare remained hotly contested and incomplete. In the new millennium, then, Australia adopted a far more shareholder-centric position on hostile takeovers, sharply limiting defenses in a manner strongly resembling the approach taken in the United Kingdom – a move that, as we have seen, was not inhibited by the social concerns of prior decades because, by the 2000s, state-based social welfare programs, notably Medicare, were firmly established. Figure 5.2 illustrates this historical progression.

Although not the focus of this book, it is worth pausing here to observe that the Australian experience in recent decades similarly demonstrates the capacity of social welfare protections to divert political pressure from labor law as well, by the very same mechanism – diminishing the social and political freight of the employment relationship tends to divert political pressure away from labor law just as it does from corporate law. This dynamic is vividly illustrated by Australia's treatment of employee entitlements in the context of insolvency. A year before the Cooney Report, another report by the Law Reform Commission – generally called the Harmer Report (again after its Commissioner) – undertook a "General Insolvency Inquiry" addressing the position of employees owed various entitlements upon the insolvency of a corporate employer. The report explains that "[t]he rationale put forward for the priority for employees is that they are in a particularly vulnerable position if their employer becomes bankrupt or is wound up." The report responds, however, that "[t]he development of a sophisticated social welfare system has to some extent diminished the significance of the rationale for the employee priority," and argues that "[t]he most effective way to ensure employees are paid in the event of their employer becoming insolvent is through the introduction of a wage earner protection fund."[254] This, as Joellen Riley explains, effectively

[254] LAW REFORM COMMISSION, GENERAL INSOLVENCY INQUIRY ¶ 155 (Report No. 45, 1988) (Harmer Report) (emphasis removed).

"is what we now have in the GEERS" program – the General Employee Entitlements and Redundancy Scheme, created by the Howard government in 2001.[255]

In response to a series of corporate insolvencies in which employee entitlements in the hundreds of millions of dollars were not paid, calls for some type of regulatory response to insulate employees from this vulnerability gained political traction.[256] In his 1999 ministerial discussion paper, Peter Reith (Minister for Employment, Workplace Relations and Small Business) noted the Harmer Report's proposal for a "wage-earner protection fund."[257] Reith proposed corporate law liability for directors seeking to dodge employee entitlements, and suggested two potential avenues to ensure payments – a "safety net" fund, or a "compulsory insurance scheme."[258]

Director liability for unpaid entitlements was ultimately incorporated into the Corporations Act, but did little to address the problem because it generally proved impossible for employees to demonstrate subjective intent to deprive them of entitlements.[259] Similarly, priority over unsecured creditors offered no solution because there was typically little left for employees after secured creditors were paid – and the notion of giving employees priority over secured creditors met stiff opposition,[260] as did other proposals aimed at forcing businesses to internalize these costs, such as mandatory insurance.[261] GEERS, aptly described by Riley as "a welfare-based safety net,"[262] essentially amounted to instrumental use of a social welfare–based strategy by the conservative Howard government to avoid political problems associated with alternative solutions through corporate law, labor law, and other regulatory domains. Mohammed

[255] Joellen Riley, *Bargaining for Security: Lessons for Employees from the World of Corporate Law*, 44 J. INDUS. REL. 491, 492, 500 (2002).

[256] *See* Mohammed al Bhadily & Robert Guthrie, *Insolvency Protection for Employee Entitlements: International Alternatives to GEER Scheme*, 2010 J. APPLIED L. & POL'Y 33, 35 (2010); Helen Anderson, *Directors' Liability for Unpaid Employee Entitlements: Suggestions for Reform Based on Their Liabilities for Unremitted Taxes*, 30 SYDNEY L. REV. 470, 476 (2008); Riley, *supra* note 255, at 491–96.

[257] *See* PETER REITH, THE PROTECTION OF EMPLOYEE ENTITLEMENTS IN THE EVENT OF EMPLOYER INSOLVENCY 5 (Minister for Employment, Workplace Relations and Small Business, Ministerial Discussion Paper, Aug. 1999).

[258] *See id.* at 6–12.

[259] *See* al Bhadily & Guthrie, *supra* note 256, at 34–35; Anderson, *supra* note 256, at 471, 484–85, 490; Riley, *supra* note 255, at 492.

[260] *See* Anderson, *supra* note 256, at 483, 493–94; KordaMentha, *Employee Entitlements* 2–4 (KordaMentha Research Unit Paper 304, Dec. 2003), http://www.camac.gov.au/camac/camac.nsf/byHeadline/PDFSubmissions/$file/KordaMentha_304.pdf; REITH, *supra* note 257, at 5, 14; Riley, *supra* note 255, at 499.

[261] *See* Anderson, *supra* note 256, at 494–95; Riley, *supra* note 255, at 500–01.

[262] *See* Riley, *supra* note 255, at 493, 498–99.

al Bhadily and Robert Guthrie plausibly suggest that "the Howard Conservative Coalition which established GEERS opted for the taxpayer-funded model, arguably not because it was the advocate of government intervention of social security but because it was unwilling to impose any impost on business to underwrite corporate failure."[263] Indeed, in this light it is unsurprising that the program has been criticized as unfairly off-loading the costs of corporate insolvency onto taxpayers and thereby incentivizing excessive corporate risk-taking.[264]

For our purposes, however, what is most interesting about the emergence of GEERS in Australia is that it vividly illustrates the interrelated nature of corporate law, labor law, social welfare policy, and other forms of regulation in addressing risks faced by employees in large corporate enterprises – and notably the potential for instrumental use of social welfare policy to relieve political pressures from these other regulatory domains. Reith underscores the linkages among these various areas of law and policy in his 1999 report, observing that labor law creates an obligation to pay employee entitlements in insolvency, which corporate law can reinforce through director liability for avoiding such payments, while social welfare–based structures can buffer losses to employees when claims nevertheless go unpaid.[265]

Commentators have drawn a close parallel between GEERS and the United Kingdom's Redundancy Payments Act (1965)[266] – which, as we have already seen, similarly represented just one of a range of regulatory responses to the vulnerability of employees in struggling companies, while facilitating stronger shareholder-centrism within corporate law. One discussion of the treatment of employee entitlements concluded that Australian employees actually do better under GEERS than employees in the United States and Canada do under their unemployment insurance programs, and that only the U.K. Redundancy Payments Scheme provides comparable protections.[267] That Australia would strengthen shareholder powers under the Corporations Act and the social safety net available to stakeholders outside corporate law almost simultaneously – a turn of events quite similar to that in the United Kingdom in the 1960s – is quite striking, suggesting the coalescence of a broadly similar political and

[263] *See* al Bhadily & Guthrie, *supra* note 256, at 48. *See also* Anderson, *supra* note 256, at 498; Riley, *supra* note 255, at 500–01.

[264] *See, e.g.*, al Bhadily & Guthrie, *supra* note 256, at 49; Anderson, *supra* note 256, at 498–99; REITH, *supra* note 257, at 8, 14; Riley, *supra* note 255, at 500–03. For a brief overview of the GEERS program, see General Employee Entitlements and Redundancy Scheme (GEERS), *Frequently Asked Questions*, http://www.deewr.gov.au/WorkplaceRelations/Programs/EmployeeEntitlements/GEERS/Common/Pages/FrequentlyAskedQuestions.aspx.

[265] *See* REITH, *supra* note 257, at 2–3, 6.

[266] *See, e.g.*, KordaMentha, *supra* note 260, at 6.

[267] *See id.* at 6.

social equilibrium. Indeed, the U.K. Redundancy Payments Scheme would seem to have loomed large in Reith's mind, as it receives far greater prominence and attention in his 1999 report than other national approaches, and he strongly emphasizes the structural similarity of his proposed fund to the U.K. approach.[268]

Although the trajectory of Australian corporate law over recent years has quite clearly been in the direction of greater shareholder orientation, however, it must be acknowledged that support for this trend is not universal – notably because of lingering concerns regarding the sufficiency of external regulatory protections for employees. As Shelly Marshall and Ian Ramsay observe, "whilst statutory protection of employee entitlements upon insolvency within company law has increased, conventional protections provided by bargaining rights and the right to strike have been eroded in labour laws since 1993" – a trend that, they suggest, has led various corporate stakeholders including employees to seek out "alternative mechanisms to make companies more accountable to stakeholders."[269] Additionally, recent corporate scandals

[268] *See* REITH, *supra* note 257, at 8, 15–18. For background on the U.K. Redundancy Payments Scheme today, see generally Directgov, *Calculating Your Redundancy Pay*, *supra* note 75; Directgov, *Entitlement to Redundancy Pay*, *supra* note 75; Directgov, *Your Rights if Your Employer Is Insolvent*, *supra* note 75. For background on Canada's employment insurance program, see generally Human Resources and Skills Development Canada, *Questions and Answers for Applicants to the Wage Earner Protection Program*, updated Feb. 15, 2012, http://www.hrsdc.gc.ca/eng/labour/employment_standards/wepp/faq.shtml; Service Canada, *Employment Insurance Regular Benefits*, updated July 23, 2012, http://www.servicecanada.gc.ca/eng/ei/types/regular.shtml. For background on U.S. state-based unemployment insurance, see generally U.S. Department of Labor, *Emergency Unemployment Compensation 2008 (EUC) Program*, Feb. 27, 2012, http://www.ows.doleta.gov/unemploy/pdf/euc08.pdf; U.S. Department of Labor, *State Unemployment Insurance Benefits*, updated Jan. 13, 2010, http://workforcesecurity.doleta.gov/unemploy/uifactsheet.asp. *See also* 11 U.S.C. § 507(a)(4)–(5) (prioritizing employees' unsecured claims in a bankrupt company for "wages, salaries, or commissions, including vacation, severance, and sick leave pay earned by an individual," as well as "contributions to an employee benefit plan," but "only to the extent of $11,725 for each individual . . . earned within 180 days before the date of the filing of the petition or the date of the cessation of the debtor's business, whichever occurs first").

[269] Shelly Marshall & Ian Ramsay, *Shareholders and Directors' Duties: Law, Theory and Evidence* 2 (Melbourne Law School Legal Studies Research Paper No. 411, 2009), http://ssrn.com/abstract=1402143. A more recent study finds that, between 1970 and 2010, worker protections through labor law remained stable while shareholder protections through corporate law increased – results suggesting that, "in the Australian case at least, increased protection for one group of stakeholders has not come at the expense of protection for other groups of stakeholders." Helen Anderson, Peter Gahan, Richard Mitchell, Ian Ramsay & Michelle Welsh, *Investor and Worker Protection in Australia: A Longitudinal Analysis*, 34 SYDNEY L. REV. 573, 580-83 (2012). The authors note that these results are consistent with my prior work on the impact of extra-corporate stakeholder protections on the evolution of U.K. and U.S. corporate governance, but add that "further research is necessary before a settled conclusion is reached as to why, and in what form, this relationship might-co-exist." *Id.* at 583. It is critical

have highlighted the heightened vulnerability of employees and others that arguably result from a strongly shareholder-centric approach to corporate decision making – notably the James Hardie scandal. James Hardie Industries Ltd, a long-time manufacturer of various building-related asbestos products, was restructured in 2001 to cordon off asbestos-related liabilities from the remainder of the business. A foundation was established to address claims relating to their asbestos products, but by 2003 it was apparent that the foundation was substantially underfunded. In response to the public outcry that ensued, James Hardie's directors "claimed that under Australian corporate law their primary duty was to the shareholders, and that it would have been impermissible for them to provide additional funds to the Foundation to support liabilities to tort claimants." The "on-going public outrage" that ensued, among other things, "forced [James Hardie] to enter into the largest personal injury settlement in Australian history," and precipitated the Parliamentary Joint Committee (PJC) and Corporations and Markets Advisory Committee (CAMAC) reports on corporate social responsibility discussed in Chapter 3.[270]

Both reports, however, concluded that the position taken in the 1989 Cooney Report remained persuasive, and that no good reason to deviate from it had been articulated. In its June 2006 report, the PJC endorsed the "enlightened self-interest" approach to corporate purpose, concluding that no change to directors' duties was required to permit regard for other stakeholders.[271] "The committee is of the view," they explained, "that no compelling case for change has been presented," and that the "focus on increasing shareholder value" remained "important, because the provision is first and foremost intended to protect those investors who trust company directors with their savings and other investment funds." At the same time, in light of the "network of legislation" addressing "the social and environmental performance of corporations," the committee added that "substantial and specific legislation provides further

to observe, however, that their study does not address worker protections provided through social welfare programs, *id.* at 579–80, which – as I explore in this chapter – help explain why Australian shareholders' corporate law protections could increase during a period when Australian workers' labor law protections did not. Once social welfare protections are brought to bear on the analysis, it would appear that overall worker protections increased during this period as well.

[270] *See* Jennifer G. Hill, *The Architecture of Corporate Governance in Australia* 6–8 (Univ. Sydney Law Sch. Legal Studies Research Paper No. 10/75, 2010), http://ssrn.com/abstract=1657810. *See also* Renee M. Jones & Michelle Welsh, *Toward a Public Enforcement Model for Directors' Duty of Oversight*, 45 VAND. J. TRANSNAT'L L. 343, 382–84 (2012); Marshall & Ramsay, *supra* note 269, at 2–4.

[271] *See* PARLIAMENTARY JOINT COMMITTEE ON CORPORATIONS AND FINANCIAL SERVICES, CORPORATE RESPONSIBILITY: MANAGING RISK AND CREATING VALUE xiv, 43, 63 (2006) [hereinafter PJC REPORT].

argument against the need for any amendment of [the] Corporations Act" to protect non-shareholders.[272] CAMAC, in its December 2006 report, likewise adopted the enlightened self-interest approach and rejected calls to broaden directors' duties,[273] concluding (like the PJC and the Cooney Committee before it) that the "more appropriate response" to social and environmental concerns was "to address particular behaviours or activities through legislation targeted at the mischief in question."[274]

Although these reports were issued during the conservative administration of John Howard,[275] it is worth noting that a "supplementary report" by Labor PJC members took a largely consistent view on the nature of directors' duties. "Labor welcomes the 'enlightened self interest' interpretation of directors' duties put forward by a range of business and legal witnesses," the supplementary report explained. They warned, however, that "[i]f there was to be a recurrence of the view from the business sector that directors duties prevented attention to legitimate stakeholder interests" (the understanding claimed by James Hardie executives), then "government would be forced to immediately review the articulation of directors' duties and ensure that no such misunderstanding were possible."[276]

Australia's ruling Labor Party remains strikingly committed to shareholder-centric corporate governance – and to robust social welfare protections outside corporate law – further demonstrating the political and social stability of this combination. As one would expect of a "Labor" party, their 2009 national platform (in the run up to their successful 2010 campaign[277]) emphasizes the general need for "[s]trong regulatory frameworks . . . to ensure that markets adhere to broader goals of social responsibility in relation to the environment, the community and the rights of employees,"[278] and favors "a strong safety net of minimum standards, consisting of ten legislated national Employment Standards and a modern award system,"[279] as well as strong state-based social

[272] *Id.* at 59–60.

[273] *See* CORPORATIONS AND MARKETS ADVISORY COMMITTEE, THE SOCIAL RESPONSIBILITY OF CORPORATIONS iv, 7, 40, 78–79 (2006). *See also id.* at 88–99, 112 (associating this approach with the COONEY REPORT).

[274] *Id.* at 8, 113. *See also* AUSTIN & RAMSAY, *supra* note 223, at 394 (citing the COONEY REPORT in support of the "enlightened self-interest" view of Australian directors' duties).

[275] *See* National Archives of Australia, *supra* note 199.

[276] PJC REPORT, *supra* note 271, at 181–82.

[277] *See* National Archives of Australia, *supra* note 199.

[278] AUSTRALIAN LABOR PARTY, NATIONAL PLATFORM AND CONSTITUTION 2009, CHAPTER 2: SECURING OUR FUTURE WITH RESPONSIBLE ECONOMIC MANAGEMENT 2 (2009) [hereinafter LABOR PLATFORM CHAPTER 2].

[279] AUSTRALIAN LABOR PARTY, NATIONAL PLATFORM AND CONSTITUTION 2009, CHAPTER 4: DELIVERING FAIRNESS FOR WORKING FAMILIES 2–5 (2009) [hereinafter LABOR PLATFORM CHAPTER 4]. For additional background on these initiatives, see Fair Work Ombudsman, *Introduction to the*

welfare protections including health care. The platform advocates a universal retirement system,[280] and describes the social function of programs such as redundancy pay and national health care in terms strongly resonating with the history described above. "Labor believes that times of economic uncertainty underscore the need for adequate social safety nets and for the protection of employee entitlements." It is observed that "[r]edundancy pay can cushion individuals and families from the immediate financial impact of the loss of work and are especially important during a period of economic downturn."[281] Similarly, universal health care is described as "a public good" serving as "the foundation of security, opportunity and equality for any society, allowing families and individuals to cope with unanticipated health issues." Although accepting the need for "both public and private health sectors" that balance "choices and guarantees of social inclusion," the platform (naturally) emphasizes that "Labor built Medicare and only Labor has supported Medicare," being "central to our vision of a fairer Australia."[282]

With respect to corporate governance, then, the platform articulates a position consistent with that taken by Labor members of the PJC report, pledging to "continue to improve corporate governance practices, the Corporations Act and related legislation to ensure that . . . [c]orporate governance addresses responsibility to employees, the environment and the community," and to "remove[] impediments to acting in a socially responsible manner," while making eminently clear that they envision no deviation from the prevailing shareholder-centric governance model. They advocate enhanced pay disclosure to ensure that companies remain "accountable to shareholders," as well as reforms to ensure that "[c]ompanies use their general meetings to appropriately communicate with shareholders" and that "[s]hareholders retain the ability to call an extraordinary general meeting of a company and . . . exercise their voting rights appropriately and regularly."[283]

There is no suggestion in the Labor platform that strong shareholder-centrism stands in tension with greater stakeholder orientation, reflecting the confidence of Australia's ruling Labor Party that stakeholders including

National Employment Standards, updated Sept. 2011, http://www.fairwork.gov.au/factsheets/FWO-Fact-sheet-Introduction-to-the-NES.pdf; Fair Work Ombudsman, *What's in a Modern Award?*, updated Sept. 17, 2010, http://www.fairwork.gov.au/awards/modern-awards/pages/what-is-in-a-modern-award.aspx.

[280] Labor Platform Chapter 4, *supra* note 279, at 8.

[281] *Id.* at 6.

[282] By contrast, the platform claims that "[t]he Liberal Party has never accepted the centrality of universal public health insurance to the provision of high quality health care to all Australians." *See* Australian Labor Party, National Platform and Constitution 2009, Chapter 6: Preparing Australia for the Health Needs of the Future 1–5 (2009).

[283] Labor Platform Chapter 2, *supra* note 278, at 9.

employees can be adequately protected through external regulation – a belief that, in turn, deflects political pressure from the corporate governance system, permitting it to focus more intently on shareholders.

II. Canada

Canada, like the other countries investigated here, performs relatively poorly in terms of both employment and unemployment protections for workers, falling near the bottom of the OECD in both respects – although within the category of common-law countries it is thought to perform marginally better than most.[284] Yet again, however, in the critical area of health care, an enormous divergence from the United States arises, with Canada's approach much more closely resembling the more comprehensive state-based approaches taken in Australia and the United Kingdom. With respect to the development of its social welfare and corporate governance regimes, the Canadian history most closely resembles that in the United Kingdom insofar as the Canadian welfare state had largely taken shape prior to the critical period of modernizing reforms in corporate law in the late 1960s and 1970s. The dynamics of Canadian corporate law reform are unique, however, in at least one critical respect: when it came time to reform Canada's corporate laws, two foreign regulatory models loomed large in reformers' minds – both the United Kingdom and the United States, the former by dint of shared legal history and the latter by dint of geographic, commercial, and cultural proximity. As this section explores, although Canadian corporate law clearly exhibits some limited degree of U.S. influence, Canada has nevertheless struck a broader social and political equilibrium strongly resembling that in the United Kingdom for broadly similar reasons, the result being relatively strong shareholders within corporate law and relatively robust stakeholder protections outside corporate law.

By World War II, a number of social welfare programs had emerged across Canada, including workers' compensation, "mothers' pensions," minimum wage laws, and "old age pensions," as well as various veterans' programs.[285] An attempt in the mid-1930s to enact "New Deal"-type national legislation addressing unemployment insurance and health care failed, however, in the face of provincial opposition and constitutional limits on federal authority,

[284] *See* Estevez-Abe et al., *supra* note 136, at 163–73 (reporting stronger employment and unemployment protections in Canada than in Australia, the United Kingdom, or the United States). Recall, however, that Australia's wage arbitration system arguably supplements its social welfare system in important respects. *See, e.g.*, Castles & Uhr, *supra* note 187, at 80; Cheffins, *supra* note 210, at 28; Esping-Andersen, *supra* note 187, at 89–90.

[285] *See* James J. Rice & Michael J. Prince, Changing Politics of Canadian Social Policy 40–47 (2000).

and similar efforts in the 1940s failed for similar reasons.[286] Under the Constitution Act, 1867, provinces possess exclusive power to regulate the "Establishment, Maintenance, and Management of Hospitals, Asylums, Charities, and Eleemosynary Institutions in and for the Province,"[287] and "the courts have interpreted the provincial power over hospitals in a very broad manner, extending provincial legislative authority to almost all areas of health care delivery" – including insurance, pharmaceuticals, and regulation of the medical profession.[288] Consequently, the movement toward universal health insurance coverage would have to begin at the provincial level.

The early innovator was Saskatchewan, which – under Premier Tommy Douglas – created the first universal health insurance plan in 1947, covering hospital-related costs through premiums charged to provincial residents and the province's general revenues. "The Hospital Services Plan was the first in North America to provide complete hospital benefits to all residents of the province," A.W. Johnson explains, including "public ward care, X-ray and laboratory services, common drugs, and other hospital services," plus "a flat per diem amount toward the cost of out-of-province hospitalization for any Saskatchewan resident." Hospitals simply took down patients' hospitalization card numbers and billed the provincial hospital services plan.[289] The political impetus for such a plan grew from the collectivist ethos of farmers in the sparsely populated Canadian west of the early twentieth century, distant from the eastern centers of economic and political power, and for whom provincial government provided the only effective pooling mechanism.[290] These dynamics were more generally reflected in the emergence of Douglas's party, the Co-operative Commonwealth Federation – the precursor of today's New Democratic Party – of which western farmers were "the backbone," and which from the start exhibited strong commitment to the development of social welfare programs.[291]

By 1949, Alberta, British Columbia, and Newfoundland had followed Saskatchewan's lead. In 1957, then, the federal government agreed to cover half the cost of such provincial plans, and by 1961, each province had a hospital care

[286] *See id.* at 50–51, 60–67. *See also* Jay Makarenko, *Canadian Federalism and Public Health Care: The Evolution of Federal-Provincial Relations*, MAPLELEAFWEB (Jan. 30, 2008), http://www.mapleleafweb.com/features/canadian-federalism-and-public-health-care-evolution-federal-provincial-relations.

[287] Constitution Act, 1867, 30 & 31 Victoria, c. 3, § 92(7) (U.K.).

[288] Makarenko, *supra* note 286, at "Provincial Powers in the Area of Health Care."

[289] *See* A.W. JOHNSON, DREAM NO LITTLE DREAMS: A BIOGRAPHY OF THE DOUGLAS GOVERNMENT OF SASKATCHEWAN, 1944–1961 145–46 (2004). On Tommy Douglas's legacy generally, see *id.* at 271.

[290] *See id.* at 5–9.

[291] *See id.* at 15, 32–33, 263–64, 270–71.

plan in place.[292] In 1962, Saskatchewan again pushed ahead by expanding its provincial health care program to cover outpatient services – over the heated opposition of physicians, who preferred a private system with means-tested supplemental programs, and actually went on strike for twenty-three days in July of that year.[293] The expanded approach, which "provided for a universal medical care plan, available to all residents of the province" – including "medical, surgical, maternity, diagnostic, and physiotherapy services, as well as specialist services upon referral" – would ultimately "become a model for medicare across Canada."[294] In 1966 the federal government again acted to facilitate such provincial plans, agreeing to expand cost-sharing arrangements to cover additional services beyond hospital care. Each province and territory established such a plan by 1972, meaning that universal health coverage was available throughout Canada by that time.[295] Although consisting of distinct provincial plans, they collectively came to constitute a national plan – referred to as "Medicare" – largely through conditions placed on the use of federal money.[296] "Canada's public health care system can be considered 'national'" insofar as the federal government's spending power allows it "to encourage the implementation of some form of public health care across the entire country," while "ensur[ing] basic criteria for the operation of these different provincial health care systems."[297]

[292] *See id.* at 318; Makarenko, *supra* note 286, at "Introduction of Provincial Hospital Care Plans"; RICE & PRINCE, *supra* note 285, at 69–70.

[293] *See* JOHNSON, *supra* note 289, at 268–69, 288. The impasse was mediated, interestingly, by a British doctor associated with the U.K. National Health Service, who had visited Saskatchewan in 1946 and participated in discussions regarding the new provincial hospital plan then taking shape. *See id.* at 295–96.

[294] *See id.* at 269, 302.

[295] *See* Makarenko, *supra* note 286, at "Introduction of Nationwide Medicare." *See also* JOHNSON, *supra* note 289, at 305; RICE & PRINCE, *supra* note 285, at 70. Although Medicare covers "necessary drug therapy administered within a Canadian hospital setting," pharmaceuticals otherwise fall to the provincial and territorial programs. *See* Health Canada, *Access to Insurance Coverage for Prescription Medicines*, updated Oct. 1, 2004, http://www.hc-sc.gc.ca/hcs-sss/pharma/acces/index-eng.php. *See also* Bea Vongdouangchanh, *Federal-Provincial Health Accord Expires in 2014, Experts Say It's Time Feds Talk about Their Plans*, HILL TIMES, Feb. 7, 2011, http://hilltimes.com/page/printpage/healthaccord-02–07–2011.

[296] *See* Makarenko, *supra* note 286, at "Federal Powers in the Area of Health Care" and "Introduction of Nationwide Medicare." *See also* Health Canada, *Canada's Health Care System (Medicare)*, updated Dec. 9, 2010, http://www.hc-sc.gc.ca/hcs-sss/medi-assur/index-eng.php; Health Canada, *Provincial/Territorial Role in Health*, updated July 27, 2009, http://www.hc-sc.gc.ca/hcs-sss/delivery-prestation/ptrole/index-eng.php. On the Parliament of Canada's taxing and spending authority, see Constitution Act, 1867, 30 & 31 Victoria, c. 3, §§ 91(1A), 91(3), 102, 106 (U.K.).

[297] *See* Makarenko, *supra* note 286, at "Federal-Provincial Inter-relationship in Public Health Care." *See also* Chaoulli v. Québec, [2005] 1S.C.R. 791, para. 16 (Can.); Taylor R. Gray,

As in many other countries, the social welfare system in Canada came under substantial pressure in the late 1970s and 1980s, and there was indeed a strong conservative push toward a more residual welfare state.[298] Between the late 1970s and 2000, federal funding (and associated conditions) diminished, and "tax point transfers" – that is, lower federal taxes permitting higher state taxes – were increasingly used in place of cash grants.[299] Nevertheless, Canadian Medicare remained universal, and social spending actually increased between 1980 and 2000 as a share of Canada's gross domestic product.[300] In 1984, the Canada Health Act banned user fees and billing (beyond public reimbursement), and established five criteria to be met by all provincial programs tracking those introduced in the 1966 Medical Care Act – "publicly administered (administered by a public agency); comprehensive (cover all medically necessary services); universal (cover all provincial residents); portable (ensuring continued coverage when persons are temporarily outside of their home province); and accessible (reasonable access to health services without financial or other barriers)."[301] So-called equalization payments help ensure consistency across the provinces,[302] and the 1999 Social Union Framework Agreement established that the provinces (except Quebec) would eliminate residency requirements and agree to use federal funds for agreed-upon purposes, and that the federal government would increase funding and refrain from acting unilaterally in the health care field.[303] Cash transfers are scheduled by legislation to be C$29 billion in 2012–2013, and over C$30 billion in 2013–2014, and tax transfers will be C$14.7 billion in 2012–2013.[304]

Over recent years, various initiatives have aimed to improve access – and particularly to reduce wait times, which remain lengthy.[305] Indeed, the growing problem of wait times led the Supreme Court of Canada, in 2005, to conclude that provincial bans on private insurance – aimed at insulating

A Corporate Geography of Canada: Insights into a Multi-Jurisdictional Model of Corporate Governance, 41 GROWTH & CHANGE 467, 472 (2010).

[298] *See* RICE & PRINCE, *supra* note 285, at 83–84, 90–95, 111, 116.

[299] *See* Makarenko, *supra* note 286, at "Changes to Federal Health Care Funding."

[300] *See* RICE & PRINCE, *supra* note 285, at 107, 125–28, 235–36.

[301] *See* Makarenko, *supra* note 286, at "Introduction of the *Canada Health Act*, 1984."

[302] *See* Health Canada, *Federal Role in Health*, updated Oct. 1, 2004, http://www.hc-sc.gc.ca/hcs-sss/delivery-prestation/fedrole/index-eng.php.

[303] *See* Makarenko, *supra* note 286, at "1999 Social Union Framework Agreement."

[304] *See* Department of Finance (Canada), *What Is the Canada Health Transfer (CHT)?*, updated Dec. 19, 2011, http://www.fin.gc.ca/fedprov/cht-eng.asp.

[305] *See* Makarenko, *supra* note 286, at "2004 Agreement on the Future of Health Care"; Health Canada, *First Minister's Meeting on the Future of Health Care 2004: A 10-Year Plan to Strengthen Health Care*, updated May 9, 2006, http://www.hc-sc.gc.ca/hcs-sss/delivery-prestation/fptcollab/2004-fmm-rpm/index-eng.php; Vongdouangchanh, *supra* note 295.

the public system from competition – could infringe an individual's rights to life and personal inviolability under provincial (and perhaps Canadian) law.[306] Notwithstanding such challenges, however, universal health coverage remains very important to Canadians socially and politically. The Supreme Court of Canada itself recognized this, stating that the five basic principles for provincial health plans "have become the hallmarks of Canadian identity," adding that "[a]ny measure that might be perceived as compromising them has a polarizing effect on public opinion."[307] This view has been echoed by Health Canada, which states that "[f]ramed by the *Canada Health Act*, the principles governing our health care system are symbols of the underlying Canadian values of equity and solidarity."[308]

As in Australia and the United Kingdom, universal health care in Canada essentially represents a victory for the political left. Although conservatives reject equation of public health care with Canadian identity – one commentator, for example, arguing that "[t]here is no greater fallacy than the idea that Canada's system of socialized medicine is essential to our system of national values"[309] – the left-leaning Liberal Party proudly touts universal health coverage as an achievement of the left, while insisting on its essential Canadianness. In its 2011 election platform, for example, the Liberal Party emphasizes that "Liberal governments have built up the foundations of equality – establishing universal medicare, a good public pension system and a Charter of Rights and Freedoms guaranteeing equality of rights and responsibilities for all Canadians."[310] The document states that "Liberal governments brought in universal medicare and passed the Canada Health Act," and asserts that "[f]or Liberals, as for most Canadians, universal access to quality, timely care regardless of your ability to pay, and regardless of which province you live in, is part of what defines Canada. It is embedded in Canadian values, and in the Liberal record."[311] This depiction of Medicare's creation as an achievement of the left would seem to be a fair historical characterization of the matter – Liberal Party Prime Ministers did, after all, lead for all but seven of the fifty years from

[306] *See* Chaoulli v. Québec, [2005] 1 S.C.R. 791, paras. 1–15, 100–08 (Can.) (majority focusing on the Quebec Charter of Human Rights and Freedoms, while the concurrence concludes that the Canadian Charter of Rights and Freedoms was violated as well).

[307] *Id.* at para. 16.

[308] *See* Health Canada, *Canada's Health Care System (Medicare)*, *supra* note 296.

[309] Michael Bliss, *Contrary History: Socialized Medicine and Canada's Decline*, CAN. MED. ASS'N J., July 17, 2007, at 224.

[310] LIBERAL PARTY OF CANADA, YOUR FAMILY. YOUR FUTURE. YOUR CANADA. 3 (2011) (Message from Michael Ignatieff). Note that unlike Australia, where the "Liberal" party represents the political right, in Canada the "Liberal" party represents the political left.

[311] *Id.* at 33.

1935 to 1984, and then again from 1993 to 2006.[312] As we have seen, the CCF (the precursor of the NDP) was in fact the first mover on universal health coverage in Saskatchewan from the late 1940s to the early 1960s, although the Liberal Party did champion its expansion nationally starting in 1963, and Medicare did indeed come "to symbolize Canada's proud and predominant social values – a humane and caring society."[313]

As in the United Kingdom, then, a relatively substantial state-based social welfare system – including universal health insurance – was largely in place by the time Canada's major effort to modernize its corporate laws arose, constituting part of the background social and political conditions before which corporate law reforms have taken place in recent decades. As Bruce Welling suggests, "[i]t seems surprising now that so little Canadian-based development of corporate law took place during [the] 100 year period" from the 1860s to 1970.[314] The Dominion Companies Act of 1934 was effectively "a composite of earlier Canadian law and of the U.K. Companies Act of 1929,"[315] and as Douglas Cumming and Jeffrey MacIntosh would observe, "[p]rior to 1975, little corporate law reform had occurred in Canada since the 1930s."[316] Welling explains that "[i]ncreasingly during this period, Canadian judges adopted English judges' statements as if they were Canadian law," leading him to conclude that "there is little to relate about the development of corporate constitutions in Canada between 1864 and 1970."[317] It was only in the 1970s – by which point the Canadian welfare state, including universal health insurance, was substantially in place – that "the most important and widespread wave of reform in Canadian corporate history" was initiated.[318]

312 *See* Parlinfo, *Prime Ministers of Canada: Political Information – Government Majorities and Minorities*, http://www.parl.gc.ca/parlinfo/compilations/federalgovernment/primeministers/Government.aspx.

313 *See* JOHNSON, *supra* note 289, at 302–05.

314 BRUCE WELLING, CORPORATE LAW IN CANADA: THE GOVERNING PRINCIPLES 53 (3d ed. 2006). *See also* FRANK IACOBUCCI, MARILYN L. PILKINGTON & J. ROBERT S. PRICHARD, CANADIAN BUSINESS CORPORATIONS: AN ANALYSIS OF RECENT LEGISLATIVE DEVELOPMENTS 3–4 (1977); Jacob S. Ziegel, *The New Look in Canadian Corporation Laws*, *in* 2 STUDIES IN CANADIAN COMPANY LAW 1, 2 (Jacob S. Ziegel ed., 1973).

315 DEPARTMENT OF CONSUMER AND CORPORATE AFFAIRS, GOVERNMENT OF CANADA, DETAILED BACKGROUND PAPERS FOR THE CANADA BUSINESS CORPORATIONS BILL 5 (1974).

316 Douglas J. Cumming & Jeffrey G. MacIntosh, *The Rationales Underlying Reincorporations and Implications for Canadian Corporations*, 22 INT'L REV. L. & ECON. 277, 280 (2002). *See also* IACOBUCCI ET AL., *supra* note 314, at 2; Ziegel, *supra* note 314, at 2.

317 *See* WELLING, *supra* note 314, at 53–54. *See also* Jacob S. Ziegel, *Preface*, *in* 1 STUDIES IN CANADIAN COMPANY LAW, *supra* note 314, at vii, vii (observing, in 1967, the long-standing reliance upon English materials to teach company law in Canadian law schools).

318 *See* WELLING, *supra* note 314, at 55.

Ontario was the first mover, initially directing its attention to securities regulation following hostile takeover and insider trading scandals that prompted pressure for reforms from the press.[319] When J.R. Kimber was appointed as Chairman of the Ontario Securities Commission in 1963, he recommended to the Attorney General that a committee be created to investigate Ontario's securities laws. This recommendation "was received with favour and the Kimber Committee was established in October, 1963."[320] The Kimber Report, issued in 1965, was considered a watershed event in the field, one observer writing (in 1965) that it "was unquestionably the most important event in securities regulation in Ontario during the past several years" – notably for its "conclusion that government should be involved in the regulation of the securities industry to a much greater extent than has previously been the case."[321] Whereas the 1947 Ontario Securities Act had "confer[red] scant authority to regulate the secondary market,"[322] the recommendations of the Kimber Report "led to important amendments not only to the Ontario Securities Act but also to the Corporations Act with respect to insider trading, take-over bids, disclosure of information to shareholders and proxy solicitation."[323]

Although "the practice in Canada was of primary concern" to the Kimber Committee, the report notes upfront that "the laws of other jurisdictions, in particular those of the United Kingdom and the United States, were considered"[324] – a dual influence shedding some light on how core features of U.K. and U.S. corporate law, respectively, resonate in the Canadian legal and political environment. U.S. models clearly exerted considerable influence in certain areas, looming particularly large in the Kimber Report's recommendations on prospectus and proxy disclosures, as well as insider trading rules.[325] Of greater interest for our purposes, however, is the Kimber Committee's response to takeovers, which as J.C. Baillie observes, was "one of the few topics dealt with in the Kimber Report concerning which there [was] no legislative code in the United States," perhaps reflecting the fact that takeover bids (unlike proxy contests) were thought to be less frequent in the United States at the time.[326]

[319] *See* James C. Baillie, *The Protection of the Investor in Ontario*, 8 Can. Pub. Admin. 172, 207–08 (1965).

[320] *See id.* at 207.

[321] *See id.* at 253.

[322] J.R. Kimber et al., Report of the Attorney General's Committee on Securities Legislation in Ontario 9 (1965) [hereinafter Kimber Report].

[323] Iacobucci et al., *supra* note 314, at 3. *See also* Philip Anisman, Takeover Bid Legislation in Canada: A Comparative Analysis 5–6 (1974).

[324] Kimber Report, *supra* note 322, at 6.

[325] *See* Baillie, *supra* note 319, at 230, 254, 264.

[326] *See id.* at 258, 262.

The Kimber Committee ultimately advocates a shareholder-centric approach to takeovers quite reminiscent of the approach taken in the United Kingdom, observing the development of the Notes on Amalgamation of British Businesses in 1959 and the development of a similar voluntary code in Canada in 1963.[327] As occurred in the United Kingdom, the Kimber Committee "concluded that the primary objective of any recommendations for legislation with respect to the take-over bid transaction should be the protection of the bona fide interests of the shareholders of the offeree company."[328] Although the Committee signals awareness of potential concerns regarding the collateral impacts of takeovers, they are effectively dismissed. "It has not been suggested to the Committee, nor is the Committee of the view," the report explains, "that the take-over bid is inherently harmful either to the general public, to the shareholders of the companies involved, or to the economy of the province or the country as a whole."[329] In this respect, it is noteworthy that the Ontario Federation of Labour was among those who submitted briefs for the Kimber Committee's consideration[330] – such that when the Committee states that it "has not been suggested" to them that takeovers might harm non-shareholders, the implication is that no such concerns were raised by this Ontario labor organization. Indeed, according to Philip Anisman, the Ontario Federation of Labour's submission to the Kimber Committee merely advocated sending information circulars to employees,[331] evidently not seeing fit to push back against the shareholder-centrism of the emerging takeover regime in any truly fundamental way.

Ontario was likewise the first mover in modernizing Canadian corporate law. In 1965, the Ontario Legislative Assembly appointed a select committee, chaired by Allan F. Lawrence, to "review The Corporations Act of the province of Ontario" and "consider the principles of the incorporation, operation, management and dissolution of corporations," an effort resulting in

[327] *See* Kimber Report, *supra* note 322, at 20–21. *See also* Anisman, *supra* note 323, at 4–5.

[328] *See* Kimber Report, *supra* note 322, at 22.

[329] *See id.* at 20.

[330] *See id.* at 72.

[331] *See* Anisman, *supra* note 323, at 172–73 n.151 (citing Ontario Federation of Labour, Letter to the Attorney-General's Committee on Securities Legislation, Jan. 20, 1964, at 2). Anisman, in his 1974 study of Canadian takeover law, observes that concerns had arisen regarding the potential impacts of takeovers – notably "depriving employees of jobs and the community in which the business was located of its benefits" – but similarly dismisses such arguments. Anisman suggests that while "liquidation of a prosperous corporation may be harmful to employees and to the community," job losses in struggling businesses would be inevitable anyway, and that "in Canada there is some substance to the argument that corporate combinations . . . can produce rationalization of business activities which will be of benefit to a developing economy" – an argument not unlike that made for facilitation of takeovers in the United Kingdom in the 1960s. *See id.* at 9–16.

the 1967 Lawrence Report,[332] which in turn formed the basis for "the major Ontario reform of 1970" reflected in the Ontario Business Corporations Act.[333] In this endeavor the Committee quite clearly felt itself to be venturing into new terrain, characterizing its task as being to examine "the fundamental principles of corporation law in its general aspects" and adding that, "[t]o our knowledge, never before in Canada has any legislative committee attempted a research and study of that nature."[334]

Much like the Kimber Committee before it, the Lawrence Committee emphasized the significant impact of U.S. models, observing that "[o]f all the materials of the various countries whose law and experience we reviewed, no materials received a closer examination and consideration than the federal and state laws of the United States."[335] Indeed, as Jacob Ziegel would observe in 1973 of the resulting Ontario Business Corporations Act, "there is very little . . . that is truly original," with "most of the new provisions hav[ing] been inspired by American and, to a much lesser extent, British precedents."[336] Strikingly, however, when it comes to the fundamental issues of power and purpose, U.S. models appear to have exerted considerably less influence than they did in more peripheral areas of corporate law.

Although little analysis is provided, the Lawrence Committee evidently saw little need to depart from the U.K. approach, preserving strong shareholder governance. For example, given the shareholders' right to elect directors, the Committee concludes that "[t]here seems to be no logical reason why the corollary right should not exist; that is, there appears no reason why the Act should not authorize the shareholders to remove directors during their term of office. Nor is there any persuasive reason why removal should require a vote in excess of the majority of the votes cast at the meeting duly called for the purpose."[337] The Committee correctly observes that this approach was consistent both with the U.K. approach and with that of "an increasing number of the United States" as of 1967.[338] It must be emphasized, however, that prior to 1967 Delaware's statute did not provide for removal, and that "[t]he 1967 revision contemplat[ing] removal . . . did not provide for the method of removal or the standards by which removal could be accomplished." In 1974, then, the Delaware statute was amended to create the structure described

[332] *See* ALLAN F. LAWRENCE ET AL., INTERIM REPORT OF THE SELECT COMMITTEE ON COMPANY LAW i–ii (1967) [hereinafter LAWRENCE REPORT].

[333] *See* WELLING, *supra* note 314, at 44. *See also* Ziegel, *supra* note 314, at 3.

[334] *See* LAWRENCE REPORT, *supra* note 332, at ix.

[335] *See id.* at vi.

[336] Ziegel, *supra* note 314, at 5.

[337] LAWRENCE REPORT, *supra* note 332, at 75. *See also* SAMUEL LAVINE, THE BUSINESS CORPORATIONS ACT . . . AN ANALYSIS 225 (1971).

[338] *See* LAWRENCE REPORT, *supra* note 332, at 75.

earlier, permitting removal by vote of a majority of shares but requiring cause to remove staggered directors unless provided otherwise in the charter[339] – the upshot being that Delaware, the U.S. jurisdiction of greatest significance for public corporations, has at no point truly fit the trend that the Lawrence Committee identified. In any event, other shareholder-centric governance rules are characterized as similarly unproblematic by the Lawrence Committee, including a low (5 percent) threshold for calling meetings, and a high degree of shareholder control over the content of corporate bylaws.[340] That the Lawrence Committee's aim was to enhance shareholders' governance powers was not lost on observers.[341] Indeed, when new legislation largely based on the Lawrence Report was first proposed in 1968, Premier John Robarts even referred to it as a "charter of rights" for shareholders.[342]

The Lawrence Report would exert substantial influence on corporate law reforms across Canada, insofar as the Ontario Business Corporations Act of 1970 formed the basis for efforts leading to the Canada Business Corporations Act of 1975 (CBCA). The Dickerson Report, which led to the CBCA, was similarly produced by a committee chaired by Robert W.V. Dickerson.[343] Like the Lawrence Committee, the Dickerson Committee found nothing socially or politically problematic about strong shareholder powers and a shareholder-centric conception of corporate purpose. Indeed, the Dickerson Committee dismissed stakeholder concerns explicitly, observing that:

> Suggestions have been made from time to time that corporation law focuses too narrowly on shareholders, and ignores the reality that others, especially the corporation's employees and creditors, are affected by and concerned with what corporations do. It follows from this, so the argument goes, that these groups should have some voice in the choice of corporate directors.

339 *See* R. FRANKLIN BALOTTI & JESSE A. FINKELSTEIN, THE DELAWARE LAW OF CORPORATIONS AND BUSINESS ORGANIZATIONS, § 4.4, at 4–10–4–11 (3d ed. 2009).

340 *See* LAWRENCE REPORT, *supra* note 332, at 77–78, 85. *See also* LAVINE, *supra* note 337, at 192–93.

341 *See, e.g.*, CANADIAN BAR ASSOCIATION, BRIEF OF THE ONTARIO COMMERCIAL LAW SUBSECTION OF THE CANADIAN BAR ASSOCIATION RELATING TO THE BUSINESS CORPORATIONS ACT, 1968 (BILL 125, 17 ELIZABETH II) AND THE BUSINESS CORPORATIONS INFORMATION ACT, 1968 (BILL 126, 17 ELIZABETH II) 39 (1969); J. Gordon Coleman, *The Rights and Obligations of Shareholders under The Business Corporations Act, 1970*, *in* LAW SOCIETY OF UPPER CANADA, DEPARTMENT OF CONTINUING EDUCATION, SPECIAL ONE-DAY PROGRAMME: THE BUSINESS CORPORATIONS ACT, 1970 E-1, E-25–E-30 (1970); Larry D. Hebb, *The Business Corporations Act, 1970: Rights and Obligations of Directors*, *in* LAW SOCIETY OF UPPER CANADA, *supra*, at D-1, D-4; LAVINE, *supra* note 337, at 359–61; Lorie Waisberg, *Analysis of Changes Made by the Business Corporations Act, 1970*, *in* LAW SOCIETY OF UPPER CANADA, *supra*, at A-1, A-19, A-22.

342 *See* Hebb, *supra* note 341, at D-21 (quoting Premier Robarts).

343 *See* WELLING, *supra* note 314, at 44–45, 55–57.

> Moreover, it is said, there is a broad public interest in corporations, and this interest should be represented in corporate boardrooms.[344]

Here the Dickerson Committee observes that concerns had been expressed regarding the social consequences of a strictly shareholder-centric approach to corporate power and purpose. Although accepting "the validity of the premise on which this argument is based," however, the Committee concludes that "we do not see any practical way, in the context of a corporations act, in which it can be implemented."[345] The Committee continues, effectively taking the position that Easterbrook and Fischel would later advocate – and which Australia and the United Kingdom would embrace in their own corporate laws – that employees and creditors could bargain for board representation and that otherwise "[t]he public interest must be reflected through government."[346]

Strong shareholder powers and orientation toward shareholders' interests are characterized throughout the Dickerson Report as logically straightforward and unproblematic. Shareholders are permitted to seize power from the board through unanimous shareholder agreements, there being "no reason in principle or policy why shareholders should not be free to agree to a different structure of management, either by a provision in the articles, in the by-laws, or in a unanimous shareholder agreement."[347] An expressly U.K.-inspired provision allowing removal of directors by ordinary resolution is deemed "elementary and necessary," particularly "in large publicly-held corporations."[348] Perhaps most strikingly, the relatively exacting disclosure obligations of the U.S. Williams Act are rejected as giving "very considerable advantages to entrenched management, enabling them to take measures at a very early stage to fend off a take-over bid," an approach based on "very different policies" from those prevailing in Canada; the Dickerson Committee advocated an approach closer to that of Ontario, which the Committee observes was based on the London City Code.[349] The resulting CBCA left practitioners remarking on the "extraordinary rights given to shareholders," including "power to participate directly and indirectly in management."[350]

[344] *See* Robert W. V. Dickerson et al., Proposals for a New Business Corporations Law for Canada, Volume I: Commentary 9 (1971) [hereinafter Dickerson Report].

[345] *See id.* at 9. *See also* Department of Consumer and Corporate Affairs, *supra* note 315, at 5.

[346] *See* Dickerson Report, *supra* note 344, at 10.

[347] *See id.* at 70.

[348] *See id.* at 74. *See also* Iacobucci et al., *supra* note 314, at 252 (characterizing the removal right as the shareholders' "most potent means of affecting the policies of the corporation").

[349] *See* Dickerson Report, *supra* note 344, at 144–45.

[350] *See* J.M. Wainberg & Mark I. Wainberg, Guidebook to Canada Business Corporations Act 33 (2d ed. 1981). *See also* Department of Consumer and Corporate Affairs, *supra*

The views on power and purpose motivating the Dickerson Committee certainly were not lost on Canadian corporate law scholars of the time. Frank Iacobucci, Marilyn Pilkington, and Robert Prichard, writing in 1977, aptly summarize the Dickerson Report's conception of corporate purpose as being that "the corporation's role is and should be profit-maximization." They further observe that newly enacted Canadian corporate legislation "does not challenge the traditional assumptions that the object of the business corporation is the maximization of profit and that the role of the corporations statute should be to enable it to do so in a fair and effective manner." Hence the statutes "impose no obligation to act in the public interest, whatever that might be, apparently assuming that the public interest in a free enterprise economy is best served by the pursuit of profit," and "make few attempts to regulate the corporate form in such a way as to implement particular social or economic policies," reflecting the view that it is "preferable to approach other social and economic goals directly, rather than through the indirect means of the corporations statute."[351] They do acknowledge "recent cases" in which courts were "willing to take a wider view" – notably, *Teck Corp. Ltd. v. Millar* – but warn that although "some courts have demonstrated a willingness to broaden the profit maximization objective, the classical approach remains firmly established," such that "directors who depart from single-minded profit-seeking are at considerable risk."[352] Observing that "shareholders form the dominant constituency within the [Canadian] corporation," they conclude that a "major theme of corporate law reform has been concerned with an appraisal and strengthening of the shareholders' mechanisms for exerting this control primarily through the democratization of the decision-making structure."[353]

To be sure, other commentators in the 1960s and 1970s did query whether sufficient attention was being paid to issues of corporate purpose in the major corporate reform efforts taking place during that period. In an article included in Jacob Ziegel's 1967 edited volume, *Studies in Canadian Company Law*, J.E. Smyth examines the social desirability of shareholder-centrism and cites cases evidencing a gradual move toward recognition of non-shareholders' interests in U.S. corporate law, in contrast with the more stark shareholder-centrism of Canadian and U.K. law.[354] In a 1970 conference sponsored by the Law

note 315, at 11 (observing that the "residual powers of shareholders to control indirectly the management of the corporation are . . . substantially increased").

[351] IACOBUCCI ET AL., *supra* note 314, at 7–10. *See also id.* at 134–46 (setting out "a normative decision-making model").

[352] *Id.* at 296.

[353] *Id.* at 132.

[354] *See* J.E. Smyth, *The Social Implications of Incorporation*, *in* 1 STUDIES IN CANADIAN COMPANY LAW, *supra* note 314, at 651, 655–65.

Society of Upper Canada on the new Ontario Business Corporations Act, L.D. Hebb observed that "some basic questions about directors' responsibilities remain unanswered," including "whether directors owe duties to anyone but the company," and more specifically whether they "owe any duties to company employees or to the community."[355] Likewise Ziegel, writing in 1973, questioned whether it was really entirely clear that "social and economic regulation" could have no place in corporate law, as the Dickerson Report suggested, observing that this position "presupposes some logical limitation to the contents of company law legislation, an argument that is difficult to sustain."[356] He further observes that neither the Ontario Business Corporations Act nor the proposals toward the CBCA had explored the meaning of the "corporation's interests" in any depth, contrasting this with the "vigorous debate" in the United States regarding "the shareholder's position in the large modern corporation."[357]

The lack of serious reflection on these issues in Canadian reforms of the 1960s and 1970s suggests not that Canadian policy makers were equivocating on shareholder-centrism, but that they effectively took it for granted that shareholders' interests ought to remain the principal metric by which to assess corporate decision making. Accordingly, the lack of concerted opposition to shareholder-centric corporate governance rules (including by organized labor) – particularly in light of the substantial completion of Canada's welfare state by the time significant corporate law reform efforts arose – provide at least indirect evidence that Canadian policy makers were generally comfortable with the capacity of extra-corporate regulation to safeguard the interests of non-shareholders, including employees. Put differently, the Dickerson Committee's conclusion that non-shareholders are best protected outside corporate law did not precipitate protests, or even substantial comment, for the same reason the equivalent position provoked neither protests nor substantial comment in the United Kingdom – extra-corporate stakeholder protections had, in fact, deflected social and political pressure for corporate law to demonstrate such regard for non-shareholders' interests.

The fundamental nature of this social and political equilibrium in Canada appears not to have changed substantially in the intervening years. As of 2000, Cumming and MacIntosh would observe "the low political profile of corporate law in Canada," such that "corporate law reform has not been an issue for provincial or federal politicians."[358] They add that "there is no

355 Hebb, *supra* note 341, at D-22.

356 *See* Ziegel, *supra* note 314, at 33.

357 *See id.* at 42–44, 56–57.

358 Douglas J. Cumming & Jeffrey G. MacIntosh, *The Role of Interjurisdictional Competition in Shaping Canadian Corporate Law*, 20 INT'L REV. L. & ECON. 141, 144 (2000).

well-organized constituency championing the cause of corporate law reform," and that it remains unlikely "to capture the interest or imagination of the median [Canadian] voter."[359] To the extent today's Liberal Party has expressed misgivings about corporate transactions such as takeovers, the root concern appears to be increasing foreign ownership,[360] and presumably the threat posed by shareholders and management alike who do not share "Canadian" values, rather than any inherent tension between the interests of shareholders and other corporate stakeholders.[361]

Although recent case law has expressed regard for non-shareholders – notably creditors – this appears to reflect an enlightened shareholder value approach much like that embraced in Australia and the United Kingdom, an approach that remains fundamentally committed to a conception of the corporation placing shareholders at the heart of the enterprise. To be sure, in *Re BCE, Inc.* the Supreme Court of Canada did state that directors' fiduciary duty "is not confined to short-term profit or share value," but rather "looks to the long-term interests of the corporation"; that "[i]n considering what is in the best interests of the corporation, directors may look to the interests of, *inter alia*, shareholders, employees, creditors, consumers, governments and the environment to inform their decisions"; and that although the "corporation and shareholders are entitled to maximize profit and share value," they may not do so "by treating individual stakeholders unfairly."[362] Recall, however, that at least for sophisticated creditors, fair treatment appears simply to amount to giving them what they bargained for in their contracts.[363] Similarly, to the degree Canadian corporate law requires boards to focus on the employees' interests, this takes the form of statutory liability for unpaid

[359] *Id.* at 149–50.

[360] *See, e.g.*, Liberal Party of Canada, *supra* note 310, at 13.

[361] The CBCA requires that 25 percent of the board (and in some cases a majority) be "resident Canadians," and permits restricting the sale of shares to resident Canadians through amendment of the articles by special resolution. *See* Canada Business Corporations Act, C.R.C, c. C-44, §§ 105(3)-(3.1), 174. The aim is to ensure that "the Canadian viewpoint would be expressed in all meetings of directors and committees of directors of corporations controlled by persons who are not resident Canadians." Department of Consumer and Corporate Affairs, *supra* note 315, at 12. *See also* Iacobucci et al., *supra* note 314, at 244–49; Christopher M. Bruner, *Culture, Sovereignty, and Hollywood: UNESCO and the Future of Trade in Cultural Products*, 40 N.Y.U. J. Int'l L. & Pol. 351, 368–70, 384–90 (2008) (discussing similar efforts to protect Canada's "cultural industries" in the trade context). Such requirements are clearly in tension with the notion that shareholder wealth maximization should be the fundamental metric for board decision making in Canada, and that other economic and social policy aims ought to be pursued through other forms of regulation. *See* Iacobucci et al., *supra* note 314, at 249.

[362] BCE Inc. v. 1976 Debentureholders, [2008] 3 S.C.R. 560, paras. 37–40, 64 (Can.).

[363] *See id.* paras. 95–114, 156–65.

wages[364] – once again, effectively amounting to an obligation not to evade contractual obligations. Both suggest an approach to stakeholders' interests differing little in substance from the shareholder-centric model historically embraced by Canadian corporate law, an approach facilitated by the relatively robust suite of stakeholder protections available outside corporate law, much like in Australia and the United Kingdom.

D. SHAREHOLDER ORIENTATION, SOCIAL WELFARE, AND POLITICAL EQUILIBRIUM

In order to illuminate more fully the intrinsic relationship between social welfare policy and corporate governance exhibited by each of the common-law jurisdictions investigated in this book, it is helpful to step back at this point to place the developments and processes described above in the broader context of modern economic history. From this perspective, the impact of social welfare policy and corporate governance on one another reflects some of the most fundamental social and political forces that have shaped industrialization in each of the countries investigated.

In each country, the relationship between social welfare policy and corporate governance represents one expression of a greater historical transition toward, and adjustment in response to, industrial capitalism. Political economist Karl Polanyi, in his classic 1944 study of industrialization, *The Great Transformation*, describes the shift from agrarian to industrial society as requiring a "double movement" in social and political terms. With the emergence of the "factory system," he explains, "[i]ndustrial production ceased to be an accessory of commerce," newly requiring "long-term investment with corresponding risks." And unless the "continuance of production was reasonably assured, such a risk was not bearable." The more complex the system grew, "the more numerous were the elements of industry the supply of which had to be safeguarded." The result was commodification of all "elements of industry," including labor.[365] The problem, of course, is that labor is bound up in people, and thus cannot truly be commodified:

[364] *See* Barry Reiter, Directors' Duties in Canada 474–80 (4th ed. 2009) (reviewing whether various Canadian employment and corporations statutes place "personal liability on directors to pay debts that are owed by their corporations to employees"). Reiter suggests that directors concerned about such liabilities can, among other things, require CEO/CFO certifications "attesting to the timely payment of employee wages," reduce the duration of pay periods, make sure that indemnification and insurance arrangements "address employee-related liabilities in a suitable way," and in the extreme, resign sooner rather than later in "cases of financial uncertainty." *See id.* at 501–04.

[365] Karl Polanyi, The Great Transformation: The Political and Economic Origins of Our Time 78 (Beacon Press 2001) (1944).

> For the alleged commodity "labor power" cannot be shoved about, used indiscriminately, or even left unused, without affecting also the human individual who happens to be the bearer of this peculiar commodity. In disposing of a man's labor power the system would, incidentally, dispose of the physical, psychological, and moral entity "man" attached to that tag. Robbed of the protective covering of cultural institutions, human beings would perish from the effects of social exposure....[366]

Any society that truly treated labor in this manner would, to put it mildly, be a deeply unstable one. As Polanyi expresses it, "no society could stand the effects of such a system of crude fictions even for the shortest stretch of time unless its human and natural substance as well as its business organization was protected against the ravages of this satanic mill."[367]

The response was a series of "protective counter-moves which blunted the action of this self-destructive mechanism" – giving rise to social and political responses that, in essence, saved industrialization from itself. "Social history in the nineteenth century," Polanyi argues, "was thus the result of a double movement: the extension of the market organization in respect to genuine commodities was accompanied by its restriction in respect to fictitious ones." While industrialism and markets expanded, "a network of measures and policies was integrated into powerful institutions designed to check the organization of the market," including with respect to its impacts on labor.[368] In this light, "the modern working class" emerged out of "immediate self-interest... to become the protectors of society against the intrinsic dangers of a machine civilization,"[369] and social welfare structures would function in a similar manner. Classic early examples included workers' compensation laws, which had already begun to emerge by the 1880s.[370] U.S. developments lagged those in Europe, but once "the lower ranges of labor could not any more be freely replaced from an inexhaustible reservoir of immigrants... the United States caught up with a century of European development," including the development of "social security for labor through unionism and legislation."[371] As Polanyi concludes of such efforts, "if market economy was a threat to the human and natural components of the social fabric... what else would one expect than an urge on the part of a great variety of people to press for some sort of protection?"[372] For Polanyi, this double movement – increasing reliance on markets, paired with social responses to blunt its human costs – reflected society's fundamental ambivalence in the face of industrial capitalism's "stunning

[366] *Id.* at 76.
[367] *Id.* at 76–77.
[368] *Id.* at 79.
[369] *Id.* at 105.
[370] *See id.* at 153–54.
[371] *Id.* at 211.
[372] *Id.* at 156.

contradictions," generating great wealth and great poverty alike, while sacrificing social security in the name of expansive freedom of contract.[373]

Though Polanyi, writing in 1944, did not phrase it in such terms, the history that he recounts is fundamentally about risk management – and approaching that history through this conceptual lens allows us to perceive more clearly the intrinsic relationship between social welfare policy and corporate law. In his 2002 book *When All Else Fails*, economic historian David Moss recounts "the government's role as a risk manager" throughout American history. In so doing, he draws together seemingly disparate aspects of the management of risk in facilitating and managing industrial capitalism, a perspective from which corporate law and social welfare structures reveal themselves to be of a piece. "Without limited liability law, bankruptcy law, government-printed money, and unemployment insurance – just to name a few pivotal risk management policies – it is doubtful that a modern industrial economy could have taken root in America."[374]

Limited liability, widely considered today to be a fundamental attribute of the corporate form,[375] emerged to facilitate industrial production in the nineteenth century by shifting unbearable risks away from investors. As Moss recounts, "the world's first limited liability statutes were enacted in the United States in the early nineteenth century," first in New York and then elsewhere, the "overarching objectives [being] business development and economic growth." Moss fairly describes this development "as one of the most valuable pieces of industrial policy ever enacted in the United States," and

[373] *See id.* at 87–89.

[374] David A. Moss, When All Else Fails: Government As the Ultimate Risk Manager 1 (Harvard University Press, 2004) (2002). Although beyond the scope of this book, it should be observed that just as the U.K. and U.S. corporate governance systems diverge in relative degrees of shareholder orientation, so their bankruptcy systems diverge in relative degrees of creditor orientation. As the United Kingdom more strongly favors shareholders while solvent and creditors once insolvent, one might generalize that U.K. law favors the residual claimant to a greater extent than U.S. law does. *See, e.g.*, John Armour, Gerard Hertig & Hideki Kanda, *Transactions with Creditors, in* Reinier Kraakman et al., The Anatomy of Corporate Law: A Comparative and Functional Approach 115, 149–50 (2d ed. 2009); Rafael La Porta et al., *Law and Finance*, 106 J. Pol. Econ. 1113, 1135–38 (1998); Marco Pagano & Paolo Volpin, *The Political Economy of Finance*, 17 Oxford Rev. Econ. Pol'y 502, 514–15 (2001). *See also* John Armour, Brian R. Cheffins & David A. Skeel, Jr., *Corporate Ownership Structure and the Evolution of Bankruptcy Law: Lessons from the United Kingdom*, 55 Vand. L. Rev. 1699 (2002). Interestingly, although early American bankruptcy laws drew heavily from creditor-friendly British models, successive nineteenth-century American statutes moved gradually toward the more debtor-friendly approach embraced today, largely reflecting the view that "a discharge in bankruptcy would prevent entrepreneurial talent (human capital) from going to waste as a result of crippling, over-hanging debt." Moss, *supra*, at 133–45.

[375] *See, e.g.*, John Armour, Henry Hansmann & Reinier Kraakman, *What Is Corporate Law?, in* The Anatomy of Corporate Law, *supra* note 374, at 1, 9–11.

as "a critical foundation of our capitalist economic system."[376] The benefit of risk reduction for shareholders, however, naturally came at the cost of risk newly borne by others, specifically creditors who consequently could look only to the corporation's assets for satisfaction of the debts owed them, be they "voluntary" creditors such as banks, or "involuntary" creditors – notably, tort victims harmed by industrial products or activities. The logic is that the benefit to shareholders of avoiding potentially bankrupting losses exceeds the cost to creditors of enduring limited losses, particularly given that creditors can simply price the additional risk of loss into their loan deals. Tort victims, for their part, clearly have no *ex ante* opportunity to negotiate the terms of the debt owed them, effectively "permit[ting] shareholders to shed (or *externalize*) a portion of their default risk for free – again increasing the appeal of equity investment, though this time at the expense of involuntary creditors."[377] Evidently, however, legislators have universally concluded that "a small amount of scattered suffering was a price worth paying to gain the full capital-mobilizing effect of airtight shareholder protection."[378] Although such risk shifting could, to some degree, be achieved through private negotiation, Moss speculates that states perceived a need for legislative action because of the impossibility of *ex ante* contracting with involuntary creditors, and the substantial transaction costs that a private regime could entail with voluntary creditors. In any event, negotiating for limited liability could prove awkward. "Why would a corporation's managers request such an extraordinary grant of immunity unless they knew the corporation's risk of default was greater than it appeared?"[379]

Viewed historically, investors' limited liability under corporate law constitutes "an exceptionally pure component" of what Moss calls "Phase I" risk management – that is, risk management policy aimed at facilitating industrialism.[380] Phase I, of course, was followed (as the name implies) by "Phase II," in the early twentieth century, focusing on risks faced by workers. This effectively represented a response to the social costs of industrial capitalism, including those unleashed by Phase I risk management techniques such as limited liability.[381] Although Moss, writing in 2002, employs a very different vocabulary, the dialectical social and political process that he describes maps quite coherently onto the "double movement" that Polanyi identified in 1944. "The dawn of the twentieth century," Moss explains, "brought an entirely new set of risks to the attention of U.S. policymakers. Industrial workers, who had once constituted but a tiny fraction of the nation's labor force, had by now grown into a large and powerful social group." Notwithstanding

[376] Moss, *supra* note 374, at 54.
[377] *Id.* at 74–75.
[378] *Id.* at 81.
[379] *Id.* at 80–83.
[380] *See id.* at 83.
[381] *See id.* at 6–7.

wage increases, workers nevertheless faced substantial financial uncertainty, and "the loss of a job – whether because of a workplace injury, illness, old age, or an economic downturn – could easily land a worker and his family in poverty." Extended families and tight-knit local communities had performed an important risk-spreading function in the predominantly agricultural economy of the nineteenth century, but "rapid urbanization left these traditional safety nets in tatters." The response, Moss explains, was to replace those family and community-based risk-spreading structures with state-based risk-spreading structures – in other words, welfare state structures, early examples of which included workers' compensation laws, unemployment insurance, and old-age insurance.[382]

The discussion presented in this chapter regarding the interrelationship between the degree of shareholder orientation in corporate law and the degree of protection of other stakeholders' interests outside corporate law tends to suggest that Polanyi's "double movement" and the balancing of Moss's "Phase I" and "Phase II" risk management policies – which broadly reflect the same social and political dynamics – have resulted in more-or-less stable political equilibria in countries that have invested more substantially in social welfare programs. In Australia, Canada, and the United Kingdom, social and political pressures have effectively been diverted from the corporate form – and the system of industrial capitalism more generally, of which the corporate form is an exemplar – through the provision of relatively robust state-based social welfare programs, including universal access to health care. Recall, however, that in the United States, industrial production and social welfare have remained in greater tension with one another – and the historical lenses offered by Polanyi's and Moss's work offer useful opportunities to assess why this is the case. Our failure in the United States to achieve so stable a social and political equilibrium as that achieved elsewhere in the common-law world could be described as giving rise to a "Phase III," in Moss's terminology, or a "treble movement," in Polanyi's. In essence, those structures aimed at facilitating industrialism have been subjected to renewed social and political pressure – particularly in times of crisis – to accommodate various stakeholders' interests, precisely because social welfare structures intended to respond to stakeholders' vulnerabilities have not been sufficiently effective.

To be sure, the United States has undertaken substantial state-based social welfare initiatives in certain areas,[383] but they differ in strength and

[382] *See id.* at 6–7. For additional background, see *id.* at 152–80 (on workers' insurance), 180–216 (on social security).

[383] *Cf. id.* at 317–19 (observing that "anti-statist sentiments" in the United States are real, but overstated).

comprehensiveness from those provided in Australia, Canada, and the United Kingdom. Sociologist Theda Skocpol, in her 2000 book *The Missing Middle*, examines "America's finest social policy achievements" – including public education, Civil War benefits, programs for mothers and their children, Social Security, Medicare, and the GI Bill – and identifies some telling characteristics of successful U.S. social policy initiatives. "Successful social programs in the United States have never been understood as poor relief or as mere personal 'entitlements,'" she observes. Rather, they "have been morally justified as a return for service to the community, or else as a preparation for individuals who would subsequently contribute to the larger community."[384] This approach, she argues, "has been a characteristic way for Americans to combine their deep respect for individual freedom and initiative with due regard for the obligations that all members of the national community owe to one another."[385] As discussed earlier, heavy reliance has long been placed upon employer-provided benefits through Charny's "employee welfare state,"[386] which is fully consistent with Skocpol's broader point, insofar as such benefits are provided as a form of reward for productive work.

As Moss recounts, the push for universal health insurance in early twentieth-century America failed because of opposition by business, doctors, and insurance companies, who decried it as a form of socialism.[387] Likewise, President Franklin Roosevelt's effort to include health insurance in the draft social security legislation met "fierce opposition from physicians and especially the American Medical Association," in response to which health insurance was removed from the bill.[388] Indeed, "Americans . . . rejected major proposals for compulsory health insurance about a half-dozen times throughout the twentieth century."[389] Approaching the success and failure of various social welfare programs from the perspective of risk management, Moss argues that such programs are most likely to flourish in the United States when they are relatively "invisible," require less state bureaucracy, and can "easily be cast in the rhetoric of contract"[390] – essentially what political scientist Suzanne Mettler has called "the submerged state."[391] This view is fundamentally compatible

[384] *See* THEDA SKOCPOL, THE MISSING MIDDLE: WORKING FAMILIES AND THE FUTURE OF AMERICAN SOCIAL POLICY 25–29 (2000) (emphasis removed).

[385] *Id.* at 27. *See also* METTLER, *supra* note 146, at 39; PRASAD, *supra* note 91, at 82–83, 94–95.

[386] *See generally* Charny, *supra* note 130.

[387] *See* Moss, *supra* note 374, at 172–76.

[388] *See id.* at 214–15. *See also* METTLER, *supra* note 146, at 99.

[389] *See* Moss, *supra* note 374, at 335.

[390] *See id.* at 17, 295, 320.

[391] *See generally* METTLER, *supra* note 146. By this term, Mettler refers to "a conglomeration of federal policies that function by providing incentives, subsidies, or payments to private

with Skocpol's suggestion that such programs flourish when they can be characterized as a form of reward for service to the community. Unlike social security, for example, which involves individual accounts resembling private insurance and a very low cost-to-expenditure ratio, "one of the main reasons why compulsory health insurance was never adopted in the United States was the expectation that, unlike other forms of social insurance, public health insurance would require deep public involvement in the provision of health care services."[392]

One consequence, as explored above, has been the renewal of social and political pressure for U.S. public companies – the principal vehicles of American industrialism – to address social risks thought not to be adequately addressed through state-based social welfare structures. Given the relative weakness of the social safety net in the United States, corporate law has – particularly in times of crisis – been expected to help make up the difference, which has predominantly taken the form of structures enabling managers to deviate from the shareholders' interests where they directly conflict with those of other stakeholders. Hostile takeovers provide the clearest example, threatening employees with job loss – a situation bringing into stark relief the extraordinary vulnerability of U.S. employees, relative to their counterparts in other common-law countries, because of their high degree of dependence on their jobs for access to social welfare protections including health care. Recent corporate governance and social welfare reforms following the financial crisis suggest that the social and political equilibrium in the United States may be evolving – a possibility explored in Chapter 6 – but it is critical to observe just how closely intertwined the foregoing history reveals corporate governance and social welfare protections to be. The far greater extent to which social welfare concerns have affected the development of U.S. corporate law reflects the fact that our political economy and public risk management strategies have followed a unique trajectory – the consequence being that the social stakes of corporate governance are higher in the United States than they are in other common-law countries. Simply put, public companies in the United States are expected to bear substantial social and political freight that their counterparts in Australia, Canada, and the United Kingdom can leave to the state.

organizations or households to encourage or reimburse them for conducting activities deemed to serve a public purpose." Among other things, this approach permits expansion of public policy without visibly expanding the government itself. *See id.* at 4.

392 *See* Moss, *supra* note 374, at 320–21.

PART III

THE THEORY'S EXPLANATORY DOMAIN

6 Stability, Change, and the Future of Corporate Governance in the Common-Law World

The aim of this chapter, broadly speaking, is to illuminate more fully the boundaries of my theory's explanatory domain, and how those boundaries might ebb and flow in the future.

First I revisit my focus on four common-law countries, distinguishing the fundamental political dynamics conditioning their corporate governance systems – and the way their corporate governance systems interact with extra-corporate stakeholder protections – from the dynamics observed in countries where blockholders predominate. Here I take Germany's bank-dominated system as the paradigm case, briefly exploring the differing regulatory posture vis-à-vis shareholders that tends to arise where this sort of blockholding is widespread. I then critique my focus on common-law countries from another angle, briefly exploring how the political and legal dynamics at work in these countries differ from those at work in a set of countries thought to exhibit similar levels of share ownership dispersal – China, the Netherlands, and Japan. The cursory comparisons drawn aim not to provide a comprehensive account of corporate governance in these additional countries, but rather to illuminate the boundaries of my explanatory domain by highlighting various ways in which historical, cultural, and political factors at work in a given country can affect the impact of the social welfare–related dynamics on which I have focused here. Put differently, my aim is not to explain these additional systems so much as to explain why I do not purport to explain them.

Conversely, then, I reexamine the inclusion of Australia and Canada, which are thought to exhibit somewhat lower levels of share dispersal than the United Kingdom and the United States do. Once again the aim is to reveal how various historical, cultural, and political factors can affect the social welfare–related dynamics on which I have focused, but in a different manner. Here the objective is to examine the degree to which their commonalities with the United Kingdom and the United States are attributable to cultural, commercial, and (in the case of Canada) geographic proximity to influential foreign regulatory models.

The remainder of the chapter, then, examines various developments that might lead the common-law countries investigated to become more or less shareholder-centric in the future – some of which are essentially extrinsic to my theory, whereas others relate to it quite closely. The potential for changes in the composition of the shareholder base to impact the degree of shareholder-centrism over time is assessed by reference to the trend toward increased foreign ownership of U.K. equities. The potential for changes in prevailing conceptions of investor identity – notably, the extent to which voters might think of themselves as "shareholders," as opposed to "employees" – is assessed through a more concerted look at the impact of Australia's compulsory superannuation program, which arguably has fostered a more widespread investor mind-set in Australian society. The potential for post-crisis austerity measures to undermine the social and political stability of shareholder-centric corporate governance rules is explored through examination of the impact of substantial welfare spending cuts on the strongly shareholder-centric U.K. takeover regime.

Finally, then, I evaluate corporate governance responses to the recent financial crisis in the United Kingdom and the United States (substantially harder hit than Australia and Canada were), each of which have adopted shareholder-centric reforms. In the United Kingdom, I argue that this response reflects the fact that grappling with excessive risk-taking of the sort that led to the crisis would effectively require redefining the U.K. corporation in the financial context, a more radical step than policy makers appear prepared to take. The results have been conceptually strained efforts to attribute the crisis to a failure of shareholder "stewardship," prompting greater reliance on shareholder-centric governance in clear tension with diminished social welfare protections for stakeholders – an outcome that my theory predicts will not remain politically and socially stable over time. In the United States, meanwhile, the shift toward shareholder-centrism largely reflects a "middle class" coalition built on the investment-related and social welfare–related concerns of the average working family – a development that has been particularly intriguing because, unlike in the United Kingdom, these developments have been accompanied by greater social welfare protections for stakeholders outside the corporate governance system. If sustained (as of this writing, a big "if"), this shift would effectively reflect movement toward a political and social equilibrium more closely approximating that adopted in the other common-law countries, with stronger extra-corporate stakeholder protections facilitating stronger shareholder powers within corporate law.

A. MAPPING THE EXPLANATORY DOMAIN

I argued in the prior chapter that the relative weakness of extra-corporate stakeholder protections in the United States has substantially impeded the emergence of a starkly shareholder-centric corporate system resembling those in Australia, Canada, and the United Kingdom, and that the traditional U.S. ambivalence toward shareholders remains powerful today. From the global comparative perspective, however, one might object that if extra-corporate stakeholder protections – including social democratic welfare-state programs – somehow correlate with shareholder orientation, then we ought to observe *even more* shareholder-centrism in, say, continental Europe. Yet, we in fact observe less. The key to grappling with this apparent inconsistency is to revisit the sequencing – that is, how and why the issue of shareholder orientation has arisen in the common-law countries investigated here.

As Martin Gelter observes, given that "concentrated ownership is the international norm and dispersed ownership the exception, one could speak of concentrated ownership as the primeval state of any corporate governance system." The upshot is that "it is not the persistence of concentrated ownership, but rather its unraveling . . . that calls for an explanation."[1] Throughout most of the world, shareholder power is simply a given – it is an incident of the substantial concentration of share ownership in the hands of one or a small number of entities. In this context, the principal political pressure brought to bear on the corporate governance system – and accordingly, the principal regulatory aim – is to counteract and contain the blockholders' innate power through various forms of stakeholder-oriented protections.[2]

Germany represents the paradigm case. In addition to offering "one of the world's most expensive, generous and encompassing systems of social provision,"[3] the German corporate governance system includes core features aimed directly at curtailing the influence of controlling blockholders while correlatively enhancing the influence of employees in the development of corporate policy. German corporate law gives shareholders substantial voting

[1] Martin Gelter, *The Dark Side of Shareholder Influence: Managerial Autonomy and Stakeholder Orientation in Comparative Corporate Governance*, 50 HARV. INT'L L.J. 129, 182 (2009).

[2] *See id.* at 154–76. *See also* Martin Gelter, *Taming or Protecting the Modern Corporation? Shareholder–Stakeholder Debates in a Comparative Light*, 7 N.Y.U. J. L. & BUS. 641 (2011).

[3] *See* Philip Manow, *Germany: Co-Operative Federalism and the Overgrazing of the Fiscal Commons*, *in* FEDERALISM AND THE WELFARE STATE: NEW WORLD AND EUROPEAN EXPERIENCES 222, 262 (Herbert Obinger, Stephan Leibfried & Francis G. Castles eds., 2005). *See also* Lynne Poole, *Germany: A Conservative Regime in Crisis?*, *in* COMPARING WELFARE STATES 153, 155 (Allan Cochrane et al. eds., 2d ed. 2001) (observing that Germany's "rights-based" social welfare system "has provided relatively high levels of benefits and health care").

power in the annual general meeting, and banks have historically held sway over German public companies because of their role as commercial lenders, their own equity holdings, and, critically, their ability to vote deposited shares when authorized by brokerage clients. At the same time, however, a German public company – termed an *Aktiengesellschaft* (AG) – has a two-tier board structure that has lent itself to the integration of employees in the development of corporate policy. The supervisory board – termed the *Aufsichtsrat* – "formulates (or at least approves) major corporate policies and strategies," and appoints the members of the management board – termed the *Vorstand* – tasked with implementing them.[4] German labor law, then, mandates "codetermination," which directly "integrate[s] employees into the firm's governance processes," reflecting "the stakeholder conception of the corporation." In general, corporations with over two thousand employees are required to give employees and shareholders equal supervisory board representation.[5] Although the efficacy of employee representation on the supervisory board has been questioned – among other things because of the fact that the board's chairman, elected by shareholders, holds the tie-breaking vote, as well as the apparent tendency of management boards to act unilaterally without seeking supervisory board approval – codetermination nevertheless remains "enormously important, symbolically and ideologically, as a feature of Germany's consensus-driven social-market economy," and is bolstered by other features

[4] *See* JOHN W. CIOFFI, PUBLIC LAW AND PRIVATE POWER: CORPORATE GOVERNANCE REFORM IN THE AGE OF FINANCE CAPITALISM 70–71 (2010). *See also* ALAN DIGNAM & MICHAEL GALANIS, THE GLOBALIZATION OF CORPORATE GOVERNANCE 269–74, 277–82 (2009); Gelter, *supra* note 1, at 158–61. For additional background on the shareholders' powers in the general meeting, see GERHARD WIRTH ET AL., CORPORATE LAW IN GERMANY 89–90, 131–52 (2d ed. 2010). For additional background on the two-tier board structure of German public companies, see *id.* at 98–131.

[5] *See* CIOFFI, *supra* note 4, at 73–74. There are in fact three distinct codetermination regimes in Germany. In companies with over five hundred employees in Germany, employees get one-third of the supervisory board seats, whereas the proportion rises to one-half in companies with over two thousand employees in Germany. In the coal, iron, and steel industries, however, a distinct regime applies under which shareholders and employees have equal representation on the supervisory board, with one additional member – "the so-called neutral member" – selected "by means of a complicated mediation procedure." *See* WIRTH ET AL., *supra* note 4, at 117–18. *See also* DIGNAM & GALANIS, *supra* note 4, at 271–72; Luca Enriques, Henry Hansmann & Reinier Kraakman, *The Basic Governance Structure: Minority Shareholders and Non-Shareholder Constituencies*, *in* REINIER KRAAKMAN ET AL., THE ANATOMY OF CORPORATE LAW: A COMPARATIVE AND FUNCTIONAL APPROACH 89, 100–01 (2d ed. 2009); Gelter, *supra* note 1, at 168–70; PETER ALEXIS GOUREVITCH & JAMES J. SHINN, POLITICAL POWER AND CORPORATE CONTROL: THE NEW GLOBAL POLITICS OF CORPORATE GOVERNANCE 160–62 (2005); MARK J. ROE, POLITICAL DETERMINANTS OF CORPORATE GOVERNANCE: POLITICAL CONTEXT, CORPORATE IMPACT 29–31, 71–72 (2003).

of the German corporate governance system.[6] Most tangibly, works councils – termed *Betriebsrat* – "wield substantial influence within the workplace, and often over entire corporate groups, through their wide and complex array of informational, consultation, and codetermination or codecision rights" under German labor law. Although obviously creating a risk of holdup problems, John Cioffi observes that works councils have "proved highly beneficial to firms as a way of coordinating labor relations in workplaces staffed by highly skilled and productive employees," as evidenced by voluntary adoption of integrated works councils for corporate groups even though German labor law requires them only at individual production facilities.[7]

Germany has, to be sure, adopted various shareholder-oriented reforms over recent decades in an effort to foster a culture of minority investing and thereby develop its domestic equity markets, but these reforms have not fundamentally altered Germany's long-standing commitment to stakeholder-centric corporate governance. For example, legislation enacted in 1998 sought to curb bank dominance by limiting their voting power, and tax reforms enacted in 2000 (effective in 2002) sought to facilitate divestment of share blocks by eliminating capital gains taxes that had previously disincentived broader dispersal of shares.[8] Reform efforts in this vein steered well clear of the codetermination system, however, reflecting "the extraordinary political sensitivity of the subject and . . . the broad popularity of codetermination among the electorate."[9] Similarly, European Union initiatives aimed at furthering the common market project have found greater support in Germany when they relate to securities regulation, as opposed to company law – a contrast vividly illustrated by fierce resistance to a proposed EU takeover directive in 2001. Inspired by the London City Code, the proposed directive prohibited defensive measures unless approved by shareholders – a proposal that German labor unions, in particular, viewed "as a means of decisively shifting power and income from employees to shareholders," leading to "a potent coalition" of management and labor "to oppose the directive and its supporters in the financial sector and government." In July 2001 the proposed directive was rejected, and a new German takeover law was enacted later that year, which among other things gave management "vast discretion to defend against

[6] Cioffi, *supra* note 4, at 70, 73–74. *See also* Enriques et al. *supra* note 5, at 101; Roe, *supra* note 5, at 30–31, 72–73.

[7] *See* Cioffi, *supra* note 4, at 74–76 (providing a summary table of "works council rights"). *See also* Dignam & Galanis, *supra* note 4, at 274–76; Gelter, *supra* note 1, at 171–73.

[8] *See* Cioffi, *supra* note 4, at 154–55, 160–61. *See also* Roe, *supra* note 5, at 80–81.

[9] Cioffi, *supra* note 4, at 155, 170–71. *See also* Dignam & Galanis, *supra* note 4, at 312–33, 409–10; Gourevitch & Shinn, *supra* note 5, at 163.

	concentrated ownership	dispersed ownership
market-based minority protections	weaker	stronger
predominant shareholders	controlling shareholders	minority shareholders
regulatory posture toward shareholders	constrain	protect
shareholder orientation in corporate law	weaker	stronger

Figure 6.1. Ownership Concentration and Regulatory Posture toward Shareholders

takeover."[10] (The directive ultimately passed in 2004, but only once the board neutrality rule was made optional.[11]) More recently, the financial crisis has only "reinforced the German government's . . . commitment to the principles of the social market economy" – reflected perhaps most clearly in stronger supervisory board oversight of executive pay.[12]

As the case of Germany vividly illustrates, in a country where blockholding predominates, the principal regulatory issue remains how to counteract the blockholders' innate power over corporate affairs through various forms of stakeholder-oriented protections – a dynamic reflected in Figure 6.1. In the common-law countries investigated here, however, the principal regulatory issue differs radically. In the development of capital markets exhibiting substantially dispersed share ownership, the principal challenge faced by lawmakers and regulators becomes inducing investors to accept the status of minority shareholders through the construction of shareholder-oriented protections.

The divergence between the United States and the other common-law countries investigated[13] strongly suggests that the process of ownership

[10] *See* Cioffi, *supra* note 4, at 143–45, 161–69. *See also* Pepper D. Culpepper, Quiet Politics and Business Power: Corporate Control in Europe and Japan 52–53, 64–70, 78–80 (2011); Dignam & Galanis, *supra* note 4, at 285–92, 334–37; Wirth et al., *supra* note 4, at 222–25.

[11] *See* Council Directive 2004/25, arts. 9(2)-(3), 12, 2004 O.J. (L142/12) (EC). For an argument that "in many Continental European countries," where highly concentrated stock ownership predominates, "the adoption of the Takeovers Directive has been . . . used as an opportunity to reduce the contestability of corporate control or as an occasion to introduce new rules and regulations that might strengthen the defensive barriers of national enterprises," see Marco Ventoruzzo, *Takeover Regulation as a Wolf in Sheep's Clothing: Taking U.K. Rules to Continental Europe*, 11 U. Pa. J. Bus. L. 135, 151–73 (2008).

[12] *See* Cioffi, *supra* note 4, at 221–22.

[13] *See supra* Chapters 3, 5.

dispersal reflects a continual balancing of emergent shareholder and stakeholder protections with one another. In dispersed ownership systems such as those in Australia, Canada, the United Kingdom, and the United States, shareholder and stakeholder regulatory protections develop in response to one another, reflecting a perpetual process of (re)calibration in which the aim is to balance shareholders' comfort with minority voting status and stakeholders' comfort with shareholder-centric corporate governance rules. Shareholder-centric protections initially fostering the dispersal of share ownership and the development of deep, liquid equity markets may, to be sure, occur initially in the financial marketplace, as the historical prominence of stock exchange listing rules in the United Kingdom and the United States vividly illustrates. Ultimately, however, the regulatory consolidation of shareholder protections inevitably takes place in a more overtly political arena where the welfare of other stakeholders looms large. The more robust the protections provided for other stakeholders (notably employees) outside the corporate governance system, the less political resistance shareholder-centric corporate governance structures will face – dynamics illustrated in each of Australia, Canada, and the United Kingdom. Conversely, where extra-corporate stakeholder protections remain weak, political opposition arises, inhibiting strongly shareholder-centric corporate governance and favoring the retention of managerial flexibility to accommodate non-shareholders' interests within the corporate governance system itself – dynamics illustrated in the United States.

The distinction between the impact of politics on corporate governance in dispersed ownership systems, on the one hand, and in concentrated ownership systems, on the other, is straightforward enough – it is effectively the difference between protecting minority shareholders and constraining controlling shareholders, respectively. It must be acknowledged, however, that the binary distinction drawn above between "dispersed" and "concentrated" ownership does tend to blur at the margin, as there is in fact a high degree of variation across countries with respect to relative degrees of ownership dispersal. For example, Peter Gourevitch and James Shinn find levels of blockholding in China, the Netherlands, and Japan equal to or lower than levels observed in the United Kingdom and the United States[14] – yet these countries have not historically exhibited the forms of shareholder orientation that I associate with a high degree of ownership dispersal. Conversely, Australia and Canada

[14] Gourevitch and Shinn measure levels of blockholding by reference to the market value of listed companies with 20-percent blockholders as a percentage of the total market capitalization of the given country's stock markets. They report 23.6 percent for the United Kingdom and 15 percent for the United States. The corresponding figures are 20 percent for the Netherlands, 5 percent for China, and 4.1 percent for Japan. *See* GOUREVITCH & SHINN, *supra* note 5, at 17–18.

exhibit somewhat higher levels of blockholding than the United Kingdom and the United States do,[15] yet Australia and Canada do exhibit the forms of shareholder orientation that I associate with a high degree of ownership dispersal. How – if at all – can these borderline cases be squared with the binary distinction drawn above?

In China, the Netherlands, and Japan, data purporting to measure ownership concentration can prove misleading – although in ways that help to illuminate the boundaries of my explanatory domain. Based on Gourevitch and Shinn's measure – which focuses on the market value of listed companies with 20-percent blockholders, expressed as a percentage of the total market capitalization of the given country's stock markets – China was found to have a remarkably low concentration level of just 5 percent.[16] As Gourevitch and Shinn acknowledge, however, data on private blockholding present an incomplete picture of Chinese securities markets. "China's experiment with publicly traded firms and stock markets is only a decade old, and therefore the state is still the dominant blockholder," holding (as of 2005) an average of 65 percent of state-owned enterprises with traded equity.[17] Efforts to assure investors that their money is safe in China's nascent securities markets have been undertaken, but notwithstanding "hortatory language in various official regulations and listing requirements about directors' responsibility for protecting the rights of shareholders, in fact China's supervisory committee, similar in function to Germany's *Aufsichtsrat*, continues to function as a rubber-stamp for the board of managing directors," who themselves are "all insiders, appointed by the party."[18]

As Li-Wen Lin and Curtis Milhaupt explain, the state maintains an extraordinary level of control over "national champions" in a wide range of important industries through "vertically integrated groups" falling under the umbrella of "a central holding company known as the State-Owned Assets Supervision and Administration Commission (SASAC)." In a given industry, a majority shareholder known as "the 'core' company of the group – which is itself 100% owned by SASAC" – essentially "coordinates the group's activities and transmits

[15] Gourevitch and Shinn report 27.5 percent for each of Australia and Canada. Similarly, they report 27 percent for New Zealand and 24.6 percent for Ireland. *See id.* at 18.

[16] *Id.* at 17–18.

[17] *Id.* at 192.

[18] *Id.* at 194–95. They speculate that such investments may remain attractive domestically relative to "their only alternatives – cash under the mattress, or deposits in the state-owned banking sector," and internationally in light of the potential "upside of buying into a large economy whose growth prospects are widely believed to range between 8 and 10 percent per annum for the foreseeable future." *Id.* at 197.

business policy to group members, who are contractually bound to promote the policies of the state."[19] For example, the governance documents of the China National Nonferrous Metals Industry Group (CNNG) "are a capsule summary of state capitalism," requiring CNNG "to undertake important functions requested by the state, including the implementation of national economic development policies, advising the government in enacting industrial policies, and in implementing corporate, industrial, and national standards."[20] This alignment of business interests and public policy is facilitated, of course, by the fact that "managers of national champions simultaneously hold important positions in the government and the Communist Party."[21] Lin and Milhaupt, like Gourevitch and Shinn, emphasize the concentration of China's brand of "state capitalism," observing that "[i]n no other developed or developing country does a single shareholder – private or public – hold control so pervasively over the leading firms in the national economy." Companies under SASAC's control "account for 62% of GDP," and include "[v]irtually every leading firm in a critical industry in China, from telecom to energy, autos to steel."[22] So pervasive a form of state-capitalism as this simply "does not fit neatly into any of the standard taxonomies," defying categorization as straightforwardly shareholder-centric or stakeholder-centric because the government is at once the controlling shareholder and the undisputed political representative of all domestic stakeholders.[23]

Meanwhile, the Netherlands – which falls between the United Kingdom and the United States, according to Gourevitch and Shinn's measure[24] – has similarly brought about far greater de facto concentration, although by very different means. The Netherlands exhibits what Gourevitch and Shinn describe as "a corporatist compromise" in corporate governance dating to the period of reconstruction following World War II. The number of listed firms with blockholders began to decline substantially in the 1960s, but as Gourevitch and Shinn explain, managers and employees of large companies have "effectively insulated listed companies from the pursuit of shareholder value" by embedding them within "a thicket of antitakeover measures, among the most

[19] Li-Wen Lin & Curtis J. Milhaupt, *We Are the (National) Champions: Understanding the Mechanisms of State Capitalism in China* 1–2 (Columbia Law and Economics Working Paper No. 409, 2011), http://ssrn.com/abstract=1952623.

[20] *Id.* at 31.

[21] *Id.* at 2.

[22] *Id.* at 34–35 & n.72.

[23] *Id.* at 51.

[24] *See* GOUREVITCH & SHINN, *supra* note 5, at 17–18 (reporting a 20 percent concentration level in the Netherlands). For various approaches to the measurement of "patient capital," including in the Netherlands, see CULPEPPER, *supra* note 10, at 29–36.

complex and sophisticated in the world."[25] Various techniques have been used to limit the voting power of public shareholders, "including preferred shares, priority shares, binding appointments, and voting caps." More dramatically, corporate managers "arranged to create a synthetic blockholder . . . by setting up an administrative or so-called trust office – an *administratiekantoor* – and transferring voting rights to these offices," which in turn publicly sold depository receipts that effectively amounted to cash-flow rights bereft of voting power.[26] This structure has been reformed to give public investors "the statutory right to obtain a proxy to exercise the voting rights on the underlying shares" in some circumstances – although, tellingly, not "when a hostile takeover is imminent."[27]

Between 1993 and 2007, placement of securities with trust offices declined, but Dutch companies still widely employ "preference shares" with enhanced voting power to ward off unwanted takeover bids,[28] demonstrating that moves aimed at enhancing the rights of public shareholders have not substantially undermined the position of Dutch labor. Indeed, although the 1971 *structuur* regime – under which "self-selecting boards [in] certain large Dutch companies . . . were legally charged with the duty to represent and harmonize the interests of shareholders and labor" – was abandoned in 2004, it was "replaced . . . with the standard northern European [co-determination] model in which employees elect one-third of the directors of large companies."[29]

[25] GOUREVITCH & SHINN, *supra* note 5, at 178–81. They explain that "many blockheld firms delisted from the exchanges" in the postwar decades, "tilting the markets towards more diffusely held firms with professional managers in the saddle." *Id.* at 181.

[26] *Id.* at 182–83. *See also* CULPEPPER, *supra* note 10, at 41–44.

[27] Luca Enriques, Henry Hansmann & Reinier Kraakman, *The Basic Governance Structure: The Interests of Shareholders as a Class*, *in* THE ANATOMY OF CORPORATE LAW, *supra* note 5, at 55, 63–64 n.50. For a discussion of "how the managers of Dutch large firms successfully defended takeover protections from the attacks of neoliberal politicians and institutional investors," see CULPEPPER, *supra* note 10, at 82–114.

[28] *See* CULPEPPER, *supra* note 10, at 42–43. "Preference" shares have enhanced voting power in the sense that they can be sold at a substantial discount to their nominal value, yet come with full voting rights. The fact that the management board can sell them to a trusted party without shareholder approval renders them an effective antitakeover device, as their sustained and widespread use demonstrates (60 percent of Dutch companies in 1993, and 57 percent in 2007). "Priority" shares, by contrast, come with special decision-making authority, which correlatively carves back at the power of the general shareholders' meeting. Like the placement of securities with trust offices, use of priority shares fell between 1993 and 2007. *See id.* at 42–43; GOUREVITCH & SHINN, *supra* note 5, at 182–83.

[29] Enriques et al., *supra* note 5, at 102–03. *See also* Enriques et al. *supra* note 27, at 56 n.4, 64; Gerhard Schnyder, *Revisiting the Party Paradox of Finance Capitalism: Social Democratic Preferences and Corporate Governance Reforms in Switzerland, Sweden, and the Netherlands*, 44 COMP. POL. STUD. 184, 195–98 (2011).

From 1971 until 2004, the supervisory boards of companies subject to the *structuur* regime selected their own members; shareholders, the managing board, and the works council alike could recommend candidates, but lacked power to appoint them directly to supervisory board positions.[30] Since 2004, however, shareholders and the works council have become more central to the process. Shareholders were granted the right to approve appointments, while the works council was granted what Edo Groenewald describes as "an enhanced right of recommendation concerning one-third of the members of the supervisory board," under which candidates can be rejected only if "unqualified for the position" or if the appointment would render the board not "properly constituted."[31] As Gerhard Schnyder concludes, "the Dutch reform of 2004 does not constitute a break with the traditionally very pronounced 'stakeholder approach,'" as public shareholders' new rights have come "mainly at the expense of the supervisory and of the management boards, whereas employees have gained in influence alongside shareholders."[32] The upshot is that the Netherlands continues to demonstrate the capacity of a strong historical, cultural, and political commitment to stakeholder-centric governance to overcome the forces that I associate with ownership dispersal – even in the face of strong demands to protect public shareholders.[33]

Japan, much like China and the Netherlands, has historically had a much higher level of de facto concentration than one would guess based purely on measures of private blockholding – although recent trends have resulted in genuine dispersal of shareholdings, giving rise to a natural experiment effectively requiring Japanese lawmakers to evaluate U.K. and U.S. corporate governance models along the dimensions discussed in this book. By Gourevitch and Shinn's measure, Japan's capital markets are the most highly dispersed of the bunch, with a concentration level of just 4.1 percent.[34] In fact, however, postwar Japan long exhibited a high degree of de facto concentration through a cross-shareholding structure called *keiretsu*. Managers effectively "created a set of synthetic blockholders" involving an "interlocking network of fellow-keiretsu managers and 'main banks,'" an arrangement thought to provide an effective means of achieving the benefits of "patient capital" – stable

[30] For an overview of the *structuur* regime, see Edo Groenewald, *Corporate Governance in the Netherlands: From the Verdam Report of 1964 to the Tabaksblat Code of 2003*, 6 EUROPEAN BUS. ORG. L. REV. 291, 294–97 (2005).

[31] For an overview of the 2004 reforms, see *id.* at 299–300.

[32] Schnyder, *supra* note 29, at 197.

[33] *See id.* at 196–97 (describing "[s]ignificant pressures for reform . . . from the stock exchange authorities" since the 1980s). *See also* GOUREVITCH & SHINN, *supra* note 5, at 178–79.

[34] GOUREVITCH & SHINN, *supra* note 5, at 17–18.

industrial relations built on promises of lifetime employment, and correlatively greater capacity to engage in long-term strategic planning.[35] Pepper Culpepper similarly notes that both the "horizontal links between allied companies as well as [the] vertical links among supplier companies and their large customers" that are commonly associated with *keiretsu* structures "could function as takeover protection," an observation consistent with the fact that cross-shareholding substantially increased in the 1960s "after the liberalization of capital flows led many Japanese managers to be concerned about the possibility of hostile takeover by foreign companies."[36]

Since the mid-1990s, however, long-term stable shareholding of the sort that held the *keiretsu* together began to decline, leading to the emergence of a nascent market for corporate control in Japan.[37] In response to Japan's ongoing economic crisis and plummeting share prices, banks were forced to unwind cross-shareholdings to remain in compliance with regulatory capital requirements – a self-reinforcing process leading one institution after another to sell as reciprocal ties dissolved. Starting in 2004, then, a handful of high-profile hostile takeover attempts caught the attention of managers, lawmakers, and even the public, leading the government to convene an advisory group – the Corporate Value Study Group (CVSG) – to address the scope of acceptable conduct, notably with respect to defenses.[38] "A major question debated by this group," Culpepper explains, "was whether to permit the use of poison pill takeover defenses, as allowed under Delaware law in the United States, or instead to adopt the strict board neutrality requirement in the City of London

[35] *Id.* at 170. *See also* John Armour, Henry Hansmann & Reinier Kraakman, *What Is Corporate Law?*, *in* The Anatomy of Corporate Law, *supra* note 5, at 1, 29–30; Roe, *supra* note 5, at 89–93. Ronald Gilson and Mark Roe argue that promises of lifetime employment in fact arose to reduce "[l]abor strife" following World War II, and that once in place, "associated institutions that could function effectively given the politically imposed lifetime employment" arose. *See* Ronald J. Gilson & Mark J. Roe, *Lifetime Employment: Labor Peace and the Evolution of Japanese Corporate Governance*, 99 Colum. L. Rev. 508, 520–24 (1999). These included reliance on bonus compensation to incentivize good performance; an early retirement age of just fifty-five years, providing a hedge against poor performance; and "closure of the external labor market" to permit employers to retain their best employees. *Id.* at 529–31. Gilson and Roe argue that "[i]t is the closed external labor market, not employers' promises to employees of lifetime jobs, that assures employers that they can earn a return if they invest in their employees' general human capital." *Id.* at 513–14.

[36] Culpepper, *supra* note 10, at 44 & n.47.

[37] *Id.* at 45–46. *See also* Gregory Jackson & Hideaki Miyajima, *Varieties of Capitalism, Varieties of Markets: Mergers and Acquisitions in Japan, Germany, France, the UK and USA* 5, 12 (RIETI Discussion Paper Series 07-E-054, June 2007), http://ssrn.com/abstract=1012210.

[38] Culpepper, *supra* note 10, at 116–18. The CVSG was chaired by Hideki Kanda, a prominent legal scholar and a coauthor of *The Anatomy of Corporate Law. See* Kraakman et al., *supra* note 5.

of the United Kingdom."[39] Ultimately the CVSG found poison pills "consistent with the principle of shareholder equality enshrined in Japanese company law," effectively opting for the Delaware approach to hostile takeovers over the more shareholder-centric U.K. approach. Culpepper speculates that "the choice of the Delaware standard appears to have been a product of both familiarity with the lawyers on the panel and an appeal to the interests of [the economic ministry], lawyers, and managers" – the ministry favoring avoidance of administrative turf battles through a more court-based approach, the lawyers favoring the familiar (many having pursued graduate legal study in the United States), and managers naturally favoring greater freedom to deploy defenses.[40]

These explanations are certainly plausible enough, although in light of the analysis presented in this book, there would also appear to be a social welfare–oriented logic to Japan's preference for the Delaware approach to takeovers. As Mark Roe has observed, the promise of lifetime employment "has been a key institution" in Japan, "one developed to support social peace" in the postwar era.[41] As such, it constitutes a core element of the Japanese social safety net in a manner not entirely unlike Charny's "employee welfare state" in the United States and Castles' "wage-earners' welfare state" in Australia.[42] The difference, emphasized by the "Varieties of Capitalism" literature, lies in the degree of employment protection historically available in Japan – a virtual guarantee long considered so dependable that, notwithstanding the weak public safety net available to workers should they lose their jobs, workers readily invested in development of firm-specific skills.[43] Indeed, Roe even goes so far as to suggest that promises of lifetime employment "in some ways [have] made Japan 'more' socially democratic than the European social democracies,"[44] which suggests

[39] CULPEPPER, *supra* note 10, at 119.

[40] *Id.* at 134–35. *See also* Jackson & Miyajima, *supra* note 37, at 23–24. Although the CVSG in fact promulgated a set of "guidelines," as a practical matter they became de facto rules through endorsement by the Ministry of the Economy, Trade, and Industry. CULPEPPER, *supra* note 10, at 137–38.

[41] ROE, *supra* note 5, at 92.

[42] *See supra* Chapter 5.B–C.

[43] *See* Margarita Estevez-Abe et al., *Social Protection and the Formation of Skills: A Reinterpretation of the Welfare State*, *in* VARIETIES OF CAPITALISM: THE INSTITUTIONAL FOUNDATIONS OF COMPARATIVE ADVANTAGE 145, 153–55, 162–63 (Peter A. Hall & David Soskice eds., 2001) (observing, in contrast with Japan, that "we would *ordinarily* expect the development of firm-specific skills to be coupled with generous protection against unemployment," as in Europe). Gilson and Roe explain that "[a]lthough the basic Japanese employment rule was 'employment at will' with notice, Japanese courts responded to the 'scarcity of employment opportunities in the chaotic post-War economy,' with an 'abuse of rights' doctrine that required that employers not dismiss employees 'abusively.'" Gilson & Roe, *supra* note 35, at 525–26.

[44] ROE, *supra* note 5, at 92.

that undermining employment stability through the threat of hostile takeovers would – perhaps even more than in Australia and the United States in the 1980s – tend to undermine social welfare stability in Japan in a profound way. In this light, it is not surprising that Japan would adopt the Delaware approach to takeover defenses, even though the U.K. approach arguably represents a more comfortable fit with the "shareholder equality" principle of Japanese company law and the administrative approach to economic regulation typically favored in Japan.[45] The ability to shut down hostile takeover attempts being critical to the maintenance of Japanese social stability, the vanishing structural defense of cross-shareholdings had to be replaced with some other form of defensive mechanism for employment-based social welfare provision to remain feasible.

Each of these cases illustrates the capacity of deeply entrenched historical, cultural, and political commitments to overcome the forces that I associate with share dispersal, effectively reconcentrating share ownership in one way or another toward the pursuit of public policies thought to require the subordination of private capital – state capitalism in the case of China, stakeholder capitalism in the case of the Netherlands, and employment-based social welfare stability in the case of Japan. By the same token, recent events in Japan illustrate that the corporate governance dynamics described in this book may nevertheless contribute to description – and perhaps even prediction – of future directions that policy makers outside the common-law world might pursue in the face of exogenous shocks requiring abandonment of the structures through which de facto concentration of shareholdings had previously been achieved.

Australia and Canada, on the other hand, pose the equal and opposite puzzle – why would these countries exhibiting somewhat higher levels of share ownership concentration nevertheless exhibit characteristics associated here with higher degrees of dispersal? It would seem that just as deeply entrenched historical, cultural, and political commitments might lead highly dispersed markets in China, the Netherlands, and Japan to favor corporate governance structures sharply diverging from those found attractive in the very different U.K. and U.S. settings, strong historical, cultural, and political ties might draw Australia and Canada closer to U.K. and U.S. approaches despite differences in their respective market structures. How, if at all, might we tease out the degree to which the purported equilibria in Australia and Canada result from similar social welfare–based dynamics, as I have suggested, as opposed to the

[45] CULPEPPER, *supra* note 10, at 134–35 (observing that the "UK City Code is plausibly more attractive" in such respects).

gravitational pull of foreign models looming large in the minds of Australian and Canadian policy makers due to cultural, commercial, and (in the case of Canada) geographic proximity?

What is perhaps most striking about the higher degree of share ownership concentration in Canadian capital markets is the fact that such empirical realities have been effectively irrelevant to corporate governance reform efforts. Indeed, until recently, the relative concentration of Canadian capital markets has not been widely understood. Ronald Daniels and Jeffrey MacIntosh, in a 1991 article, argued that "the structure and efficiency of Canadian markets has often been ignored both by academics and policy-makers," and that "when foreign approaches are emulated, [they] result in statutory and judicial approaches to corporate regulation that only crudely fit the Canadian setting."[46] Notably, although some Canadian companies resembled the British and American norm, with "a large float of publicly traded securities, high liquidity, and high institutional shareholdings," Canadian markets were in fact dominated by companies with "a much smaller float of publicly traded securities, relatively low liquidity, and low institutional ownership." This effectively impaired the efficiency of Canadian securities markets and gave rise to "a much higher risk of predatory conduct by corporate insiders" – yet no distinctions were drawn by Canadian corporate law to reflect the substantial differences between these two categories of companies.[47] In stark contrast with the United Kingdom and the United States, Daniels and MacIntosh found that just 14 percent of companies in the TSE 3000 Composite Index were widely held, while 60.3 percent had "a single shareholder with legal control" and 25.4 percent either had one shareholder with "effective control" (i.e., greater than 20 percent voting power) or "two or three shareholders . . . having the ability to combine and establish joint legal or effective control." This, they observed, meant that abuse at the hands of a controlling shareholder would presumably be a much bigger problem in Canada.[48]

Although they note that lip service had been paid to the potential distinctiveness of Canadian markets during the reform era of the 1960s and 1970s, Daniels and MacIntosh rightly observe that "this recognition has seldom (if ever) been followed up by a concrete analysis of the nature of Canadian distinctiveness

[46] Ronald J. Daniels & Jeffrey G. MacIntosh, *Toward a Distinctive Canadian Corporate Law Regime*, 29 Osgoode Hall L.J. 863, 865 (1991).

[47] *Id.* at 877–80. Recall, however, that Canada has placed distinctive emphasis on the oppression remedy, which may reflect some sensitivity to the unique problems arising in a context of concentrated share ownership. *Cf. id.* at 887 ("We applaud judicial efforts to fashion a *de facto* fiduciary duty of [controlling] shareholders through the statutory oppression remedy.").

[48] *Id.* at 884–87. Similarly, "highly interconnected corporate empires" were found to be common in Canada, exacerbating the potential for minority abuses. *Id.* at 888–90.

and its consequences, rendering the appeal to Canadian distinctiveness more rhetorical than real."[49] This charge would appear entirely legitimate, particularly with respect to share ownership concentration. If Canada's corporations and markets differ from those in the United Kingdom and the United States in so fundamental a respect as this, then why does Canada's corporate governance system resemble them so closely, globally speaking? Why look to these countries for models, rather than other systems with similar levels of ownership concentration, which often approach corporate governance in a markedly different way?

As Daniels and MacIntosh themselves suggest, during the period of reforms in the 1960s and 1970s, good data on share ownership concentration appear not to have been readily available. Indeed, accounts from the 1960s, when securities reforms began in earnest, effectively treat Canada as a dispersed ownership system. J.C. Baillie, for example, writing in 1965, discusses Adolph Berle's description of "the nature of 'passive' property ownership as it now exists in the United States," and suggests that this was "almost completely applicable to the Canadian situation as well."[50] Similarly, Frank Iacobucci, Marilyn Pilkington, and Robert Prichard, in their 1977 treatise, include a brief discussion of "the distribution of shareholdings" in Canadian public companies, but explain that "[u]nfortunately, all of the literature on which we base our conclusions . . . involves American data." Clearly they were sensitive to the potential for systematic divergence on this score, but explain that they were "unaware of equivalent Canadian studies and analysis and therefore have drawn conclusions based on foreign commentary." Although they astutely suggest that "[i]f we had Canadian data we would expect to find even less diffuse holdings," they could only speculate[51] – even as of 1977, by which point Canada's modernizing reforms had already largely occurred. The upshot is that, given the lack of good data regarding the degree of share ownership concentration in Canadian markets at the time, reformers in the 1960s and 1970s evidently confronted no empirical impediment to drawing from otherwise appealing legislative models in the United Kingdom and the United States.

It should be observed, however, that all of this goes to the appropriateness of looking to U.K. or U.S. models in the Canadian context at all, as opposed to which of the two might prove more useful to Canadian reformers. As we have seen, the U.K. and U.S. models – whatever their similarities may be from

[49] *Id.* at 908–09.

[50] James C. Baillie, *The Protection of the Investor in Ontario*, 8 Can. Pub. Admin. 172, 328 n.347 (1965).

[51] Frank Iacobucci, Marilyn L. Pilkington & J. Robert S. Prichard, Canadian Business Corporations: An Analysis of Recent Legislative Developments 139 n.18 (1977).

the global perspective – differ markedly in terms of the degree of power and centrality that shareholders ought to have. On this score, the relative impact of U.K. and U.S. models may actually tend to reinforce my conclusions when assessed in light of Canada's cultural, commercial, and geographic proximity to these countries.

The United States naturally looms quite large in Canadian commerce, accounting for approximately 72 percent of Canada's exports and approximately 62 percent of its imports in 2011.[52] Indeed, it has been estimated that approximately 75 percent of the Canadian population lives within one hundred miles of the U.S. border,[53] rendering it unsurprising that U.S. corporate law would have real impact on the reform of Canada's corporate law. What is certainly surprising, however, in light of Canada's commercial and legal ties with the United States, is the fact that U.S. models appear not to have held much attraction for Canada in the most consequential areas – the core division of power at the heart of the corporation. The adoption of relatively shareholder-centric governance structures in Canada cannot be attributed solely to foreign influence, insofar as Canada effectively had to overcome U.S. influence in order to adopt and maintain such structures. In this light, their adoption might more plausibly be interpreted as suggesting that an equilibrium involving strong shareholder powers and strong extra-corporate stakeholder protections prevailed in Canada for substantially the same reasons that it did in the United Kingdom – a preference for the relative conceptual clarity of greater shareholder-centrism, unencumbered by political pressures of the sort that have impeded the United States from moving more concertedly in the same direction.

Australia, meanwhile, resembles Canada in terms of share ownership concentration, while differing from Canada in terms of the nature and strength of cultural, commercial, and geographic ties to the United Kingdom and the United States. Like in Canada, there is a higher level of share ownership concentration than in either the United Kingdom or the United States.[54] Geof Stapledon, in a 1999 study of listed Australian companies, found that

[52] Statistics Canada, *Imports, Exports and Trade Balance of Goods on a Balance-of-Payments Basis, by Country or Country Grouping*, http://www.statcan.gc.ca/tables-tableaux/sum-som/l01/cst01/gblec02a-eng.htm (last updated May 10, 2012).

[53] *See* Christopher M. Bruner, *Culture, Sovereignty, and Hollywood: UNESCO and the Future of Trade in Cultural Products*, 40 N.Y.U. J. INT'L L. & POL. 351, 355 (2008).

[54] *See, e.g.*, Brian R. Cheffins, *Corporate Governance Convergence: Lessons from Australia*, 16 TRANSNAT'L LAW. 13, 21 (2002); Alan Dignam, *The Role of Competition in Determining Corporate Governance Outcomes: Lessons from Australia's Corporate Governance System*, 68 MOD. L. REV. 765, 770–71, 783–84 (2005); JOHN FARRAR, CORPORATE GOVERNANCE IN AUSTRALIA AND NEW ZEALAND 50 (2001); Luke Nottage, *Corporate Governance and M&A in Australia: An*

97 percent had at least one shareholder with 5 percent voting power (an institution in 34 percent of those cases), while 45 percent "had a non-institutional shareholder which controlled 20 per cent or more of the equity"[55] – a level of concentration rendering certain aspects of Australia's corporate governance system difficult to explain. Luke Nottage observes, for example, that Australia's "largely pro-bidder" takeover rules, as well as the sheer volume of successful takeovers, present "somewhat of a puzzle, since blockholders have been stronger and institutional investors have traditionally been much weaker" than in the United Kingdom.[56] Just as Daniels and MacIntosh suggested that corporate law reform efforts in Canada had paid insufficient regard to prevailing levels of share ownership concentration, Nottage suggests that Australia's "largely pro-bidder substantive law" on takeovers was built "on the assumption (without strong empirical justification . . .) that it had dispersed shareholdings as in the UK."[57]

Path dependence[58] would appear to offer a particularly compelling explanation for the long-standing resemblance of Australian company law to U.K. company law. Recall that, as the leading treatise explains, although contemporary Australian company law "is less dependent upon the United Kingdom" than it once was, it nevertheless remains the case that numerous provisions of the Corporations Act 2001 "can be traced back to some pioneer legislation in the United Kingdom," such that "the expository views of courts there can be instructive."[59] And, of course the historical, cultural, and political connection with the United Kingdom that this reflects has not been challenged or diluted by U.S. influence to the degree observed in Canada for the simple reason

Overview for Assessing Japan and the "Americanisation" Thesis 4–5 (Sydney Law School Legal Studies Research Paper No. 08/28, Mar. 2008).

55 Geof Stapledon, *Share Ownership and Control in Listed Australian Companies* 15–16 (Apr. 1999), http://ssrn.com/abstract=164129.

56 Nottage, *supra* note 54, at 18. *See also* Stapledon, *supra* note 55, at 3–14 (observing that "stock-exchange-listed companies are not as significant a part of the economy in Australia as in some other Western countries," and that "the significance of institutional investors in Australia . . . is not as great as in the UK and the US").

57 Nottage, *supra* note 54, at 18–19. *See also id.* at 4 n.2. As to the volume of successful takeovers, Nottage and Stapledon both suggest quite plausibly that Australia may have a higher proportion of "friendly" deals negotiated on terms acceptable to target management and their blockholders. *Id.* at 18; Stapledon, *supra* note 55, at 19–20.

58 On the concept of path dependence, see *supra* Chapter 4.B.i. *See also* Lucian Arye Bebchuk & Mark J. Roe, *A Theory of Path Dependence in Corporate Ownership and Governance*, 52 STAN. L. REV. 127 (1999); Adrian Kay, *A Critique of the Use of Path Dependency in Policy Studies*, 83 PUB. ADMIN. 553 (2005).

59 R.P. AUSTIN & I.M. RAMSAY, FORD'S PRINCIPLES OF CORPORATIONS LAW 2 (14th ed. 2010). *See also* Bell Group Ltd. (in liq.) v. Westpac Banking Corp. (No. 9) (2008) 70 ACSR 1, ¶¶ 4370–83 (Sup. Ct. WA) (Austl.) (tracing Australian directors' duties to their British origins).

that Australia is neither geographically nor commercially so proximate to the United States as Canada is. For example, although the United States is far and away Canada's most important trading partner, Australia's most important trading partner is China – which accounted for 19.2 percent of Australia's exports and 14.5 percent of its imports in 2009.[60]

Although the enormous influence of U.K. law in Australia is clear, however, there is nevertheless substantial reason to doubt that Australia's similar social welfare equilibrium – pairing strong shareholder-centrism with strong extra-corporate stakeholder protections – reflects path dependence on U.K. legal models. As a threshold matter, recall that the social welfare equilibrium described here embodies not simply company law, but social welfare policy (and labor law) as well. Yet, as we have seen, the employment-based social welfare policy embraced by Australia through much of the twentieth century clearly bore no resemblance whatever to the state-based social welfare system developed in the United Kingdom in the aftermath of World War II. At the same time, the resemblance in the area of company law – although concededly quite real – should not be overstated. As Rob McQueen explains, Australia's adherence to English predecessor statutes through the nineteenth and the first half of the twentieth centuries "was simply a reflection of the fact that most of the overseas trade of the Australian colonies (and later the states) was with England."[61] Prior to World War II, Australia's default to the English model was reinforced by a general "lack of domestic interest in companies legislation," given that "very few companies were formed annually in *any* of the states" (most domestic businesses opting to operate as partnerships at the time).[62] In the postwar decades Australian industry began to expand substantially, but well into the 1980s the principal issue remained administrative and regulatory harmonization across the states – a project that appears to have strongly favored ongoing substantive adherence to the prevailing English model simply to avoid provoking opposition. As McQueen explains of reform efforts in the 1980s, "[i]n their determination to both secure the passage of the legislation and to prevent (if possible) constitutional challenges to the legislation, the Commonwealth government followed the 'safe' course of only making cosmetic alterations to the existing legislation" – the idea being that "the less the substantive changes in the legislation, the less contentious it would be." This required "retention in large part of the ageing and conceptually confused

[60] Department of Foreign Affairs and Trade, Commonwealth of Australia, *Composition of Trade Australia: 2009*, at 5 (May 2010).

[61] Rob McQueen, *An Examination of Australian Corporate Law and Regulation 1901–1961*, 15 U. New S. Wales L.J. 1, 19–20 (1992).

[62] *Id.* at 21–23.

legislative structure which had existed before the introduction of a 'national' system of companies administration and regulation"[63] – but Australian reformers evidently considered this a price worth paying to achieve the benefits of a nationally integrated administrative and regulatory structure.

More substantive reforms to Australian company law have been implemented since the 1980s and, as we have seen, these hardly support the path dependence argument, appearing rather to respond to Australia's unique circumstances. To be sure, corporate governance structures arise at various points in recent Australian history that resonate strongly with U.K. and U.S. models, but the manner in which they have arisen – and changed over time – hardly suggests that any particular foreign model has overwhelmed the sensibilities of Australian policy makers. Consider again the manner in which Australia's approach to takeover defenses evolved from the 1980s through the 2000s, effectively moving from a U.S.-style approach permitting substantial latitude to deploy defenses toward a U.K.-style approach strongly empowering target company shareholders. Even if U.K. and U.S. corporate governance models – as opposed to, say, the German model – loom larger in Australian policy makers' minds due to long-standing cultural and commercial ties, the very fact of this shift, coupled with the varying macroeconomic and social welfare landscape over this time period, suggests that Australia's evolving approach to takeovers has been driven not by foreign influence, but by a pragmatic and domestically oriented assessment of the regulatory posture toward takeovers that would best serve Australian society under prevailing circumstances. Australia may have arrived at a social welfare equilibrium strikingly similar to that in the United Kingdom, and undoubtedly cultural and commercial ties have played some role in commending this approach to Australian policy makers, but the process by which they got there contradicts the notion that this can be straightforwardly chalked up to path dependence. Ironically, Australia arrived at a social welfare equilibrium resembling the U.K. approach through a long and complex process of domestic policy evolution – in multiple regulatory fields – that in fact bore virtually no resemblance to the U.K. experience prior to the turn of the millennium.

B. THE EVOLVING SHAREHOLDER BASE

The prior section of this chapter assessed the degree to which various historical, cultural, and political factors might lead countries lacking private

[63] *Id.* at 23–28. *See also* Nottage, *supra* note 54, at 8, 27–28 (speculating that "in corporate law reform, delays and complex legislation may also be associated with a long history of blockholders, who have relatively less need for changes benefiting shareholders generally").

blockholders – notably, China, the Netherlands, and Japan – to adopt corporate governance structures differing from those found in the United Kingdom and the United States, and conversely the degree to which such factors might lead countries with a substantial number of private blockholders – notably, Australia and Canada – to adopt U.K.- and U.S.-style corporate governance structures, notwithstanding the divergence in levels of share ownership dispersal. In so doing, these factors were weighed against the social welfare dynamics discussed in this book, assessing the degree to which the social welfare–based logic described here retains its explanatory power – or could offer predictive power moving forward – notwithstanding the significant impact of local history, culture, and politics in corporate governance policy formation. This section considers another set of variables that could readily impact the degree of shareholder-centrism embraced in a given country over time – the prevailing popular conception of who "the shareholders" are, and relatedly, the salience of "shareholder" as a political identity.

The prevailing conception of who "the shareholders" are can impact the degree of shareholder-centrism in a given country in any number of ways. The historical dominance of domestic institutional investors in the United Kingdom provides a particularly vivid example here. As we have seen, the relative comfort of U.K. regulators with market-based self-regulation of takeovers – effectively permitting the market to police itself – has at least partly been underwritten by the geographic concentration and, one suspects, the cultural homogeneity of "the City," London's financial district.[64] To the extent that this has permitted greater comfort with a high degree of shareholder-centrism in U.K. corporate governance, it stands to reason that geographic and cultural dispersal of shareholdings in British equities – if sufficiently substantial and sustained – could tend to undermine shareholder-centrism moving forward.

As Brian Cheffins explains, since the mid-1990s a "combination of regulation and market factors" has led pensions and insurers – the traditional stalwarts of U.K. equity markets – to diminish their holdings. Insurers began selling off U.K. equities following the dot-com bust in order to improve "the 'free asset ratios' (the excess of capital after liabilities had been accounted for) they depended on to attract investors, protect themselves against fluctuations in investment performance and make acquisitions." In 2004, then, regulations were introduced that required more conservative financial reporting of liabilities by insurance companies, which "encouraged insurers to invest in

[64] *See supra* Chapter 4.B.iii. *See also* John Armour & David A. Skeel, Jr., *Who Writes the Rules for Hostile Takeovers, and Why? – The Peculiar Divergence of U.S. and U.K. Takeover Regulation*, 95 Geo. L.J. 1727 (2007).

bonds rather than equities to bolster surpluses and achieve a higher degree of certainty with liabilities." Pension funds, for their part, began moving away from U.K. equities following the elimination of favorable tax treatment on dividends received, a change phased in between 1993 and 1997. The upshot was a dramatic drop in insurer and pension holdings between 1993, when these institutions held 52 percent of U.K. publicly traded equities, and 2006, by which point their holdings had fallen to just 26 percent.[65] Over this period they were largely replaced by other institutional investors such as hedge funds, holdings of which rose from just 0.6 percent to 10 percent over this period, although the "rise of overseas investors was even more pronounced" over this period, skyrocketing from 16 percent to 40 percent. "The new foreign owners," Cheffins explains, "included mainstream institutional investors seeking to diversify, specialist investment funds focusing on 'active' investing strategies . . . , shareholders in companies based outside Britain obtaining a UK stock market listing and even an occasional foreign investor buying up sizeable stakes in publicly traded UK companies."[66]

The changing nature of the U.K. shareholder base could hold substantial consequences for the traditionally shareholder-centric U.K. approach to corporate governance. In stark contrast with the "close-knit financial environment" characteristic of the City historically, greater dispersal of shares among investors increasingly located (and focused) elsewhere has "diminished this coherence and reduced overlap on share registers,"[67] eroding the capacity for concerted action upon which British self-regulation was historically built. At the same time, the potential for shareholder "activism" – involving public confrontations over the quality of management and direction of corporate affairs not typical of U.K. shareholder interventions historically – has emerged, and the consequences are difficult to predict.[68] Cheffins argues that "[t]here is not only 'room' for shareholder activism and private equity buyouts with the UK's current corporate governance system, but they in fact could fortify current arrangements" by imposing a strong "disciplinary mechanism" reinforcing "investor confidence in publicly traded companies."[69] At the same time, however, a lack of cohesiveness between shareholders and management

[65] Brian R. Cheffins, Corporate Ownership and Control: British Business Transformed 387–90 (2008). *See also* John Kay, The Kay Review of UK Equity Markets and Long-Term Decision Making: Final Report 10, 29–31 (2012), http://www.bis.gov.uk/assets/biscore/business-law/docs/k/12-917-kay-review-of-equity-markets-final-report.pdf [hereinafter Kay Review].

[66] Cheffins, *supra* note 65, at 390, figures at 88–89.

[67] *Id.* at 391. *See also* Kay Review, *supra* note 65, at 10.

[68] Cheffins, *supra* note 65, at 394–97.

[69] *Id.* at 402–04.

could look less favorable from the financial regulators' perspective. As one observer put it in 2006:

> There used to be a time when British chief executives could walk around the Square Mile . . . and bump into almost all their shareholders – when an investor roadshow meant going up to Edinburgh to see (Scottish-based insurers) Scottish Widows or Standard Life. Now there are not just foreign institutions but some that the company will have never heard of.[70]

The same, of course, might be said of U.K. financial regulators' posture vis-à-vis the predominant holders of U.K. equities. As Caroline Bradley observed in 1999:

> The City of London was for a long time controlled through this common culture of the governing class, regulated through unwritten and informal rules rather than formally through legislation. People still talk about the Governor of the Bank of England controlling participants in the financial markets by raising his eyebrows. This control mechanism meant that people who were regarded as part of the City were protected, and outsiders were not. The Bank of England is part of the City of London, the largest British financial centre, in a way that other central banks and bank regulators are not.[71]

Whether the gradual evaporation of this "common culture" between regulator and regulated will ultimately undermine U.K.-style shareholder-centrism – or be counterbalanced by the potential disciplinary benefits that Cheffins identifies in these developments – remains to be seen. Regardless, however, it is increasingly clear that the cultural glue that once held the City together will have to be replaced by something if the traditional U.K. reliance on market-based self-regulation is to persist in its current form.[72]

This development gestures toward the substantial impact that changes in the composition of the investor base could have on the degree of shareholder-centrism in a given country. Another that relates more closely to the theory explored in this book involves changes in the way that existing investors think about themselves, and more specifically, the degree to which thinking of themselves as "shareholders" – rather than, say, "workers" or

[70] *Id.* at 391 (quoting "the head of broking at the British arm of US investment bank Morgan Stanley" from *Americans Sweep Aside Blue-Blooded Britons*, SUNDAY TIMES, Aug. 27, 2006).

[71] Caroline Bradley, *Transatlantic Misunderstandings: Corporate Law and Societies*, 53 U. MIAMI L. REV. 269, 309 (1999).

[72] *Cf.* Landon Thomas Jr., *Once-Stodgy World of London Banking Losing Its Old-School Ways*, N.Y. TIMES DEALBOOK, July 13, 2012, http://dealbook.nytimes.com/2012/07/13/once-stodgy-world-of-london-banking-losing-its-old-school-ways/ (observing such cultural and geographic dynamics in London banking due to an influx of foreign banks and the recent shift from the City to Canary Wharf).

"consumers" – conditions their political activity. John Cioffi rightly observes that "[d]espite the increasing proportion of households holding shares, 'shareholder' is not a salient political identity" in the United States, and thus has "failed to mobilize electorates as appeals to working-class identity" have historically done.[73] This presumably reflects the fact that U.S. households often hold investments through multiple layers of institutional intermediaries (such as employer-sponsored retirement savings plans), blurring their status as beneficial investors; most U.S. investors in fact stand several removes of abstraction away from the actual investment of their funds in corporate stock.[74] The situation arguably looks quite different in Australia, however, where the employees' role in saving for their retirement – in other words, their status as beneficial investors – has been brought back into focus through a unique retirement pension program coupled with a sustained marketing effort aimed at cultivating a widespread investor political identity.

Although the rise of institutional investment obviously is not unique to Australia, the manner in which it emerged and the role it now plays in Australian society appear qualitatively unlike what we find in other countries. In 1992, Australia adopted a program of compulsory "superannuation" – that is, mandatory retirement pension fund contributions. This initiative, championed by the Keating Labor government, responded to the growing inadequacy of means-tested pension funds, and effectively built upon the incorporation of employer pensions into the awards scheme in the 1980s.[75] Compulsory superannuation has resulted in a literal explosion of managed assets in Australia, and a far greater stake in the stock market for the average Australian worker, over the last two decades. In 1993, when the compulsory program took effect, total superannuation assets stood at A$183 billion, rising to A$245 billion by 1996.[76] As of March 2011, they had multiplied to an astonishing A$1.3 trillion,[77] reflecting the fact that the mandatory employer contribution had tripled from

[73] CIOFFI, *supra* note 4, at 11.

[74] Christopher M. Bruner, *The Enduring Ambivalence of Corporate Law*, 59 ALA. L. REV. 1385, 1432–35 (2008). *But see* Martin Gelter, *The Pension System and the Rise of Shareholder Primacy* 3–5, 9–28 (Fordham Univ. Sch. of Law Working Paper Series, 2012), http://ssrn.com/abstract=2079607; *infra* Chapter 6.D (exploring the greater political salience of capital markets to employees following the shift to defined contribution pensions, and the impact of this shift on postcrisis corporate governance reforms).

[75] Jennifer Hill, *Institutional Investors and Corporate Governance in Australia*, *in* INSTITUTIONAL INVESTORS AND CORPORATE GOVERNANCE 583, 584–89 (Theodor Baums, Richard M. Buxbaum & Klaus J. Hopt eds., 1994). *See also* National Archives of Australia, *Australia's Prime Ministers*, http://primeministers.naa.gov.au/primeministers/.

[76] SUPER SYSTEM REVIEW, FINAL REPORT – PART ONE: OVERVIEW AND RECOMMENDATIONS 5 (2010).

[77] AUSTRALIAN BUREAU OF STATISTICS, 5655.0 – MANAGED FUNDS, AUSTRALIA (Mar. 2011).

an initial 3 percent of wages to its current level of 9 percent.[78] Among other things, this is thought to have substantially increased financial literacy and attention to investing across the population. "There is great support at present for the superannuation funds," one corporate recruiter has observed, "and many Australians have become quite knowledgeable about money investments as a result of their participation in this programme."[79] As the Australian Securities and Investments Commission (ASIC) explains, "[m]ost people can choose which super fund they'd like their super contributions paid into,"[80] and ASIC's "MoneySmart" provides guidance on selecting funds and identifying suitable investment strategies.[81]

This was, in fact, part of the point from the beginning, according to former Labor Prime Minister Paul Keating, who spearheaded development of the program. In 1986, as Treasurer in the Hawke government, Keating negotiated a deal with the Australian Council of Trade Unions involving "a 3 per cent superannuation payment . . . as an employer contribution in lieu of an award wage rise." Later, when the Australian Industrial Relations Commission refused to increase it, Keating – by then Prime Minister – "intervened by introducing a Superannuation Guarantee Charge in 1992," creating the compulsory program that would ultimately reach 9 percent.[82] Today "[a]lmost every employee is covered under the superannuation system," with only limited exclusions,[83] and as one press report in 2006 observed, "Mr Keating can boast of comprehensive super reforms that allowed working Australians to boost

[78] *See* Glenda Korporaal, *Keating Revels in His $1 Trillion Legacy*, AUSTRALIAN, Dec. 30, 2006, http://www.theaustralian.com.au/news/nation/keating-revels-in-his-1-trillion-legacy/story-e6frg6nf-1111112757240. For a brief overview of the mechanics of the program, see Australian Securities & Investments Commission, *Glossary – Co-Contribution*, updated June 29, 2012, http://www.moneysmart.gov.au/glossary/c/co-contribution; Australian Securities & Investments Commission, *How Super Works*, updated Mar. 12, 2012, http://www.moneysmart.gov.au/superannuation-and-retirement/how-super-works; Working In, *Australian Superannuation*, http://www.workingin-australia.com/jobs/job-tools/superannuation.aspx. Note that the level of direct investment in stocks has increased substantially as well. *Compare* Hill, *supra* note 75, at 590 (observing that in 1991 "only about 10.2% of Australian adults [were] direct shareholders in the sharemarket") *with* AUSTRALIAN STOCK EXCHANGE, 2010 AUSTRALIAN SHARE OWNERSHIP STUDY 5 (2011) (reporting that in 2010 the "level of direct participation in the Australian share market was 39%").

[79] Working In, *supra* note 78.

[80] Australian Securities & Investments Commission, *How Super Works*, *supra* note 78.

[81] Australian Securities & Investments Commission, *Choosing a Super Fund*, updated Mar. 12, 2012, http://www.moneysmart.gov.au/superannuation-and-retirement/how-super-works/choosing-a-super-fund; Australian Securities & Investments Commission, *Super Investment Options*, updated Mar. 12, 2012, http://www.moneysmart.gov.au/superannuation-and-retirement/how-super-works/super-investment-options.

[82] Korporaal, *supra* note 78.

[83] Working In, *supra* note 78.

their savings," and indeed "to get indirectly involved in the share market." As Keating himself put it in 2006, "I have always thought that owning the home was fine, but being able to share in the basic wealth of the nation in the stock market was a way of having the ordinary mums and dads having a share in the bounty."[84]

Although any form of pension investment can turn employees into stockholders (at least indirectly),[85] Australia's compulsory superannuation program arguably merges "employee" and "shareholder" identities to a considerable degree, and in a unique manner, with interesting implications for the social welfare–based theory developed in this book. Jennifer Hill rightly observes that although any employee share ownership program aims "deliberately to dissolve an 'us/them' mentality in labour relations, by blurring the boundaries between investors and employees," superannuation goes further.[86] For our purposes, what is most interesting about compulsory superannuation is that it effectively blurs not only the boundary between "employee" and "shareholder" identities, but also the boundary between "public" and "private" governance spheres, combining attributes of a state-based social welfare program with attributes of Castles' "wage-earners' welfare state," out of which it grew. While harnessing the private stock market, it is nevertheless a near-universal, government-mandated program creating an "inexorable movement towards a *de facto* national retirement income policy."[87] As opposed to facilitating shareholder-centrism by reducing the political stakes of the employment relationship and thereby defusing anti-shareholder sentiment – as I have argued state-based social welfare programs have historically done in Australia, Canada, and the United Kingdom – this unique social welfare program actively facilitates pro-shareholder sentiment. Given the hybrid approach at which Australia has arrived, involving both substantial state-based social welfare protections (notably, healthcare) and substantial employer-based social welfare protections (notably, compulsory superannuation), it is all the less surprising that Australia has adopted such strongly pro-shareholder rules over recent years. Australia's social welfare programs are at once defusing anti-shareholder

[84] Korporaal, *supra* note 78.

[85] *See, e.g.*, Simon Deakin, *The Rise of Finance: What Is It, What Is Driving It, What Might Stop It?*, 30 Comp. Lab. L. & Pol'y 67, 71 (2008); Gelter, *supra* note 74. Similarly, privatizations can be structured to turn employees, and citizens more generally, into shareholders – a clear goal of the Thatcher government's privatization of British Telecom. *See* Monica Prasad, The Politics of Free Markets: The Rise of Neoliberal Economic Policies in Britain, France, Germany, and the United States 133–34 (2006).

[86] Jennifer Hill, *At the Frontiers of Labour Law and Corporate Law: Enterprise Bargaining, Corporations and Employees*, 23 Fed. L. Rev. 204, 223–24 (1995).

[87] *Id.* at 224. *See also* Hill, *supra* note 75, at 589.

sentiment and promoting pro-shareholder sentiment – strategies similarly rooted in the politics of social welfare that strongly reinforce one another.

The capacity of this synergistic combination of private and public social welfare programs to promote shareholder-centrism remains to be seen – and of course the broader consequences of such an approach could prove difficult to predict, rendering its long-term desirability an open question. In 2010, for example, the Australian mining industry initiated an advertising campaign aimed at combatting a proposal for a substantial new mining tax. Among other things, this campaign endeavored to harness the political dynamics described above – specifically, the growing tendency of average voters to think of themselves as shareholders – by suggesting that "the average superannuation investor would be worse off if the tax goes ahead" because of the adverse impact on mining stocks. This suggestion was hotly disputed by the Association of Superannuation Funds, which estimated that "the tax would have an impact of less than 1 per cent on the superannuation account balances of an average worker," whereas "the measures funded by the proposed resources tax – to increase the superannuation guarantee from 9 to 12 per cent and cut the corporate tax rate from 30 to 28 per cent – will have a much bigger positive impact on superannuation balances."[88] Remarkably, however, Labour Prime Minister Kevin Rudd's refusal "to negotiate on the 40 percent rate of the tax or when it would kick in . . . embroiled his government in a damaging war of words with the wealthy and influential mining sector," directly prompting the Labor Party's July 2010 decision "to dump Rudd, who was falling dramatically in opinion polls, in favour of [Julia] Gillard." Shortly after taking office, Gillard's administration "backed down . . . slashing the rate and scope of the levy that had threatened to cost her government re-election."[89]

Although it would presumably be impossible to determine with any certainty the degree to which these events, and the underlying politics, are attributable to the superannuation-inspired shareholder mentality that has increasingly taken root in Australian society over the last two decades, the episode must surely have given pause to politicians across the spectrum. If indeed some critical mass of the voting public actually believed that such a tax would be a net detriment to them – perhaps being systematically more likely to focus narrowly on the short-term investment consequences of such a tax than voters twenty years earlier might have been – one might fairly question whether the

[88] Scott Alle, *Mining Tax Super Impact 0.6 Per Cent: Funds*, ABC News, June 11, 2010, http://www.abc.net.au/news/2010–06–11/mining-tax-super-impact-06-per-cent-funds/863160.

[89] Madeleine Coorey, *Australia Backs Down on Mining Tax*, Sydney Morning Herald, July 2, 2010, http://news.smh.com.au/breaking-news-world/australia-backs-down-on-mining-tax-20100702-zsdy.html.

cultivation of such a broad-based and deeply held "shareholder" identity across the electorate will necessarily serve Australia well in the long run.[90]

C. POSTCRISIS AUSTERITY

The core thesis of this book is that robust welfare-state protections available to employees outside the corporate governance system can deflect stakeholder-oriented pressures from it, permitting a higher degree of shareholder-centrism to take root and remain politically stable over time. A corollary, then, would presumably be that policies undermining those welfare-state protections could – if sufficiently substantial and sustained – tend to undermine the political stability of shareholder-centric corporate governance as well. Although it remains far too early to say what the long-term consequences of the recent financial crisis will be (the causes and consequences of which are discussed more fully below[91]), postcrisis cuts to welfare-state programs adopted in the United Kingdom, in particular, may provide a window into the long-term viability of strongly shareholder-centric corporate governance in an age of austerity.

In October 2010 it was reported that the Conservative-Liberal Democrat coalition government planned "the country's steepest public spending cuts in more than 60 years, reducing costs in government departments by an average of 19 percent, sharply curtailing welfare benefits, raising the retirement age to 66 [from 65] by 2020 and eliminating hundreds of thousands of public sector jobs in an effort to bring down the bloated budget deficit." George Osborne, Chancellor of the Exchequer, detailed substantial cuts in unemployment benefits, among other things, telling the House of Commons that "[t]oday is the day when Britain steps back from the brink." Yet, as the *New York Times* would observe, "while the government has sought to rein in welfare costs," certain "politically sacred benefits for the elderly, including free eye tests, prescription drugs and bus passes, would remain." Tellingly, so would

[90] Note that, to the extent this episode reflects a culture shift toward a narrower and more intense focus on investment returns, it would appear to be broadly consistent with evidence on changing attitudes among Australian investors generally. The Australian Securities Exchange's *2010 Australian Share Ownership Study* reported "interesting changes" from prior surveys, including "a smaller proportion of investors saying they take into account the quality of corporate governance when making investment decisions, as well as a declining proportion expressing preference for companies that are socially and environmentally responsible." Interestingly, the study also found "a decline in the proportion of investors who feel you only succeed if you invest for the long-term." Australian Stock Exchange, *supra* note 78, at 22. The study involved "a telephone survey" of "2,400 randomly selected people aged 18 years and over . . . from across all the states, covering both metropolitan and regional areas." *Id.* at 31.

[91] *See infra* Chapter 6.D.

the National Health Service (NHS), "one of the most politically delicate institutions in Britain," which would "be allocated more money, rather than less."[92] It would soon become clear, however, that Prime Minister David Cameron in fact aimed to move the NHS toward a decentralized and partially privatized model – a proposal described by the *Financial Times* in January 2011 as "the most politically risky" of the government's proposed austerity measures, given that the "NHS remains hugely popular with the public."[93] This initiative reflected a broader policy shift advocated by the coalition government – styled as "Building the Big Society" – involving proposals aimed at shrinking the national government through privatization of public services and "radical devolution of power and greater financial autonomy to local government."[94]

Cameron's Big Society met with little enthusiasm among cash-strapped city councils,[95] while proposed welfare reforms met with heated opposition across British society. Unite – "Britain's biggest union with 1.5 million members in every type of workplace"[96] – has remained a staunch opponent of the government's welfare reform agenda, touting the welfare state as "one of the UK's greatest achievements" and arguing that the government's efforts to cut benefits and privatize services "were unacceptable when they were first published and the worsening economic situation should lead to a fundamental rethink."[97] In light of "the many thousands of workers threatened with losing their jobs in the current recession," Unite has advocated improvements in "the terms of statutory redundancy payments." Joint general secretary Derek Simpson cited Unite research indicating that "in virtually every constituency in Britain, workers are dependent on statutory redundancy pay if they lose their jobs"[98] – an indication of the continuing significance of the welfare program that, as we

[92] Sarah Lyall & Alan Cowell, *Britain Plans Deepest Cuts to Spending in 60 Years*, N.Y. TIMES, Oct. 20, 2010.

[93] George Parker, *Cameron Pledge on Health Reform*, FIN. TIMES (London), Jan. 18, 2011, at 3. *See also* BBC News, *"Radical" NHS Shake-Up May Jeopardise Patient Care*, BBC NEWS, Apr. 26, 2011, http://www.bbc.co.uk/news/health-13193604?print=true.

[94] Cabinet Office, United Kingdom, *Building the Big Society*, May 18, 2010, http://www.cabinetoffice.gov.uk/sites/default/files/resources/building-big-society_0.pdf.

[95] *See* James Boxell, *Liverpool Council Quits PM's Big Society*, FIN. TIMES, Feb. 3, 2011, http://www.ft.com/cms/s/0/aad9cc8a-2fd1–11e0–91f8–00144feabdc0.html#axzz1HLzvmY9s (reporting that Cameron's Big Society was "in danger of becoming a public relations fiasco" following Liverpool's withdrawal from the program due to "more than £100m of cuts to grants for local community organisations").

[96] Unite, *About Us*, http://www.unitetheunion.org/about_us.aspx.

[97] Unite, *Welfare Reform Campaign*, http://www.unitetheunion.org/campaigns/welfare_reform.aspx.

[98] Unite, *Stop the Rot on Redundancy Pay*, http://www.unitetheunion.org/campaigns/stop_the_rot_on_redundancy_pay.aspx.

have seen, directly facilitated the adoption of a shareholder-centric takeover regime by the Wilson Labour government of the 1960s.

Proposed NHS reforms, meanwhile, have been the subject of particular union anger. Unite has strongly advocated maintenance of "a National Health Service that is publicly owned, publicly funded and publicly accountable, providing comprehensive and universal health services, free to all, before and after treatment," charging that "a 'health system' comprised of contracted, competing businesses will lead to an incentive to 'cherry pick'... the most 'profitable' patients," while "removing the private income cap... will allow organisations to prioritise attracting and treating fee paying patients," creating "a multi-tiered service, which will increase inequality."[99] In March 2012, citing the NHS as "our greatest national achievement" that had "cared for generations of working people," Unite called for a "[m]ass lobby of parliament and rally in Westminster" in opposition to the coalition government's Health and Social Care Bill, which it charged would "place [the NHS] in the hands of business" and ultimately "destroy the NHS."[100] The bill, likewise opposed by the British Medical Association, was roundly criticized at a rally in Westminster reportedly attended by "[t]housands of nurses, midwives, doctors, physiotherapists, cleaners, porters and other NHS workers." Among other things, speakers argued that the proposal "to let NHS hospitals raise as much as 49% of their income from private patients could lead to a two-tier NHS," and that the coalition government lacked "a mandate for introducing the bill, given the Conservative leader [Cameron] ruled out reorganising the NHS during the 2010 election."[101]

Although the fate of U.K. welfare reform initiatives remains uncertain at this writing, there is already evidence that postcrisis concerns regarding the vulnerability of workers may prompt reassessment of certain corporate governance structures – notably in the takeover context. In 2010, the confectioner Cadbury was acquired by Kraft Foods in a hostile takeover that came as an enormous shock to the British public for a host of reasons. The idea of Cadbury, widely viewed in the United Kingdom as "a national icon," being acquired by a "mighty conglomerate from across the ocean" prompted a general upswell of economic nationalism. At the same time, Cadbury was "freighted with cultural and historical associations that hold a powerful appeal to the

[99] Karen Reay & David Fleming, *Unite Written Response to "Equity and Excellence: Liberating the NHS,"* Feb. 16, 2011, at 2, 6–7.

[100] Unite, *Unite 4 Our NHS*, http://www.unitetheunion.org/sectors/health_sector/unite_4_our_nhs.aspx.

[101] Denis Campbell, *Save Our NHS Rally: Thousands March in Health Bill Protest*, GUARDIAN, Mar. 7, 2012.

contemporary British psyche" – its past philanthropy, attention to workers' welfare, and "commitment to contributing to the well-being of British society" helping to "remind Britons of their kinder, gentler selves, of a bygone era of fellow-feeling and community values."[102] Perhaps most significant, however, is the fact that Cadbury employees themselves, observing Kraft's substantial debt burden, feared that the takeover "could threaten tens of thousands of jobs."[103] Although the Cadbury board ultimately recommended acceptance, concluding that Kraft's offer "represents good value for Cadbury shareholders," unions remained concerned, as Kraft had made no commitments to Cadbury's 4,500 U.K. employees.[104] As Unite's deputy general secretary Jack Dromey put it, "[o]ur fear is that the Kraft takeover is not in the national interest, and in the months of this hostile takeover process, we have heard nothing from Kraft to calm fears that it is in the interest of the Cadbury workforce either." Unite added that Kraft's substantial debts could render job cuts an "irresistible imperative."[105]

Kraft's takeover of Cadbury prompted far-reaching reflections on the U.K. takeover regime, including its implicit values and impact on employees. In the wake of the battle, Cadbury Chairman Roger Carr, in a February 2010 seminar at Oxford's Saïd Business School, concluded:

> At the end of the day, there were simply not enough shareholders prepared to take a long term view of Cadbury and prepared to forego short-term gain for longer-term prosperity.... Individuals' controlling shares which they had owned for only a few days or weeks determined the destiny of a company that had been built over almost 200 years.[106]

Shortly thereafter, Lord Peter Mandelson – Secretary of State for Business, Innovation and Skills – sounded a similar theme in his March 2010 Mansion

[102] Henry Chu, *Kraft Takeover Bid of Cadbury Leaves Bitter Taste in Britain*, L.A. TIMES, Jan. 18, 2010, http://articles.latimes.com/2010/jan/18/world/la-fg-britain-cadbury18–2010jan18 (adding that, as of January 2010, "no one named Cadbury sits on the board of directors, the company has morphed into more of a modern corporation and the talk is of profit margins and vision statements"). *See also* HOUSE OF COMMONS BUSINESS, INNOVATION AND SKILLS COMMITTEE, IS KRAFT WORKING FOR CADBURY? (Sixth Report of Session 2010–12, May 12, 2011), at 19 [hereinafter HOUSE OF COMMONS REPORT] (observing the company's "Quaker tradition"); *The Value of Caring for Your Workers*, JOURNAL (NEWCASTLE, UK), Jan. 26, 2010, at 10–11.

[103] Chu, *supra* note 102.

[104] *Cadbury Agrees Kraft Takeover Bid*, BBC NEWS, Jan. 19, 2010, http://news.bbc.co.uk/go/pr/fr/-/2/hi/business/8467007.stm.

[105] *Kraft Completes Cadbury Takeover*, BBC NEWS, Feb. 2, 2010, http://news.bbc.co.uk/go/pr/fr/-/2/hi/business/8492572.stm.

[106] *Roger Carr, Cadbury: Hostile Bids and Takeovers*, Feb. 16, 2010, http://www.sbs.ox.ac.uk/newsandevents/news/Pages/RogerCarrCadbury.aspx.

House Speech, observing that "the UK has a very open market for corporate control, arguably the most open in the world," that "a takeover can have huge implications for workforces and communities as well as investors," and that "there is a strong case for throwing some extra grit in the system." Pointedly, he elaborated:

> In the case of Cadbury and Kraft it is hard to ignore the fact that the fate of a company with a long history and many tens of thousands of employees was decided by people who had not owned the company a few weeks earlier, and probably had no intention of owning it a few weeks later.[107]

Before long the City Panel would itself become involved, issuing "a statement of public criticism" of Kraft in May 2010 for carelessly stating that it could keep Cadbury's Somerdale facility operational, when in fact Cadbury's plan to close it had progressed beyond the point of no return – a breach of the City Code's requirement that statements made "during the course of an offer must be prepared with the highest standards of care and accuracy."[108] The Panel emphasized that this is particularly important with statements regarding "strategic plans for the offeree company and their likely repercussions on employment and the locations of the offeree company's places of business," which in turn affect the ability of target boards and employee representatives to formulate their own views.[109] More consequentially, however, the Code Committee of the City Panel initiated a review of the City Code itself – action acknowledged to have been undertaken "in the light of the widespread commentary and public discussion on the regulation of takeover bids for UK companies, following the takeover of Cadbury plc by Kraft Foods Inc.,"[110] including Lord Mandelson's remarks on the matter.[111]

In proposing amendments to the City Code, the Code Committee made eminently clear that its aim was to reduce bidders' "tactical advantage" and "to take more account of the position of persons who are affected by takeovers in

[107] Lord Peter Mandelson, Mansion House Speech, Mar. 1, 2010, http://webarchive.nationalarchives.gov.uk/20100304014526/http://www.bis.gov.uk/mansion-house-speech.

[108] PANEL ON TAKEOVERS AND MERGERS, KRAFT FOODS INC. ("KRAFT") OFFER FOR CADBURY PLC ("CADBURY") (2010/14, May 26, 2010) (citing Rule 19.1 of the City Code).

[109] *Id.* at 3.

[110] PANEL ON TAKEOVERS AND MERGERS, REVIEW OF CERTAIN ASPECTS OF THE REGULATION OF TAKEOVER BIDS: RESPONSE STATEMENT BY THE CODE COMMITTEE OF THE PANEL FOLLOWING THE CONSULTATION ON PCP 2011/1 (RS 2011/1, July 21, 2011), at 1 [hereinafter CODE COMMITTEE STATEMENT].

[111] PANEL ON TAKEOVERS AND MERGERS CODE COMMITTEE, CONSULTATION PAPER ISSUED BY THE CODE COMMITTEE OF THE PANEL: REVIEW OF CERTAIN ASPECTS OF THE REGULATION OF TAKEOVER BIDS (PCP 2010/2, June 1, 2010), at 13.

addition to offeree company shareholders."[112] Among other changes broadly considered favorable to target management and employees,[113] the City Code was amended to clarify that a target board "is not required by the Code to consider the offer price as the determining factor" in formulating its opinion on the offer, and that it "is not precluded by the Code from taking into account any other factors which it considers relevant."[114] Additionally, and of greater pertinence to the events prompting the review, the Code Committee decided to require so-called negative statements regarding its intentions vis-à-vis employees and production facilities, such that "[i]f the offeror has no intention to make any changes in relation to [such] matters . . . or if it considers that its strategic plans for the offeree company will have no repercussions on employment or the location of the offeree company's places of business, it must make a statement to that effect."[115] The amendments also created a presumption that the party making such statements intends to adhere to them "for a period of 12 months from the date on which the offer period ends," unless some other time frame is specified or "there has been a material change of circumstances."[116] New rules further require that the offer document and target board circular be made available to employee representatives (or employees directly),[117] and facilitate the dissemination of employees' views by clarifying that "the Code does not prevent the passing of information in confidence" to employees,[118] and by requiring the target company to circulate the employee representatives' opinion on the offer at the company's expense.[119]

[112] Panel on Takeovers and Mergers Code Committee, Review of Certain Aspects of the Regulation of Takeover Bids (2010/22, Oct. 21, 2010), at 3.

[113] *See, e.g.*, Eduardo Gallardo, *Protectionism and Paternalism at the UK Panel on Takeovers and Mergers*, Harvard Law School Forum on Corporate Governance and Financial Regulation, Dec. 11, 2010, http://blogs.law.harvard.edu/corpgov/2010/12/11/protectionism-and-paternalism-at-the-uk-panel-on-takeovers-and-mergers/; Eduardo Gallardo, *More Protectionism and Paternalism at the UK Panel on Takeovers and Mergers*, Harvard Law School Forum on Corporate Governance and Financial Regulation, Apr. 21, 2011, http://blogs.law.harvard.edu/corpgov/2011/04/21/more-protectionism-and-paternalism-at-the-uk-panel-on-takeovers-and-mergers/; Gary Green et al., *U.K. Takeover Code Changes to Strengthen Position of Takeover Targets*, World Sec. L. Rep. (BNA) (2010).

[114] Code Committee Statement, *supra* note 110, at 58–59 (quoting new Note 1 on Rule 25.2).

[115] *Id.* at 79–81 (quoting new Rule 24.2).

[116] *Id.* at 82–84 (quoting new Note 3 on Rule 19.1).

[117] *Id.* at 84–86 (discussing new Rules 24.1 and 25.1).

[118] *Id.* at 88–89 (quoting new Note 6 on Rule 20.1).

[119] *Id.* at 89–95 (discussing new Rules 2.12(a) and (d), 25.9, 30.4(b), 32.1(b), and 32.6(b)). For additional background on the review process, see generally Panel on Takeovers and Mergers, Consultation Paper Issued by the Code Committee of the Panel: Review of Certain Aspects of the Regulation of Takeover Bids – Proposed Amendments to the Takeover Code (PCP 2011/1, Mar. 21, 2011).

All the while, Parliament expressed keen interest in Kraft's takeover of Cadbury and its ramifications for takeover regulation in the United Kingdom. An April 2010 report of the House of Commons Business, Innovation and Skills Committee similarly found that "Kraft acted irresponsibly and unwisely" in its statements regarding the Somerdale facility, expressed "deep concerns over the possibility of the Cadbury takeover being motivated by a desire among institutional investors for short-term profits," and concluded that "a review of takeover regulations would be welcome." In the course of the proceeding leading to the report, however, the Committee received from Kraft "a number of undertakings, including most notably a commitment that there would be no further compulsory redundancies among manufacturing employees and no additional manufacturing facilities closures, in each case for at least two years."[120] In May 2011, then, the Committee engaged in a one-year review of Kraft's adherence to these undertakings, issuing a second report in which the Committee emphasized its frustration at the refusal of Kraft CEO Irene Rosenfeld to appear personally,[121] but otherwise expressed satisfaction with intervening events – notably the City Panel's criticism of Kraft's Somerdale statements and subsequent employee-oriented amendments to the City Code, as well as Kraft's efforts to adhere to the two-year undertakings made to the Committee in 2010.[122]

The events surrounding Kraft's controversial takeover of Cadbury and ensuing amendments to the City Code – a drama playing itself out before the backdrop of historic cuts to state-based social welfare programs – provide at least some limited evidence that heightened social welfare vulnerability of employees in a time of crisis and austerity can bring substantial political pressures to bear on shareholder-centric corporate governance structures. Although the impacts to date have included stakeholder-friendly amendments to the City Code, however, it must be emphasized that U.K. takeover regulation – and company law, for that matter – remain as fundamentally shareholder-centric as ever, a fact not lost on Britain's unions.

Unite, in an August 2010 submission to the Code Committee, took direct aim at the stark shareholder-centrism of U.K. takeover regulation:

[120] House of Commons Report, *supra* note 102, at 5–6 (summarizing the April 2010 report and associated proceedings).

[121] *Id.* at 8–10.

[122] *Id.* at 11–22. *See also* Harry Wallop, *Cadbury Acquires a Taste for US Owner Kraft at Last*, Telegraph, Mar. 4, 2012, http://www.telegraph.co.uk/finance/newsbysector/retailandconsumer/9120100/Cadbury-acquires-a-taste-for-US-owner-Kraft-at-last.html (describing Kraft's "charm offensive," focused on new research and development facilities in Birmingham); Jane Wardell, *UK Lawmakers Criticize Kraft's Cadbury Deal*, Assoc. Press, May 23, 2011, http://abcnews.go.com/Business/wireStory?id=13662749.

> Unite has serious concerns about the fact that no one involved in determining the outcome of a takeover bid is required to take account of the long-term interest of the target company.
>
> In addition, the interests of the long term stakeholder the employees, suppliers, communities and the wider interest of society are not taken into account. The outcome of the bid is decided by shareholders alone, depending on the price of shares. Whilst shareholders want the highest price for shares, far from this meaning a takeover is in the long term interests of the company, the opposite is often the case, particularly if it means being saddled with more debt.[123]

From Unite's perspective, the conduct of Kraft and Cadbury alike had only underscored these concerns, revealing the practical difficulties faced by employees in "negotiating guarantees for the workforce," or even prying accurate information out of the companies involved regarding the employment impacts of the takeover.[124] The Cadbury takeover was "subject to the most widespread media and political scrutiny of any takeover for several years," Unite suggested, because of the "parties' failure to take their obligations seriously" vis-à-vis employees.[125] Particularly galling were "problems in persuading Kraft to provide information," purportedly due to Cadbury's unwillingness to provide information to Kraft in the context of a hostile bid – a claim that Unite found less than credible, as "even without detailed information Kraft was willing to bet £11 billion on the bid."[126] Unite's May 2011 response to the proposed City Code amendments, then, "welcome[d] the amendments to the Code in which employees and employee representatives are granted more recognition," acknowledging the value of additional information on bidders' plans for target companies and their workforces and the imposition of presumptive time frames regarding their expressed intentions.[127] At the same time, however, Unite rightly observed that the Code remains fundamentally shareholder-centric, reiterating its "serious concerns . . . about the fact that no one involved in determining the outcome of a takeover bid is required to take account of the long-term interest of the target company," and calling

[123] Roger Jeary, Director of Research, Unite the Union, Unite Response to Takeover Panel Consultation, Aug. 4, 2010, at 1.

[124] *Id.* at 4–10.

[125] *Id.* at 7.

[126] *Id.* at 6–7.

[127] Roger Jeary, Director of Research, Unite the Union, Unite Response to Takeover Panel Consultation, May 27, 2011, at 6–7 [hereinafter May 2011 Consultation]. *See also* Press Release, Unite, Kraft's secrecy will risk Cadbury's future unless the government acts, warns Unite (May 23, 2011) (included as Appendix 1 to Jeary, May 2011 Consultation, *supra*) ("Unite welcomes the [Parliamentary] committee's scrutiny of Kraft, in particular the recommendation that the UK urgently needs a new takeover regime.").

for "firmer guidance" regarding penalties for failure to adhere to the Code as well as recognition by the City Panel of "the responsibility it has towards employment issues and employees in a takeover."[128]

In this light, it is all the more striking that the City Panel and the Code Committee expressly rejected the notion of revisiting the "nature and purpose" of the City Code, making only a minor amendment to the Code's introduction to clarify that the Code aims neither "to facilitate" nor "to impede takeovers" as such (as opposed to "takeover offers"). The core structure remains "designed principally to ensure that shareholders in an offeree company are treated fairly and are not denied an opportunity to decide on the merits of a takeover"[129] – a capsule summary of U.K. takeover regulation that remains as fundamentally accurate today as it was before the financial crisis, the Cadbury takeover, and the ensuing amendments to the City Code.

D. POSTCRISIS COALITIONS

It has become commonplace to speak of the financial and economic crisis that arose in 2007 as a "global" crisis,[130] which is certainly accurate enough in the sense that its effects have spanned virtually the entire globe. Not all countries, however, have been affected equally, or contributed equally to its emergence – even among countries with legal and financial cultures as similar as those investigated here. Australia and Canada have weathered the storm considerably better than have the United Kingdom and the United States – a divergence attributed, among other things, to more conservative mortgage origination practices and capital adequacy rules in the former two countries. U.K. and U.S. financial firms, on the other hand, have been at the heart of the crisis from the beginning and, accordingly, have been much harder hit in its aftermath.[131]

[128] May 2011 Consultation, *supra* note 127, at 1–2, 7.

[129] CODE COMMITTEE STATEMENT, *supra* note 110, at 97–98 (quoting amended section 2(a) of the Introduction to the Code).

[130] *See, e.g., Global Financial Crisis*, FIN. TIMES, http://www.ft.com/intl/indepth/global-financial-crisis.

[131] *See generally* Sue Konzelmann, Marc Fovargue-Davies & Gerhard Schnyder, *The Faces of Liberal Capitalism: Anglo-Saxon Banking Systems in Crisis?*, 36 CAMBRIDGE J. ECON. 495 (2012). On Australia, see also Tony D'Aloisio, Chairman, Australian Securities & Investments Commission, *Regulatory Response to the Financial Crisis* (Presentation to Asia Securities Forum) (Oct. 12, 2009); Dr. Ken Henry, Secretary to the Treasury, Commonwealth of Australia, *The Australian Financial System – Emerging from the Global Financial Crisis* (Address to the Count Financial Canberra Conference) (Mar. 15, 2010); John F. Laker, Chairman, Australian Prudential Regulation Authority, *The Global Financial Crisis – Lessons for the Australian Financial System* (Opening Remarks, Australian Economic Forum) (Aug. 19, 2009); Előd

It is hardly surprising, then, that U.K. and U.S. reform efforts following the crisis have been considerably more sweeping than those in Australia and Canada.[132] What is quite surprising, however, is that both the United Kingdom and the United States would respond to a crisis increasingly considered attributable to excessive risk-taking in financial firms with corporate governance reforms aimed at empowering shareholders.[133] This final section of the chapter examines why U.K. and U.S. reform efforts have unfolded in this manner, and how they relate to the social welfare–based dynamics explored here.

Although the causes and consequences of the crisis lie well beyond the scope of this book, there is growing evidence suggesting that, in both the United Kingdom and the United States, a number of financial and economic factors converged in the late 1990s and 2000s to create a "perfect storm" of excessive risk-taking aimed primarily at boosting short-term returns to financial firm stockholders – a development encouraged by a proliferation of investment structures allowing otherwise rational actors to ignore the substantial risks accumulating on their own balance sheets and throughout the financial system. As in other settings, limited liability leaves shareholders in financial firms strongly preferring risk-taking. This risk preference is exacerbated in financial firms, however, to the extent that creditors' incentives to monitor management are undermined by explicit government guarantees in deposit-taking institutions (in the form of deposit insurance) and implicit government guarantees in other institutions considered "too big to fail" (in the form of bailouts).[134] In the United States, competitive pressures and correlatively greater emphasis on financial firm stock price – what William Bratton and Michael Wachter have termed "management to the market"[135] – accelerated over the last four decades.

Takáts & Patrizia Tumbarello, *Australian Bank and Corporate Sector Vulnerabilities – An International Perspective* (IMF Working Paper WP/09/223, Oct. 2009). On Canada, see also Anita Anand, *How Canadian Banks Became the Envy of the World*, NEXUS, Summer 2009, at 26 (2009); Philippe Bergevin, *Canada and the United States: The Global Financial Crisis and Its Impact on Canada* (Dec. 2008), http://www2.parl.gc.ca/content/lop/researchpublications/prb0834_05-e.htm; Caroline Hepker, *G20: Why We All Want to Be Canadian Now*, BBC NEWS, June 25, 2010, http://www.bbc.co.uk/news/10409354?print=true; Lev Ratnovski & Rocco Huang, *Why Are Canadian Banks More Resilient?* (IMF Working Paper WP/09/152, July 2009).

[132] *See, e.g.*, Anand, *supra* note 131, at 27 (explaining that "Canadian financial institutions have been well-regulated" and that "other countries [are] turning to examine the Canadian financial system in redesigning their regulatory regime"); D'Aloisio, *supra* note 131, at 14 (explaining that "[t]he fact that the Australian regulatory system has been more robust, has enabled Australia to take a more measured response to these developments").

[133] *See generally* Christopher M. Bruner, *Corporate Governance Reform in a Time of Crisis*, 36 J. CORP. L. 309 (2011).

[134] *See id.* at 311–12, 315.

[135] William M. Bratton & Michael Wachter, *The Case against Shareholder Empowerment*, 158 U. PA. L. REV. 653, 659 (2010).

Since the 1970s, commercial banks have grown in size and complexity, facing greater competition because of the lifting of restrictions on branching and interstate banking. This coincided with the evolution of investment banking firms, which abandoned their risk-tempering partnership structures in the 1970s and 1980s to become publicly traded corporations, encouraging greater risk-taking behind a veil of limited liability and further fueling the increasingly shareholder-centric ethos of modern American finance. These trends effectively merged, then, in the 1999 Gramm-Leach-Bliley Act, which permitted full-service financial firms combining investment and commercial banking under one roof.[136] Meanwhile, starting in the early 1990s, these trends were reinforced by growing reliance on equity-based pay, a shift aimed at aligning managers' incentives and interests with those of the shareholders,[137] as well as the shrinking time horizon of shareholders themselves as trading increased and holding periods correlatively decreased.[138]

Mortgage securitization emerged as the culmination of these trends toward financial deregulation and pressure to maximize financial firm share price, exploding in the late 1990s and 2000s.[139] Low long-term interest rates fueled investor demand for higher-yield alternatives to treasury securities, while low short-term interest rates fueled mortgage lending and a correlative housing boom. "Mortgage-backed securities" (MBS) deriving their income from pools of mortgages, "collateralized debt obligations" (CDOs) deriving their income from pools of MBS, and even so-called CDO-squared deriving their income from pools of CDOs, were packaged by investment banks and sold to investors with varying risk tolerances by creating numerous "tranches" of these securities with varying claims on the pools' income. Typically, the marketability of these securities was bolstered by credit enhancements (such as guarantees); credit ratings from agencies such as Moody's and Standard & Poor's, purporting to assess the relative default risks involved; and the availability of "credit default swaps" (CDS) sold by entities such as AIG, contracts that purported to

[136] *See* Bruner, *supra* note 133, at 312–13; Christopher M. Bruner, *Conceptions of Corporate Purpose in Post-Crisis Financial Firms*, 36 SEATTLE U. L. REV. (forthcoming 2013), at 22, http://ssrn.com/abstract=2120594. Note that as general partners prior to incorporation, investment bankers faced unlimited personal liability for firm losses, creating a strong incentive to limit risk-taking. *See* UNIF. PARTNERSHIP ACT § 15 (1914). *See also* Bruner, *supra*, at 14–15; Malcolm Salter, *How Short-Termism Invites Corruption – And What to Do about It* 10–19 (Harv. Bus. Sch. Working Paper No. 12-094, 2012), http://hbswk.hbs.edu/item/7015.html.

[137] *See* Bruner, *supra* note 133, at 316–17. The explosion in equity-based pay was in fact catalyzed by a 1993 amendment to the Internal Revenue Code rendering executive pay beyond $1 million deductible only if performance-based. *See* 26 U.S.C.S. § 162(m).

[138] *See* Salter, *supra* note 136, at 12–13; LYNN STOUT, THE SHAREHOLDER VALUE MYTH 66–67 (2012). *See also* KAY REVIEW, *supra* note 65, at 14.

[139] For a more detailed discussion of historical trends culminating in excessive mortgage securitization, see Bruner, *supra* note 133, at 311–17.

provide insurance-like protection by transferring some of the default risk to the CDS seller in exchange for a fixed upfront payment. For a time, everyone was happy – institutional investors got attractive alternatives to government securities, home buyers got attractive mortgages with low initial rates, financial firm stockholders got higher share prices, and financial firm managers got higher bonuses.[140]

The consequences of this process are now painfully clear. The stock of outstanding securitized credit in the United States would rise almost five-fold between 1996 and 2007, securitization issuance in the United Kingdom would rise almost tenfold between 2000 and 2007, and notional amounts of outstanding CDS would rise from under $1 trillion in 2001 to over $62 trillion in 2007.[141] The securitization process became so lucrative and widespread that pressure grew to generate more and more mortgages for pooling, leading mortgage lenders to expand lending to so-called subprime borrowers with weak credit records. In 2006 and 2007, however, mortgage defaults spiked and the housing bubble burst, neither having been predicted by the rating agencies whose ratings – used to help market these complex securities – had effectively assumed low default rates and rising home values.[142] In mid-2007, the dominos began to fall as sponsoring banks were forced to acknowledge credit guarantees and other credit enhancements on their own books – revealing their true leverage to be much higher than previously reported – and the rating agencies downgraded the securities, throwing their value into question and impairing their liquidity.[143] Financial firms heavily exposed to these securities (either directly or by virtue of having sold CDS on them) began to fall one by one, leading to a wave of U.S. government-orchestrated bailouts beginning in 2008 – including through the Troubled Asset Relief Program (TARP), established through the Emergency Economic Stabilization

[140] For additional background on causes and consequences of the crisis, see generally Lucian A. Bebchuk & Holger Spamann, *Regulating Bankers' Pay*, 98 GEO. L.J. 247 (2010); Bratton & Wachter, *supra* note 135; Christopher M. Bruner, *The Changing Face of Money*, 30 REV. BANKING & FIN. L. 383, 400–06 (2010–2011); ROBERT POZEN, TOO BIG TO SAVE? HOW TO FIX THE U.S. FINANCIAL SYSTEM (2010); Frederick Tung, *Pay for Banker Performance: Structuring Executive Compensation for Risk Regulation*, 105 NW. U. L. REV. 1205 (2011); ADAIR TURNER, FIN. SERVS. AUTH., THE TURNER REVIEW: A REGULATORY RESPONSE TO THE GLOBAL BANKING CRISIS (2009), http://www.fsa.gov.uk/pubs/other/turner_review.pdf.

[141] POZEN, *supra* note 140, at 5, 47–49, 71–73; TURNER, *supra* note 140, at 14. *See also Summaries of Market Survey Results*, INT'L SWAPS AND DERIVATIVES ASS'N, http://www.isda.org/statistics/recent.html.

[142] *See* Christopher M. Bruner, *States, Markets, and Gatekeepers: Public-Private Regulatory Regimes in an Era of Economic Globalization*, 30 MICH. J. INT'L L. 125, 145–46 (2008); POZEN, *supra* note 140, at xi–xix, 58–65. For general background on the rating agencies and their role in global bond markets, see Christopher M. Bruner & Rawi Abdelal, *To Judge Leviathan: Sovereign Credit Ratings, National Law, and the World Economy*, 25 J. PUB. POL'Y 191 (2005).

[143] POZEN, *supra* note 140, at, 51–53, 60; TURNER, *supra* note 140, at 20–22.

Act signed into law in October 2008 by President George W. Bush, which permitted the Secretary of the Treasury to purchase up to $700 billion worth of "troubled assets from any financial institution."[144]

In the United Kingdom, meanwhile, the crisis unfolded in a similar manner. Lord Adair Turner, Chairman of the U.K. Financial Services Authority, observes in his review of the crisis that, although mortgage securitization caught on somewhat later than in the United States, the United Kingdom "experienced a credit and property cycle similar to that seen in the US," with "rapid credit growth in the household sector." He explains that banks in the United Kingdom were "as exposed as US banks and investment banks to the loss of confidence, disappearance of liquidity, and fall of assets prices which gradually gathered pace from summer 2007," and observes that just as in the United States (though in stark contrast with the experiences of Australia and Canada), the U.K. government ultimately bailed out a number of large British financial institutions.[145]

The upshot is that the United Kingdom and the United States experienced broadly similar crises for broadly similar reasons, and in each country intense scrutiny has fallen upon financial firm management – in many instances fueled by public outrage at continued payment of bonuses in financial firms dependent on government support.[146] Corporate governance practices and executive compensation structures have been closely scrutinized in the wake of the crisis as the public and regulators alike seek to determine how such reckless practices could have become so endemic to the financial system, and how we prevent such a catastrophe from occurring again. Although the empirical literature on corporate governance in the financial context was not previously well developed,[147] a growing body of postcrisis research increasingly tends to

[144] Emergency Economic Stabilization Act of 2008, H.R. 1424, 110th Cong. §§ 101, 115 (2008). *See also* Bruner, *supra* note 133, at 314–16. For in-depth analyses of the various bailouts, see generally Steven M. Davidoff & David Zaring, *Regulation by Deal: The Government's Response to the Financial Crisis*, 61 ADMIN. L. REV. 463 (2009); POZEN, *supra* note 140.

[145] TURNER, *supra* note 140, at 14, 18, 29, 32, 35; *Adair, Lord Turner*, FIN. SERVS. AUTH., http://www.fsa.gov.uk/pages/About/Who/board/turner.shtml. *See also* Andrew Grice, *£850bn: Official Cost of the Bank Bailout*, INDEP., Dec. 4, 2009, http://www.independent.co.uk/news/uk/politics/163850bn-official-cost-of-the-bank-bailout-1833830.html; Konzelmann et al., *supra* note 131; George A. Walker, *Financial Crisis – U.K. Policy and Regulatory Response*, 44 INT'L LAW. 751, 753–55 (2010); Edward Walker-Arnott, *Company Law, Corporate Governance and the Banking Crisis*, INT'L CORP. RESCUE (Special Issue) 3, 3 (2010).

[146] *See* Grice, *supra* note 145; David Ellis, *Goldman's Blankfein Collects $9 Million Bonus*, CNN.COM (Feb. 5, 2010), http://money.cnn.com/2010/02/05/news/companies/blankfein_bonus/.

[147] *See, e.g.*, Renee Adams, *Governance and the Financial Crisis* 5 (Eur. Corp. Governance Inst., Finance Working Paper No. 284/2009, 2009), http://ssrn.com/abstract=1398583; Luc Laeven & Ross Levine, *Bank Governance, Regulation and Risk Taking*, 93 J. FIN. ECON. 259, 259 (2009);

suggest that equity-based pay resulted in greater risk-taking in financial firms leading up to the crisis. The broader association of investor protection with greater risk-taking in nonfinancial firms was already empirically documented and broadly understood,[148] and postcrisis empirical studies have reported similar findings.[149] Luc Laeven and Ross Levine, for example, find that "banks with more powerful owners tend to take greater risks,"[150] and Renee Adams finds, among other things, that "banks with TARP funds have more independent boards, larger boards, more outside directorships and greater incentive pay for CEOs."[151] Similarly, Andrea Beltratti and René Stulz find that "banks with more pro-shareholder boards performed worse during the crisis,"[152] and Rüdiger Fahlenbrach and Stulz find that "banks led by CEOs whose interests were better aligned with those of their shareholders had worse stock returns and a worse return on equity" during the crisis – findings that may suggest that "CEOs focused on the interests of their shareholders in the build-up to the crisis and took actions that they believed the market would welcome."[153]

Jonathan R. Macey & Maureen O'Hara, *The Corporate Governance of Banks*, 9 FRBNY ECON. POL'Y REV. 91, 91 (Apr. 2003).

[148] *See* Kose John et al., *Corporate Governance and Risk-Taking*, 63 J. FIN. 1679, 1708 (2008). *See also* Tung, *supra* note 140, at 1217 n.60 (observing that management equity ownership is associated with higher bond premia, suggesting greater perceived risk among bondholders); Bebchuk & Spamann, *supra* note 140, at 262 (observing that "CEOs who are insulated from shareholder pressure and do not receive high-powered pay are less prone to engage in risk-taking"). On the "notable shortage of reliable results showing that shareholder primacy actually works better" in performance terms, see STOUT, *supra* note 138, at 48–50 (emphasis removed). *See also* KAY REVIEW, *supra* note 65, at 14–21 (discussing negative consequences of short-termism in corporate decision making and the role of shareholders in promoting it).

[149] *See* Simon Deakin, *The Corporation as Commons: Rethinking Property Rights, Governance and Sustainability in the Business Enterprise*, 37 QUEEN'S L.J. 339, 341–43 (2012) ("Emerging empirical research suggests that evidence of a link between shareholder-oriented corporate governance and bank failure is more than just circumstantial . . . .").

[150] Laeven & Levine, *supra* note 147, at 273. *See also* Jeffrey N. Gordon, *Executive Compensation and Corporate Governance in Financial Firms: The Case for Convertible Equity-Based Pay* 6–7 (Columbia Law Sch. & European Corp. Governance Inst. Working Paper No. 373, 2010), http://ssrn.com/abstract=1633906 (arguing that undiversified blockholders and managers in financial firms prefer risk-taking to a greater extent than diversified shareholders do, given the latter group's greater exposure to systemic risks).

[151] Adams, *supra* note 147, at 13.

[152] Andrea Beltratti & René M. Stulz, *Why Did Some Banks Perform Better during the Credit Crisis? A Cross-Country Study of the Impact of Governance and Regulation* 3 (Eur. Corp. Governance Inst. Working Paper Series in Fin., Working Paper No. 254, 2009), http://ssrn.com/abstract=1433502.

[153] Rüdiger Fahlenbrach & René Stulz, *Bank CEO Incentives and the Credit Crisis* 1–2 (Fisher Coll. of Bus. Working Paper Series, Working Paper No. 2009-03-013, 2010), http://ssrn.com/abstract=1439859.

It is entirely comprehensible that reform efforts have emphasized stabilizing the banking system and curbing risk-taking in the future.[154] In light of what we know about how the crisis unfolded, however, including the growing empirical literature examining corporate governance dynamics in financial firms, we might have anticipated that reforms would aim to divorce financial firm managers' interests from the short-term risk-taking preferences of equity holders to the maximum degree possible – say, by retaining equity-based compensation while imposing a longer-term view through deferral mechanisms,[155] or better yet by substantially reducing the impact of stock price on pay,[156] an approach that would seem particularly attractive in light of recent findings suggesting that "bank CEOs' inside debt holdings preceding the Financial Crisis are significantly positively associated with better stock returns and accounting return on assets," and significantly negatively associated with risk-taking.[157]

Indeed, the history of corporate governance in banking might reasonably have led us to expect postcrisis reformers to take aim at the architecture of the modern financial firm itself. Historically, U.S. corporate law drew a clearer distinction between financial and nonfinancial firms, consciously aiming to constrain risk-taking in banks by imposing heightened fiduciary duties on directors and exposing shareholders to some measure of personal liability – the former taking the form of a more robust duty of care, and the latter taking the form of so-called double liability rules under which the stock of a failed bank could be assessed to the tune of its sale price to create a fund for the benefit of creditors, giving the shareholders a strong incentive to monitor

[154] *See generally* Dodd-Frank Wall Street Reform and Consumer Protection Act, H.R. 4173, 111th Cong. (2010) [hereinafter Dodd-Frank Act]. *See also* Davidoff & Zaring, *supra* note 144; *Tackling the Financial Crisis*, HM TREASURY, http://www.hm-treasury.gov.uk/fin_finstability_actions.htm. For incisive critiques of the Dodd-Frank Act, see generally STEPHEN M. BAINBRIDGE, CORPORATE GOVERNANCE AFTER THE FINANCIAL CRISIS (2012) (concluding that the Act's corporate governance reforms "lack strong empirical or theoretical justification," and that "each erodes the system of competitive federalism . . . by displacing state regulation with federal law"); DAVID SKEEL, THE NEW FINANCIAL DEAL: UNDERSTANDING THE DODD-FRANK ACT AND ITS (UNINTENDED) CONSEQUENCES (2011) (arguing that the Act's special treatment of large financial institutions and reliance on ad hoc regulatory responses will undermine its efficacy).

[155] *See, e.g.*, Sanjai Bhagat & Roberta Romano, *Reforming Executive Compensation: Focusing and Committing to the Long-Term*, 26 YALE J. ON REG. 359 (2009); POZEN, *supra* note 140, at 277–81; DAVID WALKER, A REVIEW OF CORPORATE GOVERNANCE IN U.K. BANKS AND OTHER FINANCIAL INDUSTRY ENTITIES: FINAL RECOMMENDATIONS 21–22 (2009), http://webarchive.nationalarchives.gov.uk/+/http://www.hm-treasury.gov.uk/d/walker_review_261109.pdf.

[156] *See, e.g.*, Bebchuk & Spamann, *supra* note 140, at 283–85; Gordon, *supra* note 150, at 11–14; Tung, *supra* note 140, at 1226–41.

[157] Frederick Tung & Xue Wang, *Bank CEOs, Inside Debt Compensation, and the Financial Crisis* 4 (Emory Pub. Law Research Paper No. 10–98, 2010; Emory Law and Econ. Research Paper No. 10–63, 2010), http://ssrn.com/abstract=1570161.

risk-taking in order to avoid later assessment.[158] In this light, some have advocated bringing such risk-reduction strategies to bear upon today's systemically important financial institutions in order to reduce directors' intense focus on share price and to focus the minds of shareholders themselves on constraining risk-taking, rather than encouraging it.[159]

Surprisingly, however, postcrisis corporate governance reforms in both the United Kingdom and the United States have sought to empower shareholders, evidently in the belief that more powerful shareholders would constrain excessive risk-taking by reckless managers. In the United Kingdom, this view found its most vivid expression in the new "Stewardship Code" for institutional investors, which aims expressly to reinforce the shareholders' governance supremacy, to encourage institutions to exert themselves, and correlatively to render management more directly answerable to shareholders.[160] The idea – as Sir David Walker describes it in the review of corporate governance in U.K. banks where he initially proposed such a code – is that institutional investors "who have significant rights of ownership and enjoy the very material advantage of limited liability should see these as complemented by a duty of stewardship," exercise of which may at the same time "offer a means of increasing absolute returns by addressing issues in the company in a timely and influential manner and thus improving long-run performance."[161] Evidently the Financial Reporting Council (FRC) agreed, implementing Walker's

[158] *See* Bruner, *supra* note 136, at 7–15. For additional background on the duty of care in banking, see Patricia A. McCoy, *A Political Economy of the Business Judgment Rule in Banking: Implications for Corporate Law*, 47 CASE W. L. REV. 1 (1996). For additional background on double liability rules, see Jonathan R. Macey & Geoffrey P. Miller, *Double Liability of Bank Shareholders: History and Implications*, 27 WAKE FOREST L. REV. 31 (1992). Double liability was the rule for national banks from the 1860s until the advent of deposit insurance in the 1930s, following which double liability rules at the state level declined as well. *See* Bruner, *supra* note 136, at 14, 26–27. Note that Australia, Canada, and the United Kingdom also employed multiple liability regimes. *See generally* Lewis T. Evans & Neil C. Quigley, *Shareholder Liability Regimes, Principal–Agent Relationships, and Banking Industry Performance*, 38 J. L. & ECON. 497 (1995); John D. Turner, *"The Last Acre and Sixpence": Views on Bank Liability Regimes in Nineteenth-Century Britain*, 16 FIN. HIST. REV. 111 (2009).

[159] *See* Bruner, *supra* note 136, at 32–34 (advocating "revisiting the fundamental issue of whether shareholder interests and incentives really constitute a socially beneficial touchstone for corporate governance in financial firms"); Peter Conti-Brown, *Elective Shareholder Liability*, 64 STAN. L. REV. 409 (2012) (advocating an elective regime permitting shareholders in systemically important banks to choose either double liability or heightened capital requirements); Claire Hill & Richard Painter, *Berle's Vision beyond Shareholder Interests: Why Investment Bankers Should Have (Some) Personal Liability*, 33 SEATTLE U. L. REV. 1173 (2010) (advocating personal liability for investment bankers through contract or assessable stock); Jonathan R. Macey & Maureen O'Hara, *Solving the Corporate Governance Problems of Banks: A Proposal*, BANKING L.J., Apr. 2003, at 326 (advocating financial firm fiduciary duties focused on "fixed claimants").

[160] *See* WALKER, *supra* note 155, at 17–19.

[161] *Id.* at 70.

proposal first through amendments to the U.K. Corporate Governance Code – a best practices code that applies not just to financial firms, but to all listed companies, on a "comply or explain" basis[162] – and ultimately through a self-standing Stewardship Code.[163] The revised U.K. Corporate Governance Code further states that "[a]ll directors of FTSE 350 companies should be subject to annual election by shareholders,"[164] a change that the FRC describes, together with the Stewardship Code, as "part of a drive to improve engagement between boards and shareholders," and specifically to "increase accountability to shareholders."[165] More recently, a push arose in mid-2012 "to give shareholders a binding vote on a company's policy for director pay," a move aimed at bolstering the preexisting say-on-pay votes (nonbinding shareholder votes on executive compensation packages) already held annually.[166]

The Stewardship Code itself, issued in July 2010 and revised in September 2012, explains that the aim is to "enhance the quality of engagement between institutional investors and companies to help improve long-term returns to shareholders and the efficient exercise of governance responsibilities" through a "comply or explain" approach resembling that of the U.K. Corporate Governance Code.[167] The Stewardship Code's seven principles, then, urge institutional investors to (1) disclose their stewardship policies, (2) adopt a "robust" conflict of interest policy, (3) actively "monitor their investee companies," (4) adopt "clear guidelines on when and how they will escalate their

[162] Financial Reporting Council, The UK Corporate Governance Code, 2012, at 1–5 (U.K.) [hereinafter UK Corporate Governance Code]; Financial Services Authority Handbook, Listing Rules 9.8.6(5)–(6), 9.8.7 (U.K.).

[163] Financial Reporting Council, 2009 Review of the Combined Code: Final Report, 2009, at 34 (U.K.); Financial Reporting Council, Revisions to the UK Corporate Governance Code (Formerly the Combined Code), 2010, at 5, 10 (U.K.) [hereinafter Revisions to the UK Corporate Governance Code]. *See also* Marc Moore, *Introduction*, INT'L CORP. RESCUE (Special Issue) 1, 1 (2010) (observing the "absorption of many of the (originally industry-specific) Walker recommendations by the Financial Reporting Council into the draft new edition of the generic UK Corporate Governance Code").

[164] UK Corporate Governance Code, *supra* note 162, at 16.

[165] Revisions to the UK Corporate Governance Code, *supra* note 163, at 2–5.

[166] *See* Amy L. Goodman, *Binding Say on Pay in the UK*, HARVARD LAW SCHOOL FORUM ON CORPORATE GOVERNANCE AND FINANCIAL REGULATION, July 9, 2012, https://blogs.law.harvard.edu/corpgov/2012/07/09/binding-say-on-pay-in-the-uk/ (emphasis removed). *See also* DEPARTMENT FOR BUSINESS INNOVATION & SKILLS (U.K.), DIRECTOR'S PAY: GUIDE TO GOVERNMENT REFORMS (June 20, 2012); DEPARTMENT FOR BUSINESS INNOVATION & SKILLS (U.K.), DIRECTOR'S PAY: CONSULTATION ON REVISED REMUNERATION REPORTING REGULATIONS (June 2012); Ali Qassim, *U.K. Plans to Introduce Binding Shareholder Votes on Director Pay Policy, Exit Payments*, Corp. L. Daily (BNA) (June 29, 2012).

[167] Financial Reporting Council, *UK Stewardship Code*, http://www.frc.org.uk/Our-Work/Codes-Standards/Corporate-governance/UK-Stewardship-Code.aspx. *See also* Financial Reporting Council, The UK Stewardship Code, 2012, at 1–4 (U.K.) [hereinafter UK Stewardship Code].

stewardship activities," (5) be prepared "to act collectively with other investors" in so doing, (6) adopt a "clear policy on voting" and disclosure thereof, and (7) make periodic reports "on their stewardship and voting activities."[168] With regard to escalation of institutional investor involvement, the FRC indicates that "if companies do not respond constructively when institutional investors intervene," institutions should consider responses ranging from further discussions with senior management and the board to "intervening jointly with other institutions on particular issues" – potentially including public statements, submission of shareholder resolutions, and "in some cases proposing to change board membership"[169] – an approach to escalation hewing closely to a preexisting code promulgated by the Institutional Shareholders Committee.[170]

The United States, for its part, has pursued a more ambitious reform agenda. TARP firms were subjected to pay restrictions and Treasury oversight, as well as say-on-pay votes.[171] In May 2009, then, Senator Charles Schumer of New York introduced a bill to "provide shareholders with enhanced authority over the nomination, election, and compensation of public company executives" through a "Shareholder Bill of Rights Act."[172] This act, if enacted, would have introduced a number of strongly shareholder-centric reforms, including an express grant of authority for the SEC to expand shareholder access to the company's proxy statement for director nominations (typically referred to as proxy access); say-on-pay (and golden parachute) votes; as well as listing rules requiring independent board chairs and annual board elections by majority (rather than plurality) vote.[173] Some of these proposed reforms did in fact make their way into the Dodd-Frank Act, signed into law by President Barack Obama in July 2010, which includes say-on-pay (and golden parachute) votes, additional disclosure of how executive compensation relates to corporate performance, a three-year clawback of incentive-based compensation following accounting restatements, and clear authority for proxy access.[174] The Dodd-Frank Act also requires risk committees in certain larger financial firms and

[168] UK Stewardship Code, *supra* note 167, at 6–10.

[169] *Id.* at 8.

[170] Financial Reporting Council, Implementation of the UK Stewardship Code, 2010, at 1–2 (U.K.). *See also Shareholder or Shareowner?*, Hermes Equity Ownership Servs., http://www.hermes.co.uk/files/pdfs/shareowner_or_shareholder_311003.pdf.

[171] Emergency Economic Stabilization Act of 2008, H.R. 1424, 110th Cong. §§ 111, 302 (2008); American Recovery and Reinvestment Act of 2009, H.R. 1, 111th Cong., 123 Stat. 115, § 7001 (2009).

[172] Shareholder Bill of Rights Act of 2009, S.1074, 111th Cong., preamble, § 1 (2009) [hereinafter SBRA].

[173] *Id.* §§ 3–5.

[174] Dodd-Frank Act, *supra* note 154, §§ 951, 953, 954, 971.

imposes additional regulation for incentive-based pay in financial firms that regulators believe "could lead to material financial loss to the covered financial institution."[175]

The SEC, having received a green light from Congress, revived a stalled push for shareholder proxy access, adopting a new rule to this effect in August 2010.[176] The SEC's new proxy access rule would have, under certain circumstances, permitted shareholders or groups maintaining 3 percent voting power for three years to include their own nominees in the company's proxy statement for up to 25 percent of the board (or at least one seat). At the same time, the SEC's rule on shareholder proposals was amended to facilitate proposals relating to nomination procedures.[177] The proxy access rule effectively would have been mandatory, permitting states or companies to opt out only through the extreme step of prohibiting shareholder nominations entirely.[178] Styled in the adopting release as an effort to "facilitate the effective exercise of shareholders' traditional State law rights to nominate and elect directors to company boards,"[179] the SEC's proxy access rule was nevertheless quite controversial from the start, prompting two heated dissents. Commissioner Troy Paredes argued that the rule "confers upon shareholders a new substantive federal right that in many respects runs counter to what state corporate law otherwise provides,"[180] and Commissioner Kathleen Casey described the adopting release itself as "a jiu-jitsu exercise . . . purporting to give deference to state law and to increase shareholder choices under state law, when in fact the rules do exactly the opposite."[181]

Predictably, the proxy access rule was challenged in court by the U.S. Chamber of Commerce and the Business Roundtable, and in October 2010 the

[175] *Id.* §§ 165(h), 956.

[176] Securities and Exchange Commission, Facilitating Shareholder Director Nominations, 74 Fed. Reg. 29024 (June 18, 2009) (proposed rule); Securities and Exchange Commission, Facilitating Shareholder Director Nominations, 75 Fed. Reg. 56668 (Sept. 16, 2010) (final rule) [hereinafter Proxy Access Release]. On prior SEC initiatives leading to this recent effort, see BAINBRIDGE, *supra* note 154, at 224–28.

[177] Proxy Access Release, *supra* note 176, at 56674–77 (summarizing the new Rule 14a-11 and amendment of Rule 14a-8 under the Securities Exchange Act of 1934).

[178] *Id.* at 56678.

[179] *Id.* at 56668.

[180] Troy A. Paredes, Commissioner, Securities and Exchange Commission, Statement at Open Meeting to Adopt the Final Rule Regarding Facilitating Shareholder Director Nominations ("Proxy Access") (Aug. 25, 2010), http://sec.gov/news/speech/2010/spch082510tap.htm.

[181] Kathleen L. Casey, Commissioner, Securities and Exchange Commission, Statement at Open Meeting to Adopt the Final Rule Regarding Facilitating Shareholder Director Nominations (Aug. 25, 2010), http://sec.gov/news/speech/2010/spch082510klc.htm. *See also* BAINBRIDGE, *supra* note 154, at 229–31; Christopher Bruner, *Proxy Access Forum: Christopher Bruner*, CONGLOMERATE BLOG, Aug. 26, 2010, http://www.theconglomerate.org/forum-proxy-access/.

SEC stayed its implementation pending resolution of the matter.[182] Ultimately the rule was struck down by the Court of Appeals for the D.C. Circuit, which found that the SEC had failed "adequately to assess the economic effects" of the rule.[183] The opinion is striking in its disdain for the SEC's effort – particularly given that Congress had all but mandated the rule.[184] The court chastised the SEC for focusing "exclusively and heavily upon two relatively unpersuasive studies" supporting its position while disregarding "the numerous studies submitted by commenters that reached the opposite result,"[185] and rejected the SEC's attempt to square its rule with corporate federalism.[186] In the last sentence of the body of the opinion, the court goes so far as to call the SEC's application of the rule to investment companies "unutterably mindless."[187]

The court emphasized that the amendment to the shareholder proposal rule aimed at facilitating proposals relating to nominating procedures was not challenged,[188] which taken alone (following the court's rejection of the proxy access rule) effectively brings the federal regime very close to the opt-in regime adopted by Delaware in 2009.[189] In September 2011, the SEC confirmed that it would not seek rehearing or Supreme Court review regarding the proxy access rule, but emphasized that the amended shareholder proposal rule would give shareholders "the opportunity to establish proxy access standards on a company-by-company basis." SEC Chairman Mary Schapiro stated that she remained "committed to finding a way to make it easier for shareholders to nominate candidates to corporate boards," reflecting her belief that this would "make boards more accountable for the risks undertaken by the companies they manage," but that she wanted "to be sure that we carefully

[182] Securities and Exchange Commission, Facilitating Shareholder Director Nominations, 75 Fed. Reg. 64641 (Oct. 20, 2010); Jessica Holzer, *SEC Awaits Court Ruling on Proxy Rule*, WALL ST. J., Oct. 4, 2010.

[183] Business Roundtable v. SEC, 647 F.3d 1144, 1148–49 (D.C. Cir. 2011).

[184] *See* Dodd-Frank Act, *supra* note 154, § 971(a) (expressly permitting, but not mandating, an SEC rule requiring that a company's proxy "include a nominee submitted by a shareholder").

[185] *Business Roundtable*, 647 F.3d at 1150–51.

[186] *Id.* at 1151, 1155–56 (rejecting the SEC's discounting of the costs of the rule "as a mere artifact of the state law right of shareholders to elect directors," while not similarly discounting the benefits).

[187] *Id.* at 1156.

[188] *Id.* at 1153.

[189] *See* DEL. CODE ANN. tit. 8, § 112. As J. Robert Brown has observed, this move was made preemptively, in anticipation of a federal rule. *See* J. Robert Brown, *The SEC, Access and the Need to Preempt Delaware Law*, THERACETOTHEBOTTOM.ORG (Apr. 23, 2009), http://ww .theracetothebottom.org/preemption-of-delaware-law/the-sec-access-and-the-need-to-preempt-delaware-law.html.

consider and learn from the Court's objections as we determine the best path forward."[190]

In any event, the logic of reform efforts such as those pursued by Senator Schumer and Chairman Schapiro, and those enacted through the Dodd-Frank Act, is appealingly simply. In a binary corporate governance system in which all power resides either with the board or with the shareholders,[191] attributing a problem to one power constituency presumptively suggests that the solution must lie with the other. This, in effect, undergirds Chairman Schapiro's commitment to proxy access – to the extent that reckless managers proximately caused the crisis, it must follow that strengthening shareholders through reforms such as proxy access would address the problem by "mak[ing] boards more accountable for the risks undertaken by the companies they manage." This, of course, echoes the position taken by the SEC in its adopting release, which suggests that the crisis "heightened the serious concerns of many shareholders about the accountability and responsiveness of some companies and boards of directors to shareholder interests," and presents proxy access as a way to "significantly enhance the confidence of shareholders who link the recent financial crisis to a lack of responsiveness of some boards to shareholder interests."[192] A similar logic clearly motivated Senator Schumer's proposed "Shareholder Bill of Rights Act," which would have stated as "findings" of Congress that "among the central causes of the financial and economic crises . . . has been a widespread failure of corporate governance," and that "a key contributing factor . . . was the lack of accountability of boards to their ultimate owners, the shareholders."[193]

Institutional shareholders themselves, meanwhile, have similarly advocated augmenting their own power as an antidote to excessive risk-taking. For example, the Council of Institutional Investors (CII), in a December 2008 letter to Speaker of the House of Representatives Nancy Pelosi, argued that "the current crisis represents a massive failure of oversight." The letter concludes that "[i]n order to restore trust and ensure that such a crisis never happens again, regulators and investors must be given the tools necessary to guarantee robust oversight and meaningful accountability of corporate managers and

[190] Press Release, Statement by SEC Chairman Mary L. Schapiro on Proxy Access Litigation, 2011–179, Sept. 6, 2011, http://www.sec.gov/news/press/2011/2011–179.htm.

[191] Matthew Bodie contrasts the marginalization of employees in corporate governance with their central role in theories of the firm. *See generally* Matthew T. Bodie, *Employees and the Boundaries of the Corporation*, *in* Research Handbook on the Economics of Corporate Law 85 (Claire A. Hill & Brett H. McDonnell eds., 2012).

[192] Proxy Access Release, *supra* note 176, at 56669–70.

[193] SBRA, *supra* note 172, § 2.

directors." In the case of investors, ICC advocated "a number of key corporate governance reforms" to "empower shareowners to anticipate and address unforeseen future risks."[194]

This view likewise prompted the new U.K. Stewardship Code, Walker suggesting in his proposal that greater involvement by institutional investors "may offer a means of increasing absolute returns by addressing issues in the company in a timely and influential manner and thus improving long-run performance."[195] A similar view animated Australia's adoption of the "two strikes" rule in June 2011, Senator Don Farrell, suggesting in his second reading speech that "the global financial crisis highlighted a number of issues relating to remuneration structures" and implying that greater shareholder influence over executive pay could mitigate "the dangers of remuneration structures that focus on short-term results, reward excessive risk-taking and promote corporate greed."[196]

This position appears highly suspect in light of the growing postcrisis empirical literature, which tends to suggest that strong emphasis on the interests of risk-preferring shareholders results in more risk-taking, not less – a tension clearly discernible in efforts to reform incentive-based pay in large financial firms. In April 2011, seven financial regulators jointly proposed rules to implement § 956 of the Dodd-Frank Act, which imposes limits on incentive-based compensation structures in certain financial firms.[197] The proposed rules, if enacted, would apply to large financial firms (with $1 billion in assets), prohibiting "any" incentive-based pay arrangement "that encourages inappropriate risks" through "excessive compensation" or "that could lead to material

[194] Letter from Jeff Mahoney, General Council, Council of Institutional Investors, and others, to the Honorable Nancy Pelosi (Dec. 2, 2008), at 1–2, http://www.calpers-governance.org/docs-sof/marketinitiatives/initiatives/cii-corporate-governance-reform-advocacy-letter.pdf [hereinafter Mahoney Letter].

[195] WALKER, *supra* note 155, at 70. *See also* Institutional Shareholders' Committee, *Code on the Responsibilities of Institutional Investors* (Nov. 16, 2009), http://institutionalshareholders committee.org.uk/sitebuildercontent/sitebuilderfiles/ISCcodeexpressrelease161109.pdf; Institutional Shareholders' Committee, *Improving Institutional Investors' Role in Governance* (June 5, 2009), http://institutionalshareholderscommittee.org.uk/sitebuildercontent/sitebuilderfiles/ISCImprovingInstitutionalInvestorsRoleInGovernance50609.pdf (advocating "improvements that could be made to corporate governance in the wake of the banking crisis").

[196] Cth, Parliamentary Debates, Senate, 14 June 2011, 3 (Don Farrell, Senator) (Austl.).

[197] *See* Dodd-Frank Act, *supra* note 154, § 956; Securities and Exchange Commission, Incentive-Based Compensation Arrangements, 76 Fed. Reg. 21170 (Apr. 14, 2011) (proposed rule jointly issued with Department of the Treasury, Office of the Comptroller of the Currency and Office of Thrift Supervision; Federal Reserve System; Federal Deposit Insurance Corporation; National Credit Union Administration; and Federal Housing Finance Agency) [hereinafter Joint Rule Proposal].

financial loss," and requiring that the arrangement "[b]alances risk and financial rewards." Illustrative options provided in the proposed rule include "using deferral of payments, risk adjustment of awards, reduced sensitivity to short-term performance, or longer performance periods." For larger firms (with $50 billion in assets), deferral is literally required, as is board determination of which nonexecutives are in a position "to expose the [firm] to possible losses that are substantial in relation to the covered [firm's] size, capital, or overall risk tolerance" (such as "traders with large position limits"), for whom the board must specifically approve the pay structure and ensure that it "effectively balances the financial rewards to the covered person and the range and time horizon of risks associated with the covered person's activities."[198]

It remains to be seen as of this writing whether this rule will be adopted. Regardless, however, it bears emphasizing that the notion of balancing risk and reward, particularly through "reduced sensitivity to short-term performance" pressures, is clearly in tension with the shareholder-empowerment theme animating postcrisis corporate governance reforms more generally. This may help explain why a lengthy joint effort of seven financial regulators provides so little concrete guidance on how large financial firms are to achieve this goal. In observing that its suggestions "are not exclusive, and additional methods or variations of these approaches may exist or be developed," and in speculating that new methods "for making compensation sensitive to risk-taking are likely to evolve during the next few years,"[199] the seven regulators obliquely acknowledge that this is where we in fact ought to be directing our efforts – a project in no respect furthered by empowering risk-preferring shareholders, as most of the Dodd-Frank Act's corporate governance reforms tend to do.

In his review of corporate governance in British banks, Walker grapples with this fundamental tension more directly, if ineffectually. Walker recognizes that banks, like other types of companies, must balance the shareholder-centrism of company law with legitimate concerns regarding the broader consequences of bank failure, yet rejects the notion of broadening bank directors' duties beyond narrow shareholder-centrism.[200] He concludes that "the UK unitary board structure and the Combined Code of the FRC remain fit for purpose," and advocates maintenance of a single corporate governance code for financial

[198] Joint Rule Proposal, *supra* note 197, at 21215–16.

[199] *Id.* at 21179. For additional background on the proposals, see *id.* at 21172–83; Henry Oehmann, Nicole Jordan & Jack Katz, *Beyond Banks: New Incentive Compensation Rules Reach Entire Industry*, MONDAQ BUS. BRIEFING, May 9, 2011; Kathleen Wechter, Pamela Baker & Martin Moderson, *Guidance Issued on Financial Institutions Incentive-Based Compensation Arrangements*, MONDAQ, June 8, 2011.

[200] WALKER, *supra* note 155, at 23, 29, Annex 3.

and nonfinancial firms alike, "with some additional [bank]-specific elements to be taken forward through the FSA."[201] Although he rightly acknowledges that bank shareholders may have supported greater leverage for "the very high returns that could be generated," and that short-term equity market pressures "in many cases led to both encouragement and greater acceptance of increased leverage," he nevertheless suggests that shareholders could be expected to act as responsible "stewards," providing "guidance" and "pressure" to maintain bank managers' focus on the long term – an odd suggestion, given his expression of hope that greater exposure to management might itself be the mechanism by which to "moderate shareholder focus on short-term performance."[202]

Even if shareholder empowerment made sense as a crisis response in the financial context, however, it remains entirely unclear why this would support doing the same in nonfinancial public companies. Brian Cheffins, in his study of companies removed from the S&P 500 in 2008, found that "institutional shareholders were largely mute as share prices fell," whereas "directors of troubled firms were far from passive, as they orchestrated CEO turnover at a rate far exceeding the norm in public companies." These findings, Cheffins suggests, indicate that "corporate governance functioned tolerably well in companies removed from the S&P 500," such that "the case is not yet made for fundamental reform of current corporate governance arrangements."[203] Cheffins's conclusion would appear all the more compelling in nonfinancial firms, given that financial firms "not only suffered the largest share price declines, they also dominated the roster of companies removed from the index."[204]

That U.K. and U.S. policy makers would react to the crisis by empowering shareholders thus seems doubly difficult to explain. This regulatory response does not add up in the context of financial firms because the excessive risk-taking that led to the crisis appears to have stemmed from strong equity market pressures to boost short-term returns. Nor does it add up in the context of nonfinancial firms, which were not the problem in the first place (and where risk-taking incentives and the finance literature similarly contradict the rationale underlying the reforms adopted). How do we account for these postcrisis

[201] *Id.* at 11. *See also id.* at 19–22 (recommending, among other things, board risk committees, deferrals, and clawbacks).

[202] *Id.* at 13, 25–27. *See also* KAY REVIEW, *supra* note 65, at 9–21, 44–49 (similarly recognizing the dangers of short-termism while calling for greater "stewardship"); John Plender, *Banking: Rarely Pointed Finger*, FIN. TIMES, Jan. 17, 2010 (arguing that "the proposition that [greater shareholder engagement] could prevent a recurrence of the crisis is questionable").

[203] Brian R. Cheffins, *Did Corporate Governance "Fail" during the 2008 Stock Market Meltdown? The Case of the S&P 500*, 65 BUS. LAW. 1, 1 (2009) (emphasis removed).

[204] *Id.* at 51–52.

developments, then, and how do they relate to the social welfare–based drivers of corporate governance and shareholder-orientation discussed in this book?

In the case of the United Kingdom, reforms favoring shareholders largely reflect the lack of practical alternatives within a corporate legal system that effectively defines the corporation as an association of shareholders. In this light, Walker's call for greater "stewardship" by British institutional shareholders was the furthest thing from revolutionary – indeed, it was intended to be precisely the opposite. The Stewardship Code aims not to change British corporate governance, but to reinforce its long-standing structure. Again, Walker emphasizes "the importance of discharge of the responsibility of shareholders as owners, which has been inadequately acknowledged in the past,"[205] and that "those who have significant rights of ownership and enjoy the very material advantage of limited liability should see these as complemented by a duty of stewardship."[206] The Financial Services Authority, in implementing a new rule requiring large U.K. banks to maintain policies promoting "effective risk management" – a rule imposing no limits on shareholders' influence over pay policies – similarly explains that they "recognise the vital importance of the role of shareholders in monitoring and controlling remuneration risks."[207] In each instance, the rhetorical move is the same – reinforcement of authority is styled as imposition of a duty, a move aimed at massaging the fundamental tension arising from empowering the very constituency whose interests most strongly skew in the direction of exactly what we want to prevent.

This form of corporate governance response to the financial crisis underscores what we have already observed – that the U.K. corporate entity is defined by shareholder-centrism, that the U.K. board's power is entirely derivative of a shareholder-granted mandate, and that the purpose of the U.K. corporation is purely and simply to advance the shareholders' interests. In this light, use of the word "stewardship" to describe U.K. shareholders' role is perfectly descriptive as a theoretical matter, virtually connoting an entitlement – in fact, a duty – to manage management.[208] The evidence from the crisis suggests that, if

205 Walker, *supra* note 155, at 12.

206 *Id.* at 70.

207 Fin. Servs. Auth., Reforming Remuneration Practices in Financial Services: Feedback on *CP09/10* and Final Rules 7 (Aug. 2009), http://www.fsa.gov.uk/pubs/policy/ps09_15.pdf. *See also* Bebchuk & Spamann, *supra* note 140, at 279–80; Michael McKee & Michelle Monteleone, *Reward Structures under Fire in the UK Financial Services Sector*, Int'l Corp. Rescue (Special Issue) 15, 16–18 (2010).

208 *See* Oxford English Dictionary Online, steward, *v*. (including "To manage, administer") (2d ed. 1989). As a practical matter, however, this characterization remains open to doubt. *See* Roger Barker, *Responding to the Crisis: A UK Corporate Governance Perspective*, Int'l Corp. Rescue (Special Issue) 12, 14 (2010) ("For many diversified institutional investors, corporate engagement is simply too costly and too time-consuming to become a viable ownership

anything, British policy makers would do better to curb shareholder influence in financial firms, but such a move would amount to far more than a "reform" initiative – it would literally require redefining the U.K. corporation in the financial context. British policy makers evidently found it far more comfortable to conclude that strict shareholder-centrism remains an appropriate lodestar for U.K. corporate governance, but that it simply was not being done correctly. Hence the FRC opined in December 2009 that the U.K. Corporate Governance Code and associated guidance "require some updating," but "remains broadly fit for purpose," the crisis merely revealing problems with "the way that the Code has been applied" – notably, a lack of "effective engagement between companies and shareholders." The notion of "sector-specific provisions" for banks is expressly rejected in order to "maintain the integrity of a single Code for companies,"[209] reflecting a strong aversion to redefining the corporation in the financial context. Avoidance of the core challenge, however, not only fails to address the true problems in financial firm governance that precipitated the crisis, but may ultimately undermine the political and social stability of U.K. corporate governance – particularly given that reinforcement of shareholder-centrism has coincided with austerity measures outside corporate governance that diminish social welfare protections available to employees.[210] The theory set forth here suggests that such trends, if substantial and sustained, could leave the U.K. corporate governance system incapable of weathering future crises for lack of the robust social welfare structures that historically supported the shareholder-centric U.K. conception of the corporation.

In the United States, the crisis similarly prompted reforms aimed at empowering shareholders – yet there is a critical distinction. Whereas postcrisis shareholder empowerment in the United Kingdom reinforces the status quo, such reforms in the United States sharply deviate from the status quo. U.S. shareholders quite clearly have not been conceptualized as active "stewards" of corporate governance – they are expected to trust their managers to act in their interests, and at most to sue them if they fail to do so. In this regard

strategy."); Brian R. Cheffins, *The Stewardship Code's Achilles' Heel*, 73 MOD. L. REV. 1004, 1020 (2010) (arguing that, given domestic institutions' waning stock ownership, a "presumption of Stewardship Code effectiveness . . . arguably harks to a bygone age"); Financial Reporting Council, *supra* note 170, at 6 (expressing "hope" that foreign investors will "commit to the Code"). On U.K. institutions' historical tendency to intervene principally in times of poor performance, see Sridhar Arcot et al., *Corporate Governance in the UK: Is the Comply or Explain Approach Working?* 30 INT'L REV. L. & ECON. 193, 193, 199 (2010); Bernard S. Black & John C. Coffee, Jr., *Hail Britannia?: Institutional Investor Behavior under Limited Regulation*, 92 MICH. L. REV. 1997, 2047 (1994); WALKER, *supra* note 155, at 75.

[209] Revisions to the UK Corporate Governance Code, *supra* note 163, at 2, 6.

[210] *See supra* Chapter 6.C.

shareholder-centric reform initiatives clearly represent a departure from the traditional U.S. conception of the shareholders' role. In fact, however, this development is rooted in social and political dynamics fully consistent with those explored in this book. Specifically, postcrisis shareholder-empowerment in the United States reflects a populist backlash against perceived managerial recklessness, a dynamic that – just like the reaction to hostile takeovers in the 1980s – has been reinforced by the fragmentation of our federal system and fueled by the relative weakness of social welfare protections available to employees.

As we have seen, regulation of a U.S. corporation's internal affairs has traditionally been left to the state of incorporation – a choice-of-law rule that has been hotly criticized as antidemocratic, permitting one state (say, Delaware) to regulate the governance of corporations that in all practical respects reside and conduct their business in another state (say, California).[211] Although it is increasingly clear that Delaware faces little meaningful competition from other states in attracting foreign incorporations,[212] Washington, DC is another matter. Indeed, Congress possesses ample authority to federalize corporate law as and when it likes – a constitutional capacity that looms particularly large in times of crisis, as the core securities statutes, the Sarbanes-Oxley Act, and the Dodd-Frank Act all variously illustrate. At such times, Delaware – keenly understanding the vulnerability of its position[213] – rationally seeks to lay low and weather the storm as best it can. As Edward Rock and Marcel Kahan have

[211] William Cary, writing in 1974, decried "the present predicament in which a pygmy among the 50 states prescribes, interprets, and indeed denigrates national corporate policy as an incentive to encourage incorporation within its borders, thereby increasing its revenue." William L. Cary, *Federalism and Corporate Law: Reflections upon Delaware*, 83 YALE L.J. 663, 701 (1974). For more recent critiques of the legitimacy of Delaware's dominance, see generally Kent Greenfield, *Democracy and the Dominance of Delaware in Corporate Law*, 67 LAW & CONTEMP. PROBS. 101 (2004); Daniel J.H. Greenwood, *Markets and Democracy: The Illegitimacy of Corporate Law*, 74 UMKC L. REV. 41 (2005); Renee M. Jones, *Legitimacy and Corporate Law: The Case for Regulatory Redundancy*, 86 WASH. U. L. REV. 1273 (2009).

[212] *See, e.g.*, Lucian Arye Bebchuk & Assaf Hamdani, *Vigorous Race or Leisurely Walk: Reconsidering the Competition over Corporate Charters*, 112 YALE L.J. 553, 578 (2002); Robert Daines, *The Incorporation Choices of IPO Firms*, 77 N.Y.U. L. REV. 1559, 1570–74 (2002); Marcel Kahan & Ehud Kamar, *The Myth of State Competition in Corporate Law*, 55 STAN. L. REV. 679, 687 (2002). Roberta Romano argues, however, that Delaware faces "defensive" competition aimed at keeping locally headquartered companies incorporated in their home states. Roberta Romano, *The States as a Laboratory: Legal Innovation and State Competition for Corporate Charters*, 23 YALE J. ON REG. 209, 214 (2006). *See also* BAINBRIDGE, *supra* note 154, at 21–25.

[213] *See, e.g.*, Leo E. Strine, Jr., *Breaking the Corporate Governance Logjam in Washington: Some Constructive Thoughts on a Responsible Path Forward*, 63 BUS. LAW. 1079, 1084 (2008) ("No substantial argument can be made that Congress does not have the constitutional authority to enact a preemptive corporate law governing publicly traded corporations operating in interstate commerce.").

argued, "the biggest threat facing Delaware is the emergence of some major crisis that focuses public attention on the peculiar mode of U.S. corporate lawmaking . . . and undermines the public faith in Delaware's ability to handle the job"[214] – an approach that they detect in Delaware's response to the current crisis. As they observe, the terms of J.P. Morgan Chase's government-orchestrated acquisition of Bear Stearns almost certainly exceeded the scope of deal protections permissible under Delaware law – yet Vice Chancellor Donald Parsons agreed to stay the Delaware action and permit litigation to proceed in New York, notwithstanding Delaware's substantial interest in "maintaining the integrity of the fabric of Delaware corporate law."[215] The most plausible explanation for this uncharacteristic deference to New York, they suggest, was that it in fact represented deference to Washington. As Rock and Kahan query, "how could Delaware even contemplate enjoining a transaction that was supported, indeed, arguably driven and financed by the Federal Reserve with the full support of the Treasury – a transaction that may have been necessary to prevent a collapse of the international financial system?" As a political matter, the question answers itself. Delaware effectively could not hear the case, so it withdrew – an implicit acknowledgment of "Delaware's lack of political legitimacy" with regard to issues of broad national interest.[216]

Congress unquestionably possesses superior political legitimacy on matters affecting numerous constituencies across the country, but as Mark Roe observes, "when Washington acts on corporate law, it brings with it another strain of public policy: American populist sentiment and national public opinion." In Washington, Roe elaborates, there are "more interest groups, and broader ideas of efficiency, fairness, and sometimes power leveling" at work than one encounters in Delaware, which generally focuses more intently on the corporate power constituencies – shareholders and the board.[217] These political forces are readily discernible in the shareholder empowerment initiatives described earlier, which reflect a strong "populist" backlash against

[214] Edward Rock & Marcel Kahan, *How to Prevent Hard Cases from Making Bad Law: Bear Stearns, Delaware and the Strategic Use of Comity*, 58 EMORY L.J. 713, 715 (2009). *See also* Mark J. Roe, *Delaware's Competition*, 117 HARV. L. REV. 588, 601 (2003).

[215] Rock & Kahan, *supra* note 214, at 714–16. *See also In re* The Bear Stearns Companies, Inc. Shareholder Litigation, C.A. No. 3643-VCP, 2008 Del. Ch. LEXIS 46 (Del. Ch. 2008).

[216] Rock & Kahan, *supra* note 214, at 744. *See also* Lawrence A. Hamermesh, *The Policy Foundations of Delaware Corporate Law*, 106 COLUM. L. REV. 1749, 1752, 1770–71 (2006); Jones, *supra* note 211, at 1275–77. *But see* Christopher M. Bruner, *Managing Corporate Federalism: The Least-Bad Approach to the Shareholder Bylaw Debate*, 36 DEL. J. CORP. L. 1 (2011) (arguing that Delaware remains best positioned overall to address fundamental issues of corporate law).

[217] Mark J. Roe, *Delaware and Washington as Corporate Lawmakers*, 34 DEL. J. CORP. L. 1, 17, 33 (2009). *See also* BAINBRIDGE, *supra* note 154, at 27–40; Jones, *supra* note 211, at 1298–1300; Strine, *supra* note 213, at 1081.

corporate managers[218] that left lawmakers and regulators with little to gain from careful assessment of the complex factors resulting in excessive focus on stock price for the benefit of shareholders, let alone the critical differences between financial and nonfinancial firms. Institutional shareholders, meanwhile, naturally seized upon an opportune political moment to gain greater governance power.[219]

The true relevance of these reforms to the theory developed in this book, however, is the degree to which they were driven by the politics of the American "middle class." Although perhaps impossible to define with any specificity, the "middle class" label has, in the context of postcrisis reform efforts, come generally to stand for the investment-related and social welfare–related goals and concerns of the average working family,[220] and as such creates a conceptual bridge between the incentives and interests of "employees" and "shareholders." To be sure, the employee-shareholder distinction has blurred somewhat in recent decades because of the shift from defined benefit to defined contribution pensions, which has effectively transferred investment risk from employers to employees, rendering capital markets more politically

[218] *See, e.g.*, BAINBRIDGE, *supra* note 154, at 36–39; Bhagat & Romano, *supra* note 155, at 359–63; Cheryl Bolen et al., *White House Seeks Tough Limits on Size, Trading Activities of Large Financial Firms*, 42 Sec. Reg. & L. Rep. 117 (BNA) (Jan. 25, 2010). *See also* Jeffrey N. Gordon, *"Say on Pay": Cautionary Notes on the U.K. Experience and the Case for Shareholder Opt-In*, 46 HARV. J. ON LEGIS. 323, 338, 355–56 (2009).

[219] *See* BAINBRIDGE, *supra* note 154, at 270; Bratton & Wachter, *supra* note 135, at 656. *See also* Press Release, California Public Employees' Retirement System et al., *Public Plan Investors Announce Market Regulation Reform Principles – Transparency, Regulatory Independence and New Agency to Prevent Systemic Risk Are Critical for Restoring Confidence in Capital Markets* (Mar. 10, 2009), http://www.calpers.ca.gov/index.jsp?bc=/about/press/pr-archive/pr-2009/mar/regulation-reform-principles.xml; Letter from Lochiel Crafter, Chief Executive Officer, Australian Reward Investment Alliance et al., to the Honorable Barack Obama, President of the United States et al. (Feb. 13, 2009), at 1, http://www.calpers-governance.org/docs-sof/marketinitiatives/initiatives/financial-reform/2009-02-13-us-financial-market-and-cg-reforms.pdf; Carl C. Icahn, *The Economy Needs Corporate Governance Reform*, WALL ST. J., Jan. 23, 2009, at A13; Mahoney Letter, *supra* note 194; Erik Krusch, *Proxy Disclosures: More Say and Less Pay*, WESTLAW BUS. CURRENTS, Jan. 28, 2010.

[220] *See, e.g.*, Ann Belser, *Middle Class Finding It's Harder to Make Ends Meet*, PITTSBURGH POST-GAZETTE, Jan. 31, 2010, http://drummajorinstitute.org/library/article_print.php?ID=7276; Claire Suddath, *The Middle Class*, TIME, Feb. 27, 2009, http://www.time.com/time/printout/0,8816,1882147,00.html; Claire Suddath, *Obama's Middle-Class Task Force Has No Middle Class*, TIME, Mar. 4, 2009, http://www.time.com/time/printout/0,8816,1882913,00.html; WHITE HOUSE MIDDLE CLASS TASK FORCE, ANNUAL REPORT OF THE WHITE HOUSE TASK FORCE ON THE MIDDLE CLASS 9–10 (Feb. 2010), http://www.whitehouse.gov/sites/default/files/microsites/100226-annual-report-middle-class.pdf [hereinafter MCTF ANNUAL REPORT]; WHITE HOUSE MIDDLE CLASS TASK FORCE, FINANCING THE DREAM: SECURING COLLEGE AFFORDABILITY FOR THE MIDDLE CLASS 1 (2009), http://www.whitehouse.gov/assets/documents/staff_report_college_affordability1.pdf [hereinafter FINANCING THE DREAM].

salient to the middle class.[221] This trend has not, however, rendered employee and shareholder interests coextensive; for example, potential harms to target firm employees in hostile takeovers remain far more visible and acute than any pension investment benefits accruing to employees more generally.[222] Nevertheless, as political scientist Peter Hall explains, "[w]hen debates can be configured so as to engage some identities more deeply than others, actors can be induced to join coalitions they might not otherwise support"[223] – dynamics vividly illustrated by postcrisis calls for reform in the interests of the "middle class." This framing of the reform agenda tends to unify a diverse constellation of issues, from availability of health care following job loss, to the safety of savings for education and retirement[224] – concerns that have long been associated with the middle class,[225] and that remain intimately bound up with American corporate governance because of reliance on corporate employers as a means of providing social welfare protections.

Social welfare programs that have historically flourished in the United States have, as sociologist Theda Skocpol explains, tended to rest upon a

[221] *See* Gelter, *supra* note 74, at 3–5, 9–28.

[222] *Cf. id.* at 27–28 (observing that even if "a proposed policy that facilitates hostile takeovers" might generate greater pension returns, this "does not imply that workers no longer need to care about their job"). *See also id.* at 30–31 (observing that "employees may be more skeptical about increasing the actual decision-making power of shareholders, particularly in decisions with redistributive effects between capital and labor," but that hostile takeovers "are no longer politically as salient as they were in the 1980s").

[223] Peter A. Hall, *Historical Institutionalism in Rationalist and Sociological Perspective*, *in* EXPLAINING INSTITUTIONAL CHANGE: AMBIGUITY, AGENCY, AND POWER 204, 212 (James Mahoney & Kathleen Thelen eds., 2010).

[224] *See, e.g.*, DRUM MAJOR INSTITUTE, MIDDLE CLASS HOUSEHOLDS ARE FEARFUL FAMILIES 1–2, 9–10 (2008); *About the Middle Class Task Force*, WHITE HOUSE MIDDLE CLASS TASK FORCE, http://www.whitehouse.gov/StrongMiddleClass/about; FINANCING THE DREAM, *supra* note 220, at 6; MCTF ANNUAL REPORT, *supra* note 220, at iii, 9–11; Andrea Batista Schlesinger & Amy Traub, *A Strengthened Middle Class*, NEW PROGRESSIVE VOICES, http://newprogressivevoices.org/strengthenedmiddleclass/; WHITE HOUSE MIDDLE CLASS TASK FORCE, WHY MIDDLE CLASS AMERICANS NEED HEALTH REFORM 1 (2009), http://www.whitehouse.gov/assets/documents/071009_FINAL_Middle_Class_Task_Force_report2.pdf. *See also* David U. Himmelstein et al., *Medical Bankruptcy in the United States, 2007: Results of a National Study*, 122 AM. J. MED. 741 (2009); Michael Luo & Megan Thee-Brenan, *Poll Reveals Trauma of Joblessness in U.S.*, N.Y. TIMES, Dec. 14, 2009, http://www.nytimes.com/2009/12/15/us/15poll.html?_r=1&pagewanted=print; Richard Morin, *America's Four Middle Classes*, PEW RESEARCH CENTER, July 29, 2008.

[225] *See, e.g.*, THEDA SKOCPOL, THE MISSING MIDDLE: WORKING FAMILIES AND THE FUTURE OF AMERICAN SOCIAL POLICY 6–11, 124–41 (2000); ELIZABETH WARREN & AMELIA WARREN TYAGI, THE TWO-INCOME TRAP: WHY MIDDLE-CLASS MOTHERS AND FATHERS ARE GOING BROKE 57–63, 78–95 (2003). *See also* John M. Broder, *Problem of Lost Health Benefits Is Reaching into the Middle Class*, N.Y. TIMES, Nov. 25, 2002, http://www.nytimes.com/2002/11/25/us/problem-of-lost-health-benefits-is-reaching-into-the-middle-class.html.

reward-for-service rationale, "support[ing] people who serve the community and the nation" – an approach exemplified by Social Security and the G.I. Bill.[226] Conversely, then, it is not surprising that in a time of crisis we observe a corollary to this rationale – the characterization of growing middle-class vulnerability as evidence of a fraying "social contract."[227] These dynamics have been fully in evidence in postcrisis reform efforts, which have tended to promote both shareholder-centric corporate governance and greater social welfare protection for working families in these terms. Senator Schumer's proposed Shareholder Bill of Rights Act, for example, would have included as a "finding" of Congress that boards' failures "to appropriately analyze and oversee enterprise risk, and most importantly, to prioritize the long-term health of their firms and their shareholders," ultimately led to "losses that have been borne by millions of Americans who are shareholders through their pension plans, 401(k) plans, and direct investments."[228] This characterization of the causes and effects of the crisis resonates particularly powerfully because it builds directly on the distinctly American reward-for-service social welfare rationale, while simultaneously drawing upon traditional "employee" and "shareholder" incentives and interests. In this light, the aim would seem to be to forge an employee-shareholder coalition against management via pension fund investment in a manner like that discussed by Gourevitch and Shinn.[229]

President Obama, in a similar spirit and presumably for similar reasons, created a "Middle Class Task Force" (MCTF) led by Vice President Joseph Biden, a body describing itself as "a major initiative targeted at raising the living standards of middle-class, working families."[230] The MCTF has pursued a range of reform initiatives across numerous regulatory contexts, although for our purposes their common significance is that all are effectively brought together by the corollary of the reward-for-service social welfare rationale – in each case the core claim being that rewards for the middle class must be brought back into balance with their service to the nation and the economy. In its report on the American Recovery and Reinvestment Act, the MCTF describes the defining "challenge we face" as being to formulate and implement policies that "create the glue to reconnect the living standards of middle-class families to the economic growth they themselves are creating" – a broader initiative

[226] Skocpol, *supra* note 225, at 24–43 (describing attributes of successful social welfare programs in the United States).

[227] *Cf.* Schlesinger & Traub, *supra* note 224 (describing the postwar "social contract" among "businesses, workers, and government").

[228] SBRA, *supra* note 172, §§ 2(2)–(3).

[229] Gourevitch & Shinn, *supra* note 5, at 205–28. *See also* Gelter, *supra* note 74, at 26–39.

[230] *About the Middle Class Task Force*, *supra* note 224.

described as "one of the main reasons for the creation of the [MCTF]."[231] Likewise the MCTF's 2010 annual report explains that "in order to reconnect the growth of American prosperity and productivity with the growth of middle-class living standards, we . . . need to ensure that middle-class families have access to the things they need in order to succeed: affordable child and elder care, opportunities for higher education, secure retirement savings options, and of course, quality, affordable health care."[232]

Not surprisingly, the Obama administration has consistently drawn upon the unique capacity of the "middle class" concept to forge a substantial and powerful employee–shareholder coalition in the wake of the crisis. President Obama remarked shortly after signing the Dodd-Frank Act into law that the administration's "overall economic plan" aims to make "our middle-class more secure," a broad goal at once embracing initiatives including education tax credits, health insurance reform, and "Wall Street reform" to address "the recklessness and irresponsibility that led to the worse recession of our lifetime."[233] Similarly, at a December 2011 speech in Kansas, President Obama argued that "the basic bargain that made this country great" – the notion that "if you gave it your all, you'd take enough home to raise your family and send your kids to school and have your health care covered, put a little away for retirement" – had "eroded," rendering this "a make-or-break moment for the middle class." In this context, the Dodd-Frank Act, including shareholder-centric corporate governance reform, is identified as a response to recklessness in financial firms and a means of reorienting them toward "what should be their core purpose: getting capital to the entrepreneurs with the best ideas, and financing millions of families who want to buy a home or send their kids to college." Strikingly, however, President Obama turns to a more stakeholder-oriented conception of the corporation later in the same speech, arguing that economic recovery would "require American business leaders to understand that their obligations don't just end with their shareholders."[234] Toggling in this manner between shareholder- and stakeholder-centric rhetoric renders all the more clear that the utility of the "middle class" concept in postcrisis politics is its capacity to help forge an employee–shareholder coalition. The White House Web site,

[231] White House Middle Class Task Force, The American Recovery and Reinvestment Act: Helping Middle-Class Families 5 (2009), http://www.whitehouse.gov/assets/documents/staff_report_ARRA-FINAL.pdf.

[232] MCTF Annual Report, *supra* note 220, at 9.

[233] Remarks of President Barack Obama as Prepared for Delivery: Weekly Address (July 24, 2010), http://www.whitehouse.gov/the-press-office/weekly-address-president-obama-praises-new-wall-street-reform-law-says-gop-plan-wil.

[234] *Text: Obama's Speech in Kansas*, N.Y. Times, Dec. 6, 2011, http://www.nytimes.com/2011/12/07/us/politics/text-obamas-speech-in-kansas.html?pagewanted=all.

meanwhile, presents "Security for the Middle Class" as a major component of its efforts to promote jobs and the economy – a category of policy initiatives including both passage of "the most far reaching reform of Wall Street in history" to "prevent the excessive risk-taking that led to the financial crisis," and passage of "comprehensive health insurance reform" to address the "rising health care costs" that have "forced too many individuals into bankruptcy to get their families the care they need."[235]

Financial reforms, including shareholder empowerment initiatives, and social welfare reforms, including greater access to health insurance, are not only politically compatible, but are to some degree politically interdependent due to corporate employers' historical role as the principal means of delivering such social welfare benefits in the United States.[236] The substantial nexus between these policy domains is vividly illustrated by the posture of the California Public Employees' Retirement System (CalPERS), which not only manages pension funds for California public employees, but manages their health care benefits as well. As the nation's "largest public pension fund," CalPERS has been a prominent voice in favor of shareholder-centric corporate governance reforms, and as the nation's "second largest public purchaser" of health care (after the U.S. federal government), CalPERS has likewise been a prominent voice in favor of health care reforms.[237] Given the traditional reliance on employer-based health insurance coverage in the United States, it is unsurprising that an entity in CalPERS' position would adopt a twofold "mission . . . to advance the financial and health security for all who participate in the System."[238] CalPERS' mission and its postcrisis reform advocacy alike

[235] *Security for the Middle Class*, http://www.whitehouse.gov/economy/middle-class (White House Web site).

[236] This does not, however, mean that shareholder empowerment straightforwardly advances middle class interests. Based on Federal Reserve and IRS data, William Bratton and Michael Wachter demonstrate that "even as shareholding has diffused downward to lower income individuals the shareholders' overall socio-economic status has remained largely unchanged." They conclude that "there is nothing inherently democratic (or progressive) about the shareholder interest in corporate politics." *See* William W. Bratton & Michael L. Wachter, *Shareholders and Social Welfare*, 36 SEATTLE U. L. REV. (forthcoming 2013).

[237] CAL. PUB. EMPS' RETIREMENT SYS., CALPERS APPLAUDS SENATE ON HEALTH CARE REFORM ACTION (Dec. 24, 2009); CAL. PUB. EMPS' RETIREMENT SYS., FACTS AT A GLANCE: CORPORATE GOVERNANCE (Jan. 2010); CAL. PUB. EMPS' RETIREMENT SYS., FACTS AT A GLANCE: GENERAL (Jan. 2010); CAL. PUB. EMPS' RETIREMENT SYS., FACTS AT A GLANCE: HEALTH (Jan. 2010); CAL. PUB. EMPS' RETIREMENT SYS., FACTS AT A GLANCE: INVESTMENTS (Jan. 2010); *CalPERS Presses for Financial Market Reform*, CAL. PUB. EMPS' RETIREMENT SYS., http://www.calpers-governance.org/marketinitiatives/initiatives/financial-reform; Memorandum from Ann Stausboll, Chief Executive Officer, California Public Employees' Retirement System, to California Congressional Delegation, H.R. 4173 "Wall Street Reform and Consumer Protection Act of 2009" (Dec. 9, 2009).

[238] CAL. PUB. EMPS' RETIREMENT SYS., FACTS AT A GLANCE: GENERAL, *supra* note 237, at 1.

illustrate the compatibility and interdependence of investment, corporate governance, and social welfare policy in the United States – fundamental political linkages that remain as substantial as ever in the wake of the crisis.

Given the financial and economic uncertainties that define the postcrisis political landscape, it is unsurprising that shareholder-centric corporate governance reforms in the United States have emerged hand in hand with substantial social welfare reforms aimed at reducing the vulnerability of employees in the event of job loss. Postcrisis opinion polls have made painfully clear that loss of access to affordable health care looms large among employment-related concerns[239] – an entirely comprehensible development, given the catastrophic consequences that major medical expenses can impose upon those without adequate insurance coverage. As nominee for Secretary of Health and Human Services Kathleen Sebelius explained to a Senate committee in April 2009, about half of recent foreclosures had at least partially resulted from uninsured medical expenses.[240] Similarly, the MCTF's 2010 annual report observed that "the rising cost of health care and health insurance is one of the primary strains on middle-class family budgets," yet "families are losing insurance at an alarming rate." The report cites data indicating that from 1997 to 2006 "half of Americans under the age of 65 found themselves without health insurance at some point," and that in 2009, "an average of 15,000 Americans lost their private health insurance each day, often because of job loss or because their employer dropped their coverage."[241] As Gallup would report in December 2010, "[a] new low of 44.8% of American adults report getting their health insurance through an employer in November, down from 50% in January 2008, when Gallup began tracking it."[242]

Health insurance reforms signed into law by President Obama in March 2010 were clearly the most direct response to these trends, aiming to extend

[239] *See, e.g.*, PEW RESEARCH CENTER, MORE WORKERS ANTICIPATE PAY CUTS, LAYOFFS: AS JOBS CRISIS SPREADS, WORRIES CLIMB THE ECONOMIC LADDER 10, 15–16 (2009), http://people-press.org/reports/pdf/492.pdf; Lydia Saad, *Americans Rate National and Personal Healthcare Differently*, GALLUP (Dec. 4, 2008), http://www.gallup.com/poll/112813/Americans-Rate-National-Personal-Healthcare-Differently.aspx. *See also* John Fairhall & Kate Steadman, *The New Uninsured*, WASH. POST, Feb. 3, 2009, at HE01; Francesca Lunzer Kritz, *Staying Insured after Job Loss*, L.A. TIMES, Jan. 19, 2009, at F1.

[240] *Harry and Louise Ride Again*, ECONOMIST, Apr. 4, 2009, at 36, 36. *See also* Himmelstein et al., *supra* note 224 (finding that "62.1% of all bankruptcies in 2007 were medical," and that from 2001 to 2007, "the share of bankruptcies attributable to medical problems rose by 49.6%").

[241] MCTF ANNUAL REPORT, *supra* note 220, at 9. *See also* David A. Hyman, *Employment-Based Health Insurance: Is Health Reform a "Game Changer?"* 9 (University of Illinois Law and Economics Research Paper no. LE10–010, June 2010), http://ssrn.com/abstract=1624311 ("The standard estimate is that every 1% increase in unemployment results in 2.1 million Americans losing their [employment-based health coverage].").

[242] Elizabeth Mendes, *In U.S., New Low of 44.8% Get Healthcare from Employer*, GALLUP (Dec. 17, 2010), http://www.gallup.com/poll/145277/new-low-healthcare-employer.aspx.

social welfare protections precisely when shareholder powers were also being extended in corporate governance. Although the United States remains a long way from universal coverage, maintaining a fundamentally employer-based system leaving well in excess of ten million Americans uninsured (even in the best case scenario), the Patient Protection and Affordable Care Act (PPACA) has been projected to "help extend coverage to 32 million previously uninsured Americans and contribute greatly to the stability and security of coverage of those who already have it"[243] – though the U.S. Supreme Court's equivocal resolution of the inevitable constitutional challenge to the statute cast doubt on this optimistic claim.[244] In any event, the White House meanwhile promotes the new health care law in a manner fully consistent with the middle class politics and traditional reward-for-service narrative described above, styling the mandate as a response to the fact that the "average US family and their employer pay $1000 a year extra in health insurance costs to cover care for the uninsured," and emphasizing that the PPACA "gives hard-working families the security they

[243] Karen Davis, Cathy Schoen & Kristof Stremikis, Mirror, Mirror on the Wall: How the Performance of the U.S. Health Care System Compares Internationally 15, 17 (2010 update). For analyses of the PPACA, its impact on employer-based coverage, and its budget consequences, see Tom Baker, *Health Insurance, Risk, and Responsibility after the Patient Protection and Affordable Care Act*, 159 U. Pa. L. Rev. 1577 (2011); United States General Accountability Office, *The Federal Government's Long-Term Fiscal Outlook: Fall 2010 Update*, Nov. 2010, at 3, 8; Hyman, *supra* note 241; David Leonhardt, *Opposition to Health Law Is Steeped in Tradition*, N.Y. Times, Dec. 14, 2010, http://www.nytimes.com/2010/12/15/business/economy/15leonhardt.html.

[244] Although the mandate to buy health insurance (or pay a penalty) – the statute's central cost-spreading strategy – was upheld under Congress' taxation power, the strategy of forcing Medicaid expansion by threatening states with the loss of existing payments should they decline was rejected by the Court. *See* Adam Liptak, *Supreme Court Upholds Health Care Law, 5–4, in Victory for Obama*, N.Y. Times, June 28, 2012, http://www.nytimes.com/2012/06/29/us/supreme-court-lets-health-law-largely-stand.html?pagewanted=all. *See also* Adam Liptak, *In Health Case, Appeals to a Justice's Idea of Liberty*, N.Y. Times, Mar. 30, 2012 (discussing oral arguments regarding the mandate's consistency with Congress' authority to regulate interstate commerce).

For a sampling of the spirited debate regarding the mandate's constitutionality, compare Randy Barnett, Nathaniel Stewart & Todd Gaziano, *Why the Personal Mandate to Buy Health Insurance Is Unprecedented and Unconstitutional* (Heritage Foundation Legal Memorandum No. 49, 2009) (arguing that the mandate exceeds the commerce authority, and that to be brought within the taxing authority the money would have to flow through the federal budget) with Brian Galle, *Conditional Taxation and the Constitutionality of Health Care Reform*, 120 Yale L.J. Online 27 (2010), http://yalelawjournal.org/2010/5/31/galle.html (arguing that the mandate represents a permissible form of "conditional taxation") and Brian Galle, *Is the Health Care Legislation Constitutional?*, Prawfsblawg (Mar. 27, 2010, 10:25 AM), http://prawfsblawg.blogs.com/prawfsblawg/2010/03/the-health-care-legislation-is-constitutional-part-i-nec-proper.html (arguing that the mandate falls within the commerce authority).

	1980s	2000s
perceived crisis	hostile takeovers	reckless risk-taking
blame assigned	shareholders	board
oppositional coalition	employee-board	employee-shareholders
power	board	shareholders
purpose	stakeholders	shareholders

Figure 6.2. Crises and Employee Coalitions

deserve."[245] These concerns impacted regulatory actions in other policy domains as well – including, for example, the bailout of the American auto industry. As of March 2009, the "three Detroit auto makers provide[d] health care for more than one million Americans, including union retirees and their dependents," complicating negotiations over the fate of the struggling Chrysler and General Motors[246] and essentially rendering the auto bailout a social and political imperative.[247]

The intrinsic relationship between the degree of shareholder-centrism in corporate governance and the degree of protection available to employees outside it – taken together with Gourevitch and Shinn's emphasis on the role of political coalitions in corporate lawmaking – point toward an underlying historical continuity, notwithstanding the apparent fundamental shift in favor of shareholders. Even though antitakeover laws in the 1980s and postcrisis corporate governance reforms in the 2000s starkly contrast in outcome – the former favoring stakeholders whereas the latter favor shareholders – the underlying political dynamics in the two instances are virtually identical, similarly underscoring the critical role of employee interests. In each case, as Figure 6.2 illustrates, a crisis threatened financial and social welfare stability for working "middle class" families; the given crisis was conceptualized as

[245] *A More Secure Future: What the New Health Law Means for You and Your Family*, http://www.whitehouse.gov/healthreform/relief-for-americans-and-businesses (White House Web site). *See also Security for the Middle Class*, http://www.whitehouse.gov/economy/middle-class (White House Web site).

[246] Matthew Dolan, *Obama Seeks Concessions from UAW Retirees*, Wall St. J., Mar. 31, 2009, at A4. *See also* Toni Johnson, *Healthcare Costs and U.S. Competitiveness* (Council on Foreign Relations, updated Mar. 26, 2012), http://www.cfr.org/publication/13325/.

[247] *See The Obama Autoworks*, Wall St. J., Mar. 31, 2009, at A20; Steve Lohr, *In U.S., Steps toward Industrial Policy in Autos*, N.Y. Times, May 20, 2009; *Text: Obama's Speech in Kansas, supra* note 234. *See also* Skeel, *supra* note 154, at 35–40 (criticizing the Chrysler and GM bailouts for "commandeering the bankruptcy process . . . to distinguish among otherwise similarly situated creditors, deciding which to pay and which not to pay").

a corporate governance problem, with blame assigned to one or the other power constituency, the shareholders or the board as the case may be; an employee coalition emerged in opposition to that power constituency; governance power shifted in favor of the board or the shareholders, as the case may be; and regulatory emphasis shifted in favor of stakeholders or shareholders, as the case may be. In the 1980s, hostile takeovers prompted an employee–management coalition to contain premium-seeking shareholders, and in the 2000s, an employee–shareholder coalition has formed to contain perceived managerial recklessness – yet the underlying social welfare concerns, and associated political dynamics, are virtually identical.[248]

Although it remains far too early as of this writing to draw firm conclusions, it is worth observing that these ongoing postcrisis developments will help illuminate the predictive power of the theory developed in this book in at least two respects. Continued movement in this direction would effectively amount to a shift toward a form of social welfare equilibrium in the United States more closely resembling that historically observed in Australia, Canada, and the United Kingdom – stronger shareholder powers and greater shareholder centrality within corporate governance, and stronger stakeholder protections outside it. At the same time, the divergence between the postcrisis responses of the United Kingdom, which has strengthened shareholders yet weakened protections for stakeholders, and the United States, which has strengthened shareholders while strengthening protections for stakeholders, gives rise to a natural experiment of sorts. Assuming, again, that these policy trajectories continue in the future (far from certain as of this writing, on either side of the Atlantic), the theory developed in this book suggests that the latter approach will exhibit greater social and political stability in the face of future crises.

[248] Mark Roe presciently foresaw such a possibility, observing in 1994 that "[a]nti-finance 'populism' is not what it once was as a political force." He adds that "if the political contest is seen as pitting responsible institutions against greedy managers, we could imagine the resulting rules as not hurting shareholder activism badly. The attention to managerial salaries in the media suggests that modern 1990s' 'populism' can target managers as well as institutions." MARK J. ROE, STRONG MANAGERS, WEAK OWNERS: THE POLITICAL ROOTS OF AMERICAN CORPORATE FINANCE 285 (1994). *See also* Bruner, *supra* note 136, at 15–32 (discussing pro-employee populism in nonfinancial firms and pro-depositor populism in financial firms, and evaluating pro-shareholder populism in the wake of the crisis against this historical background).

7 Conclusions

Although common-law jurisdictions do, globally speaking, exhibit the relatively greater share dispersal and shareholder-centrism that the comparative corporate literature ascribes to them, generalizations regarding the so-called Anglo-American, Anglo-Saxon, or common-law corporate governance model obscure more than they illuminate. Australia, Canada, the United Kingdom, and the United States do exhibit substantial similarities in their business cultures, financial structures, and legal traditions, yet they nevertheless diverge markedly in terms of the degree of governance power granted to shareholders and the degree to which corporate (or company) law in a given country prioritizes the shareholders' interests.

As we have seen, U.S. shareholders are considerably less powerful and less central to the corporate enterprise than are their U.K. counterparts, and their Australian and Canadian counterparts – although somewhere between these extremes – fall closer to the latter approach than the former. In this book I have argued that external regulatory structures affecting the incentives and interests of other stakeholders in widely held public corporations – particularly social welfare protections available to employees – have exerted an underappreciated but critical impact on the degree of shareholder-centrism exhibited by each of these countries. In the United Kingdom, where state-based social welfare protections have (to date) remained relatively robust, less political pressure has been brought to bear on the corporate governance system to show regard for the interests of non-shareholders. In the United States, meanwhile, weaker state-based social welfare protections have left the corporate governance system exposed to greater stakeholder-oriented political pressures – particularly in times of perceived social and economic crisis. Australia, for its part, provides its own uniquely striking illustration of these dynamics, exhibiting susceptibility to stakeholder-oriented political pressures in a period of social welfare instability, and then moving strongly in the direction of U.K.-style shareholder-centrism once state-based social welfare protections stabilized. Canada, then, falls somewhat closer to the middle of the spectrum, although quite decidedly breaks toward U.K.-style shareholder-centrism in the most consequential areas of corporate governance – a striking tendency given the geographic, commercial, and cultural proximity of influential U.S. models during the period of greatest reform activity.

That legal systems so similar as these should diverge so markedly on fundamental issues at the very heart of corporate governance vividly demonstrates that corporate law cannot be fully understood in a disciplinary and regulatory silo. Neither can corporate governance structures be understood in a historical, cultural, and political vacuum. Ironically, economic theories of corporate governance – including the "nexus of contracts" theory that has garnered such broad adherence over recent decades – acknowledge this fact, although they cannot begin to accommodate the social and political forces that the broader political economy brings to bear on corporate governance. The metaphorical "contract" embodied in corporate law's default rules – with shareholder wealth maximization its core term – is implicitly held constant, while all other aims are to be pursued through external regulatory regimes and (real) contractual negotiations by reference to that fixed corporate form.[1] As the analysis presented in this book demonstrates, the reality in each of the countries investigated contradicts this implicit subordination of social welfare concerns and associated politics. To the contrary, corporate governance and social welfare policy are, and long have been, deeply intertwined, each impacting the other in numerous and complex ways as a given society continually calibrates (and recalibrates) the role of public corporations in the achievement of broader political and social goals. Building on insights of political theories of corporate governance developed by legal scholars and political scientists over recent decades, I have endeavored to illuminate more fully the political foundations of shareholder power in the common-law world – which I have argued substantially consist of larger political and social equilibria involving ostensibly unrelated domains of law and policy. In essence, Australia, Canada, and the United Kingdom have struck upon equilibria involving greater reliance on external regulation to protect the social welfare of employees, freeing up the public corporation to focus on generating returns for shareholders. The United States, in contrast, has historically expected corporate employers to bear considerably greater social and political freight – one consequence being greater reluctance to prioritize shareholders' interests when they come into direct conflict with those of other corporate stakeholders, particularly employees.

[1] *See, e.g.*, Frank H. Easterbrook & Daniel R. Fischel, The Economic Structure of Corporate Law 36–39 (1991).

Given the historical, cultural, and political contingency of the equilibrium struck in each country, the analysis presented here provides no basis upon which to claim that any one approach is "optimal" or to be regarded as inherently superior; the normative metrics will vary from country to country, not least because prevailing views on distributive justice will vary from one society to another, and from one historical period to another.[2] By the same token, however, the analysis presented here provides no basis upon which to claim that the varying equilibria that I describe constitute "functionally equivalent" means of social welfare protection; even societies as similar as these can and do vary enormously in the degree of social welfare protection thought desirable. Indeed, in the United States, ambivalence regarding the appropriate governance role of shareholders and the degree to which we ought to prioritize their interests reflects a more fundamental ambivalence regarding the appropriate means and ends of social welfare provision – a cultural and political tension manifesting itself quite clearly in the debate over health care reform.

"Something about health care," Gerald Seib observed in the *Wall Street Journal* in 2009, "calls forth from the national psyche a deep, almost inexplicable schizophrenia"[3] – a complex reaction attributable to a number of American cultural traits. Seib, for example, emphasizes ambivalence not only regarding the government and its capacities, but also regarding the traditional employer-based system. Reliance on employers for health care has "fostered a view of employers as either paternalistic guardians who look after our health for mutual benefit, or as powerful overlords with an obligation to do so." For decades the consequence was legislative paralysis, not because the majority favored the current system, but because "the two starkest alternatives to the status quo" – reliance on oneself, or reliance on the government – "both scare people."[4] David Leonhardt of the *New York Times* similarly identifies in the health care debate a "tension between two competing traditions in the

[2] *See supra* Chapter 2.

[3] Gerald F. Seib, *U.S. Psyche Bedevils Health Effort*, WALL ST. J., Aug. 4, 2009, at A2.

[4] *Id. See also* Jackie Calmes & Dalia Sussman, *Poll Finds Wariness about Cutting Entitlements*, N.Y. TIMES, Jan. 20, 2011, http://www.nytimes.com/2011/01/21/us/politics/21poll.html (reporting that "Americans overwhelmingly say that in general they prefer cutting government spending to paying higher taxes," but that this preference "dissolves when they are presented with specific options related to Medicare and Social Security, the programs that directly touch the most people and also are the biggest drivers of the government's projected long-term debt"); *Poll Responses on How to Cut the Deficit*, N.Y. TIMES, Jan. 20, 2011, http://www.nytimes.com/interactive/2011/01/20/us/poll-graphic.html?ref=politics; Timothy Stolzfus Jost, *Why Can't We Do What They Do? National Health Reform Abroad*, 32 J.L. MED. & ETHICS 433, 438 (2004) (attributing health care reform failures to "the cultural aversion of Americans to the use of government to solve problems," and the correlative belief "that private know-how and entrepreneurialism can solve all problems").

American economy" – a "laissez-faire tradition that celebrates individuality and risk-taking," and a "progressive tradition that says people have a right to a minimum standard of living," perspectives that "have never quite reconciled themselves."[5] This tension emerges not only across the electorate, but as a form of cognitive dissonance in the minds of the growing number of individuals who disfavor government handouts, yet increasingly rely on them in the wake of the crisis. Binyamin Appelbaum and Robert Gebeloff of the *New York Times* report that "as more middle-class families . . . land in the safety net . . . anger at the government has increased" proportionately. "They are frustrated that they need help, feel guilty for taking it and resent the government for providing it" – a potential explanation for the striking trend that "[s]upport for Republican candidates, who generally promise to cut government spending, has increased since 1980 in states where the federal government spends more than it collects. The greater the dependence, the greater the support for Republican candidates."[6]

The upshot of such skepticism toward government and favoritism toward the private sector, as Timothy Jost observes, is that in contrast with the greater consensus exhibited by other developed countries, "Americans are far more ambivalent about universal coverage."[7] This is readily detectable in the Patient Protection and Affordable Care Act (PPACA) itself, which, as Tom Baker observes, "some might regard . . . as the unnatural union of opposites – solidarity on the one hand and markets, choice, and individual responsibility on the other." He adds that "[p]ublic ownership and pure, tax-based financing are technically easier and almost certainly cheaper routes to health care solidarity, but they come at a cost to the status quo that Congress was not prepared to pay."[8] "In the case of health care," Baker concludes, "the moral and political conversation about risk and responsibility is long underway. The [PPACA] reflects and contributes to that conversation, but it makes no radical changes."[9]

[5] David Leonhardt, *Opposition to Health Law Is Steeped in Tradition*, N.Y. Times, Dec. 14, 2010, http://www.nytimes.com/2010/12/15/business/economy/15leonhardt.html.

[6] *See* Binyamin Appelbaum & Robert Gebeloff, *Even Critics of Safety Net Increasingly Depend on It*, N.Y. Times, Feb. 11, 2012 (reporting on the research of Professor Dean P. Lacy, a political scientist at Dartmouth College). *See also* Suzanne Mettler, The Submerged State, How Invisible Government Policies Undermine American Democracy 39–40 (2011) (observing "the paradox surrounding submerged features of American social policy: clearly, many citizens who might say they oppose government spending are in fact themselves beneficiaries of social programs").

[7] Jost, *supra* note 4, at 438.

[8] Tom Baker, *Health Insurance, Risk, and Responsibility after the Patient Protection and Affordable Care Act*, 159 U. Pa. L. Rev. 1577, 1579–80 (2011).

[9] *Id.* at 1621.

Given the interconnectedness of corporate governance with underlying social welfare protections available to employees, U.S. corporate law's ambivalence regarding shareholders would appear to be grounded in a much deeper ambivalence regarding the appropriate roles of public and private spheres in meeting society's basic needs. The rootedness of social welfare policy and (through it) corporate governance in fundamental social values and distributive politics contradicts glib descriptive claims of "functional equivalence" across societies and legal systems, and likewise precludes sweeping normative claims regarding the regulatory "optimality" of any particular approach. The analysis offered here does, however, illuminate fundamental dynamics of the formation of corporate governance systems in the common-law world that raise important considerations for policy makers in each of these countries to consider when calls for reform arise – as they naturally will following crises of one form or another. Corporate governance long has been, and remains, just one part of a much broader political economy – and reforms to the fundamental power balance and priorities of the public corporation can have social, political, and regulatory impacts reaching far beyond corporate law. Confident as proponents of shareholder-empowerment, in particular, may be that accountability to shareholders optimizes the efficiency and performance of public company governance, policy makers would do well to closely scrutinize such initiatives before the backdrop of their own country's political economy and social welfare regime. Even among countries as closely related as those explored here, shareholder-centric reforms may not translate from one society to another as coherently as their proponents would have us believe.

John Stuart Mill, writing in 1840, observed of the raging debates over the social impacts of industrialism that "the besetting danger is not so much of embracing falsehood for truth, as of mistaking part of the truth for the whole."[10] The same might be said of contemporary debates over the appropriate role of shareholders and their interests in corporate governance – which too often proceed on the assumption that a correct answer may be deduced from legal premises internal to corporate law, or that an optimally efficient balance may be derived from economic characteristics inherent to the corporate form. The reality is that those legal premises and economic characteristics – however fixed, stable, and cosmically inevitable they may seem to their proponents – are, and always have been, contingent and contestable.

To be sure, there is nothing to prevent lawmakers and regulators in any given country from augmenting shareholders' powers without augmenting extra-corporate stakeholder protections; diminishing extra-corporate stakeholder

[10] Raymond Williams, Culture and Society 50 (1993) (1958) (quoting Mill).

protections without introducing capacity for boards to show regard for stakeholders' interests or even augmenting shareholders' powers while simultaneously diminishing extra-corporate stakeholder protections. As a matter of legislative and regulatory competence, such moves clearly can be (and recently have been) made. Lawmakers and regulators keen to increase shareholder-centrism and/or cut social welfare spending in a substantial and sustained manner should, however, think hard about the risks – the substantial social and political instability that could readily result, and the difficulty of predicting how, when, and at what cost the inevitable correction would come. In light of the manner in which corporate governance has historically evolved in Australia, Canada, the United Kingdom, and the United States – and the significant impact that social welfare concerns can exert upon corporate governance where shareholders' and stakeholders' respective interests are thought to conflict – such initiatives will eventually be tested by one form of crisis or another, and very likely found wanting. Something has to give, and ultimately does.

Index